How Media Ownership Matters

How Media Ownership Matters

RODNEY BENSON
MATTIAS HESSÉRUS
TIMOTHY NEFF
JULIE SEDEL

OXFORD
UNIVERSITY PRESS

OXFORD
UNIVERSITY PRESS

Oxford University Press is a department of the University of Oxford. It furthers the University's objective of excellence in research, scholarship, and education by publishing worldwide. Oxford is a registered trade mark of Oxford University Press in the UK and certain other countries.

Published in the United States of America by Oxford University Press
198 Madison Avenue, New York, NY 10016, United States of America.

Library of Congress Cataloging-in-Publication Data
Names: Benson, Rodney, author. | Hessérus, Mattias, 1977– author. |
Neff, Timothy, author. | Sedel, Julie, author.
Title: How media ownership matters / Rodney Benson, Mattias Hessérus,
Timothy Neff, and Julie Sedel.
Description: New York : Oxford University Press, 2025. |
Includes bibliographical references and index.
Identifiers: LCCN 2024021264 (print) | LCCN 2024021265 (ebook) |
ISBN 9780199931316 (paperback) | ISBN 9780199931293 (hardback) |
ISBN 9780197790281 (epub)
Subjects: LCSH: Mass media—Ownership. | Mass media—Political aspects. |
Mass media—Social aspects.
Classification: LCC P96.E25 B46 2024 (print) | LCC P96.E25 (ebook) |
DDC 302.23—dc23/eng/20230610
LC record available at https://lccn.loc.gov/2024021264
LC ebook record available at https://lccn.loc.gov/2024021265

DOI: 10.1093/oso/9780199931293.001.0001

Paperback printed by Marquis Book Printing, Canada
Hardback printed by Bridgeport National Bindery, Inc., United States of America

Online Appendix Tables are available at: https://rodneybenson.org/publications/how-media-ownership-matters/online-appendix

Contents

Illustrations

Figures

Tables

Appendix Tables

Online Appendix Tables

Introduction: Understanding Media Ownership

Consider these real-life vignettes of how media ownership matters.

ProPublica, a nonprofit news outlet, pores through a vast "trove of data" to reveal that many of America's wealthiest citizens—Elon Musk, Jeff Bezos, and George Soros among them—in some years legally "owed not a single dollar in income tax to the US Treasury," sparking a "national conversation about potential changes in the law."[1] *SVT*, Sweden's public television channel, has an investigative magazine show called *Mission: Investigation* (*Uppdrag granskning*). Its hard-hitting, public service-oriented investigations of business and government include a story about suspected bribing of foreign clients by Sweden's largest and partly-state-owned telecommunications company, resulting in the resignations of the company's board and CEO.[2]

Shortly after Go.com, the "internet arm" of the stock market-traded Walt Disney company, purchased a five percent stake in Pets.com, the "Pets.com sock puppet" (a cute "mongrel dog") starts appearing on news programs of the *ABC* television network, also owned by Disney; while some *ABC* journalists insist that they did not know of the investment and vigorously deny "advanc[ing] the cause of Pets.com," a prominent journalism school dean argues that news divisions should avoid even giving "the appearance of the cross promotion of corporate interests."[3] In France, an independent filmmaker releases a documentary called *Thanks Boss!* (*Merci Patron!*) about workers laid off at a factory owned by the stock market-traded luxury goods company LVMH. The French newspaper *Le Parisien*, also owned by LVMH and its dominant shareholder Bernard Arnault, is criticized for not publishing an article about the documentary.[4]

When the company owning the French newspaper *Le Journal du Dimanche* announces that its new editor will be a controversial journalist seen as sympathetic to the far right, the newspaper's journalists launch a strike in protest. In the ensuing public debate, critics suggest that Vincent Bolloré, the dominant shareholder of the stock market-traded company in the midst of buying the newspaper, is seeking to transform the publication from a forum for diverse opinions into a partisan instrument of ultra-conservative causes and candidates—just as he is accused of having done at the cable channel *C-News*.[5] In Sweden, Jonas Nordling, editor-in-chief of the left-leaning, partly labor union-funded *Dagens Arena*, proudly describes the news outlet he leads as "a partisan medium" and a "resistance movement."[6]

How Media Ownership Matters. Rodney Benson et al. Oxford University Press. © Rodney Benson, Mattias Hessérus, Timothy Neff, and Julie Sedel 2025. DOI: 10.1093/oso/9780199931293.003.0001

These examples help illustrate three types of civically consequential modes of ownership power. The first two concern *public service orientation*, which includes a commitment to holding the powerful to account. The second set of cases, accusations of promoting or suppressing information according to the interests of media owners, are examples of alleged *economic instrumentalism*. And the third set of partisan actions and remarks (purported or openly affirmed) points to *political instrumentalism*, using a media outlet to promote a particular partisan agenda.

Let us return to the sets of vignettes again, but this time to pay attention not only to *what* the owner is doing (or supposedly doing) but *what kind* of owner is being described: nonprofit and public in the first; stock market-traded conglomerates (including one with a dominant shareholder) in the second; and a stock market-traded dominant shareholder-controlled company and an activist civil society association in the third. In each case, in other words, not only a different individual owner, but a different type of owner is involved. In this book, we argue that this type or "form" of ownership is not just coincidental; it is crucial in explaining these incidents. Media ownership, as a material and symbolic configuration of power, plays a central role in the news-making process.

However, owners do not act alone. Media must also be funded, whether by advertising, paying subscribers, donors, or taxpayers. They also must find an audience and keep that audience coming back for what they have to offer. These factors are analytically distinct from ownership, but they often group together with certain ownership forms: for instance, taxpayer funding for public media, advertising funding for stock market-traded media, and elite subscribing or donating audiences for civil society-owned media—although there are exceptions, and many news outlets rely on multiple revenue streams.

The purpose of this book is to understand the structural incentives and disincentives that lead media outlets with different ownership forms, funding, and audiences to provide news and views in certain ways and not in others, often with crucial civic consequences for the societies in which they operate. News media ownership matters because journalism matters. When a community's newspaper is shut down or deprived of resources for public affairs reporting, political corruption rises.[7] When news organizations promote a political candidate or cause, they intensify pre-existing political beliefs and mobilize supporters who may tip the balance of an election.[8] And when information about the outside business interests of media owners is not fully revealed, citizens may be exposed to increased financial, health, and safety risks.[9]

The Approach

In this book, we argue that research on media ownership needs to go beyond statistics on market concentration and anecdotes about powerful moguls. Instead, we can learn more about the exercise of ownership power by examining and comparing different types of ownership. These *ownership forms* introduce distinct institutional logics—"unique organizing principles, practices, and symbols that influence individual and organizational behavior"[10]—into the journalistic field. We identify four major ownership forms—*market, private, civil society*, and *public*—and various subforms.

Next, we analyze these forms in context, first in relation to the social logics (education, income, etc.) shaping the beliefs and practices of the people who produce and consume news media. These aspects are captured well in Pierre Bourdieu's field theory and his conceptions of habitus and production-reception homologies, to be discussed further.[11] But what is often missing from this type of analysis is the element of contingency and uncertainty.[12] As Todd Gitlin's classic research on television entertainment showed, cultural producers never know for sure what will attract an audience or generate sustainable revenues.[13] Thus, we also pay attention to *media management*; that is, how individual owners, business managers, and senior editors strive to balance financial and other goals through strategies of *funding-audience adjustment*. As a result, while ownership forms, funding, and audiences are analytically distinct, they often tend to group together in *ownership complexes*.

Terms like ownership form and owner are shorthand for complex configurations of finance and management. An owner may be an individual, a family, employees, a dominant shareholder, a dispersed collection of shareholders, a cooperative, or a nonprofit foundation or association, among other possibilities. Some civil society-owned outlets are essentially devoid of an owner who extracts profits or attempts to impose an editorial line and instead are governed by their self-constituting boards of directors. Even when a particular individual is deemed to be the sole owner or dominant shareholder, such ownership is usually organizationally mediated.[14] Our focus on ownership form makes room for such particularities while capturing the systematic institutional affordances, incentives, and constraints that each form or subform embodies. Acting in relation to these structural conditions, various owners and/or their delegated board members or managers attempt to exercise effective "allocative" and "operational" ownership power.[15]

We agree with the US Public Broadcasting Service's (*PBS*) public editor who wrote in response to an attempt by *YouTube* to lump *PBS* in with Russia's *RT*, China's *CCTV*, and any number of other "state" broadcasters receiving taxpayer public funding: "Funding (whatever form it takes) is a poor proxy for anything, particularly the quality of editorial content."[16] Indeed, funding and the other economic underpinnings of journalism are not in themselves a "proxy" for quality (however defined), and neither funding nor other dimensions of ownership power completely override the professional judgment and agency of journalists to report and comment on current events. Instead, we argue that the ownership complex (which, of course, is quite different at *PBS* than at *RT* or *CCTV*) *shapes the environment* in which journalists do their work: it does not determine, but it may influence—whether by enabling or constraining—the kind of news content that will be produced.

Likewise, our framework is not an attempt to replace other distinguished approaches to "explaining" the news. We do not deny that broad social and ideological currents, as well as various news "sources," powerfully shape journalism and public discourse, an approach pioneered in critical cultural studies by Stuart Hall, Raymond Williams, and others.[17] Nor do we dismiss the myriad of other factors influencing the production of news—from the micro-level to the macro-level—persuasively identified by distinguished scholars such as Michael Schudson, Erik Neveu, Pamela Shoemaker, Steve Reese, Barbie Zelizer, and Frank Esser.[18] Rather, our goal is to highlight one cluster of the forces shaping news—ownership, and its close relation to funding and audiences—and take this focused analysis as far as we can to see what it reveals. The questions we ask, the dimensions of news production we study, and the methods we deploy are carefully selected to focus on ownership.

For example, we take it as a given that national political, economic, and cultural context will shape the news, but the purpose of this book is not primarily to compare media systems per se. Rather, comparative research allows us to overcome nationally specific assumptions about who or what can be a media owner. In addition, in our statistical analysis, our *primary* focus is not on how ownership differs cross-nationally, but how given ownership forms and related complexes of funding-audience adjustment are similar or different to other forms/complexes in the *same* national field. If we find patterns that produce statistically significant results aggregated across three distinct media systems, we can be more certain of how—and how much—ownership forms and complexes do indeed matter.

Finally, our approach is engaged with normative questions but we do not make any a priori assumptions about the motives or the civic effects engendered by various types of owners. Shareholders in media companies may be banks, wealthy individuals, employees, churches, or political parties. Nonprofit associations may be established by individuals and groups representing a wide range of perspectives. The journalistic "outcomes" of these different ownership forms, subforms, and hybrid combinations may well be multiple and potentially contradictory. As foreshadowed by our opening examples, we foresee three major ways in which ownership forms and complexes may make a civically meaningful difference in the production of news. We identify these outcomes as *modes of power* for *public service orientation, political instrumentalism,* and *economic instrumentalism.*

The Research

To answer how ownership matters and to put our theoretical framework to work, we conducted research in three western industrial democracies: the United States (US), Sweden, and France. These three western nation-states share many common characteristics as relatively prosperous capitalist democratic polities with broadly similar intellectual and cultural heritages. Yet they also represent each of the three western "media systems" identified by political scientists Daniel C. Hallin and Paolo Mancini in their classic work *Comparing Media Systems.*[19] These media systems—*liberal* (US in the most distilled form, but also arguably Canada, Ireland, and the UK), *polarized pluralist* (Italy, Spain, Greece, and to a certain extent France), and *democratic corporatist* (Sweden and other northern European countries)—have historically embodied distinct configurations of market structure, state intervention, and journalistic professionalism and politicization.

According to Hallin and Mancini, the US represents the most market-dominated field (far more so than others in the liberal model), while in France and Sweden, the state plays a larger role in supporting non-commercial public media and in subsidizing commercial media. Sweden, nevertheless, also has a relatively thriving commercial sector and among the highest rates of news readership and trust in the world. A comparison of the US, Sweden, and France thus allows us to investigate how ownership functions across diverse media environments—a question not fully explored by Hallin and Mancini—both to more confidently generalize our findings and to appropriately contextualize them. In the book's conclusion, we discuss how our approach and findings relate to previous and potential future research on other world regions, including across the Global South.

A multi-country comparative approach also allows us to help expand the global ownership "imaginary." Unique ownership forms in our three countries include philanthropic-supported nonprofits like *ProPublica* in the US; audience-only funded, journalist-founded *Mediapart* in France; and political party/partisan affiliated foundation-owned newspapers in Sweden, just to name a few. Different terminologies have emerged to identify how journalists and their publics identify owners as either "bad" ("industrial" owners in France, "conglomerates" and "hedge funds" in the US) or "good" ("nonprofits" in the US, "independent" media in France, "public service" radio and TV in Sweden). Formally identical ownership forms may be inflected differently in each of the countries, as they function in relation to their distinctive, historically shaped national fields. And outlets that are formerly or informally associated with the same global companies—*HuffPost*, *Slate*, *Vice*, and *Metro*, in our study—may partner with local owners associated with different ownership forms or subforms in each country.

Including these three journalistic fields in our study—distinctive in many ways, yet also partially integrated—thus broadens the range of ownership variation and allows us to systematically identify both similarities and differences across ownership forms and national fields. The total sample of more than fifty news outlets is large enough to facilitate quantitative calculations while remaining manageable for deeper, qualitative analysis. Appendix Table AI.1 provides a list of our sample of US, French, and Swedish news organizations, categorized by the four broad ownership forms—market, private, civil society, and public.

After providing historical context, we focus our structural analysis on the 2010s and early 2020s, with special attention to 2016 and surrounding years when we conducted extensive content analysis. Given the rapid change of media, descriptive findings are bound to be soon out of date. What matters for the rigor of our explanatory analysis, however, is that our depiction of ownership forms and other structural variables (such as audience characteristics and primary funding) are derived as much as possible from the same time period as our content analysis. In other words, one simply has to choose a time period and try to hold to it. As we will see, the 2010s and early 2020s have been an important turning point in the rise and fall (and rise, again) of new media ownership forms and funding-audience strategies. Even as it recedes into the past, we believe that an in-depth understanding of this particular historical moment will continue to be valuable for any understanding of where journalism has been and where it is going.

To facilitate a focused and theoretically useful comparison, within limits that attempt to reflect the actual structure and composition of each national field, we hold constant for some factors while incorporating variation in others. We focus on general interest outlets, and thus, except for passing discussions to provide context, we exclude smaller, more specialized news outlets and business news outlets. We do not analyze the online versions of weekly or monthly magazines, focusing instead on outlets that, regardless of medium, tend to post on a daily basis. We include outlets with audiences either elite (high education and income) or mass omnibus (slightly below to slightly above the mean levels of education and income). We also consider outlets with the high economic capital that accrues from large audiences and revenues and/or the high symbolic capital that accompanies journalistic prizes: some outlets possess one type of capital more than the other, some are able to combine the two (see Chapter 2). Our sample comprises variation in funding and in the political views of audiences and owners.

Our approach incorporates multiple methods, both qualitative and quantitative. Over a period of more than a decade, capturing processes of change as well as continuity, we conducted more than one hundred in-depth, semi-structured interviews with owners, founders, top managers, and editors across all ownership forms in each country. Many of these interviews are excerpted in this book, noting the title of the person at the time of the interview. We gathered data on owner and audience characteristics and funding for all the outlets in our study, derived from proprietary surveys, company annual reports, direct requests to news organizations, and database searches. We supplemented this research with systematic reviews of reports from professional associations, industry groups, or research institutes; trade journal articles; and published memoirs or interviews with news industry insiders. Finally, we conducted an original quantitative content analysis of each outlet's news website measuring dimensions of public service orientation, partisan favorability and intensity, and economic instrumentalist self-promotion. For the analysis of public service-oriented and partisan news, we drew a "constructed week" sample consisting of general news, economic news, and opinion articles for each outlet on each sample day, beginning in December 2015 and concluding in June 2016. This procedure generally provided us with fifty to seventy-five articles per outlet, categorized by topic and genre, and hundreds of mentions of individuals and organizations, categorized by institutional affiliation, partisan leaning, and valence (positive, negative, or neutral/mixed). For the analysis of economic instrumentalist promotion, we drew *the entire universe* of published articles available in databases for periods ranging from 2015 to 2019—hundreds of thousands of articles—to identify all mentions of owners and associated economic interests; we then drew subsamples to code for valence of the mentions.

We primarily analyze news content variables for each news outlet *in relation to other outlets in the same national field.* This method allows us to see the effects of ownership in national context and to see if such nationally relational effects aggregate in a statistically significant way across three leading western democracies.[20] (For more detailed information about methods and sources, see Appendix II: Methods, hereafter referred to as Methods Appendix.)

No doubt there are gaps in the story we tell, corners of the media world we did not adequately explore, new developments we missed. We invite others to use what they can from this book—whether conceptual, methodological, or empirical—to help make sense of what will likely be, for better or worse, more decades of transformation in the economics of journalism. Further, although our focus is on news media, we hope that our investigations can help inspire and guide research on ownership over the production of all types of cultural goods—from music to film to visual art, popular entertainment, and more—that make our individual and collective lives fulfilling in every sense of the word.

The Rest of the Book

The remainder of the book consists of seven chapters and a conclusion. In Chapter 1, we develop further the theoretical themes and original conceptual framework previewed in the Introduction. (Readers more interested in the empirical analysis may choose to skip ahead to Chapter 2.) We show why a focus on media concentration or individual media moguls will not tell us everything we need to know about the power of media ownership. We explain what we mean by "forms of ownership," an approach heralded but not fully theorized or empirically investigated by scholars such as James Curran, C. Edwin Baker, and Robert Picard and Aldo van Weezel. We develop this approach theoretically by linking it to: the institutional logics framework of Roger Friedland, Patricia Thornton and others; Pierre Bourdieu's field theory; and the media management school of economics led by Eli Noam, Lucy Küng, and others. Against all-or-nothing claims about the power of ownership, we insist that ownership must be understood both in *context* (historical, social, economic, symbolic) and as part of a *complex* of interrelated factors that tend to assemble together, largely due to the conscious strategies adopted by owners and managers. We conclude by defining and clarifying three normatively consequential modes of power—the concrete ways in which ownership ultimately matters—public service orientation, political instrumentalism and partisanship, and economic instrumentalism.

In Chapter 2, we fill in this framework by retelling the history of news media in the US, Sweden, and France through the lens of ownership forms. We thus document which ownership forms emerged first, their unique and shared characteristics across the countries, and how they developed and changed over time. Our goal is to demonstrate the distinct institutional logics of each ownership form and the kind and degree of variation for which they each make room. In the last half of the chapter, we identify the economic, social, and symbolic logics that organize and differentiate media across and within ownership forms in each of the national fields.

Chapters 3 and 4 shift the focus to media management, first to decisions about investing or cutting spending and then to the process of what we call *funding-audience adjustment.* We show how particular funding-audience adjustment strategies—matching the optimal amount and type of funding with a target audience—tend to be affiliated more consistently with some ownership forms than others. This analysis allows us to identify *ownership complexes* as subgroupings consisting of ownership form, primary funding, and audience demographics.

Chapter 5 analyzes public service orientation in action. We measure the news content of fifty-one news websites across the three countries for amount and type of public service-oriented *information* and *pluralism.* Using standardized scales that measure these amounts in relation to other news outlets in the same national field, we search for patterns in any strong associations between public service-oriented news content and ownership forms, funding, and audiences.

Chapter 6 examines the relationship between ownership complexes and political instrumentalism. It draws on in-depth interviews and other insider sources to explore how ownership forms, funding-audience adjustment strategies, organizational legacies, and formal or informal professional groups or procedures facilitate, shape, or hinder political instrumentalism. The chapter concludes with a quantitative analysis of partisan slant or favorability—in attention, valence (left versus right-leaning), and intensity (degree of imbalance regardless of direction)—for fifty-one news outlets across the three countries.

Chapter 7 examines economic instrumentalism as it manifests in the self-promotion of positive information and the suppression of negative information about ownership economic interests. Drawing on a modified sample of US, Swedish, and French news outlets' total news output over twenty- to twenty-one-month periods, we quantitatively measure how often owners, major shareholders, donors, and associated companies and organizations appear in news coverage and whether those mentions are positive or negative. We also systematically search journalistic professional and trade publications for any economic instrumentalism "public scandals" that have emerged over the past decade. We conclude this chapter with a discussion of the special methodological challenges posed by an investigation of economic instrumentalism and consider how economic instrumentalist goals may be achieved by owners even in the absence of self-interested promotion or suppression of news content.

In the Conclusion, we bring together the many research strands of the book to answer the question posed at the outset: how does media ownership matter? We review how the answer is different depending on the mode of power and identify similarities and differences across three national journalistic fields. We highlight the book's unique theorization of ownership complexes (forms and funding-audience adjustment strategies) and how it provides a unifying *lingua franca* to organize and make sense of a fragmented but growing body of research on media ownership. The chapter concludes with an exploration of emerging questions and promising new research across the globe.

In sum, the deceptively simple question of how media ownership matters is really two questions, both complex and multi-faceted. One is a question of what is at stake. It leads us to analyze the types of concrete outcomes of ownership that matter to the life of a democratic society: information, accountability, and voice; partisan engagement, the risk of imbalance in attention and criticism or praise; and economic self-dealing. The other is a question of influence. How much and in what ways do different ownership forms, in interaction with funding and target audiences, actually shape the news? In the remainder of this book, we will attempt to answer these difficult and often politically charged questions as fully and honestly as we can.

1
Ownership Forms and Modes of Power: A New Framework

In the broad public debate, media ownership is often about the concentrated market share of big corporations, like AT&T or Disney, or the assumed influence of individual moguls, like Rupert Murdoch or Vincent Bolloré. What tends to be ignored are the organizational infrastructures underneath these big names. As media economics scholar Benjamin Compaine has asked: "Are there patterns of ownership that matter?"[1] The purpose of this book is to identify these patterns and to investigate how they matter for the kind of news that gets produced. In this chapter, we explain how a theory of institutional logics can be used to develop a rigorous framework for identifying distinct ownership "forms." However, ownership power is also shaped by potentially cross-cutting social influences and the basic uncertainty that besets any strategy to produce cultural content for an audience. We thus add to our conceptual toolkit theories of social fields and media management strategies of funding and audience adjustment. Having identified how ownership matters in its concrete functioning, we conclude this chapter by turning to the question of how it matters in its normatively consequential outcomes, or what we call its "modes of power": public service orientation, political instrumentalism and partisanship, and economic instrumentalism.

Beyond Media Concentration and Moguls

For some critics of media market concentration, the primary issue is not the form of ownership, but rather the number of outlets available to the public and the number of companies owning these outlets, with the ultimate danger being monopoly control.[2] The central concern of this approach is aptly summed up in Ben Bagdikian's quote of British Lord Acton for the final edition of his classic text, *The Media Monopoly*: "Power corrupts; absolute power corrupts absolutely."[3] Yet Bagdikian failed to see the need for a pluralism of *forms* of media. He saw "commercial" control as the only possibility and expressed little interest in public or nonprofit alternatives. Commercial control, he wrote, "is far from perfect, but it is less bad than any other system."[4] This overriding concern with ownership concentration over form generated notable blind spots. To offer

How Media Ownership Matters. Rodney Benson et al. Oxford University Press. © Rodney Benson, Mattias Hessérus, Timothy Neff, and Julie Sedel 2025. DOI: 10.1093/oso/9780199931293.003.0002

just one example: with its wide reach and substantial resources, the public BBC increases the concentration of the British journalistic field, but it does not thereby decrease the civic quality of the offering, in fact the contrary occurs according to most research.[5]

When discussing concentration, we also need to be clear about what we are measuring and how levels of concentration vary historically across sectors and nation-states. In the successive editions of his book between 1983 and 2004, Bagdikian documented a decrease in the number of companies controlling the majority of US media from fifty to just five.[6] However, this statistic does not capture significant differences across media sectors. Indeed, concentration in ownership of local television news in the US may be reaching historic highs, with the Sinclair chain owning the legal limit of stations reaching thirty-nine percent of all US households.[7] However, the total newspaper print circulation controlled by the largest chain, Gannett/Gatehouse, at just over ten percent as of 2019, was still less than that controlled by William Randolph Hearst's newspaper empire in 1935, with some fourteen percent of total US daily newspaper circulation and twenty-three percent of the Sunday circulation.[8]

Columbia University economist Eli Noam, leading an international team of scholars, places the US in global perspective in *Who Owns the World's Media? Media Concentration and Ownership around the World.*[9] Noam presents this project as a way to provide empirical evidence to settle the ongoing debate between the "pessimists," such as Bagdikian, and the "optimists," such as Compaine.[10] Noam and colleagues amassed an impressive collection of data for thirty countries that together make up sixty-three percent of the world's population, eighty-two percent of the world's GDP, and ninety percent of world media revenues,[11] a sample that includes the nation-states at the heart of our study: the US, France, and Sweden. One of Noam's astounding findings, at least in light of Bagdikian's well-known critical portrayal of US media, is that the US has the *least* concentrated news media ownership among all thirty countries. As Table 1.1 shows, the US is much less concentrated in news media ownership (attention and revenues) than Sweden and France, which are ranked in the middle of Noam's sample.[12]

The most concentrated national media systems are China, Egypt, South Africa, Russia, Turkey, and Mexico—all with authoritarian systems or weak democracies. However, the least concentrated media systems are not necessarily the strongest democracies: immediately following the US as the least concentrated news media systems (either for revenues or attention) are Argentina, Japan, Spain, Canada, Belgium, Poland, Taiwan, Germany, Finland, Brazil, and Switzerland. If we examine the rankings provided by Reporters Without Borders (RSF), we see only a very loose connection between media "freedom" and low news media industry concentration. Of the aforementioned Noam-ranked lowest concentration countries, only Finland is listed among the top ten for media freedom among the 180 countries in the RSF's report from the same

Table 1.1 National News Media Ownership Concentration

	HHI News Media by Attention (30 Country Rank: Least Concentrated)	HHI News Media by Revenues (30 Country Rank: Least Concentrated)
US	828 (1)	839 (1)
Sweden	2,629 (14)	2,442 (11)
France	2,688 (17)	2,459 (14)
30 country average	3,006	2,818

Note: Figures and rankings are from Noam (2016c, 1317, Table 38-7, "Weighted Country HHIs, 2011 or Most Recent"). HHI (Herfindhal-Hirschman Index), a measure of market concentration, has a low score (indicating even distribution) that varies depending on the number of units and a high score of 10,000 (indicating a monopoly).

Table 1.2 Top Five Largest Audience Online News Websites by National Field and Ownership Form

	Stock Market Widely Held	Stock Market Dominant Shareholder	Private	Civil Society	Public
US	*HuffPost* (1) *CNN* (2)	*New York Times* (3) *Fox News* (4) *NBC News* (5)	—	—	—
France		*Le Figaro* (2)	*Le Monde* (1)	*Ouest-France* (4) *20 Minutes* (5)*	*France Télévisions (FranceTVInfo)* (3)
Sweden	*Aftonbladet* (1) *Svenska Dagbladet* (5)	—	*Expressen* (2) *Dagens Nyheter* (4)	—	*SVT* (3)

Sources: Sweden: https://www.similarweb.com/top-websites/sweden (2020 data, accessed June 17, 2020); France, www.similarweb.com/top-websites/france (2020 data, accessed June 17, 2020); US (June 2019, eBizMBA Rank, from Quantcast data, hard copy preserved by authors). For Sweden and France, the top original (non-aggregator) news sites were identified among the top 50 websites listed.
*51 percent owned by SIPA Ouest-France.

period, while the US (#32), Spain (#36), Taiwan (#47), Japan (#53), Argentina (#54), and Brazil (#108) are ranked much lower.[13]

Having data on media concentration levels is useful, but we can deepen our understanding of concentrated media power by paying attention to ownership *forms*. If we look closely at the largest audience news websites in the US, France, and Sweden (Table 1.2), we immediately see that they embody different forms of media ownership. The largest US news websites are all stock market-traded, whereas the dominant media in France and Sweden are more evenly distributed across forms, including private, civil society, and public.[14]

As concentration increases, competition is assumed to decrease, in turn presumably reducing the pluralism of voices and viewpoints in the public sphere. US media regulation has long assumed the benefits of competition, that "truth" will emerge from vigorous competition in a "marketplace of ideas." Journalists generally relish competition and believe that it makes their journalism better.[15] Some research studies and policy analyses support this view, especially for low or moderate levels of competition.[16]

However, pluralism can also be accommodated *within* large conglomerates that earn profits by providing differentiated products for different audiences, including ideological differentiation.[17] We see this kind of intra-corporation pluralism in Comcast's ownership of both the US centrist *NBC* broadcast channel and the left-liberal *MSNBC* cable channel, or the Norwegian Schibsted's ownership of two sharply opposed Swedish newspapers, the social democratic popular tabloid *Aftonbladet* and the liberal-conservative morning daily *Svenska Dagbladet.*

Under some conditions, competition may actually serve to decrease pluralism. Media scholar Pablo Boczkowski found that as online competition increased between two leading Argentinian newspapers during the early 2000s, there was an "intensification of monitoring" by the rival newsrooms, which ultimately contributed to an increasing overlap in their selection, presentation, and narration of news.[18] French economist Julia Cagé and colleagues discovered that in the highly competitive French online news ecosystem, copying was rampant, and less than one-third of news content produced was original.[19] In a long-term historical study of French regional newspapers, Cagé also found that increased competition in local markets tended to decrease the production of public affairs news and, ultimately, local election voter turnout.[20] Conversely, public or philanthropic subsidies that provide a buffer from market competition seem to be part of the reason why news outlets like the *BBC*, the *Guardian*, the *Christian Science Monitor*, and *ProPublica* are able to provide substantial amounts of original public affairs news content.[21]

If raw competition is not able to reliably generate diverse journalistic content, what can? If institutional logics theory is correct, we should find that different *forms of owners* with distinct market or non-market values and incentives will expand the pluralism of practices, voices, and viewpoints in the news.[22] In addition, if Pierre Bourdieu is right that there is a "homology" or parallel relationship between the reception and production of news, then we should find that outlets with different kinds of audiences (varying in their income, education, or other "social properties") will also tend to differ in the types of news that they produce.[23] In other words, these theories suggest that it's not the *competition*, it's the institutional and social *composition* that produces the greatest pluralism.

* * *

The focus on individual media owners, sometimes called "moguls" when they are perceived to be very powerful, overlaps in some ways with media concentration.[24] After all, one way to become a mogul is to corner a market. But most moguls do not have monopoly power. And the power that they do have, according to Jonathan Knee, Bruce Greenwald, and Ava Seave of the Columbia University Business School in their book *The Curse of the Mogul*, is often counterproductive to financial success. They define a mogul as "any media company executive or owner with significant influence over significant operations."[25] According to Knee and colleagues, "good" moguls focus on the bottom line and maximum profits; "bad" moguls care more about getting a good table at the best restaurants, socializing with the celebrity "talent" that they employ, or winning prestigious prizes like the Pulitzers.[26]

It only takes a slight shift in perspective to see that when a mogul cares more about prestige than profits, public service-oriented journalism could be the beneficiary. This is the stance of journalism professor Dan Kennedy in his book, *The Return of the Moguls*.[27] Surveying a landscape in which stock market-traded and hedge fund-owned newspapers maximize profits through deep cuts in professional staff, Kennedy argues that a new generation of moguls, like Jeff Bezos, Amazon founder and *Washington Post* owner, and John Henry, owner of the Boston Red Sox baseball team and the *Boston Globe*, offers a welcome alternative. (Their closest French counterpart might be Xavier Niel, dominant private shareholder of *Le Monde*; there does not seem to be a contemporary Swedish example.) Whether or not they are truly motivated by civic mindedness, the result for Kennedy is clear: the new owners are investing needed funds and hope into previously moribund newsrooms, and while still demanding profitability in the long term, have made it clear that maximum profits are not their only measure for success. Kennedy acknowledges, but mostly dismisses, worries that some moguls indifferent to profits may have more nefarious motivations, such as using their media properties to advance their political and economic interests. This critique is especially widespread in France. *Bosses of the National Press: All Bad*, the translated title of a French book by journalist Jean Stern, offers a starkly different portrayal of moguls.[28] In fact, both Kennedy and Stern may be right: as we will see, owners may, in some instances, be serving the public good even as they also try to serve their own interests.

Much of the previous research on individual owners, whether called moguls or not, has focused on this question of influence, but with little or no attention to ownership forms.[29] The assumption has generally been that ownership power is synonymous with domination and thus the best owner is simply the owner who "interferes" least. This is the kind of power that sociologist Steven Lukes has termed "power over," consistent with Weberian and Marxist theories. But Lukes, drawing from Parsons, Arendt, and Foucault, argues that there is another conception of power—a "power to"—that is fundamental to generating the capacity to act.[30] This notion of "power to" contributes to a different conception of ownership power. It would not deny the value of journalistic autonomy; however, it also calls attention to the generative role that owners (whether journalists or non-journalists) may play in providing the resources and the infrastructures journalists need to do their job.

Because contemporary societies are highly pluralistic, encompassing a range of value-laden "institutional logics," this conception of power also accords to institutionally diverse owners the civically positive potential to expand the pluralism of voices, viewpoints, and styles of communication in the journalistic field. As Raymond Williams documents in *The Sociology of Culture*, cultural production has from its historical beginnings relied on some form of external support, whether from religious or aristocratic patronage, the market, or the state. Each of these "institutions," as Williams calls them, continues to live on in some form in the present, creating not only different degrees of autonomy but also distinct structural incentives for diverse ways of producing culture.[31] To fully assess the two faces of ownership power—domination and capacity to act—we need analytical categories adequate to the challenge. We turn now to this crucial task.

Typologies and Institutional Logics of Ownership Forms

Beyond the focus on media concentration and moguls, research on media ownership has often suffered from a lack of analytical clarity and comprehensiveness. As noted, Bagdikian's *The Media Monopoly* puts the onus on "big corporations" but makes no distinction between stock market-traded and privately held ownership.[32] In *Manufacturing Consent*, Edward Herman and Noam Chomsky identify "size, ownership, and profit orientation" as the first of five filters shaping the news.[33] They acknowledge the existence of commercial variants—such as stock market-traded, stock market-traded with a dominant shareholder, non-news media conglomerate ownership (such as General Electric), and direct family or individual control—but insist that the commonalities far outweigh the differences. They are all large, "profit-seeking" businesses, controlled by "very wealthy people or by managers who are subject to sharp constraints by owners and other market-profit-oriented forces"; and they "are closely interlocked, and have important common interests, with other major corporations, banks, and government."[34]

These claims are not entirely wrong, but they are incomplete.[35] Bagdikian and Herman and Chomsky also tend to be US-centric. They see public ownership of the media as small and irrelevant, based on the minor position occupied by US public media, as well as potentially dangerous, with government intervention representing either another form of top-down control or an alliance with corporate power to limit media freedom. Other classic US studies, by Herbert Gans, Gaye Tuchman, Todd Gitlin, and Charlotte Ryan, acknowledge the complexity and contradictions of large-scale commercial media, and the (small) possibilities for social movements to influence news media. Overall, though, they convey an impression of the media as an almost monolithic whole, governed by a singular commercial/professional media logic.[36] If they had spent more time looking abroad, they might have seen that there were in fact alternatives.[37] With the twenty-first-century financial collapse of journalism, interest in new economic models has dramatically increased but our theories of ownership have not kept up.

Media ownership research needs a fresh start, focused on *variation* in ownership forms.[38] We need a new framework sensitive to national contexts yet capable of identifying broad ownership types that transcend any single country case study.[39] Fortunately, there have been notable efforts in this direction, which we build upon.

British media sociologist James Curran proposed, in 1991, an elegant model, both descriptive and prescriptive, of a media system composed of structurally distinct sectors: a central hub of "public service TV" (like the *BBC*) surrounded by spokes of sectors of civic (associational), professional (journalist-controlled), private enterprise, and social market media (smaller private media partially supported by the state to promote "competition and consumer choice").[40] Curran, in turn, influenced the American legal scholar C. Edwin Baker. In a 1994 policy paper for the Harvard Shorenstein Center on Media, Politics, and Public Policy, Baker noted that much of the US research on media ownership up to that time had been "too narrow," focusing on relatively minor differences between "chain-owned" and "independent" newspapers or television stations. "Why?" He exclaimed. "Why not analyze additional ownership forms?" To really answer the question of how ownership matters, Baker felt, research needed to explore whether "worker ownership, or non-profit foundation ownership, or public ownership as well as . . . various non-ownership mechanisms of control within privately owned-media" would be more oriented toward democratic values.[41]

In a subsequent book on media concentration, Baker concluded that the "best way to respond to the problems" of concentration "is some version" of Curran's multi-sector proposal. Paraphrasing Curran, Baker concluded: "Strength lies in structural diversity. An ideal media realm will be pluralist in the types of media entities that it supports. Policy should encourage their operation *on the basis of different principles* . . . . [P]olicy should provide support, often varying kinds of financial support, for sectors not adequately nourished by the market."[42] For both Curran and Baker, because of the structural inevitability of "market failure" (the tendency of commercial media to underproduce public affairs information and overproduce sensationalist news for the broad public), strong noncommercial media are an essential part of any civically healthy media ecology.[43] Media economists, such as Simeon Djankov, Robert Picard, Aldo van Weezel, and Eli Noam, have also created useful ownership typologies, each with their own distinct categories and definitions.[44]

Nevertheless, there is still conceptual work to be done to isolate the forms that operate "on the basis of different principles." Fortunately, the "institutional logics" theory first proposed by sociologists Roger Friedland and Robert Alford, and subsequently developed by organizational scholars Patricia Thornton, William Ocasio, and Michael Lounsbury, provides a way forward.[45] Institutional logics theory captures well the contemporary experience of a pluralistic world in which many different standards and values compete for our attention and allegiance. It follows that media ownership is more likely to make a substantial difference in the kind of journalism that gets produced the more it is aligned with a distinct institutional logic.

In institutional logics theory, the social world is understood to consist of the "potentially contradictory" institutional orders of market, corporation, family, profession, religion, community, and the (democratic) state.[46] As we signaled in the Introduction, each of these logics provide "unique organizing principles, practices, and symbols that influence individual and organizational behavior."[47] These logics are "socially-constructed, historical patterns of cultural symbols and material practices, including assumptions, values, and beliefs, by which individuals and organizations provide meaning to their daily activity, organize time and space, and reproduce their lives and experiences."[48]

As such, a *market* logic driven outlet would emphasize maximization of profit; a media outlet owned by a *religious* organization would motivate action through adherence to shared sacred values; and an outlet owned by a *community*-driven owner, such as a political party or nonprofit association, would emphasize its commitment to the community's values and ideology. We would also witness distinctive practices at a *family*-controlled outlet, even if traded on the stock market, given the importance of institutional logics of family reputation, honor, and loyalty. For Thornton and colleagues, a *state* logic—presumably operative in public media—is legitimized by "democratic participation" and oriented toward increasing the common good.[49] Outside of the enforcement of democratic laws and norms, however, a state logic could operate to one-sidedly serve the interests of elites and the government in power.[50]

Institutional logics may operate at the level of journalistic staff as well as owners and top managers, either in a complementary or contradictory fashion. Regardless of ownership form, we would expect that most journalists would organize their work in relation to a *professional* institutional logic, emphasizing craft, expertise, reputation, and status; however, if the owners and top managers are also journalists, we would expect a journalistic professional institutional logic to be even more strongly embedded in the news outlet's practice. At outlets with non-journalist owners, as noted, we would expect not a total rejection of journalistic professionalism, but rather a hybridization or mixing of professional and other institutional logics.[51]

For example, a media outlet owned by a religious organization, if it hopes to be taken seriously in the professional journalistic field, would need to find a way to combine shared sacred values with journalistic professional values. The journalistic field, to use Bourdieu's terminology, *refracts* this attempted religious field intervention through its own dominant journalistic logic. The institutional logics approach, however, allows us to keep the focus on the *something new and different* that a non-journalistic owner is introducing into the journalistic field. Mary Baker Eddy, the founder of the US Christian Science church-owned *Christian Science Monitor*, did just that when she committed the *Monitor* in the early twentieth century to the practice of journalism that would "injure no man, but bless all mankind"—in other words, deeply contextualized journalism about social problems, international as well as national, that avoided any sensationalistic or partisan bias.[52]

News outlets owned by political parties, party-linked foundations (as in Sweden), social movements, or trade unions will likely attempt to join a particular community's ideological commitment to an otherwise professional practice of journalism: combining these logics may be more legitimate in some national journalistic fields (Sweden, France) than in others (the US) given their distinct histories of journalism and relations to the state and civil society.

In some cases, the unique logic of an ownership form may be quite subtle but nevertheless highly consequential for democracy. As journalism scholar David Ryfe persuasively argues, the emergence in the US of nonprofit 501(c)(3) ownership has generated new practices of journalism because of the philanthropic funding afforded by this ownership form. In particular, philanthropic funders' concern with policy or social change "impact" over maximizing audiences or revenues incentivizes news that is less frequently updated; less exclusive (encouraging collaboration and sharing among outlets); and more exclusively focused on public affairs, investigative, and in-depth reporting.[53]

Drawing on institutional logics theory, we should be on the lookout for a variety of ownership forms and subforms, but how any particular organization or individual acts is partially contingent and cannot be answered in advance of close empirical research.

* * *

To help us understand ownership in relation to distinctive institutional logics, we posit the existence of four broad ownership forms: market, private, civil society, and public. For each of these forms, we pay attention to their articulation of material and symbolic logics, as manifested in autonomy from market pressures, relations between ownership and management control, substantive value systems, and synergies with particular types of funding or audiences. Each of these forms (and subforms, to be discussed) embody dominant logics or constellations of logics.

Market ownership refers to any owner primarily subject to a profit-maximizing *market* logic, chiefly stock market and private equity/hedge fund ownership. Stock market ownership, by definition, would seem to fully embody the market logic, but it has not always done so exclusively. Through the 1970s, many stock market-traded companies were effectively controlled by managers primarily motivated by internal bureaucratic and status concerns (a *corporation* institutional logic) and, as such, they were partially insulated from pressures to increase share prices and maximize profits. In such conditions, it makes sense to emphasize the "principal–agent" relationship: the ever-present possibility that the agents (managers) supposedly acting on behalf of the owners/shareholders (principals) will "shirk" their responsibilities and serve their own corporate interests.[54] Beginning in the 1980s, however, according to economic sociologists Neil Fligstein and Adam Goldstein, large institutional investors and financial managers implemented new ways to realign the interests of managers with those of profit-maximizing shareholders through a "shareholder value" conception of corporate control. Top managers were increasingly paid in stock shares rather than salaries, thus closely tying their total compensation to company financial performance (as indicated in rising share prices). In the process, financial markets came to reward corporations and their managers with higher share prices primarily when they cut costs through consolidation, outsourcing, and benefit reductions. Employee "layoff announcements," in particular, were interpreted "as a signal of shareholder-friendly management whereby the number of workers would decline and their salaries would be added to corporate profits."[55] In addition, the convention of publicly released quarterly reports, eagerly awaited by market actors, created a short-term focus that disincentivizes managers from taking any losses while waiting for long-term investments to pay off.

"Private equity," according to Fligstein and Goldstein, "is the main mechanism through which the tenets of shareholder value have spread to new domains beyond [stock market] publicly traded corporations."[56] The terms "private equity" and "hedge fund" are often used interchangeably in public discourse and by journalists. They refer to subtle distinctions important to finance professionals, but their shared characteristics have been more consequential for journalism.[57]

Compared to stock market-traded companies, private equity and hedge funds do not face the same quarterly pressure to maximize short-term profits: instead, their typical maximum time horizon is around three years. Nevertheless, they exist to generate superior financial returns, which eventually translate, as we will see in Chapter 3, into aggressive staff layoffs and other budget cuts. There are also significant interconnections between private equity, hedge funds, and stock market ownership. Hedge funds and private equity firms are among the largest institutional shareholders in stock market-traded media companies. Such large shareholdings have entitled them to seats on the companies' boards of directors, which they have used to push for policies that prioritize maximum profits over all other goals.[58]

One subform of market ownership, however, has the potential to resist profit maximizing pressures: stock market-traded companies in which a dominant shareholder—an individual or often a family—controls a majority or strong plurality (generally at least 30 percent) of voting shares.[59] Reflecting this domestic or *family* logic of "unconditional loyalty," the extended Sulzberger family that controls a majority of voting shares of the New York Times Company holds regular retreats to maintain close ties and reinforce shared values, such as their long-standing professional and civic commitment to invest in quality news.[60] At other outlets, families with a controlling interest may be driven more by partisan political or religious motivations. Nevertheless, because their wealth is ultimately rooted in the issuance of publicly traded shares, the dominant shareholding family of a stock market-traded company can never entirely ignore pressures to increase stock prices and dividends through profitable operations.

Private ownership is distinguished from *market* ownership in at least two major ways. First, it is usually a more concentrated form of ownership, residing either with a wealthy individual, a family, or a small group of investors. Second, although aspiring to generate positive net revenues to support operations, private owners have no obligation to "maximize shareholder value" and thus have greater discretion to balance profit targets and timelines with amenities of status, political influence, or civic duty. Private ownership is often linked to multi-generational *family* stewardship, but also incorporates employee ownership, as well as start-ups in which individual founders are supported by venture capital or angel investors. There can be significant variation within this form, including cross-nationally. As we will see in the next chapter, at US employee-owned outlets, management has generally been delegated to non-journalist business managers operating according to *market* and *corporation* logics, with a mandate to preserve employment and private shareholder values for retiring employees.[61] In France, employee ownership has generally involved more active journalistic entrepreneurial management and control, and thus a strong journalistic *professional* logic. Venture capital investors (often organized as limited liability partnerships, or LLPs) have a lengthy time horizon before they expect profitability, up to ten or more years.[62] As competition has increased for the "next big thing," venture capital has often granted founding entrepreneurs near total autonomy. One of the largest VC firms, the Founders Fund, even bragged on its website that "it has never removed a single founder" and that it gives entrepreneurs with "audacious vision" veto-proof authority over their boards of directors.[63]

Civil society refers to the associational and organizational sector that operates between the market and the state, without being entirely independent of either. Civil society ownership thus encompasses a range of distinct institutional logics: *professional* (primarily journalistic, but also academic), *religion*, and *community* (party-partisan, labor union, national public policy, or local civic foundation). What unites these diverse institutional logics under the rubric of civil society is a strong mission-driven orientation and a certain distance from profit pressures.[64] As such, this ownership form inverts the logic of the market by placing the pursuit of profit below that of professional, partisan/activist, or religious ideals. These non-market logics are expressed in many ways: in the values expressed in their organizational bylaws and mission statements; in the non-business backgrounds of a relatively high proportion of their founders, board directors, and managers; and typically, in governmental dispensation from tax liability for the organization and donors. Beyond the specific institutional logics, there are two important sets of overlapping oppositions within the civil society ownership form: first, between outlets that provide general news for a broad audience and those outlets that provide more topic-specific or partisan slanted information for a more targeted audience; and second, between outlets funded commercially (advertising, subscriptions, or other sales) and those funded through non-commercial sources, such as large scale philanthropy, small donations, and/or partial government subsidies (although some outlets receive both commercial and non-commercial funding, with varying mixtures). To be clear, we are concerned with the relatively public-facing media produced by these organizations and not the internal newsletters or magazines they may produce solely for their members.[65]

Public ownership ranges from having a more democratic nonpartisan state logic in most western democracies to a non-democratic partisan state logic in authoritarian nation-states. Public media, by definition, have strong civic missions, although the particular understandings of that mission may vary cross-nationally. In many countries, there has also long been a strong nation-building emphasis, an effort to create and foster a common culture; in recent decades, to varying degrees, this unifying thrust has co-existed with an effort to acknowledge and celebrate diversity. In principle, it is the form most insulated from market pressures, but partial reliance on commercial funding or competition with commercial outlets may lessen such autonomy. In most cases (the US and New Zealand are exceptions), the majority of funding derives from citizen payments (general taxes or a dedicated fee), but public media outlets may vary both within and across countries in their specific mix of public, advertising, and philanthropic funding.[66] In contrast to elite commercial and some civil society media, news content will be widely available and not restricted by paywalls on the basis of the civic principle of universal access to all citizens.[67] Conversely, even in democracies, public media can be subject to political pressure from the government in power or opposition parties, as well as from their audiences. Public media journalists will be more autonomous in their professional judgments and more accountable to civic responsibilities when "arms-length" administrative buffers and depoliticized allocation of resources are clearly designed with these purposes in mind.[68]

In sum, each of these four broad forms of ownership—market, private, civil society, and public—express distinctive institutional logics or collections of logics. At this juncture, we must also note two important subforms that may cross these ownership forms: the first, the "conglomerate" subform; the second, the "current/legacy journalist control" subform of non-ownership control. Conglomerate ownership refers to any outlet owned by a major company with control of significant non-news media holdings. This subform can be linked to either market or private ownership and has important implications for economic instrumentalism (see the discussion of "performance" in this chapter's final section).[69] Current/legacy journalist control encompasses any outlet founded and majority-owned by journalists; controlled if not directly owned (as in the case of nonprofits) by journalists; and/or if not currently controlled, retaining some journalistic legacy rights of control (such as, in France, veto power over appointment of director). This expression of a professional logic as a power over or counter-power within ownership forms, a kind of "non-ownership mechanism of control" as suggested by Baker, is consistent with Thornton and colleagues' premise that institutional logics are modular and can exist in combination in particular empirical cases.

From Ownership in Context to Agentic "Ownership Complexes"

Media ownership forms must be understood and analyzed in context. As Michael Schudson succinctly stated: "Ownership is important. Ownership is not everything."[70] But which context? Beyond the obvious importance of national context and professional journalistic traditions, two of the most important factors that vary within national fields are audiences and funding.

Following Gans's assessment in his classic *Deciding What's News*, it was long assumed that journalists knew little about, and cared even less about, their audiences. With the rise of sophisticated audience metrics closely monitored by editors (even if not all reporters), the notion that audiences do not influence the news is harder to maintain. Indeed, a key focus, and contribution, of contemporary journalism research has been to show how perceptions of audience demand are shaping news production.[71] Even in the pre-digital era, Bourdieu demonstrated the tight links between circuits of news production and consumption. He argued that the "social space"—the entirety of social relations in a society—is organized around two fundamental oppositions: between those actors (individuals and organizations) that possess significant material and symbolic resources (*capital*) and those who do not, and between those whose capital is primarily cultural versus those whose capital is primarily economic. Bourdieu posits that there will be a parallel or "homologous" relationship between the social positions that actors occupy in a field and the discursive "position-takings" that they adopt; he also expects production and reception to be homologous.[72]

The notion of homology suggests that there will be a match between the positions (of economic success or professional prestige) that news outlets occupy, the news content that they produce, and the audiences that these outlets attempt to reach. We can sense this recognition of a "matching" for example, when owner/publisher Arthur Sulzberger Jr., described the *New York Times* as producing "quality journalism" for "quality audiences."[73] Such pairings may or may not accord with ownership forms, but if they do, it will probably be at least in part because the forms tend to align with particular social positions in the field. Thus, Bourdieu's field theory provides both important social context for analyzing ownership and an alternative hypothesis for why and how news outlets differ in the kind of news that they produce.

Funding can be linked to both institutional and social class logics. Advertising tends to express the interests of profit-generating *markets* as inflected by the caution of large corporations anxious to avoid controversy that might damage the value of their brands;[74] at the margins, nevertheless, some small niche advertisers can support *community* logics expressed in alternative cultural and political content.[75] Corporate advertisers tend to prefer affluent and younger audiences with the disposable income and inclination to spend, but to the extent that advertising-funded media provide "free" access to their content, these outlets will attract larger and more economically diverse audiences than subscription-funded media.[76] While paying audiences have been hailed as a way to avoid undue advertiser pressure, they also introduce their own types of influence: providing an incentive to produce unique, high quality stories not available elsewhere, but also, potentially increasing political pressures to pander to subscribers' pre-existing partisan views. Large-scale philanthropy tends to express the class and political interests of economic capital old (early twentieth-century industrial titans) and new (Silicon Valley) converted into cultural capital: donations are usually justified as *civic* but may also express various *market*, *corporation*, and *community* logics.[77] Public (taxpayer) funding, facilitated by the state, is justified by a civic or democratic *state* logic, but if not adequately protected from political pressures can serve to promote some communities over others or reproduce the political status quo.

What is missing so far in this framework—of ownership forms structurally linked to institutional logics but also influenced by their audience social positioning and their types of funding—is the contingent and never entirely predictable work of management and editorial strategy. Building on Graham Murdock's classic categorization of ownership influence as either allocative or operational,[78] two dimensions of media management strategies seem crucial: first, budgeting; and second, matching funding sources to target audiences to create a sustainable revenue flow, however sustainability is defined, through a process of *funding-audience adjustment*.

Allocative power sets goals and priorities and establishes the level of resources available for any given purpose. Allocative power can be focused on cutting (reducing costs and services) or creating (adding or modernizing products and services), with variable effects on the "sustainable provision of journalistic value," as journalism scholars Michael Brüggemann, Frank Esser, and Edda Humprecht found in their study of the responses of German publishers to the financial crisis of the late 2000s.[79] Allocation also involves decisions to expand (purchase additional outlets or related businesses), ostensibly to achieve economies of scale and greater efficiencies, but if fueled by excessive debt may put the enterprise at risk.

Meanwhile, it is in the operational realm that Bourdieu's "production-reception" homologies are produced. Decisions about how to fund the outlet can shape the size and type of the targeted audience, and vice versa. At US privately owned outlets with venture capital backers, for instance, investors have tended to follow the template of the immense success of Google, in particular its prioritization of scale before monetization and the ultimate massive payoff it achieved through advertising. As a result, they encouraged digital media outlets (like *HuffPost* or *BuzzFeed*) to develop and target their content for mass audiences rather than subscription-paying elite audiences.[80] Whether or not reporters are aware of this process of matching content to audiences and funding, their editors definitely are.[81] Jenny Wiik's large survey of Swedish journalists found that when asked whether responding to an audience's desire for diversion and relaxation should be a priority, sixty-two percent of managing editors said "yes" compared to only thirty-six percent of reporters.[82] In a recent study of journalists' "imagined audiences" that included the *Chicago Tribune*, Jacob Nelson found that most reporters still adhered to a vague "mass" conception of their audience, but that a top editor and marketing manager he spoke with were well-informed about their audience demographics, which they knew to be primarily "rich" and "white" in a city with a significant working-class and minority population.[83]

Matching supply with demand is an art as much as a science, subject to uncertainty and frequent trial and error. It has to be a priority not only at profit-maximizing outlets but also at civil society outlets that prize their professional or political autonomy, as attested by the memoirs of the editors of the British *Guardian* and the US left-leaning political magazine *The Nation*.[84] At the Swedish "red-green" *Dagens ETC*, editor-in-chief Andreas Gustavsson places readers at the heart of the newspaper's financial strategy and journalistic mission: "We communicate extremely actively with the readers several times a week. [If you are a subscriber or crowdfunder] you get a personal letter from me where I tell you what is going on and I also ask if we should invest in economic journalism now, or should we hire a climate journalist . . . The readers have a great influence on what we do."[85]

One powerful example helps show how ownership form shapes but does not determine funding-audience adjustment strategies: the long and uneven road to the *New York Times*'s now highly admired national and international digital subscription model. The *New York Times*'s ownership subform—stock market-traded, but with a dominant shareholder—made it possible for the owning family-appointed publishers to take the long view and risk short-term losses, but it did not dictate the particular strategies that they would pursue.

The *New York Times*'s first attempt to create a national edition, in the 1980s and early 1990s, had only limited success because national advertisers refused to support it, preferring instead national magazines like *Time* and *Newsweek*. When Arthur Sulzberger Jr., father of the current publisher, took the reins in the early 1990s, he initially made a distinctive break with his own father's attempt to target the newspaper to elites, no matter their location.[86] Instead, Sulzberger Jr. pursued a "return to New York" and a more "populist" approach that would attract all those who had so far resisted the allure of the *New York Times*, with "expanded coverage of sports, metro, and Downtown [culture]."[87] International and public affairs reporting, of course, remained strong, as part of the historic "franchise" of the *New York Times*, central to its quest for influence as well as the prestige of its economic brand. By the mid-2000s, however, the collapse of print advertising and circulation ultimately doomed this approach, tipping the *New York Times* as close to bankruptcy as it had ever been since its earliest years. In 2011, the maverick who had broken with the elitist *New York Times*'s tradition pivoted again, and famously re-embraced it for the internet age with his then controversial decision to require subscriptions for access to the newspaper's website. Within a decade that decision had created tremendous synergies in social, symbolic, and economic capital for the *New York Times*, generating resources for a renewed expansion in public affairs, investigative, and international reporting, which continues to be built on by Arthur Jr.'s son, A. G. Sulzberger.[88] This historical sketch demonstrates not only the contingency of funding-audience adjustment strategies, but also how central they are to owner involvement in the news, even at those news organizations such as the *New York Times* where publishers are widely praised for granting enormous autonomy to their journalists.

We refer to this strategic capacity of owners to bring together configurations of ownership forms, audiences, and funding mechanisms as an ownership-led *complex* oriented toward producing a certain kind of news content. The term "ownership complex" emphasizes the crucial role of ownership forms and particular owners in producing a working project out of an array of structural factors and contingent situations.[89] In Chapter 4, we will deepen our understanding of the news outlets in our study as we situate each of them in particular ownership complexes of institutional form, funding, and audience.

***

Picard and van Weezel cautioned, at the end of their survey of types of ownership, that "Good and poor performance can result under all forms."[90] In his careful analysis of Sweden's news media landscape, explicitly referring to Picard and van Weezel, Jonas Ohlsson, director of the University of Gothenburg's Nordicom research center, came to much the same conclusion.[91] We interpret this statement in a number of ways. First, it is an expression of the uncertainty—the contingency—of social relations. Despite similar structuring influences, media owners and managers may respond in different ways. Local circumstances matter.[92] In other words, even when there are patterns, there will be exceptions. We absolutely expect this to be the case.

However, we also see Picard and van Weezel's wording as a pithy, if perhaps unintended, expression of the limitations to date of the dominant typologies of ownership. If it remains difficult to systematically link performance and ownership, one way forward is to develop more coherent and internally consistent categories of ownership forms and the context in which they operate. This section has aimed to achieve this goal.

Finally, their assessment raises the crucial issue of "performance" but does not clearly define what is meant by the term, let alone what is meant by good or bad. Picard and van Weezel, as well as Ohlsson, are primarily focused on economic and managerial variables related to efficient and sustainable economic performance. To the extent that they mention "public interest," Picard and van Weezel assume that it will correlate with sound management and "financial strength." To their credit, they call for more "systematic and controlled comparisons."[93] However, we will not get very far unless our comparisons analytically disentangle economic performance from civically consequential journalistic performance. We cannot assume that these two aspects of performance are seamlessly integrated. Financial success can just as easily be at the expense of "quality" journalism as in support of it. Conversely, some civically valuable journalistic endeavors may struggle to achieve commercial viability. What we urgently need is a careful elaboration of the journalistic outcomes that matter for society writ large. This is the focus of the next section.

Performance and Modes of Power

To fully answer the question of what constitutes "good" or "bad" performance, the researcher must go beyond the empirical object of study to identify normatively what is at stake.[94] Journalism has long enjoyed certain legal rights because of the conviction based in political philosophy that it performs a range of tasks necessary for the optimal functioning of democracy. Journalists are criticized when they are perceived as falling short of these ideals. Comparative scholars themselves do not need to adopt a strong specific normative position, but if they want to conduct research that makes clear what is at stake, the link between practices and a range of normative evaluative standards must be specified. Cross-national or regional differences in understandings of particular terms like "pluralism" or "diversity" should be acknowledged, but need not prevent the development of a generalizable assessment of journalistic performance.[95] We suggest that there exist three broad types of normatively consequential journalistic performance—what we term *modes of power*—each with multiple facets: public service orientation, political instrumentalism/partisanship, and economic instrumentalism. It is important to emphasize that these modes of power are analytical constructs or Weberian ideal types: in practice, specific actions undertaken by media owners may include elements of one or more of these modes of power.

Serving the public is today considered the ethical heart of journalistic professionalism, and often is referred to simply as journalistic "quality," but in fact this singular "quality" is composed of multiple elements that may or may not coincide in a single text or image or news outlet's body of coverage. We deploy *public service* as an abstract term, acknowledging that it also has a narrower application to "public service broadcasting" in many western European countries. Public service is both an ideal and a commitment to provide resources for civic ventures that may or may not have an economic return. It is a relatively modern invention, arising in the early twentieth century as part of a broader civic movement reshaping government, the academy, the professions, and eventually journalism across many western societies, taking slightly different forms in each national journalistic field.[96] Public service *commitment* is evident in moments of crisis when a media outlet risks significant financial loss or legal threat to pursue an investigation, and yet decides to do so anyway. In the 1970s, when the *Washington Post* decided to publish the Pentagon Papers (following the *New York Times*'s prior brave decision to be the first to publish) despite intense White House pressure and potential financial losses, it demonstrated this kind of public service commitment. Public service *orientation* is manifested in the ongoing day-to-day investment in reporting and analysis that realizes the civic mission of comprehensively and accurately informing the public, challenging corrupt or unjust power regardless of party, and providing a debate forum for a range of voices and viewpoints. Throughout this book, we thus refer to the basic building blocks of public service orientation as civically relevant *information* and *pluralism*.

It is also useful to make a distinction between staff journalistic-led public service orientation present at virtually all news organizations, even those with the most venal or partisan proprietors, and owner-led public service orientation, in which the owner (whether individual or collective) consistently and vocally defines the mission or brand in public service terms and provides the resources to support these goals. Sociologist Jeffrey Alexander has argued that public service-oriented journalism will endure in the US, despite the financial crisis that has led to significant cutbacks at most news organizations, because of the ideal of public service that suffuses the profession, akin to a cultural "dark matter."[97] However, if ownership forms and complexes matter, we should find the expression in practice of this cultural dark matter to vary across outlets. In particular, news organizations with owner-led public service reinforcement should produce the strongest and most consistent public service orientation.

Political instrumentalism refers to overt or covert attempts by an owner to direct a media outlet to promote or attack politicians, social movements, and/or issues of special concern. Political instrumentalism has been an important part of news from its earliest years, although the legitimacy of its exercise waned through the twentieth century; in the twenty-first century, the political use of news media in an increasingly fragmented and polarized media environment now seems to be once again on the rise. Political instrumentalism is sometimes referred to as an *amenity potential* that makes ownership of a media outlet worthwhile even if it generates few or negative net profits. Economists Harold Demsetz and Kenneth Lehn define amenity potential as "nonpecuniary income associated with the provision of general leadership and with the ability to deploy resources to suit one's personal preferences," such as "believing that one is systematically influencing public opinion."[98] Political party ownership or affiliation is not necessary for a media outlet to engage in political instrumentalism. Any individual or organizational owner whose priorities are political as well as economic may wish to politically instrumentalize their news outlet, although in practice they may restrain themselves because of professional norms of balance or the fear of negative publicity. As we discuss in Chapter 6, partisan slant in coverage can also be the result of commercial strategies not driven by any conscious political intent.

Economic instrumentalism concerns an owner's use of a media outlet to maximize profits or to otherwise support their economic interests through increased access to policymakers or self-interested news coverage. Such news coverage may either *promote* synergistic products and divisions, investors, funders, and business allies, or *suppress* negative information about the same. Many of the owners/publishers in David Bowers's classic survey study actively encouraged news coverage promoting their activities or those of their friends and business partners and discouraged stories that might lead to a decrease in newspaper revenue. These owners were engaging in economic instrumentalism.[99]

In cases when owners' business and political interests are closely linked, the lines between economic and political instrumentalism can be difficult to draw. Taking into account the relations to powerful donors, such mixed modes of power can operate at civil society nonprofit media as much as at commercial media.[100] Ties to investors and funders that fundamentally compromise the capacity of a news outlet to independently report on their activities may be appropriately labeled "media capture," to use the term adopted by international communications scholar Anya Schiffrin and many leading media economists.[101] In principle, however, outlets may engage in economic (or political) instrumentalism without being wholly captured.

To be clear, modes of power may have both civically positive and negative aspects. Outlets that exhibit positive performance in one mode may or may not be positive in the others, and vice versa. Public service orientation is often associated with widely praised investigative or in-depth journalism, although some libertarian thinkers have dismissed such practices as paternalistic (presuming to give the people what they "need" rather than what they "want"). Political instrumentalism is often perceived today as unprofessional partisanship and bias, but the value of the causes it promotes also depends on the eye of the beholder; a national journalistic field dominated by partisan media outlets may achieve higher external pluralism (ideological diversity across a range of outlets) than one consisting only of less partisan public service-oriented outlets. Economic instrumentalism almost always embodies conflicts of interest and lack of transparency, and thus represents a clear violation of civic norms. However, a media outlet that promotes positive information or suppresses negative information about its owner's economic interests could nevertheless offer critical, in-depth coverage of actors or issues outside those interests.

Conclusion

In this chapter we have outlined our unique approach for studying media ownership. We began by identifying the need to transcend the classic but tired debates about media concentration and media moguls. Instead, we argue for a renewed and more rigorous focus on the *forms of ownership* that operate, in C. Edwin Baker's words, on the "basis of different principles"—in other words, which have the structural potential to make a difference in the kind of journalism that gets produced. We thus specify a new typology of ownership forms undergirded by their unique constellations of institutional logics—*market*, *private*, *civil society*, and *public*—as well as the subforms of conglomerate and current/legacy journalistic control. Further, we argue for the need to situate ownership forms not only in their social *context* of audiences and funding, but to understand this context as part of an *ownership complex* actively manipulated in conditions of uncertainty by owners and managers to sustain operations in service of their missions, whether commercial or non-commercial. We identify three major ways in which media ownership ultimately matters: the normatively consequential *modes of power* of *public service orientation*, *political instrumentalism*, and *economic instrumentalism*.

We turn now to a closer look at the history and contemporary material and symbolic structures of journalism in the US, Sweden, and France—the three national cases underlying our study—with a focus on how these national fields shape and are in turn shaped by media ownership.

2

Media Ownership in Three Democracies

In this chapter, we make concrete our four primary forms of ownership—market, private, civil society, and public. For each form, considered in roughly chronological order of development, we briefly trace its distinctive history and identify the major owners and news outlets that exemplify the ownership form and its variants in the US, Sweden, and France. Focusing mainly but not exclusively on the outlets highlighted in our study (see Appendix Table AI.1), we analyze both the material and symbolic dimensions of their institutional logics. We conclude by situating the news outlets in their national fields by their economic and symbolic power, as expressed in audience size and professional prizes, along with the social properties and partisan preferences of their owners and audiences. The information provided in this chapter provides crucial context for the analysis to follow in the rest of the book.

Ownership Forms in Historical Context

Private

Private media ownership today refers to companies with legal designations such as "C" Corporation (Inc.) and LLC (limited liability company) in the US; SA (société anonyme, or public limited company), SAS (société par actions simplifiée, or simplified joint stock company), and SCOP or SCIC (société co-operative) in France; and AB (aktiebolag, essentially the same as Inc. or SA) in Sweden. It would also include the société en commandite or LLP (limited liability partnership), sometimes used in France and the US. In contrast to market ownership, discussed in the next section, such companies are not traded on the stock market or subject to the intense profit pressures of hedge fund or private equity control.

From its beginnings, a major opposition within the private form of ownership has been between owners who are journalists (or in associated professions in printing and publishing) and those who are not. In all three countries in our study, most of the earliest newspaper owners, starting in the late 1600s and early 1700s, were printer-publishers, sometimes closely allied with the monarchy or other officials.[1] As democratic freedoms expanded during the 1700s

How Media Ownership Matters. Rodney Benson et al. Oxford University Press. © Rodney Benson, Mattias Hessérus, Timothy Neff, and Julie Sedel 2025. DOI: 10.1093/oso/9780199931293.003.0003

in all three countries (only briefly in Sweden and France, before being durably revived in the late 1800s), some owners were allied to political groups or were politicians themselves. These "publicists" were small businesses with political allegiances, due to their owners' commitments, their audience's demands, or both. In Sweden, throughout the 1800s many newspapers were closely aligned to "liberal," pro-market, anti-monarchical political currents. In promoting these ideas, private owners often also advanced their class and business interests.[2] Explicitly partisan, independent, small, privately held newspapers are now rare in all three countries, disappearing earliest in the US, while surviving in much diminished numbers in France and Sweden. Sweden's *Dagens ETC*, a left-wing daily launched in 2014, was owned by its founder Johan Ehrenberg (the driving force behind the journalism brand ETC starting in 1976). In 2020, Ehrenberg followed in the footsteps of many Swedish private newspaper owners and announced plans to transfer ownership of the news outlet to a (civil society) foundation designed to safeguard the purpose and ideology of the publication in perpetuity.[3]

Over the course of the nineteenth century, increased audience demand, the rise of advertising funding, and new printing technologies made possible significantly larger scale operations. At first, owners capable of making such investments came from the ranks of publicists and the emerging profession of "journalist" (differentiated earliest and most clearly as a separate profession in the US[4]). As late as the 1880s, leading US newspaper publishers, such as Joseph Pulitzer, had built their businesses from within, starting as printer's assistants and reporters. Even so, outside wealth was beginning to play a larger role in the industry. Pulitzer had to purchase the *New York World* in 1883 from railroad magnate Jay Gould. William Randolph Hearst, Pulitzer's chief competitor in the newspaper wars of the early 1900s, inherited his wealth from his father, a successful silver miner who became a US Senator from California.[5] During the first half of the twentieth century, most US newspapers continued to be owned by companies founded by family publishers largely devoted to the business of newspapers—in effect, combining *market*, *family*, and nascent *profession* and *corporation* institutional logics. By the early 1960s, around one-third of all US daily newspapers (and nearly half of the total circulation) were part of large multi-outlet, but still privately held, "chains," such as Hearst, Advance, Scripps-Howard, Gannett, Knight-Ridder, Times-Mirror, and McClatchy.[6]

In Sweden, private family ownership likewise was a major form of ownership over the course of the twentieth century, although it was rivaled by (civil society) political party and trade union ownership to a greater degree than in the US and France. Swedish family-owned newspapers tended to have strong political party allegiances. There was a brief period in the 1920s when originally non-news media owners dominated the national press: Wenner-Gren (vacuum cleaners, refrigerators), Kreuger (matchsticks), and Bonnier (book publishing).[7] Of the three, only the Bonnier family still owns newspapers (notably national newspapers *Dagens Nyheter* and *Expressen*, and many regional papers). The Bonnier Group was, for many decades, joined by other multi-generational family group owners, all focused on newspaper holdings, notably the Ander family's NWT, the Hamrin family's Hallpressen group, later Hall Media (including *Jönköpings-Posten*), and the Hjörne family's Stampen group (including *Göteborgs-Posten*).[8] Bonnier, however, is by far the dominant owning company in Sweden, a position that increased after 2019 when Bonnier, together with the foundation-owned Amedia, bought a number of foundation-owned regional newspapers. In 2020, again with Amedia, they bought Hall Media.[9] In 2019, the stock market-traded Polaris company became the Stampen group's dominant shareholder.[10]

In France, although there have been some notable wealthy private owners of major Parisian newspapers—such as Émile de Girardin and Jean Prouvost—no press chains of significant size emerged until Robert Hersant began developing one from the 1960s through the mid-1990s. His private Socpresse group eventually owned *Le Figaro*, the popular daily *France-Soir*, and more than twenty regional newspapers. At the time of Hersant's death in 1996, Socpresse was reported to be in significant debt.[11]

In general, non-news media (conglomerate) company investment in news outlets developed earlier and in more dramatic fashion in France than in the US and Sweden. According to press historian Jean Chalaby, "The first great motive for a French person to invest in a newspaper was the desire to acquire a means of influence. This is the reason why many contractors, bankers, and politicians owned newspapers."[12] In the decades leading up to World War I, France had some of the highest circulation newspapers in the world; there is some debate about how profitable they were (advertising revenues were significantly less than in the US), but what is certain is that their private "joint stock" ownership was unstable and brought in rotating rounds of outside investors.[13] During the 1920s and 1930s, these investors—and in some cases direct owners—came from a range of business sectors, including railroads, public works, textiles, cosmetics, the iron and steel trust, and even foreign governments, all of whom used newspapers to promote their intertwined economic and political interests. Corruption was rampant.[14]

Collaboration with the Nazi and Vichy regimes during World War II further discredited not only particular industrial investors but also the very idea of capitalist ownership. After the war, the French state committed to building a press system independent of commercial and especially external industrial power, but it paid little attention to the problem of providing adequate capitalization.[15] There followed an intense but brief post-war flowering of "independent" private newspapers, many of them led by ex-resistance fighters (e.g., *Franc-Tireur*, 1941–1957; Albert Camus's *Combat*, 1941–1974). *Le Monde* was launched in 1944 when General Charles de Gaulle felt France needed a new newspaper of reference untainted by wartime collaboration: he invited Hubert Beuve-Méry, a journalist who had worked at the prestigious newspaper *Le Temps* before the war, to serve as its first editor-in-chief. Beuve-Méry and *Le Monde*'s journalists quickly established their political independence from de Gaulle as well as their effective ownership control. In the wake of the May 1968 protests, the politically engaged *Libération* was founded by Jean Paul Sartre and Serge July in 1973. During the 1980s and early 1990s, *Libération* significantly expanded its circulation with the support of advertising and outside investors.

More than three decades later, most of France's leading national newspapers are once again controlled by non-news media industrialists and bankers.[16] In 2010, three years after the departure of *Le Monde*'s elected journalist director, Jean-Marie Colombani, who had heavily borrowed to create a multi-outlet group, the newspaper was on the brink of bankruptcy. It was purchased by three private investors: Xavier Niel, founder and CEO of telecommunication company Iliade/Free; Matthieu Pigasse, a CEO of the Lazare bank; and Pierre Bergé, an heir to the Yves-Saint Laurent fortune and president of the Pierre Bergé-Yves Saint-Laurent Foundation.[17] Niel, Pigasse, and Bergé's ownership of *Le Monde* was mediated through Le Monde Libre, a société en commandite (limited partnership). From 2005 to 2014, the banker Edouard de Rothschild was the controlling shareholder of *Libération*; in 2014, the telecommunications magnate Patrick Drahi became the newspaper's dominant shareholder. As discussed in the next section, other leading industrial owners of media—of *TF1*, *Le Figaro*, and more recently, the financial newspaper *Les Echos* and the popular daily *Le Parisien* (as well as *Libération*, via Drahi's traded Altice, as of 2016)—are linked to stock market-traded companies, a change from the inter-war period.

In the US, the non-news media conglomerate subform has been most prevalent in national network (*CBS*, *NBC*, *ABC*) and cable (*CNN*, *MSNBC*, *Fox News*) television; for a relatively brief period, a conglomerate owned the digital-only outlet *HuffPost*. In all these cases, as discussed in the next section, conglomerates have been traded on the stock market. In Sweden, the private Bonnier corporation and the Norwegian stock market-traded company Schibsted are also multi-sectoral conglomerates.

In the digital era, venture capital (VC) supported start-ups constitute a unique subform of private ownership in which founders, without a large personal financial stake, can retain significant or even exclusive control for an extended, although not unlimited period of time (usually up to a decade). In journalism-related investments starting in the early 2000s, VC has tended to support digital projects that exploit internet affordances of interactivity, virality, and user-generated content, and that are designed to attract younger audiences who have abandoned traditional media.[18] Large-scale venture-based start-ups have been a mostly US-based phenomenon. Major US VC-backed digital start-ups include *Vice* (originally founded in 1994 as an alternative print magazine in Montreal, shifting to international multi-media via digital, and later cable in 2006), *Huffington Post* (founded 2005, rebranded as *HuffPost* in 2017),[19] and *BuzzFeed* (in 2006). In Sweden, the online-only free news website *Nyheter24* (News24) was founded in 2008 by a former manager of the gaming company Ladbrokes and an executive at the PR/marketing agency Starcom, with support from VC.[20] Large media conglomerates may have VC divisions that invest in digital start-ups. Bonnier invested in the online-only news website *KIT*, founded in 2014, repurposed in 2019 as a PR firm focusing on social media.[21] US-based media conglomerate owners AT&T (*CNN*), Comcast (*NBC*), Disney (*ABC*), and Fox made substantial VC investments in digital native companies such as *BuzzFeed*, *Vice*, and *Vox*.[22] VC investors have not been allergic to supporting politically engaged media, especially on the left (although not the far left). The *Huffington Post* was launched explicitly as a Democratic alternative to the right-wing *Drudge Report* by founders Arianna Huffington, Kenneth Lerer, Jonah Peretti, and astonishingly, Andrew Breitbart (the eventual founder of the right-wing *Breitbart News*), who had previously worked for the *Drudge Report*.[23]

BuzzFeed, begun as Peretti's side-gig while he was still at the *Huffington Post*, is a prime example of private VC logic at work. Even though external venture capitalists eventually invested more than eighty percent of the privately held company's capital, founder and CEO Peretti retained significant control of business strategy and spending, which included his decision to launch and maintain for many years the never profitable *BuzzFeed News*. When *BuzzFeed* finally went "public" (through a SPAC or special purpose acquisition company listing) in 2021, Peretti was in enough of a position of strength to negotiate sixty-five percent of voting shares in the post-SPAC stock market-listed company. However, almost as soon as it was listed, the increased profit pressures inherent to stock market ownership finally forced his hand to close *BuzzFeed News*.[24]

In recent years in the US, individual billionaires with non-news media interests have begun buying up financially struggling legacy newspapers and magazines: most notably, the *Washington Post* by Amazon founder Jeff Bezos in 2013; the *Boston Globe* by Boston Red Sox baseball team owner John Henry in 2013; the *Minneapolis Star Tribune* by Minnesota Timberwolves basketball team owner Glen Taylor in 2014; the *Las Vegas Review-Journal* by casino operator Sheldon Adelson in 2014; the *Los Angeles Times* and *San Diego Union-Tribune* by biotech entrepreneur Patrick Soon-Shiong in 2018; and *Time* magazine by the Salesforce software company founder Marc Benioff in

2018.[25] Similar to *Le Monde*'s controlling shareholders, these billionaires' ownership in some cases has been facilitated through mediating legal entities, such as an LLC, or limited liability corporation: Nant Capital, in the case of Soon-Shiong's ownership of the *Los Angeles Times*, and Nash Holdings, as Bezos's vehicle for ownership of the *Washington Post*. Likewise, as with non-news media owners in France, concerns have been raised about their motivations and potential conflicts of interest, which we will address in Chapter 7 on economic instrumentalism.

A final private ownership subform is employee ownership, which simply means that employees purchase or are given private stock as part of their compensation sufficient to collectively gain voting control of the company. In the US, fourteen employee-owned dailies were established during the twentieth century, most notably the *New York Sun* and regional newspapers such as the *Milwaukee Journal*, the *Omaha World-Herald*, the *Kansas City-Star*, the *Hartford Courant*, and the *Cincinnati Enquirer*.[26] In all these cases, employee ownership was created as a way for a retiring owner to ensure continued local control and, in some cases, to reward loyal employees. Employee ownership of newspapers did not lessen the need to efficiently manage the enterprise and maintain some level of profitability. In practice, employee-owned companies, at least in the US, delegated management to "executives with the power and vision to accumulate the capital needed for improvements, expansion, and the repurchase of stock [the latter, as required, when employees retired]."[27]

As with private family ownership, profit pressures for employee-owned newspapers are less intense compared to stock market ownership; to the extent that they are locally owned newspapers (as opposed to "group" or "chain" owned papers), research has shown that they do more to emphasize "community service" and local news coverage.[28] Some of the largest US employee-owned newspapers won prestigious Pulitzer prizes for journalistic excellence while they were employee-owned (*Milwaukee Journal-Herald*, *Kansas City Star*), but some did not (*Hartford Courant*, *Cincinnati Enquirer*), and some won Pulitzers after they were no longer employee-owned (the *Courant*, the *Enquirer* [2], and the *Star*).[29] At most, one can say that employee-owned newspapers in the US are generally not among the lowest quality newspapers (as measured by Pulitzer Prizes), but they are not self-evidently among the very best either.

In France, employee ownership has involved a more thorough-going attempt to prioritize journalistic professionalism over market logics and provide journalists with effective management control. *Le Monde* became fully employee-owned and controlled from 1969, when its autocratic but revered founding editor Hubert Beuve-Méry revised the charter to provide for sixty percent employee ownership (forty percent journalists, nine percent other employees, and eleven percent management).[30] This arrangement lasted in increasingly diluted form until 2010, when, as noted, it was sold to three outside investors. *Libération* began as an employee-owned newspaper, but it lost its majority employee control with a restructuration of capital in the early 1980s.[31] The 1980s were years of notable journalistic achievements for both newspapers, and *Le Monde* in particular conducted substantial investigative reporting.[32] However, the French version of employee ownership often intensified internal conflicts; unlike in the US, management was not delegated, and at *Le Monde* the director (a combination of the publisher and editor-in-chief in the US) was elected by the newspaper's journalists.[33] Employee ownership in Sweden is rare, exemplified by the worker cooperative association-owned *Fria Tidningar* (see section on civil society ownership).

Ultimately, employee ownership has been difficult to sustain over the long-term, whether because of a tendency toward economic mismanagement (as at *Le Monde* or *Libération*, with *Mediapart* a significant exception, as discussed below), or the desire, especially manifest in the US, of employees facing retirement to cash out like any other owner and sell to the highest bidder.[34] As of 2020, no major employee-owned daily newspapers remained operative in the US. However, in France, employee ownership in hybrid form—directed and at least partially financed by founding journalists, supplemented by external "angel" or relatively small-scale VC investors[35]—has revived in recent years for several online-only news outlets: *Rue89* (in 2007),[36] the investigative website *Mediapart* (in 2008),[37] and *Slate.fr* (in 2009).[38] All of these outlets were primarily founded by ex-journalists, often from *Le Monde* and *Libération*. Both *Rue89* and *Slate.fr* were influenced by and loosely linked to the US *Slate* (discussed in the section on market ownership).[39] Given its reinvestment of profits into news operations, as well as its expressed intention as early as 2016 to shift to nonprofit status, we analyze *Mediapart* as a civil society-owned outlet (see the section on civil society ownership).

In sum, private ownership encompasses a broad range of subforms, which merit close attention for their particularities: individual journalist or news media company control versus conglomerate non-news media outside control, as well as individual, family, or employee ownership, and joint stock or VC minority or majority shareholders with varying levels of control. The pressure for profit maximization can vary, but it is generally less intense than with market ownership. Non-commercial amenity potential goals are also common. Along with civil society ownership, discussed below, private ownership may encompass a great deal of variation, depending on the social characteristics (education, income, professional background, political leaning) of the individuals involved (who have a greater discretion of action than in other forms); the particular mix of family, market, corporation, or profession institutional logics; and legal contracts or organizational specifications.

Market

The market ownership form is composed of outlets subject to the most profit-maximizing pressures: stock market-traded companies, private equity firms, and hedge funds. In the contemporary period, stock market-traded outlets generally have the legal designations of "C" Corporation (Inc. in the US), SA (société anonyme, or public limited company in France), or AB/AB (publ.) (aktiebolag/publikt aktiebolag in Sweden; except for the Norway-based Schibsted, which is ASA, allmennaksjeselskap, which in Norwegian means a publicly traded stock market company). These are generally the same company types also prevalent in private ownership, the only difference being that they have taken the additional step of publicly listing themselves on the stock market. Hedge funds and private equity companies in the US, where they are most commonly found as media owners, tend to be LLCs (limited liability corporations).

In the US, the first media outlet owned by a stock market-traded company was also the first commercial radio network: *NBC* (National Broadcasting Company), owned by RCA (Radio Corporation of America), the hot "tech" stock of the 1920s. *ABC* (American Broadcasting Network) was created as a private company in 1943, when the FCC (Federal Communications Commission) forced *NBC* to divest itself of its smaller, so-called "blue network." By the early 1950s, *ABC* was owned by the stock market-traded United Paramount Theatres. Government regulation—especially through public interest programming requirements and the Fairness Doctrine requiring balanced news coverage—somewhat muted profit pressures during these decades, even if FCC chairman Newton Minow famously referred to US commercial television in 1961 as a "vast wasteland."[40] In the 1980s, profit pressures intensified as stock market-traded media adopted the "shareholder value" standard for managerial policy and compensation.[41] *NBC* was sold to General Electric in 1985, and then to Comcast in 2013. Comcast is stock market-traded, but CEO Brian L. Roberts, son of the founder, owns all of the Class B "super voting" shares, which effectively grants him a dominant plurality of thirty-three percent of all voting shares.[42] *ABC* merged with Capital Cities, a smaller newspaper and television company, in 1985; the combined Capital Cities/ABC Inc. was purchased in 1996 by the stock market-traded entertainment conglomerate Disney.[43]

The remaining of the Big Three, *CBS*, was initially majority privately owned by William S. Paley, the heir to a cigar manufacturing company that was the network's largest advertiser, starting in 1928.[44] In 1937, *CBS* was listed on the New York Stock Exchange, with Paley remaining the largest shareholder and chairman until the late 1980s.[45] In 1995, *CBS* was purchased by the stock market-traded electrical equipment manufacturer Westinghouse, and in 1997, Westinghouse changed its name and relisted itself on the stock market as CBS

Corporation to reflect its transformation into a media company.[46] Two years later, *CBS* was purchased by the stock market-traded company Viacom, *CBS*'s syndication service established in the 1950s; Viacom's majority shareholder was the movie theater company National Amusements, privately held by Sumner Redstone and his daughter, Shari Redstone. National Amusements (effectively Shari Redstone since Sumner's death in 2020) remains the dominant shareholder of Viacom (renamed Paramount Global in 2022) and thus *CBS*, controlling eighty percent of shares.[47]

With the rise of cable news in the 1980s and 1990s, additional national television news operations rose to prominence: *CNN*, *Fox News*, and *MSNBC*. *CNN* was founded in 1980 as part of the privately held Turner Broadcasting Company, based in Atlanta, Georgia. Stock market-traded conglomerate Time Warner bought Turner Broadcasting, and thus *CNN*, in 1996. In 2018, Time Warner, renamed Warner Media, was purchased by the stock market-traded telecommunications conglomerate AT&T; and in 2022, Discovery, Inc. (owner of several cable channels, including the Discovery Channel) purchased Warner Media to become the new stock market-traded company Warner Bros. Discovery.[48] *Fox News* was founded in 1996 by the stock market-traded News Corporation, controlled by dominant shareholder Rupert Murdoch. Official ownership of *Fox News* switched to various reorganized companies in the Murdoch empire, namely 21st Century Fox from 2013 to 2019, and Fox Corporation beginning in 2019, with continued Murdoch family control of more than one-third of stock market-traded shares.[49] *MSNBC* was originally a partnership between Microsoft (MS) and *NBC* (General Electric), and since 2005 has been wholly operated by *NBC* (and thus Comcast, since 2013).[50]

Stock market ownership of US newspapers generally arose out of multi-newspaper groups or "chains," after several decades of family ownership. Newspaper chains begun in the 1920s and 1930s had, by the 1960s, come to control nearly half of all US newspaper circulation. As these chains arose and grew bigger, the heirs of the founding families felt compelled to sell their newspapers to pay inheritance taxes. Prices for the newspapers rose dramatically in response to competition between competing chain buyers. Stock market ownership thus became increasingly common in the 1960s "in order to generate capital to finance acquisitions, to reduce indebtedness, and to fend off hostile takeover attempts,"[51] in addition to being driven by the belief that stock market ownership would lead to greater financial discipline and profits.

The first US newspaper company to sell shares ("go public") was Dow-Jones (*Wall Street Journal*) in 1963, followed in relatively quick succession by Times-Mirror (*Los Angeles Times*) in 1964, Gannett and New York Times Co. in 1967, Knight and Ridder (then separate companies) in 1969, and the Washington Post Co. in 1971. A second wave began in the 1980s, with Tribune (in 1983), Pulitzer (in 1986), McClatchy (in 1988), and others joining the stock market through the end of the century.[52] As of 1998, seventeen stock market-traded companies owned twenty-one percent of all US daily newspapers, including twelve of the twenty highest circulation newspapers, with a combined circulation of forty-four percent of total national circulation. Private chains (such as Hearst) controlled another thirty percent of national circulation, with the remaining one-quarter of newspapers independently owned by a single, usually local, owner.[53] During the 1990s, bolstered both by deep budget cuts and economies of scale gained from consolidated operations across outlets, stock market-traded companies owning multiple newspaper properties were highly profitable: operating profit margins (revenues minus expenses before interest and taxes) averaged nineteen percent, with Gannett (the largest chain and owner of *USA Today*, launched in 1982) highest at twenty-eight percent.[54]

Pressures to maximize profits combined with a series of heavily debt-driven mergers to destabilize the US newspaper industry. Internet-driven dramatic declines in print circulation and advertising revenues, combined with the worldwide financial crisis of 2008, pushed already fragile companies into bankruptcy. The New York Times Co., Dow Jones (*Wall Street Journal*), and the Washington Post Co., controlled by family dominant shareholders, were generally better able than widely held stock market-owned firms (such as Times-Mirror, Tribune, Knight-Ridder, or Gannett) to resist debilitating cuts in their editorial budgets. The 2010s saw a complete reversal of the 1960s trend, as companies delisted from the stock market and were bought up by wealthy individuals, as discussed in the previous section, or "investment companies" (private equity or hedge funds). By 2014, of the US newspapers owned by the largest twenty-five companies (2,199 papers), thirty-six percent were owned by private individuals or companies, forty-seven percent were owned by private equity or hedge fund investment companies (an increase from twenty percent in 2004), and seventeen percent were owned by stock market-traded companies: thus, although stock market ownership had declined, sixty-four percent remained under what we have termed *market* ownership (hedge fund/private equity and stock market combined).[55]

A handful of US online start-ups have eventually become stock market-listed companies, although not particularly profitable ones. Since 2011, the *Huffington Post* has had stock market ownership: first, under AOL (2011 to 2015), then Verizon (2015 to 2021), and finally, by the recently listed *BuzzFeed* with Jonah Peretti as controlling shareholder (2021 to the present).[56] Widely held stock market ownership has not generally been associated with online-only media at the start-up phase, with one major exception: *Slate*. It was founded in 1996 by Microsoft, under the leadership of Bill Gates, who hired former *New Republic* editor Michael Kinsley as editor and gave him creative license to create an early model of online journalism.[57] *Slate* enjoyed the financial runway accorded to an experiment in an uncertain technological and market context, eventually attaining break-even revenues. In 2004, when Microsoft judged that *Slate* no longer fit with the company's "strategic priorities," it found a buyer in the stock market-traded Washington Post Co. Since 2013, when the dominant shareholding family, the Grahams, sold the *Washington Post* to Bezos, *Slate* has remained part of the family's remaining stock market-traded investments under the umbrella of Graham Holdings.[58]

Stock market ownership of news media has historically been much less common in France and Sweden—and indeed across western Europe—than in the US, but that has started to change in France. *TF1*, the former leading public service channel sold by the French state in 1987, is directly traded as part of the TF1 Group on the Euronext exchange; its largest shareholder, with forty-four percent of shares, is Bouygues, a widely held stock market traded company (the Bouygues family does not hold a controlling plurality of voting shares).[59] In 2015, the TF1 Group became the controlling shareholder of the free daily newspaper *Metro* (previously owned by the Swedish stock market-traded company Kinnevik), and relaunched the paper as an online only website rebaptized *Metronews*, which was closed in the summer of 2016.[60]

Since 2004, *Le Figaro* has been owned by the Dassault Group (controlled by the Dassault family), the dominant shareholder in the stock market-traded arms manufacturer Dassault Aviation.[61] There have also been some recent shifts from private to dominant shareholder stock market ownership in France. In 2015, the popular daily *Le Parisien*, long privately owned by the Amaury family, was purchased by the stock market-traded luxury goods company LVMH, with Bernard Arnault as the dominant shareholder; since 2007, Arnault/LVMH has also been the owner of the financial newspaper *Les Echos*, which it purchased from the British stock market-traded publishing company Pearson (and subsequently merged with *Le Parisien* into the company Les Echos Le Parisien). In the summer of 2016, *Libération*, owned by shifting constellations of private individual investors since the 1980s, officially became part of telecommunications mogul Patrick Drahi's SFR media company, in turn owned by the stock market-traded Altice, of which Drahi is the dominant shareholder.[62] From 2011 until 2021, *Le Huffington Post* (rebaptized *Le HuffPost* in 2017) was jointly owned by the stock market-traded Verizon (owner of US *HuffPost*, until its 2021 sale to BuzzFeed, Inc.), the privately held Le Monde Group, and former Lazard investment banker Matthieu Pigasse's private holding company, Les Nouvelles Editions Indépendantes.[63]

In Sweden, until very recently, the most important stock market-traded owner has been the Norwegian conglomerate Schibsted. From the late 1990s until 2024 (see Ch. 3), it owned the elite newspaper *Svenska Dagbladet* (ideologically closely aligned with the "liberal conservatism" of the Swedish Moderate party) and the popular tabloid *Aftonbladet* (ideologically "independent social democratic" and still minority-owned by the trade union LO), as well as the largest classified advertising site in Sweden, Blocket. We classify Schibsted as a widely held stock market-traded company because its largest shareholder at the time of our study (with twenty-six percent of shares), the Tinius Trust, while influential, did not have effective control over the voting shares. According to the Schibsted website, "the main task of the Trust is . . . to be a guarantor for a free press."[64]

The leading Swedish commercial TV channel, *TV4*, founded in the early 1990s, became fully owned by the private Bonnier company in 2007.[65] Since 2019, *TV4* has been owned by the stock market-traded telecommunications firm Telia.[66] For most of its history, news programming was a much lower priority for *TV4* than for public *SVT*.[67]

The free urban daily *Metro*, the first in the sprawling Sweden-based global group Metro International, was founded in 1995 by the stock market-traded Kinnevik company, with the Stenbeck family as dominant shareholder; in 2017, it was sold to the privately held company Custos.[68] Abroad, it has also often changed ownership: While the French version (*Metronews*) continued with stock market ownership under the TF1 Group until it was closed, the US version of *Metro* was privately purchased from Metro International in 2009 by a former Metro International CEO, Pelle Törnberg, to become part of the private Seabay Media Holdings (continuing to operate under license to Metro International).[69]

Private equity and hedge funds together represent the other major subform of the market ownership form. An increasingly dominant owner of US newspapers, this subform is oriented toward maximum profitability, but is free of stock market requirements for quarterly public reports. Private equity and hedge fund investors have been a major driver of debt-driven mergers of US newspaper companies since at least the early 2000s, ostensibly to achieve sustainable economies of scale but which in fact have often led to bankruptcies. Regardless of how the inevitable corporate restructuring plays out, these investment companies reap significant financial benefits from management fees, tax breaks, conversion of debt into equity ownership, and sales of major physical assets, such as historic company headquarters in prime downtown locations.[70] As mentioned in Chapter 1, private equity or hedge fund ownership in principle can tolerate periods of unprofitability (up to three to five years, shorter than for VC), and, as we will see, it occasionally does so during periods of uncertainty. However, when in profit "harvesting" mode, US hedge fund and private equity owners have made deep cuts in newsrooms to reach their high profit targets. Examples of leading news media companies of this subform are New Media/Gatehouse (owned by Fortress Investment Group's Private Equity Team) and

Digital First Media (owned by hedge fund Alden Global Capital). Most of their holdings are in small newspapers; however, Alden's properties also include major regional newspapers such as the *Denver Post*, the *Chicago Tribune*, and the *Baltimore Sun*.[71] Demonstrating the synergy between private equity firms/hedge funds and the stock market, in 2019, Gatehouse merged with the stock market-traded Gannett to form the largest US newspaper chain, retaining the Gannett name, which continues to be stock market-traded.[72] To date, private equity/hedge fund owners have not become notable actors in the Swedish and French journalistic fields.

Civil society

Civil society ownership includes churches and other religious groups, labor unions, political parties, arts societies, and various types of nonprofit associations, foundations, or trusts, thus encompassing a constellation of institutional logics. Civil society-owned outlets may sometimes share the same organizational legal form as private outlets (SA or SAS, Inc., or AB), but often, their owning entities will have some kind of tax-advantaged or mission-designated nonprofit status. In the US, such legal entities include the 501(c)(3) nonprofit corporation or association (with no owners with redeemable shares or who receive dividends) and the "public benefit" B corporation, which incorporates non-commercial purposes into its bylaws (but still allows for shareholders who may receive profits). In France, they include média associatif (owned by an association of the law of 1901, established in that year to support voluntary associations); fonds de dotation (endowment fund, mid-way between a foundation and an association); and l'entreprise solidaire de presse d'information (solidarity enterprise, a designation created in 2015, that provides tax benefits to investors and requires a media outlet to reinvest a certain percentage of any surplus revenues in the organization).[73] The Swedish stiftelse (foundation) is like the US 501(c)(3) and the French 1901 association in that it has no shareholders, and is governed by a legal charter that requires it to defend a particular purpose, often ideological or partisan, in perpetuity.[74] The Swedish kooperativ (cooperative) association is another subform, represented by *Fria Tidningar* from 2001 to 2016.[75]

Among the earliest and most long-standing civil society-owned outlets in many western democracies are those founded by churches. Each of our national field samples includes a leading religious organization owned newspaper. In the US, the respected *Christian Science Monitor* was founded in 1908 by the First Church of Christ, Scientist, and still receives the majority of its funding from the church. In Sweden, the most prominent religiously owned newspaper is *Dagen*, founded in 1945 by the Pentecostalist leader Lewi Pethrus, who went on to found the Christian Democrats party in 1964.[76] It is now read by Christians of all denominations and owned by the Norwegian company Mentor Medier, whose largest shareholders include various Christian evangelical or "Free" churches and organizations.[77] France's *La Croix*, founded in 1883, is part of the Bayard Presse group, owned by the Catholic Assumptionist Order. These three publications have attracted journalists and managers with experience at other leading news outlets; while having a strong core readership of their co-religionists, they have also attempted to reach broader audiences.

For more than a decade, starting in the mid-1990s, *La Croix*'s editor was a prominent former *Le Monde* journalist, Bruno Frappat. In Sweden, Tomas Brunegård, previously CEO of the Stampen Group (including *Göteborgs-Posten*), chairman of the Swedish Newspaper Publishers Association, and president of the World Association of Newspapers and News Publishers (WAN-IFRA), served as a board member and chairman of *Dagen*'s owning company, Mentor Medier. As we discuss in Chapter 4, the *Christian Science Monitor* took the lead in the US in going "digital first," dramatically expanding its online audience to increase advertising revenues, but eventually pulling the plug on the project due to insufficient revenues.

Political party ownership (along with strong party affiliation for privately owned newspapers discussed previously) has diminished in all three countries over the past two centuries. Direct political party control of Swedish newspapers, whether through a local chapter or the national organization, was once common for the Center Party (previously Agrarian Party) and Social Democratic Party, but since the early 2000s these papers have closed or been bought out by family or nonprofit foundation owners.[78] In contrast, most conservative and liberal newspapers have been historically owned by individuals or families, as in the Bonnier-owned *Dagens Nyheter*, which was the organ of the (Liberal) People's Party until 1972 and subsequently has described itself as "independent liberal."[79]

Foundation ownership is one of the most distinctive features of the Swedish media landscape. According to Jonas Ohlsson, the foundation is a "legal entity created to administer an ownership stake, generally resulting from an endowment, in a newspaper company."[80] Such foundations first arose between the 1940s and 1970s largely as a way to ensure the survival of party or privately held partisan newspapers.[81] A newspaper foundation, Ohlsson explains, is distinct from private ownership in that "it is a non-profit entity, has no owners, [and] has a specific (non-commercial) objective." The foundation's assets are "managed by a board of trustees": unlike the "boards of directors of stock corporations, which are elected by the shareholders, the foundation board of trustees is often self-elective, constrained only by the law and the foundation charter."[82] These charters generally require the foundations to promote in perpetuity particular ideological positions: as it happens, these positions have most often been "[classic pro-market] liberal or conservative."[83] Even though Swedish foundations are not-for-profit, they may reward top managers and editors at the newspapers they own with high salaries and benefits.[84] The number of foundation-owned newspapers experienced a spectacular increase between 2000 and 2017, rising from eighteen to fifty, while private newspapers fell from sixty-one to thirty-nine and party newspapers declined from twenty-two to four.[85]

Leading foundation-owned newspapers have included *Norran* (located in Skellefteå, owned by the liberal foundation Stiftelsen Skelleftepress), *Barometern* (published in Kalmar, owned by Gota Media, in turn owned by two conservative foundations, Stiftelsen Barometern and Tore G Wärenstams stiftelse), and *Gefle Dagblad* (based in Gävle, until 2019 part of the Mittmedia group, in turn owned by the liberal foundations Stiftelsen Pressorganisation and Nya Stiftelsen Gefle Dagblad). A few foundations started chains, owning and operating multiple newspapers, and like their US chain counterparts used economies of scale to operate more efficiently, which in some cases has (contrary to their supposed missions) lessened their delivery of locally produced news content.[86] Swedish foundation ownership has not prevented mismanagement: in fact, according to Ohlsson, the combination of non-professional boards with strong executives has given the CEOs of foundation-owned companies more freedom than in privately held companies to take risks, which in the case of Mittmedia nearly led to bankruptcy.[87]

Amid such management missteps and a continued decline in print circulation and advertising revenues, the seeming solidity of foundation ownership has been called into question. In 2019, in desperate need of new capital and facing the possibility of having to close the newspapers, the liberal foundations owning *Gefle Dagblad* and other Mittmedia chain newspapers sold out to Bonnier News with the Norwegian foundation-owned Amedia group as a minority shareholder.[88] Because Bonnier has traditionally been associated with the liberalism of the Liberal party, the sale was interpreted by Mittmedia's owning foundations as not violating their mission to safeguard the papers' liberal political orientation.[89] The CEO of Bonnier News publicly stated that "they will work to maintain the political profiles that these newspapers have," and while the contractual details have not publicly emerged, it seems likely that they included provisions ensuring political continuity.[90]

Perhaps even more surprising, *Norran* was sold due to continuing losses even though its liberal foundation owner Stiftelsen Skelleftepress had deep financial reserves that in principle could have been used to support the paper.

The new owner, NTM (owned by a foundation with ideological links to the Moderate party), was required by the sale contract to preserve *Norran*'s liberal political line, and if it ever decides to close the title or sell it, to first offer Stiftelsen Skelleftepress the right of repurchase.[91] This arrangement—selling, with certain contractual provisos, to a larger newspaper chain perceived as better equipped to successfully navigate a challenging economic environment for local newspapers—was seen by *Norran*'s foundation owner as fulfilling its aim to "protect the brand's eternal existence."[92]

Other than *Le Figaro*, launched in 1826, and the just mentioned *La Croix*, the leftist *L'Humanité*, founded by the socialist Jean Jaurés in 1904, is among France's oldest continuous publications and has long been closely associated with the French communist party (PCF), although it no longer presents itself as the party's official organ. As of the early 2000s, individual shareholders associated with the PCF held forty percent of the capital, followed by nonprofit "1901 associations" of "readers" and "friends," corporate investors like TF1 and Hachette (which pulled out sometime before 2016), and employees.[93] In 2016, *L'Humanité* adopted the legal form of l'entreprise solidaire de presse d'information (solidarity enterprise for informational press), providing tax breaks for small contributors.[94] This legal form has also been adopted by the in-depth reporting subscription-only news website *Les Jours* and the satirical magazine *Charlie Hebdo*, both broadly on the left but not linked to any party.[95] The major governing parties have not had closely affiliated daily newspapers since the closing of the Gaullist *La Nation* in 1974 and the Socialist *Le Matin de Paris* in 1987.[96] *Ouest-France*, founded in 1944 and based in the city of Rennes, is the country's largest print circulation newspaper. Long owned by the Hutin family, since 1990 it has been owned by a nonprofit association with a religious, center-right political mission that parallels in part the *Christian Science Monitor* or some of the Swedish partisan foundation-owned newspapers.[97]

Commercial newspapers operated by non-partisan foundations, trusts, or associations represent another subform of civil society ownership. In the US, this subform applies to the *Philadelphia Inquirer*, since 2016, owned by the Lenfest Institute for Journalism; the *Salt Lake Tribune*, since 2019, constituted as its own 501(c)(3) nonprofit association, but still allowed to take advertising and subscriptions for revenues, which together made up twenty-seven percent of its revenues in 2020, as well as donations; and the *Tampa Bay Times*, owned by the Poynter Institute.[98] There are some subtle differences in ownership between these outlets. The *Tampa Bay Times* and *Philadelphia Inquirer* are owned by nonprofit associations, but remain for-profit companies, whereas the *Salt Lake Tribune* is the first US formerly commercial newspaper to wholly constitute itself as a nonprofit association. In 2022, a hybrid model between partially taxpayer-supported public media and civil society nonprofit ownership emerged when the Chicago public radio station WBEZ announced that it would purchase the *Chicago Sun-Times* and convert the paper to a nonprofit.[99]

The online-only *Mediapart*, introduced previously as a partially employee-owned news organization, is difficult to classify. While it has been very successful commercially, attaining 218,000 paying subscribers by the end of 2020 and regularly earning annual profits in excess of fifteen percent, *Mediapart* has always reinvested all of its revenues back into its news operations and is managed by its mostly journalist founders.[100] In 2016, lead founder and director Edwy Plenel indicated to us his intention to officially change *Mediapart*'s ownership to a fonds de dotation à but non lucratif (nonprofit endowment fund), which occurred in 2019.[101]

Nonprofit news outlets relying primarily on donations represent a final subform of civil society ownership. In the US, there has been an extraordinary growth in such organizations since the early 2000s in direct response to massive newsroom cutbacks at commercial media.[102] "Nonprofit" in the US context refers to a special tax designation (501(c)(3)) that allows for organizations with a civic mission to avoid paying taxes and for donors to deduct contributions from their taxable income. Churches, humanitarian organizations such as the Red Cross, and other charitable or educational projects have long enjoyed the status; news media, until recently, did not. The US Internal Revenue Service has tended to grant such status only to newly created media that receive little or no commercial revenues such as advertising (such funding is allowed, but it is fully taxed, unlike donations) and whose journalistic mission and activities can qualify as "educational," which means in practice that the news outlet cannot endorse political candidates in elections. However, the agency has approved nonprofit status for news organizations that, other than abiding by the prohibition on explicit endorsements, are overtly partisan.[103]

The first major entirely philanthropically funded US news nonprofits were two outlets solely focused on investigative reporting: the *Center for Investigative Reporting* (later referring to itself as *CIR/Reveal*), founded in 1977, and the *Center for Public Integrity (CPI)*, launched in 1989.[104] With the rise of the internet, a new wave of online-only nonprofits emerged in the 2000s, notably local/regional news websites *Voice of San Diego* (in 2005), *MinnPost* (in 2007), and *Texas Tribune* (in 2009). The national *ProPublica*, created in 2008, has been a pioneer in developing "data journalism"; it was the first online-only news organization to win a Pulitzer Prize for its reporting.[105] Standardization of the US nonprofit sector was furthered by the creation of the Institute for Nonprofit News (INN) in 2009.[106] As of the INN's 2020 survey, there were more than 250 US digital native nonprofit news outlets that generate estimated annual revenues of $500 million and provide jobs for more than two thousand journalists—not insignificant, but a small portion of the forty thousand newspaper positions that have disappeared since 2008.[107]

In Sweden and France, in contrast, there is very little philanthropic support for civil society-owned news media.[108] In Sweden, *Dagens Arena* receives most of its support from LO, a large trade union.[109] *Kvartal*, which describes itself as a "politically independent online magazine" providing a forum for constructive "public debate" and "analysis," was launched in 2016 via the creation of the fundraising foundation Stiftelsen Kvartal. Its founding editor, Peter Santesson, described the project as "rooted in the Swedish school of progressive pedagogics—the idea that learning is a pleasure." Until recently, it relied for funding on large and small individual donations, but in 2022 *Kvartal* became privately owned, with editor-in-chief Jörgen Huitfeldt as one of the investors.[110]

French journalists and media scholars do not make as sharp of a distinction between commercial and nonprofit media as in the US. In France, the closest comparison to the US INN is SPIIL (Syndicat de la Presse Indépendante d'Information en Ligne, or the Union for Independent Online Informational Press), founded in 2009. According to SPIIL's director, a news outlet is "independent if its principal investor works in the media field," a principle that is implemented loosely for the association's more than fifty members.[111] SPIIL's members have included well-known public affairs outlets like *Mediapart* and *Témoignage Chrétien*, more niche news outlets like *Reporterre* and *Basta!*, and many nonpolitical commercial lifestyle websites, such as *Wine LR*, *SportBusiness Club*, and *Jeu de Golf*. Most of SPIIL's members rely on funding from advertising and paying audiences like other commercial media. The only French "news" organization that actually refers to itself as a nonprofit is *The Conversation*, the French version of the originally Australian website featuring explanatory articles by academics (edited by journalists) on major issues of the day.[112] *Reporterre* (environment) and *Basta!* (global economic and social issues) have relied on foundation funding as well as other donations. Both outlets are owned by associations of the law of 1901 with a tax-advantaged status comparable to US 501(c)(3) organizations.[113] Both are very small-scale operations, similar to most US local nonprofits, with less than a dozen full-time journalists each.

Public

The state—or an agency or foundation established by the state—ostensibly acting on behalf of the public at large (the citizenry) is a final type of owner, generally of legacy radio and television media and their contemporary online extensions. We distinguish public or "public service" media (as they are referred to in France and Sweden) from "state" media, even though the state is involved in both, by the degree of democratic accountability and professional autonomy accorded to journalists through regulatory mechanisms. While journalists working for state media in authoritarian societies struggle and sometimes succeed in achieving some degree of unauthorized professional autonomy,[114] our focus is on state-licensed legacy audiovisual media that enjoy legally enforced protection from political interference. Even in strong democracies, however, the provision of resources and the effective force of such legal protections varies and is often contested by the political parties in power. Public media in our study can also be distinguished by their sources of funding (see Chapter 4), whether wholly from dedicated citizen paid "license fees" (Sweden's *SVT/SR* through 2018); general tax revenues (a public service fee, paid via taxes, in Sweden as of 2019); a mix of license fees (or, as of 2023, a proportion of the Value Added Tax) and advertising (*France Télévisions*); or a mix of general tax revenues, philanthropy, and business sponsorships (the US's *PBS* and *NPR*).[115] Similar to civil society-owned media, public media do not face profit pressures, even when they have commercial revenues, because they have no owners or shareholders to pay. Because of their universalizing mandates to reach as much of the public as possible, however, public media may face pressures to demonstrate that they are generating sizeable audiences.

Swedish public radio AB Radiotjänst (now Sveriges Radio or *SR*) was founded in cooperation with the government in 1924. The government telegraph agency, Telegrafstyrelsen, provided the broadcasting technological infrastructure, while ownership oversight was shared between representatives of the press and radio industries.[116] Newspapers were supportive of license fee-funded public radio as a way to keep advertising revenues for themselves. In the negotiations over the development of public TV (*SVT*) in 1956, newspapers relinquished some of their participation in the ownership to civil society associations.[117] In 1994, the old ownership structure of *SVT/SR* (and *UR*, the Swedish Educational Broadcasting Company) was replaced with three foundations (now one).[118] The governing party in power appoints the chairperson of the board that oversees the foundations, while the other twelve members, by law required to represent all major political parties, are appointed by the government with suggestions from Parliament. Board terms are eight years (except for the Chair, who serves four years) and they are staggered so that half the board leaves every four years.[119]

The combination of board oversight and foundation ownership is designed to ensure an "arms-length" relationship between public media *SVT/SR* and the government in power.[120] *SVT* and *SR* are also autonomous from one another and sometimes take different approaches to the news, as we will see. Influenced by the UK's *BBC*, the *SVT* is governed by a multi-year charter that codifies its mission and sets the terms of its relationship with the government. From the start, Swedish public media have been governed by the principle of governmental non-interference in programming, within the expectation that programs will be impartial and balanced and will promote public "education" and "enlightenment."[121] Swedish public media are well-resourced, with ninety-six percent of their revenues derived from public funding, totaling $112 per capita. In a comparison of public funding for public media in twelve leading democracies, Sweden is ranked fifth, behind Norway, Germany, Denmark, and Finland (compared to seventh for France, at $82 per capita, and a distant twelfth for the US, at $3). Even when non-public funding, such as advertising, philanthropy, or programming sales, are included, Sweden is ranked fifth with $117 per capita, behind Denmark, Norway, the UK, and Germany (with France likewise remaining in seventh place, with $102 per capita, and the US, again last, with $9 per capita).[122]

France initially followed the German policy of having the state "retain control over the transmission of radio signals" while allowing "private control over program-making."[123] In 1933, the French government created the regulatory agency PTT (Postes, Télégraphes et Téléphones) that took direct control over Radio Paris, the largest commercial station, and established a British-style license fee. In the late 1930s, amidst growing fears of a German threat, a conservative-led government assumed direct control of commercial as well as state/public channels. The occupying Nazis and collaborationist Vichy regime then used this centralized radio system for their own purposes from 1940 to 1944.[124] After the war, the French state's monopoly control over radio and subsequently television was justified by the need to protect broadcasting from private interests in the name of the "general interest." In reality, television quickly became the instrument of the government in power, especially under the presidency of Charles de Gaulle from 1958 to 1968.[125]

While state controls began to loosen during the 1970s, significant change did not occur until after the election of Socialist President François Mitterrand in 1981: the law he signed the following year strengthened the autonomy of public television and radio and allowed the creation of the first commercial television channels (*Canal+* in 1984; *La Cinq* [channel 5] in 1985). The legislative elections of 1986 led to a period of "cohabitation" (between the socialist president and a government otherwise controlled by the right): this period saw a further expansion of commercial TV with the creation of *M6* [channel 6] and the sale of the leading public channel, *TF1*, to the stock market-traded Bouygues company. *France Télévisions* is now the umbrella organization for public channels: most notably *France 2* (now the main national public channel), as well as *France 3*, *France 4*, *France 5*, *France Info* (shared with *Radio France*), *France Média Monde* (*France 24* news channel, *RFI* world radio, and the Arabic-language *Monte Carlo Doualiya* radio), *LCP-Assemblée nationale*, and *Public Sénat*. French public media also include: the Franco-German cultural channel *Arte*, launched in 1992, whose programming includes documentaries and a fifteen-minute evening news program; and the *Radio France* group, including the general news-oriented

France Inter (along with *France Info*), as well as *France Culture* and other specialized channels.[126]

From 1989 through 2021, French public television and radio was overseen by the Conseil superieur de l'audiovisuel (CSA, or the High Council on Broadcasting, which became ARCOM, Autorité de régulation de la communication audiovisuelle et numérique, in 2022). In 2013, new regulations specified that the CSA board was to be composed of seven members, serving staggered six-year terms of office: the chair, appointed by the President of the Republic; three appointed by the Senate president; and three by the National Assembly (lower house of Parliament) president.[127] As of January 2022, the ARCOM board has been composed of nine commissioners: the chair, appointed by the President of the Republic; three members appointed by the Senate president; three members appointed by the National Assembly president; one member appointed by the vice president of the Conseil d'Etat; and one member appointed by the First President of the Cour de Cassation (French Supreme Court).[128] *France Télévisions* and *Radio France* also each have their own conseils d'administration (boards of directors), led by their respective presidents (appointed by ARCOM) and composed of slightly different mixes of members, including external experts, appointed by ARCOM, the State, the National Assembly, the Senate, and employees.[129]

US public media are actually a hybrid of civil society and public ownership forms. As noted, the earliest US radio and television broadcasters were private or stock market-traded rather than public, creating a path-dependent dominance of these ownership forms in this legacy medium.[130] Small, local educational radio and television channels grew up in the margins of a dominant commercial system. The Public Broadcasting Act of 1967 created the nonprofit Corporation for Public Broadcasting (CPB) to facilitate (but not directly produce) national programming of "high quality, diversity, creativity, excellence, and innovation" for the hundreds of preexisting local public radio and television channels.[131] CPB's nine-member board of directors is appointed entirely by the US President, subject to Senate approval, but terms are lengthy (six years) and staggered in two year increments; no more than five members can belong to the same political party.[132] *PBS* (Public Broadcasting Service), a 501(c)(3) nonprofit, is directly governed by the *PBS* board of directors, whose members are elected by *PBS* member stations across the US: the *PBS* board appoints the *PBS* president, who serves as the CEO.[133] *NPR* (National Public Radio), also a nonprofit 501(c)(3), is governed by a board of directors, partly elected by member stations and partly selected by the board.[134]

The CPB allocates funding to independent program producers and to local stations affiliated with *PBS* and *NPR*. Government funding was very limited from the start and is controlled by Congressional annual appropriations. More than half of the US public media system's funding comes from large foundation gifts, business corporation sponsorships, and donations from viewers, who tend to have much higher levels of income and education than the citizenry as a whole.[135] *PBS*'s television market share is two percent, compared to thirty-five percent for *SVT* in Sweden and thirty percent for the ensemble of French public channels.[136] With commercial radio's virtual abandonment of news, *NPR* remains the leading US producer of national news for radio, and its website has often been among the top twenty US news websites (while *PBS NewsHour* is not among the top fifty).[137]

* * *

During this chapter, in addition to tracing the history of four broad ownership forms—market, private, civil society, and public—we have also mentioned in passing various subforms that may exist within different ownership forms. The first is *conglomerate* ownership (by a major company with significant non-news media holdings, which it controls), which may appear in both market and private forms. In the structural and content analysis that we provide in the following chapters, outlets with this subform include *ABC News* (Disney); *CNN* (AT&T); *HuffPost* (Verizon); *Fox News*; *CBS News*; *Le Figaro* (Dassault); *TF1* and *Metronews* (TF1 Group, with Bouygues company as largest shareholder); *Le HuffPost* (partly Verizon); *Le Parisien* (LVMH/Arnault since 2015); *Libération* (Altice/SFR since 2016); *Svenska Dagbladet* and *Aftonbladet* (Schibsted); and *Dagens Nyheter*, *Expressen*, and *KIT* (Bonnier). Institutionally overt *partisan-affiliated* media, found in private and civil society ownership forms, constitute a second subform. In our sample, these include *Dagens ETC*, *Norran*, *Barometern*, *Gefle Dagblad*, and *Dagens Arena* in Sweden, and *L'Humanité* in France (we did not include in this category outlets, such as *Fox News* or *Le Figaro*, with dominant shareholders well-known for their strong partisan sympathies). A third subform is *current/legacy journalist control*, a non-ownership mechanism of control. In our study, outlets with this subform include contemporary journalist-founded and led (but not "owned") US nonprofits *ProPublica*, *CIR/Reveal*, *MinnPost*, and the *Texas Tribune*; journalist-founded and majority owned (as of the first half of 2016) private or civil society-owned outlets *Mediapart*, *Dagens ETC*, *Vice US* and *Vice France*, *Slate.fr*, the *New York Times*, and *Ouest-France* (the latter two by founding families in which members continue to work as journalists as well as assuming management responsibilities); and "legacy" newspapers *Le Monde* and *Libération*, in which journalists as a collective at one point had effective ownership control, lost it, but have retained certain internal administrative rights (guarantees of independence from owner interference in news content, the right to collectively veto the appointment of a director, etc.).

Having established this historical context, let us now turn to an analysis of how outlets with the same ownership forms compare with one another, first in their mixes of institutional logics, and second in their amount and proportion of economic and cultural capital, both at the level of production and reception. In the structural analysis that follows, to the extent possible we focus on 2016 and surrounding years, the time period for our content analysis. With hindsight, it is also becoming clear that the 2010s and early 2020s constituted a critical moment in the contemporary history of journalism, setting in motion dramatic economic changes that continue to transform the news media landscape. Our detailed structural mapping of this period provides a baseline for future analyses.

Ownership Forms and Institutional Symbolic Logics

Even if the ownership forms we have just discussed originally embodied distinct institutional logics, there is no guarantee that these differences have persisted or that their symbolic expressions entirely parallel their material infrastructures. Over time, professionalization and commercialization may have produced homogenizing effects. This is the thesis of political scientists Timothy Cook and Bartholomew Sparrow, who have described contemporary journalism as constituting a singular "political institution."[138] We can put their thesis to the test by looking at news outlets' "mission" or "about" statements on their websites: these statements effectively express each outlet's institutional values. In successive rounds of close reading and analysis of these statements, we identified the following institutional logics: market (audience-responsive, entertainment, or no statement); two professional/journalistic logics, informational and pluralist;[139] democratic (focused on the civic goal of strengthening democracy); community/partisan (whether linked to party, trade union, or social movement); and religious. The categories are not mutually exclusive, acknowledging that organizations may embody multiple logics. (See Methods Appendix for more information about our sampling and analysis of mission statements.)

Many stock market-traded media, such as *ABC News*, *CBS News*, *Fox News*, and *TF1* (*MYTF1News*) offer little or nothing in the way of a mission statement. Their "About" or "Media Kit" tabs convey a *market* logic, asserting excellence by emphasizing size, reach, or awards (in this last case, an expression of extrinsic acclaim rather than an intrinsic embrace of journalistic excellence for its own sake). The idea that a mission—or the lack thereof—connotes a particular understanding of journalism was evident when, in France, the former CEO of *TF1* told us that he rejected the validity of the word "mission" that had been used by *TF1*'s public media competitor France 2: as such, he universalized his view that media exist only to serve market ends.[140] At *CBS News*, the "About" tab links to parent company Viacom, with headlines that subsume news into a broader conception of profit-making communication or entertainment, such as "Connecting with Everyone, Everywhere," "Telling Stories that Inspire," and "Driving Value for Our Shareholders." *Fox News* has no "About" tab, but inside the "Media Relations" link that is clearly speaking to advertisers, *Fox News* defines its mission solely in terms of its size and reach as "America's News and Much More" (alluding to its global popularity) and the "number one network in all of cable."

The mission of *audience responsiveness*—giving the readers want they want—is explicitly articulated as a primary mission by several stock market-traded media outlets, such as *HuffPost* (both in the US and France), France's *Metronews*, as well as private online-only outlets like *BuzzFeed* and Sweden's *Nyheter24*. *HuffPost* "listen[s] to [its] readers and covers the topics that matter to them"; *BuzzFeed* covers "what you care about"; and *Nyheter24* wants to "help you find what is most relevant to you." After emphasizing the same theme, *Metronews* (France) explicitly mentions *entertainment* as a part of its mission: "Metronews continuously delivers news in all its dimensions, in a mode close to our readers, educational and entertaining."

Information is often the sole theme mentioned at many stock market-traded and private media, sometimes only obliquely. *CNN* proclaims that it has a "mission to inform . . . not just what happened, but why, and what it means to you," implicitly referencing the ideal of in-depth news. At the *Los Angeles Times*, there is only an indirect reference to information, when it vaunts its "140 years" of "covering Southern California." The *New York Times*'s mission is more detailed, but it is buried deep inside the website. Inside a tab labeled only "NYTco," a headline proclaims "We seek the truth and help people understand the world." Within this section, inside a separate link labeled "Journalism," the *New York Times* articulates a strongly expertise-driven three-pronged vision: "We hire expert journalists and allow them the time and resources to create in-depth, independent, original reporting"; "we report without fear or favor, and our investigations result in concrete, meaningful action"; and "our Opinion report helps people imagine the world as it could be, through rich discussion and intelligent debate" via "Opinion journalists [who] are experts in their fields." There is no explicit mention by the *New York Times* of *pluralism* in relation to non-journalists interviewed or authoring "op-ed" articles.

Public media emphasize both a strong journalistic and democratic/civic mission, although some more explicitly than others and in different combinations: *PBS (PBS NewsHour)* and *SVT* emphasize information; *NPR* and *FranceInfo* (the latter, by 2021, combining French public TV and radio online) highlight information along with pluralism; and *SR* mentions information, pluralism, and *democracy*.

Private and civil society ownership are distinctive for the greatest mixing of missions, with some cross-national nuancing: informational, pluralist, democratic, *partisan*, and *religious*. The privately held *Washington Post* provides a "Mission Statement" that reproduces the "seven principles" established by owner/publisher Eugene Meyer in 1933, which include "tell[ing] the truth" and "discerning the important affairs of America and the world." Its policy statement on the use of sources emphasizes that "we must strive always to get a rich variety of voices into our work." *ProPublica* promises to "expose abuses of power using the moral force of investigative journalism," which is "critical to our democracy." *CIR/Reveal* likewise emphasizes its efforts to "unearth . . . original stories that hold people and institutions accountable" and contribute to "new laws and policies, better-informed conversations and community-driven solutions." Regional nonprofits like *MinnPost* and the *Texas Tribune* describe themselves providing high quality information and analysis, as well as promoting pluralism and serving democracy.[141] *Ouest-France*, while mentioning a historical commitment to a particular understanding of Catholic social humanist values (which has led it to oppose euthanasia, cloning, abortion, and a range of medical interventions), emphasizes a broad democratic mission to provide quality information, especially local and regional, to refuse "sensationalism," and to promote "pluralism."[142]

In France, detailed "charters" defining missions (of information, pluralism, and democracy) as well as specifying internal rules guaranteeing the "independence" of newsrooms from their owners (the latter, a feature seemingly less common at US[143] and Swedish news outlets) are offered by *Mediapart*, *Le Monde*, *Libération*, and the public *Franceinfo* website. In the "Le Monde Group Code of Ethical and Professional Conduct," whose link is provided at the bottom of the homepage, the preamble stresses the "essential principles of independence" (including *from* its actionnaires, or shareholders) before articulating any particular journalistic mission. In the third paragraph, it then offers this mission statement: "The vocation of the outlets in the Le Monde Group is to furnish . . . quality, precise, verified, and balanced *information*. Journalists must offer a critical perspective on the news and echo the *pluralism* of opinions." *Mediapart*, at the beginning of its very lengthy "charter," also places nearly equal emphasis on information and pluralism: "The mission of Mediapart is to be of service to the right to know and the liberty to speak, for the sake of the truth of the facts and the pluralism of opinions."

In France and especially Sweden, given the stronger tradition and ongoing legitimacy of a partisan press, stock market-traded, private, and civil society-owned news outlets are more likely than in the US to express a *partisan* mission, separate or alongside other ideals. In its "publishing mission," Sweden's Schibsted-owned elite national daily, *Svenska Dagbladet*, announces that its purpose is to "inform, enlighten, critically examine and to promote opinions." Expressing the journalistic structural autonomy that prevails at most Swedish newspapers, *Svenska Dagbladet* notes that "the editor-in-chief of the general editorial office is the responsible publisher and leads the newspaper's publishing operation. . . . The editorial page is independent of political parties with the designation independent moderate ["moderate" in the sense of Sweden's major "liberal conservative" party]; it is edited on a value foundation of combined liberalism and conservatism." After noting that it is "independent, autonomous from parties, organizations, and spheres of economic power," Bonnier-owned *Dagens Nyheter*, Sweden's other major elite newspaper, flatly states its ideology in a way that would be anathema (at least officially) at mainstream US news outlets: "DN's political orientation is liberal." The regional family-owned *Jönköpings-Posten* (today part of Bonnier News Local) describes itself as "independent bourgeois" (in the Swedish context, an umbrella term for center-right parties with conservative and/or liberal heritage). The until recently privately held, but heavily government subsidized, *Dagens ETC* has no mission statement but proclaims a slogan that succinctly captures its left environmentalist stance: "Red newspapers for a greener Sweden." France's communist *L'Humanité* affirms an exclusively partisan mission, pointing to "its role as a large and credible alternative newspaper in service of social transformation" whose website is to be developed as "a resource center for militant action, open to traditional and new forms of contestation." Somewhat surprisingly, none of the Swedish foundation-owned newspapers in the sample (originally created with partisan missions) highlighted a strong partisan mission on their individual or group website. We will have more to say about these foundation-owned papers' brand of partisan journalism in Chapter 6.

Religious organization-owned newspapers in each country emphasize their religious identities, but to different degrees and in different ways. The Swedish *Dagen* places its Christian identity front and center, proclaiming that it "covers what happens in Swedish and international Christianity and follows societal issues from a Christian perspective." The *Christian Science Monitor*, in a list of frequently asked questions in its "About Us" section, responds "No" to the question of whether the *Monitor* is a religious newspaper. However, it makes clear that its constructive solutions-oriented approach is "rooted in Christian Science, a Bible-based religion" (with a link to a separate Christian Science website). Nearly invisible at the very bottom of the homepage is a small tab titled "A Christian Science Perspective" that opens to a page with numerous religious commentaries. The French Catholic *La Croix*'s mission statement, hidden at the bottom of its homepage in a "press" marketing report, simply defines the newspaper as a "Catholic general and political information media" outlet and states that it "seeks to shed light on the facts that are promising for the future and for hope."

Table 2.1 shows how mentions of each of these institutional logics varies across ownership forms. More than half of stock market-traded outlets (both widely

Table 2.1 Ownership Forms and Missions: Percentages of Outlets with Mentions

	Market	Informational-Professional**	Pluralist-Professional	Democracy	Partisan	Religious
Market (All Stock Market)# (15)	53.3 (8)*	60.0 (9)	20.0 (3)	6.7 (1)	6.7 (1)	0.0 (0)
Private (16)	18.8 (3)	81.3 (13)	25.0 (4)	31.3 (5)	18.8 (3)	0.0 (0)
Civil Society (14)	0.0 (0)	92.9 (13)	50.0 (7)	42.9 (6)	14.3 (2)	28.6 (4)
Public (6)	0.0 (0)	100.0 (6)	66.7 (4)	66.7 (4)	0.0 (0)	0.0 (0)
Total Sample (51)	21.6 (11)	80.4 (41)	35.3 (18)	31.4 (16)	11.8 (6)	7.8 (4)

Source: Authors' analysis of outlet mission or "about" statements on websites. Categories are *not mutually exclusive* and thus percentages may add up to more than 100 percent.

*Ownership forms with the highest mentions of each mission type are highlighted.

**Informational-Professional indicates mention of "informational" mission (news/information and/or investigation); Pluralist-Professional indicates mention of "pluralist" mission.

#Stock market widely held and stock market dominant shareholder subforms are nearly the same and thus are not reported separately.

held and dominant shareholder subforms) embrace the *market* logic, compared to about twenty percent of private outlets, and no civil society (despite some being commercially funded) or public media. The *informational* professional mission is the most often mentioned across all ownership forms, starting at sixty percent with the market form and rising steadily as ownership forms become less commercialized. *Pluralism* and *democracy* are mentioned more often at civil society-owned and public media than at stock market-traded or privately held outlets. Private and civil society-owned outlets have the widest range of missions, including *partisan* missions (in France and Sweden) and *religious* missions (in all three countries, although only linked to civil society-owned media).

There are also some cross-national differences (not shown in Table 2.1). In the US and France, stock market-traded outlets are most distinctive compared to other outlets: information and democracy logics are less prominent, while market logics are more prominent. In Sweden, however, there is no such opposition and an overall lesser difference in how often information or market logics appear across all ownership forms. In all three countries, mentions of pluralism tend to be higher as one moves from more to less commercial ownership forms, but the increase is sharper and the overall focus on pluralism is higher in Sweden and especially France than in the US.

In sum, we find that symbolic missions tend to closely parallel the material organizational elements of institutional logics identified in our historical analysis.

Ownership Forms and Economic and Cultural Capital

Let us now situate ownership forms in relation to the economic and cultural capital they wield: Which news outlets reach the largest audiences, and which reach smaller, more niche audiences? Which are most celebrated for journalistic excellence by their peers? How much overlap do we find between the outlets high in such cultural capital and those high in economic capital? Do we see any connection between these patterns and media ownership forms?

In attempting to answer these questions, we consider both original data for our sampled news outlets and secondary data sources generated at the national level. Our sampled outlets (see Appendix Table AI.1) provide a close approximation of the largest audience media in each country (overlapping with about sixty-seven percent, on average, of the Reuters Institute Digital News Report's lists of outlets with the largest audiences), supplemented by a purposive sample of additional news outlets chosen to assure wide representation of ownership forms and subforms within each national field.[144] Thus, even when referring only to our national samples, we can be assured of a certain degree of representativeness of the national fields as a whole.

Figures 2.1 and 2.2 show 2016 Reuters Institute survey data identifying the largest online and offline audiences for news media in the US, France, and Sweden, expanding on the data we presented in Chapter 1 (see Figure 1.2, on the top five audience size news websites in each country). For the Reuters data, we present the accumulated percentage of online and offline weekly usage by ownership form (Stock Market-WH refers to "widely held" and Stock Market-DS refers to "dominant shareholder"). Audience size can be considered a proxy for economic capital: *roughly* for online-only outlets (given that massive audiences at outlets like *HuffPost* and *BuzzFeed* have not translated into massive revenues and large newsrooms); *more reliably* for legacy print and audiovisual outlets, whose sizes of offline audiences parallel more closely their levels of revenues and staffing. In Figure 2.1, we see that in the US, the news websites with the largest audiences are stock market widely held, followed by stock market dominant shareholder, and private ownership. In France, all ownership forms are represented among the most widely used online media, with the largest weekly audiences reached by stock market dominant shareholder, private, and civil society-owned media. Finally, in Sweden, we see a strong audience dominance of private ownership (especially Bonnier-owned titles), followed at some distance by stock market-traded Schibsted's two large newspaper websites (*Aftonbladet*

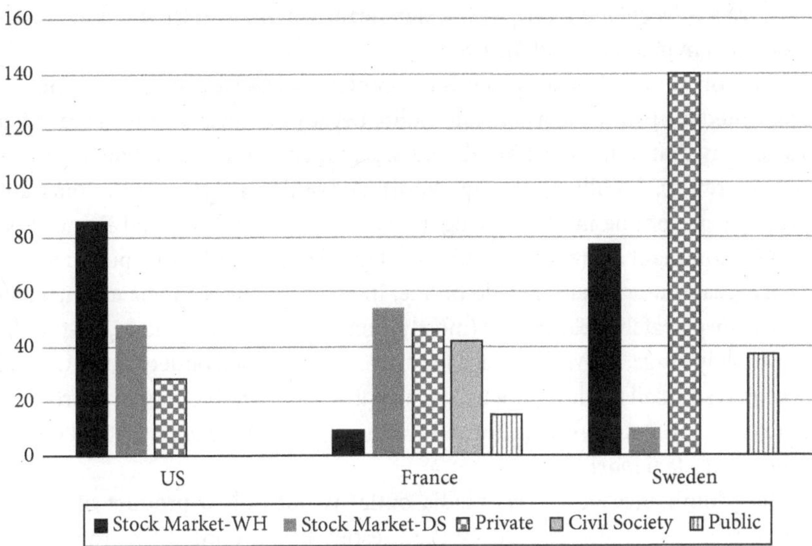

Figure 2.1 Top News Websites by National Field and Ownership Form: Accumulated Percentages of Public with Weekly Use

Source: *Reuters Institute 2016 Digital News Report* (Newman et al. 2016); accumulated percentages for ownership forms or national totals may exceed 100 given that percentages are not mutually exclusive: respondents may report weekly use of multiple outlets.

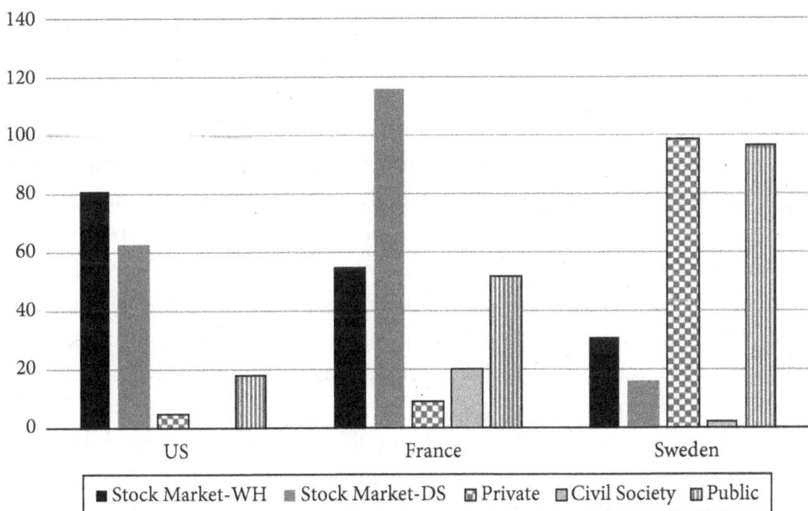

Figure 2.2 Top TV, Radio, and Print News Outlets by National Field and Ownership Form: Accumulated Percentages of Public with Weekly Use

Source: *Reuters Institute 2016 Digital News Report* (Newman et al. 2016); accumulated percentages for ownership forms or national totals may exceed 100 given that percentages are not mutually exclusive: respondents may report weekly use of multiple outlets.

and *Svenska Dagbladet*), and with a significantly higher reach of public media websites than in France and the US.

This portrait of audience reach is incomplete unless we also examine offline legacy media—print, television, and radio. Legacy audiovisual media are still a crucial way that older, more rural, and less affluent audiences follow the news (see Figure 2.2).[145] Offline, stock market-traded outlets are even more dominant than they are online in the US (slightly favoring widely held) and France (especially dominant shareholder). Across all three countries, offline public media attract greater usage than they do online. In Sweden, public media are virtually even with privately held media (mostly Bonnier) in having the highest audience weekly usage.[146] Weekly usage for civil society-owned outlets in the US and Sweden is so small on the national level that it is barely legible in both charts: it is more visible in France, especially online, due to the relative popularity of *Ouest-France* and *Mediapart*.[147]

The prominence of a news media outlet is not only a product of its audience reach; it is also shaped by the prestige it is accorded by professional practitioners. Journalistic prizes are a strong indicator of such cultural capital: we thus analyzed the distribution of major national journalistic prizes across the three countries between the early 2000s and 2020 (see Methods Appendix for more information). News outlets with high prestige may not directly reach as many people, but they may disproportionately influence powerful actors in fields of government, business, NGOs, and universities. Their news and opinion articles may also disproportionately circulate on social media and be republished by other legacy media, significantly extending their reach. For the US, we examined the Pulitzer Prizes (public service, investigative, and explanatory awards) and Peabody Awards (any awards to US news organizations), the former primarily awarded to newspapers, and the latter primarily to TV and radio, although both increasingly including online journalism in recent years. For France, we analyzed the Albert Londres separate prizes for print and audiovisual journalism. For Sweden, we assessed the Stora Journalistpriset (founded by Bonnier in 1966): as of 2002, it has included four prizes each year (all of which we tabulated), each equally available to print, audiovisual, and online journalism, for "investigation," "storytell[ing]", "innovator of the year," and "grand journalism prize" (see Figure 2.3).

For TV/radio, we immediately see that public media appears much higher in cultural capital than it did in economic capital (audience size). In France, public media received all the audiovisual prizes offered, leaving none for commercial media; in Sweden, public media received nearly half of all prizes, and the commercial *TV4*, included in both the stock market and private categories (reflecting a shift in owners) received just seven percent (not shown separately in figure). In the US, in contrast, while public media received a third of the Peabody

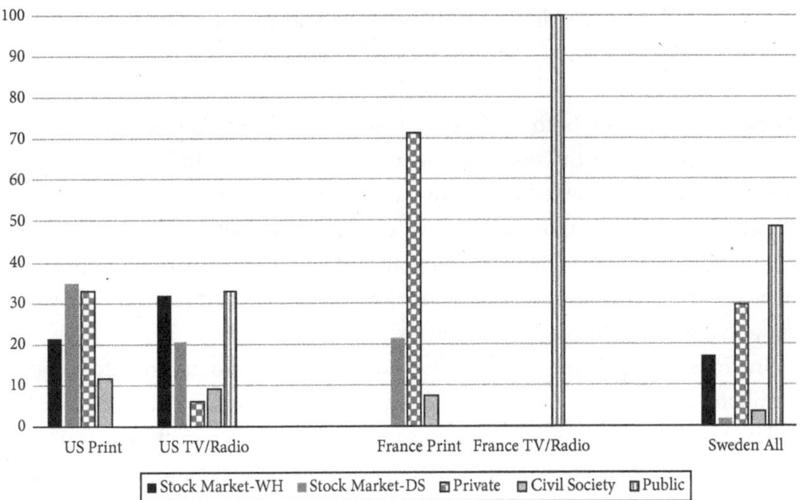

Figure 2.3 Professional Prize Winners by National Field and Ownership Form: Percentages

Source: Authors' calculations based on prize winners listed on awards websites, approx. 2000 to 2020.

Awards, stock market widely held and dominant shareholder-controlled outlets (including *ABC News*, *CBS News*, *NBC News*, and *CNN*) together earned more than half.

As for newspapers, privately held outlets are the most frequent prize winners both in Sweden (especially *Dagens Nyheter*) and France (*Le Monde*). In the US, in contrast, most of the prizes were won by stock market dominant shareholder owned (chiefly the *New York Times*) and privately held papers (numerous, but most often the *Washington Post* after it was sold to Bezos). However, many stock market widely held outlets, including the Tribune-owned *Los Angeles Times* and some Gannett-owned newspapers, also won prizes.

Civil society-owned outlets were less numerous prize winners in all three countries, perhaps partly because of their smaller size and the fact that many of them are digital natives and have only belatedly been made eligible for prizes. In the US, at least, the trend seems to be upward. *ProPublica* won awards in all of our three sampled Pulitzer categories, and the *Texas Tribune* and *CIR/Reveal* as well as *ProPublica* won Peabody Awards. Analyzing a slightly different set of Pulitzer Prizes—public service, investigative, and local—journalism policy expert Steve Waldman reports that, from 2013 to 2023, "even though the majority of papers are owned by chains, sixty-seven percent of the winners or finalists were either family-owned newspapers (forty-five percent) or nonprofit (twenty-three percent)."[148]

Ownership Forms and Characteristics of Audiences and Owners

Ownership forms are both institutional and social. Journalism scholar Stephen Lacy captured this distinction, and the importance of both dimensions, when he raised the question of whether "the impact [on news] is due to the characteristics of individual owners and managers or to some systematic impact inherent in the different types of ownership and management."[149] In addition to individual owners—and board members where they exercise ownership power—we would also add the importance of the characteristics of audiences.

Previous research on news media owners, shareholders, investors, board members, and managers has shown that they are disproportionately wealthy and highly educated.[150] Available data suggest that social characteristics of board members and managers reinforce institutional logic differences: in other words, one finds a greater prevalence of business training and professional backgrounds at stock market or private media versus a greater prevalence of academic, non-profit, journalistic, or governmental backgrounds at civil society-owned and public media.[151]

News consumption has increasingly become a practice reserved for wealthier, more highly educated persons. Despite the internet's early egalitarian hype, one sociological study found that one in six Americans never go online and that those who do tend to have significantly higher income and education levels.[152] The online audience is further split between "news avoiders" and "news seekers," with the latter group tending to be even more elite than internet users as a whole, with higher education and income levels, and more left-leaning political views.[153] In US surveys, while newspaper print subscribers were found to be more than twice as likely to have a college degree as non-subscribers, digital subscribers were also shown to have higher levels of education and income than print subscribers.[154]

About three-fifths of the news outlets in our sample have relatively "elite" audiences in level of education and income (see Methods Appendix for data sources); the remainder of outlets have "omnibus" audiences with education or income levels close to their respective national averages. There are clear differences across ownership forms: almost two-thirds of private and civil society-owned media are targeted to elite audiences. In contrast, only one-third of public media and about one-half of all stock market-owned media have elite audiences. Conglomerate-owned media are similar to stock market-traded media, and nearly ninety percent of current/legacy journalist-controlled media have elite audiences. (See the outlet-level coding for elite or omnibus audiences in Appendix Table A2.1). As for cross-national differences (see Figure 2.4), we see the following: In the US, as ownership becomes less commercial—moving toward civil society and public—audiences become more elite.[155] Sweden moves

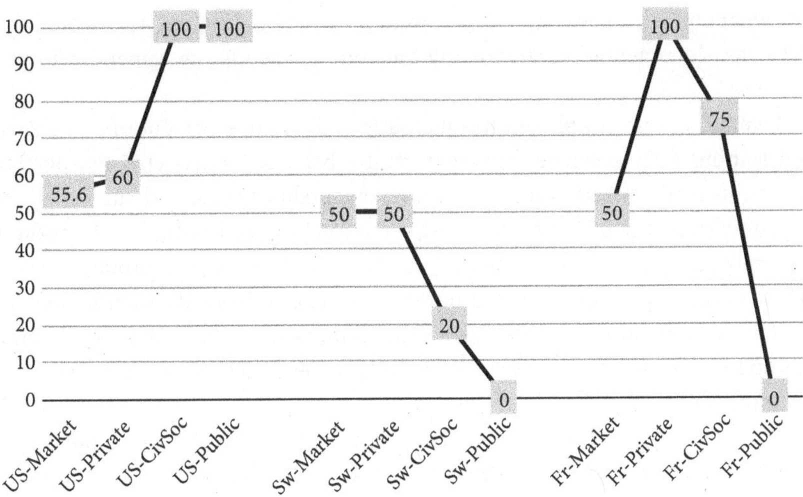

Figure 2.4 Outlets with Elite Audiences by National Field and Ownership Form: Percentages

Percentages of outlets with omnibus audience not shown in figure.

in the opposite direction: its civil society-owned and public media are less elite. France combines elite private and civil society-owned media with omnibus public media. Overall, in our samples, Sweden has a higher proportion of omnibus audience media than the US and France—consistent with the fact that Sweden remains among the world's leaders in rates of newspaper readership, digital subscriptions, and public trust in media.[156]

Do partisan preferences of audiences and owners also cluster in patterned ways across ownership forms? We measured audience partisan preferences from public or proprietary survey data. Owners' political position-takings (whether individual or family for private and stock market dominant shareholder forms, or board members for stock market widely held, civil society, and public outlets) were gleaned from their party or associational memberships, individual or organizational public statements, or publicly reported political campaign contributions. Public media outlets (at least those in our sample) have been administratively designed to be politically neutral or balanced, and we thus designated the political positioning of their ownership as such; this roughly balanced character was also generally evident in the composition of their governing boards. In our assessments of partisan preferences, we were sensitive to the particular ideological and political party spectrum in each country: thus, "right" and "left" are to be understood for each outlet's audience or owners as nationally specific.[157] (For data sources, see Methods Appendix; for an outlet-by-outlet listing of owner and audience characteristics and primary funding, see Appendix Table A2.1; for documentation supporting the coding, see Online Appendix Tables, Series 2.1–2.4).

Overall, in our sample of fifty-one outlets, thirty-one percent of owners are left-leaning, forty-seven percent are neutral or balanced, and twenty-two percent are right-leaning. Across national fields, ownership forms, and subforms, the highest percentage of owners tend to be neutral/balanced, with the exception of current/legacy journalist-controlled outlets, where the highest proportions are left-leaning. Civil society-owned outlets also tend to have left-leaning owners, except in Sweden, where, because of the dominance of [pro-market] "liberal" foundation-owned newspapers, civil society ownership is more often associated with the right.

Audiences' partisan preferences roughly parallel those of owners, but with a greater tilt to the left.[158] Fifty-three percent of the outlets included in our study have audiences that are majority left-leaning in their views; thirty-seven percent are balanced with a roughly equal mix of left and right-leaning audiences; and ten percent have majorities of right-leaning audiences. Across all ownership forms, most outlets have left-leaning audiences followed by or tied with those with balanced audiences. Stock market-owned outlets (and the conglomerate subform) have the most even distribution of left, balanced, and right audiences. Current/legacy journalist-controlled outlets have almost exclusively left-leaning audiences (ninety-three percent) (see Table 2.2).

Not shown in the table, we note that left audiences are most common in our US (seventy-one percent of outlets) and French (sixty percent) samples, while balanced audiences (sixty-seven percent) dominate in Sweden; conversely, right-leaning audiences are slightly more common in Sweden and France (thirteen percent of outlets for both) than in the US (five percent).

Conclusion

In this chapter, we have traced the historical development and contemporary distribution of ownership forms in the US, Sweden, and France. We have provided evidence of both nationally distinct and cross-nationally similar patterns across ownership forms in their institutional logics and missions, economic and cultural capital, audience demographics, and owner and audience partisan preferences.

In the US, stock market ownership arrived relatively early in the twentieth century and continues to be the economically dominant ownership form for commercial television and radio. It is now a less common ownership form than in the recent past for the legacy print press. Private equity/hedge fund ownership (also

Table 2.2 Owner and Audience Partisan Preference by Ownership Form and Subform: Percentage of Outlets

	Left Owner	Neutral/ Balanced Owner	Right Owner	Left Audience	Balanced Audience	Right Audience
Total Sample (51)	31.4 (16)	47.1 (24)	21.6 (11)	52.9 (27)	37.3 (19)	9.8 (5)
Market (All SM) (15)	20.0 (3)	53.3 (8)*	26.7 (4)	40.0 (6)	33.3 (5)	26.7 (4)
Private (16)	37.5 (6)	43.8 (7)	18.8 (3)	68.8 (11)	31.3 (5)	—
CivSoc (14)	50.0 (7)	21.4 (3)	28.6 (4)	50.0 (7)	42.9 (6)	7.1 (1)
Public (6)	—	100.0 (6)	—	50.0 (3)	50.0 (3)	—
SM-WH (8)	12.5 (1)	62.5 (5)	25.0 (2)	37.5 (3)	37.5 (3)	25.0 (2)
SM-DS (7)	28.6 (2)	42.9 (3)	28.6 (2)	42.9 (3)	28.6 (2)	28.6 (2)
Conglom. (12)	8.3 (1)	58.3 (7)	33.3 (4)	33.3 (4)	33.3 (4)	33.3 (4)
Journ. Control (15)	80.0 (12)	20.0 (3)	—	93.3 (14)	6.7 (1)	—

Source: See documentation in Online Appendix Tables, Series 2.2 and 2.4.

*Dominant owner and audience partisan preferences for each of the four main ownership forms are highlighted.

driven by a strong market logic), concentrated in a few large chains, has now become dominant, except at a handful of major national and regional newspapers privately purchased by billionaires. Private online start-ups tend to be effectively controlled by their founders with support from VC. Compared to other western industrial democracies, public media arrived late (not until the 1960s) and were designed to compensate for market failure, providing educational and news programming that commercial media would not. The number of civil society-owned news outlets, most of them digital-only, has expanded dramatically during the twenty-first century, although they continue to lag behind market and private media in their funding, staffing, and audience sizes. Civil society-owned and public media are increasingly intertwined, both relying heavily on philanthropy funding and serving niche cultural elite audiences.

In France, there is a greater stigma associated with large-scale commercial enterprises: anti-capitalist public attitudes are among the highest in the world.[159] Further, both advertising spending and media readership are lower in France on a per capita basis than in the US and Sweden.[160] The result is a publicly subsidized journalistic field with very few profitable news outlets and with profitability and quality often perceived in opposition to one another. The distinction between those outlets with journalist control (whether through ownership or other contractual means) and those without it is particularly meaningful in France: some degree of structurally guaranteed journalist control is present at many prominent French privately held outlets.

In Sweden, as in the US, commercial enterprise is accepted as civically legitimate, and privately held and stock market-traded media have historically been profitable, fueled by a strong advertising market in the past and continued relatively high levels of readership and paid subscriptions. Swedish levels of public trust in media are almost twice as high as in France and the US.[161] While many newspapers are historically linked to political parties (through party, foundation, or family control), partisanship is tempered by strong journalistic professionalism, including a commitment to the "watchdog" role of holding the powerful to account. As in France and the US, national elite dailies are among the most prestigious, but to a greater extent than in the other two countries, entirely taxpayer funded public TV and radio dominate the field in resources, audiences, public trust, and status within the profession.[162]

Across our three-country sample of news outlets (roughly representative of each national field), market logics are symbolically affirmed most often at stock market-traded outlets, while pluralist and democratic missions are embraced most frequently at public and civil society-owned media. Private media, along with civil society-owned media, highlight in their mission statements the greatest variety of distinct purposes. These patterns are most consistent in the US and France. In contrast, in Sweden, the differences across ownership forms are less pronounced, with the exception of a stronger affirmation of partisanship at private and civil society-owned outlets.

We also analyzed how ownership forms in the three countries are positioned in their fields in relation to the volume and proportion of economic and cultural capital. Stock market-traded and private media have the largest audiences in all three countries, but in France and Sweden, public and civil society-owned media also reach substantial audiences. In all three countries, private and public media have tended to win the most professional prizes, but small civil society-owned outlets are beginning to become more visible, especially in the US. Stock market-owned media, mainly in the US and Sweden, have also won a fair share of journalistic prizes, especially at outlets serving elite audiences.

Finally, we analyzed the social positioning of audiences and the political positioning of both audiences and owners as they varied across ownership forms and national fields. In contemporary high-choice media environments, any news consumption (as opposed to entertainment) has become a relatively elite activity. As measured by education and income, most of the outlets in our sample serve elite audiences, but this tendency is strongest in private and civil society-owned media. Nevertheless, public media in Sweden and France, along with some stock market-traded media in all countries, reach omnibus audiences. Owners and audiences in the sample roughly parallel one another in their partisan preferences, in both cases leaning more left than right (except in Sweden), but with owners most often expressing neutral or balanced preferences.

In sum, this chapter has provided historical background and structural data necessary to understand basic characteristics of news media ownership in three leading western democracies. Nevertheless, the ability and inclination to generate the funding and audience interest necessary to achieve public service, partisan, or economically instrumentalist purposes also depends on particular owners and managers. In the next two chapters, we turn our attention to the range of strategies deployed—with a focus on their relation to public service orientation—and how these vary across ownership forms and national fields.

3
Harvesting Profits versus Investing in News

Just as at any other organization, news media owners and their designated managers play a key role in making decisions about budgeting: when and how much to invest in staff and infrastructure, when and how much to cut. But a news outlet is not just any organization. It is accorded a special ethical and legal status because of the central role it is expected to play in a democracy by providing vital public affairs information and a forum for public debate. Decisions to invest or not to invest in the news can have major consequences beyond the fate of an individual news outlet. In this chapter, drawing on interviews and public remarks of CEOs, publishers, editors, and reporters, along with other primary and secondary sources, we examine the structures, contingencies, and contradictions that shape these decisions.[1] In other words, we analyze both the dominant logics of ownership forms and the situations in which those logics may be temporarily suspended, subverted, or transformed.

Market Ownership: Tendencies toward Cost-Cutting and Exceptions

We begin by considering the market ownership form—stock market-traded or hedge fund/private equity—for which profit maximization takes priority over public service. The Aspen Institute's Charlie Firestone, an influential convener of media industry conferences, said he asked journalists working for stock market-traded outlets at one such conference, " 'Why are you doing this, why can't you be more, just live with a little bit smaller [profit] margin?' And that was never fully answered, but the answer was 'we're looking over our shoulder, we're a public company, we have to perform.' "[2] Large-scale research confirms the many insider testimonies linking a profit-driven approach to a lesser investment in news production. One study of seventy-seven US newspapers found that newspapers with stock market-traded ownership had significantly higher profits—and smaller newsrooms—than privately held newspapers.[3]

Isaac Josephson, a former *ABC News* vice president for product development, a role that placed him squarely at the intersection of editorial and business

How Media Ownership Matters. Rodney Benson et al. Oxford University Press. © Rodney Benson, Mattias Hessérus, Timothy Neff, and Julie Sedel 2025. DOI: 10.1093/oso/9780199931293.003.0004

divisions, defines the constraints in this way: "When you're part of a [stock market] traded company there's an emphasis on short-term growth . . . [and] an expectation to grow every year."[4] As an executive producer of *ABC Evening News* from the 1980s through the late 2000s, Paul S. Mason was in a prime position to gauge the competing imperatives of producing news for a stock market-traded media organization: "You've got latitude to do some of the things you might consider to be important, but at the same time you have to keep an eye on ratings, expenditure, what are your costs, what's your P and L [profit and loss]."[5]

Executives at *TF1*, the only major French news outlet directly traded on the stock market, emphasize in similar fashion the primary importance of generating profits. As former *TF1* CEO Patrick Le Lay recalls, tellingly identifying himself fully with the channel he led for more than two decades beginning with the privatization in 1987: "I was listed on the stock exchange. I was on the CAC 40 [equivalent of the US Dow listing of the thirty largest stocks]. I had the analysts' meeting, the general shareholders' meeting. They are the ones who judge me." Le Lay added, "My first obligation was for the company to make money."[6]

Executives at Schibsted, until 2024 a stock market widely held owner of the leading Swedish national newspapers *Aftonbladet* and *Svenska Dagbladet*, are more publicly circumspect about profit seeking. Long Schibsted's largest shareholder, with twenty-six percent ownership, the Tinius Trust ostensibly set policy, highlighting the company's civic commitment to journalism.[7] However, a different message was conveyed inside the organization. *Aftonbladet* played a key role in driving traffic to Blocket, the company's highly profitable classified advertising site.[8] Even so, in the mid-2010s Schibsted refused *Aftonbladet* Editor-in-Chief and CEO Jan Helin's request to link the two and thus provide a "new model for financing journalism." Instead, according to Helin, the executives decided to reorganize the company to leave the Trust in charge of only the low profit-margin "publishing" division (the news operations) and create a new company for classified advertising, preventing any possibility of the latter helping to fund the former (a step they finally took in full in 2024[9]). Helin was repeatedly told by Schibsted officials that "no, no, you need to safeguard your bottom line," that "[profit] margins were really important," and that "the only way to keep up the margins now is . . . to cut the costs."[10]

With this profit-maximizing priority, *Aftonbladet* was forced to pursue a "really hard cost cutting strategy" with reductions in its investigative and specialized reporting and an increasing focus on sensationalist breaking news.[11] Helin's experience was echoed by other journalists we spoke with, such as Emanuel Karlsten, a former *Aftonbladet* digital consultant. Karlsten said that pressure to maximize value for stockholders each quarter forced *Aftonbladet* "to downsize, constantly downsize."[12] Helin eventually left to start a new position as programming director of the public *SVT* television channel.

To be fair, Schibsted has not always seemed to prioritize profit above all else. It held on to the elite liberal-conservative newspaper *Svenska Dagbladet* for more than two decades, even though it was scarcely sustainable even with press subsidies. Jonas Ohlsson, director of the Nordicom media research center and a leading ownership scholar, argues that if Schibsted were only interested in maximizing profit, "they would have sold *Svenska Dagbladet* a long time ago [or] wouldn't have bought it in the first place."[13] However, Schibsted's ultimate decision to sell both *Svenska Dagbladet* and *Aftonbladet* to the Tinius Trust, transformed into the sole owner of a separate non-traded company, speaks to the tensions generated inside a stock market-traded company by any holdings (in this case, legacy newspapers) unable to maximize shareholder value.

Some hedge funds, the US-based Alden Global Capital in particular, have taken cost-cutting to even greater extremes than stock market-traded companies. Alden's owners are famously secretive, but in an interview with the prestigious US magazine *The Atlantic*, co-owner Heath Freeman justified Alden's purchases as a way of saving newspapers in bankruptcy or on the verge of being closed: "These papers were in many cases left for dead by local families not willing to make the tough but appropriate decisions to get these news organizations to sustainability. These papers would have been liquidated if not for us stepping up."[14] The problem, for many critics, is that while hedge fund (or private equity) ownership may provide temporary help of a sort, this business model ultimately subjects newsrooms to unnecessarily deep cuts in the interest of enriching shareholders. Geneva Overholser, a former editor-in-chief in the Gannett chain who gained prominence for her public criticisms of the company's excessive focus on profits, now says that hedge fund ownership is even worse for journalism than stock market-traded ownership.[15] A study by University of North Carolina researchers found that "Alden-owned newspapers have cut their staff at twice the rate of their competitors."[16]

Two newspapers in the same Minnesota metropolitan market—one (the *St. Paul Pioneer Press*), owned by Alden Capital, the other (the *Minneapolis Star Tribune*, included in our study), privately held by a local billionaire—provide an instructive comparison.[17] As the second largest paper in the region, the *St. Paul Pioneer-Press* has long been in a precarious position, given that when there is direct competition advertisers tend to gravitate toward the market leader (this is the structural problem Sweden's subsidies for "second" papers were originally designed to address, keeping the smaller circulation papers alive on behalf of the democratic principle of pluralism).[18] Yet, at one point, it looked like the *Minneapolis Star Tribune* might be the first of the two to perish. In 2009, it filed for bankruptcy, and five years later it was purchased by local billionaire, Glen Taylor.[19] Under Taylor's ownership, the newspaper has had a smaller decline in print advertising and circulation revenues than US newspapers on average and, despite being in only the sixteenth largest metropolitan area in the US, it has built the seventh largest digital subscriber base. Taylor's willingness to forgo maximum profits seems to have been essential in lessening cuts (staff is down to 250 from an all-time high of 350) and in encouraging high quality reporting, with the *Minneapolis Star Tribune* earning two Pulitzer Prizes over the past decade. In contrast, to maintain maximum profits, the *St. Paul Pioneer Press*'s journalistic staff has been cut from a high of 260 to fifty. In 2017, Alden reported that the *St. Paul Pioneer Press* had earned revenues of $10 million, for a thirteen percent profit margin.[20]

In an era of economic and technological disruption, cost-cutting might seem to be the safest path to avoid bankruptcy in the face of declining audiences and advertising revenues. In fact, cost-cutting rather than investing—at least for market-owned outlets—is less of a cautious approach than the time-tested path to maximum profitability. As media scholar Victor Pickard reminds us, it was during the 1980s and 1990s, well before the rise of the internet and the financial crises of 2008 and 2020, that US stock market-traded newspapers first began to aggressively "cut costs to inflate profits instead of reinvesting in news gathering capacities for the long term."[21] During the early 2000s, this focus on profits and consolidation through debt-fueled mergers and acquisitions diverted funds from crucial early investments in digital infrastructures. Journalism scholar Margaret Susca found that stock market-traded company annual reports during this time period "made no mention of investments" in the digital transition, instead highlighting generation of "cash required for [outside] investing activities."[22]

Is it possible for stock market-traded or private equity-owned media, despite their profit-maximizing focus, to nevertheless invest in journalism? Drawing on her experience at both US commercial (notably Gannett) and public news media, Colorado public media leader Laura Frank said, "In every newsroom that I've ever been in, there's been a very strong sense of public service, that we want to do those stories that make a difference." The main difference, she added, is that "in corporate owned [stock market-traded] media you have to increase profits at a rate that keeps Wall Street happy. That's a real thing, that's a real pressure," which ultimately becomes "an issue of resources" or pressure to "do more stories" without extra time or compensation.[23] In other words, to attain their profit targets, stock market-traded media do not necessarily give up on "quality" journalism, but they may invest less in it or foster working conditions that make it all but impossible to maintain the highest standards. In this way, a professional journalistic logic is preserved, as sociologist Jeffrey Alexander has argued, but as Alexander does not acknowledge, often only in a superficial way: the symbolic ideal loses a substantial portion of its material substance in practice.[24]

It is nevertheless the case that some media owners and managers who profess little or no interest in quality journalism may intermittently or inadvertently underwrite the conditions for it. There are at least two scenarios when even stock market-traded or private equity/hedge fund owners may invest (or at least not substantially cut) public service-oriented news at a level comparable to their less profit-driven counterparts.

One situation is the liminal moment following a purchase when the best way forward is uncertain. Belying its reputation for harvesting profits (or "overharvesting" in Susca's more apt phrasing[25]), the early years of Alden Capital's ownership of the Digital First group created a brief opening for investing. The long-time journalist and news media entrepreneur John Paton was initially brought in as a member of the board of directors of one of the two companies that were ultimately merged to become Digital First. The companies were in bankruptcy, and he and other board members were asked to provide advice to the bankers who held the debt. At one point, Paton says, the banks said, "Look, would you be CEO when the company comes out of bankruptcy? It was very clear to me then that we'd have to expand that company pretty dramatically if we were going to have any success.... We invested in technology, we invested in cameras, we invested in you name it, you know, to be able to try and have an audience."[26] With much fanfare, Paton launched "Project Thunderdome," hiring seventy journalists for a central New York City-based hub that would provide original national and international news for the other newspapers in the chain. Prominent journalists hired to head up the operation included former *Washington Post.com* editor-in-chief Jim Brady.

At first, the ultimate goal—as Paton himself had executed with a group of Spanish-language newspapers he built up and then sold for a profit—was to sell the debt-free Digital First to an outside buyer. But around the time of the sale, most of the likely large American newspaper companies who might have been interested went into bankruptcy or were seriously in debt themselves. "So with fewer buyers and fewer exits," Paton says, "fewer exit opportunities on the horizon, you know, they started to go into harvesting mode." Making Digital First truly profitable from its digital operations was not seen as an option because that strategy would have required more investment and more time, with no certainty of pay-off. Alternatively, even though print circulation and advertising steadily declined each year, if costs were kept low enough, a primarily print-oriented operation could generate profitable revenues for a decade or more until the operation was finally permanently closed. In Paton's words:

> Hedge Funds take high risks. [But] it's a high price to pay if they want to start driving cash. I mean, they were really open and honest, they basically said, hey, we'll back this whole thing that you're doing, "digital first", etc. But then they wanted money to come in faster than it was coming in. It was faster, obviously, for them, for cash return to gut the costs, take the cash back off the table, and just keep doing that until at some point it gets where it couldn't be done, and they sell it off.

In the end, Paton says, he "left because the hedge funds wanted to start milking them for cash, and I didn't want to do that, I wanted to grow the companies." Editor-in-Chief Brady told one interviewer, "If you work for a company owned by a hedge fund, it's like walking through a minefield. Any step can be the one where you hit the mine. Any day it could end, and you know that."[27] In other words, this market ownership subform is not entirely antithetical to public service-oriented journalism, if CEOs and editors who care about the journalism are given some room to maneuver, but it is not a form of ownership likely to sustainably foster strong public service orientation over the long haul.

If the first exception to the challenges of combining market ownership with investing in public service orientation is this early period of experimentation during the start-up phase, a second exception is when a small news media operation operates in the shadow of a much larger media conglomerate distracted by other opportunities and challenges. This was the case for the *Huffington Post* after it was purchased by Verizon in 2015, according to one staffer.[28] Verizon did not exactly invest in the soon renamed *HuffPost*, but it also did not engage in aggressive harvesting: while staff departures were rarely "backfilled," there was no Alden Capital-level aggressive elimination of jobs. Verizon also owned *Yahoo News* (as of 2017), which, because of its scale and greater use of algorithmic curation and aggregation, was a far larger and more profitable business than *HuffPost*. Verizon Media (the Verizon division in direct contact with *HuffPost*) and *HuffPost* had different visions of news. Verizon Media managers sought to cut back on *HuffPost*'s original reporting for a "voices" vertical (black voices, Latino voices, queer voices, etc.) and shift funding to a "trends" team that searched for and produced stories based on topics trending on the internet in the hope of boosting page views. Although the company was able to begin instituting some of these changes, Verizon Media managers and staff often did not return the calls or emails of *HuffPost* staff, and there were little to no consequences when directives were not executed. In the words of the *HuffPost* staffer:

> Even though there were different visions, there wasn't a lot of commitment to actually seeing them through. . . . If [Verizon directives] didn't happen, they didn't care that much, because we made up a much smaller audience and much less revenue than Yahoo. So, any minute of [a Verizon Media manager's] time was much better spent on the Yahoo brands than on HuffPost and holding [HuffPost staff] accountable to any goals.[29]

Almost from the moment Verizon bought *HuffPost*, there were rumors that it would eventually unload the unprofitable outlet, and scarcely five years after the purchase, it sold *HuffPost* to *BuzzFeed*. *HuffPost*'s ability to function inside a vast corporate bureaucracy, relatively unscathed for at least a few years, calls to mind media scholar Josh Braun's research showing that large corporations are not "monolithic" systems. Instead, in his analysis of *MSNBC*'s diverse news operations, Braun found a decentered, internally fragmented, "heterarchic" organization in which different divisions have their own "provincial" concerns that may or may not be shared with other actors working on the same projects.[30]

All in all, widely held stock market-traded and hedge fund/private equity ownership place a premium on short-term profit maximization, making long-term investment in public service-oriented news—especially if it might require sustained periods of losses—less likely. Thus, these ownership forms are not entirely antithetical to *any* public service orientation, but they tend to work at crosscurrents to it. For Paton, with his thirty-five years of experience as an editor and executive working with all types of commercial media, the best ownership model "hands down" is the individual or family private owner or dominant shareholder that has the discretion to invest over taking the short-term gain.[31] Leading media management scholars draw from successful case studies the lesson that "a degree of cushioning [protection] from market forces appears to be positively correlated with creativity" not only in journalism but across the cultural professions.[32]

The Discretion of Dominant Shareholders and Private Owners

Among "legacy" stock market-traded print news companies, the dominant shareholder-controlled *New York Times* is perhaps most well-known for taking the long-term investing approach. That's not to say, however, that the Sulzberger family owners have been indifferent to profits. While never aspiring to the stratospheric profits of Gannett and other stock market-traded chains, the *New York Times* attained profit margins of fifteen percent and higher during the 1980s. Faced with flagging profits of less than five percent in the early 1990s, the family-selected publisher, Arthur Sulzberger Jr., instituted several rounds of layoffs and promoted a "holistic vision" of "anticipating and meeting the desires of the customer."[33] After making some ill-timed investments right before the financial crash of 2008, including a new skyscraper headquarters, the company was forced to take a large high-interest loan from Mexican telecommunications billionaire Carlos Slim (ultimately paid back early in full in 2011). During this crisis period, the family—with the crucial support of a dual stock structure that gave them majority control of voting shares—successfully fended off multiple hostile take-over attempts.[34]

As alluded to earlier, the Sulzbergers allowed the *New York Times*'s stock price to tumble and stopped taking dividends so that they could build an ambitious digital subscription model that took at least five years—and the commercially fortuitous election of a populist president *New York Times* readers loved to hate (see Chapter 6)—to become profitable. While 2021 net profits of eleven percent were lower than those of some stock market-traded or private equity companies engaged in intensive harvesting, the *New York Times*'s strategy seems to have created a successful path to long term economic sustainability. Investing rather than cutting its way to profitability, by 2021, the *New York Times*'s full-time staff of seventeen hundred journalists was the highest in its history and substantially larger than any other US news organization.[35]

However, not all dominant shareholders are able or willing to invest over the long term in quality journalism, and even when they are, what seem like savvy steps taken to diversify a company's finances may turn out later to be a major liability. Under the Graham family, with a similar dual-stock structure as at the *New York Times*, the *Washington Post* endured successive waves of cuts and lost some of its top national political reporters to the online start-up *Politico*. Partly propped up for a time by its ownership of Kaplan, a large and highly profitable educational testing and for-profit college company, this hedge collapsed when Kaplan and its competitors came under government scrutiny (during the supposedly sympathetic Democratic administration of Barack Obama) for misleading students into assuming massive debt for nearly worthless degrees. With both its media and education businesses in free fall, the Graham family sold the *Washington Post* to Amazon founder Jeff Bezos for the relatively paltry sum of $250 million. On the eve of the sale to Bezos, Katharine Weymouth, the last of the Graham family publishers, commented ruefully: "If journalism is the mission, given the pressures to cut costs and make profits, maybe [a stock market-traded company] is not the best place for the *Post*."[36] What she did not say is that the Grahams were evidently also less willing than the Sulzbergers to forgo sustained low share prices or lost dividends.

As an individual private owner, Bezos has had even more discretion to take the long view; he refocused the *Washington Post* on its natural "brand" strength in US national politics and made sure that the newspaper had the technological tools to compete digitally with the *New York Times* and other national media, first through aggressive social media distribution and subsequently through a digital subscription plan similar to that of the *New York Times*.[37] Bezos's financial backstopping, as we will discuss in the next chapter, has continued even after this initial growth spurt stalled after the 2020 presidential election.[38] Likewise, local billionaire owner Glen Taylor is widely credited with providing the support that has made the *Minneapolis Star Tribune* one of the most successful regional newspapers in the US. As Suki Dardarian, editor and senior vice president of the *Minneapolis Star Tribune*, recounts:

> The paper had been through a lot of trauma, layoffs, buyouts, ownership that was in flux, and we had a great board of directors that went out looking for someone to purchase the *Minneapolis Star Tribune* and they identified Glen, who was a Minnesota born and bred self-made multi-billionaire. He had purchased the basketball team to keep it here in town, and he purchased the newspaper to keep it in town. He said, 'The people of Minnesota deserve a great newspaper and I want to be part of that.' And, the paper has gotten measurably better every year. . . . At a time when this industry is under collapse, to have that kind of support, there is so little we have to worry about from that perspective, which gives us the chance to focus on trying to be relevant to our audience.[39]

Large privately held corporations represent another type of private ownership. Prominent examples include the Newhouse family's privately controlled Advance Publications (owner of Condé Nast magazines such as *The New Yorker*) and Hearst, controlled by the descendants of William Randolph Hearst and owner of the *Houston Chronicle*, the *San Francisco Chronicle*, and various other regional newspapers, as well as magazines, television, and multimedia properties. Josephson, whom we heard from earlier about his experiences at *ABC*, has also worked at companies with significant newspaper properties, early in his career at the stock market-traded Tribune Company and from 2019 to 2021 as head of product for Hearst Newspapers. Similar to what we saw with *HuffPost* under Verizon's ownership, Josephson said that newspapers were sheltered somewhat at Hearst because it "counted on other areas of the company for profit."[40] Josephson adds:

> The newspaper business was a point of pride, and a reminder of their origins. That's not to say we were not pressed for profit (or at least break-even status) and year over year growth. But the margin pressure was modest. The overall revenues represented a very low single-digit percentage of the company's total revenue, and everyone was just fine with that.[41]

Private owners with venture capital investors are able to wait for profitability to emerge over a relatively long period of time, thus making possible highly creative and potentially civically beneficial experimentation and innovation at online start-ups like *Vice*, *Vox*, *HuffPost*, and *BuzzFeed*.[42] Even so, at companies backed with venture capital, there will eventually come a day when the investors want to cash out. This pressure seems to have been largely behind Jonah Peretti's decision in 2021, fifteen years after the company's founding, to transform *BuzzFeed* into a stock market-traded company despite its weak financials. As part of the less rigorous SPAC (special purpose acquisition company) public listing used by *BuzzFeed*, the company's largest investors, including NBC Universal (in turn owned by the Comcast telecommunications giant), were able to win back a sizable portion of their initial investments.[43]

To be clear, investing is no guarantee of achieving either quality public service news or long-term economic sustainability. After acquiring a controlling share with an investment of 20 million euros in *Libération* in 2004, Edouard de Rothschild invested new capital for a year and a half, without micro-managing the organization, at the end of which time period the money had been exhausted and the newspaper was still losing more than a million euros per month.[44] In 2006, he issued an ultimatum that he would only invest additional funds under certain conditions: the long-time director, Serge July, would have to depart; additional staff layoffs would be put in place by the new director, Laurent Joffrin; and the newspaper's journalists would have to give up some of their statutory voting rights over the management and direction of the newspaper.[45] New owners in principle willing to invest may also initially insist on staff or other cuts, especially if they are needed to balance the budget in the context of declining revenues. This strategy was adopted after 2010 by the new owners of *Le Monde*, through cuts to "legacy" operations (especially in non-journalistic support, such as printing staff and facilities) and to salaries and benefits of top editors and managers, joined with modest new investments in digital operations.[46]

Despite their shortcomings, commercial owners—both via privately held and market-traded entities—have historically been the single largest source of investment in the news. A 2012 report for the British regulatory agency Ofcom found that private, for-profit companies (including some stock market-traded companies such as News Corporation) accounted for a greater proportion of the UK national investment in news (sixty-eight percent) than the well-funded public *BBC* (twenty-one percent).[47] This comparison combines the investments of more than one thousand newspapers spread across the UK, which likely included some overlap in articles published. In addition, a focus on raw investment tells us nothing about the specific editorial content that is being produced and highlighted on the webpages of media outlets, which is the ultimate focus of our study. Nevertheless, these statistics highlight the sheer magnitude of commercial support for news and the difficulties of fully replacing it with public and civil society ownership and funding.

The Freedom and Fragility of Civil Society and Public Media

Commercially funded civil society-owned media with no need (or legal ability) to generate profit have not faced the same pressure to cut costs as stock market-traded or privately owned media outlets. One powerful illustration of how this ownership form can open up a space to invest is provided by the experience of the *Philadelphia Inquirer*, after the owner donated the newspaper to a 501(c)(3) nonprofit news organization bearing his name—the Lenfest Institute for Journalism—in 2016. The newspaper itself was a state-licensed "public benefit" B corporation (in which social impact is legally recognized as a purpose of the company equal in importance to economic profits). With this combination of nonprofit and public benefit ownership, the *Philadelphia Inquirer* was able to break from decades of budget cuts to double its investigative journalism team and expand other reporting projects.[48] However, the president of the nonprofit Poynter Institute, which owns the *Tampa Bay Times*, has publicly stated that nonprofit ownership "doesn't guarantee journalistic excellence . . . it's an arrangement that frees you from the pressures of Wall Street, but it can bring you other pressures," which in the case of the *Tampa Bay Times*, have traditionally included the need to generate dividends to help support the educational operations of the Poynter Institute.[49]

As Sture Bergman, CEO of the foundation-owned VK Media, owner of the Umeå newspaper *Västerbottens-Kuriren*, sees it, "The legal form of foundation-owned newspaper has a lot of advantages, if run correctly. We don't have to make a profit for somebody else." Bergman adds that whereas newspaper companies with private owners must "rationalize in order to pay off the acquisitions made by the owner and send money forward, we don't have to do that. We can look after the common good in our community."[50] For the most part, however, Swedish foundation-owned newspapers have not been known for long-term investment strategies, in part because many foundation owners are "poor" with no assets of their own beyond their media holdings. *Norran*'s owner (until 2019), the Stiftelsen Skelelftepress foundation, is an exception, with extensive assets in real estate and other investments.[51] During more prosperous times, *Norran* had been expected to produce fifteen percent profits, but during the difficult transition to digital, the foundation was able to drop percentage expectations altogether. At the limit, according to *Norran* CEO Anders Westermark, the foundation owner could subsidize the paper with its real estate or other profitable investments, but it largely avoided doing that (choosing, as noted in chapter 2, to sell the newspaper rather than use its assets for this purpose).[52]

In France, foundation ownership did not protect *Ouest-France* from losing money from its outside investments (including the free daily *20 Minutes*). However, within three years, through a combination of cost-cutting and improvements to its online website that increased both total traffic (increasing digital advertising) and digital subscriptions, France's largest circulation newspaper restored its profitability.[53]

In contrast, the greatest problem for US nonprofit news outlets is not losing money from ill-timed or poorly executed business strategies, but rather generating any revenues in the first place. Compared to leading commercial national news outlets, such as the *New York Times*, with annual news budgets of $200 million or more, or the strongest commercial regional newspapers like the *Minneapolis Star Tribune* with newsroom budgets as high as $30 million, two-thirds of US nonprofits have budgets under $1 million.[54] Even at local/regional newspapers owned by hedge funds, the total number of journalistic staff may still far exceed those of nonprofits in the same market. For example, after Alden Capital purchased the *San Diego Union-Tribune* in the summer of 2023, it cut newsroom positions from 108 to around seventy-five (more than a thirty percent cut, but also part of a long-term trend, with the new total just eighteen percent of what it had been in 2006). This staffing level was nevertheless still nearly ten times the eight journalists employed by the largest local nonprofit, the *Voice of San Diego* (*VoSD*).[55] An important difference, of course, is that while a high percentage of the *San Diego Union-Tribune*'s staff may be involved in non-public affairs news reporting or editing wire services, all of *VoSD*'s full-time journalists are focused on original, local, in-depth public affairs reporting. Studies of multiple US nonprofits, both local and national, have shown that they spend a much higher proportion of their revenues on news and editorial operations than legacy commercial media: two-thirds compared to around fifteen percent at most legacy commercial newspapers.[56] With the continued emptying out of stock market-traded and hedge fund-owned newsrooms—not to mention the rise in "news deserts" with no local newspaper at all—any lingering advantage in commercial media resources compared to philanthropy-supported nonprofits may only be temporary.[57] Already, a handful of large national nonprofits, most notably *ProPublica* with 2021 revenues of nearly $46 million, a "cumulative reserve" of $44 million, and a journalistic workforce (including multiple regional editions) of around 150, are as well or better resourced and staffed as all but a handful of their commercial peers.[58]

Public media, by definition, are expected to invest public resources in public service-oriented journalism. Their capacity to do so varies depending on the level of national and local government funding. US public media have long suffered from budget levels that have not kept pace with inflation; French public media have experienced significant cuts both in public and permitted advertising funding. Of our three countries, Sweden's public media are by far the most generously and securely funded. One Swedish study found that while the total number of news journalists across Sweden had decreased by twenty-four percent from 2013 to 2019, there had been no decline in the size of the newsrooms of Sweden's public service broadcasters (TV and radio).[59]

At *SR* public radio, Klas Wolf-Watz, national news editor-in-chief, sees both the old "license fee" and the recent shift to general tax revenue funding as key to public radio's ability to serve the public: "We have a predictable funding model, I mean we know pretty well fairly far in advance what kind of money we have to work with . . . it gives us a stable ground to stand on when it comes to how to build the operation. If you are dependent on ads and subscriptions, there is perhaps less possibility to plan for the future."[60] Likewise, Charlotta Friborg, *SVT* national news editor-in-chief, sees predictable and steady budgeting as an important support for quality journalism:

> I have worked in the world of newspapers for many years and [I know] what it has looked like. . . . Perhaps it is about to change, but [at most newspapers] every fiscal year starts with at least a 10% cut. Here I can focus on journalism and journalistic content. Of course that provides a sense of calm and a focus on content, rather than on cutting down on the workforce.[61]

* * *

In this chapter, we have shown that two ownership forms, with diametrically opposed logics, provide the greatest certainty in levels of funding for public service news. It is almost certain to be low (especially in proportion to total revenues) at stock market-traded and hedge fund-owned media, with some exceptions depending on temporary circumstances. And it is almost certain to be relatively high at Sweden's well-funded version of public media. In between, most private and civil society-owned media are clear about the need to invest in public service-oriented news but struggle to generate adequate and sustainable funding. In the next chapter, we will explore the range of funding-audience adjustment strategies adopted by news outlets to navigate in this uncertain and often inhospitable environment.

4

Achieving Sustainability: Funding-Audience Adjustment Strategies

Le Monde founding publisher Hubert Beuve-Méry is famous for his insistence that "we are poor and we intend to stay that way," an approach that did not always endear him to his underpaid journalists but which may have played a key role for many years in ensuring the newspaper's autonomy from political and economic pressures.[1] Paralleling this attitude at many news organizations was the long-held belief that the editorial and commercial sides of the news operation ought to be kept apart. This tradition was strong in the US—where, for example, separate elevators were long provided at the *Chicago Tribune* for the news and business side employees.[2]

France's storied *Libération* refused any advertising for the first decade of its existence in the 1970s. Demonstrating the persistence of founding traditions, many *Libération* journalists have continued to feel unease about the commercial aspects of the newspaper, including advertising or marketing studies of the audience. One step director Laurent Joffrin felt he had to take—when he was brought in by owner Edouard de Rothschild in 2006 to impose financial discipline and increase revenues at a newspaper that was annually spending millions of euros more than it was earning (a tradition that had endured during most of the newspaper's history)—was to change this attitude:

> When I arrived at *Libération* [in 2006], there wasn't any advertising, it was Chernobyl. Well, one of the reasons, there were a lot of reasons, but the biggest was that the newspaper was not doing well and it even had the reputation of being bankrupt.... No one wanted to put advertising in a newspaper that was at risk of closing. So, I had to reassure [the advertisers] about the future of the newspaper, and the other situation was that culturally, *Libé* was hostile to advertising. Every time that management asked for something, the staff said no. And, when I came in, I told them, I said, "Each time that the management asks for something, the answer is 'yes'. Except if it poses enormous ethical problems." Thus, I reconciled, at bottom, the newspaper and the advertising market. To keep it alive![3]

How Media Ownership Matters. Rodney Benson et al. Oxford University Press. © Rodney Benson, Mattias Hessérus, Timothy Neff, and Julie Sedel 2025. DOI: 10.1093/oso/9780199931293.003.0005

The traditional journalistic view that there should be a "wall" between the business and editorial sides of the operation emerged during a period of historically unusual prosperity for the newspaper industry, from the 1950s through the 1980s.[4] This model was eventually undermined in the US at stock market-traded companies, like Gannett, that brought in MBA-trained managers who increased coordination between the two sides to meet profit-maximizing targets.[5] By the late 2000s and early 2010s, financial pressures were also increasing at private and civil society-owned outlets without the same intense profit pressures. In the contemporary context of fears for the economic survival of any "quality" journalism at all, more and more journalists, as well as their outlets' owners and managers, have adopted a more "strategic" or "entrepreneurial" approach that reconciles the professional/civic and the economic, searching, in effect, for a "win–win."[6]

"Every media owner has to ask this classic question," says Jonas Nordling, former chair of the Swedish Journalists Union and editor-in-chief of the Swedish civil society-owned outlet *Dagens Arena*:

> Do you do journalism to make money, or do you make money to do journalism? These are the two choices one has. And as long as the money is fully reinvested into the editorial side, I think it is completely reasonable that you can actually go bananas any way commercially within the boundaries of the law because you do it to get more money to run the business with. While if you only run the business for an owner to extract a large amount of capital each year for the shareholders, then it is more appropriate to discuss the driving forces behind the actual journalism.[7]

Maybe "bananas" is a good way to describe the myriad ways that news organizations find to try to balance the economic, political, professional, and civic dimensions of their journalistic enterprises. Paraphrasing a former editor-in-chief of *Expressen*, Bo Strömstedt, *Norran* CEO Anders Westermark believes that a "really good company is created in the dialectic between the figures and the letters."[8] In *Dagens Arena*'s case, this "dialectic"—or "bananas" strategy—includes a precarious mix of large and small donations, audience subscriptions, and internal subsidies from divisions within the organization that are generating significant revenues, all of which sustain but do not generate profits for the civil society-owned outlet.

In his memoir, former *TF1* executive and *Le Figaro* editor-in-chief Étienne Mougeotte sees the attempt to "satisfy the audience" as the thread that runs through his long career, which also included leading other commercial French newspapers and radio channels: "In everything that I was able to accomplish in my career, one finds a common point: the will to satisfy the public. Each media outlet has its own. It is always specific: *Le Journal du Dimanche* isn't *Le Figaro*,

Tele 7 Jours isn't *TVMag*, *Europe 1* isn't *Radio Classique* and *TF1* isn't *Arte*. I am sometimes asked how I succeeded here or there. The reply is always the same: obsession and respect for the public."[9]

Indeed, as many of our interviewees told us, one of the major preoccupations of owners and their appointed top managers is fitting what they are able to offer to what their current or prospective audiences want. As Johan Hansson, CEO of the Stampen group that owns *Göteborgs-Posten*, sees it, the job of "the owners [is] to figure out what the audience wants."[10] But, he added, there is a fundamental difference between what the drive-by free audience wants and what the renewing subscribing audience wants:

> We have changed our strategy, and that was part of my assignment as well, that we were more focused before on clicks and the number of visits, because we didn't charge for the content, and in that case . . . then celebrity news and those types of things often get a lot of clicks. But if you look at [celebrity news], people are not willing to pay for it, because they can get it for free somewhere else. But what we have found is that when we want to charge for the content it has to be content that you can't find anywhere else.[11]

For commercial and some civil society-owned media, this distinction between appealing to advertising-subsidized audiences versus paying (usually subscribing) audiences is a fundamental dividing line in the strategies we identify in our qualitative research, alongside the difference between relatively elite and omnibus audience targeted socio-demographics. In principle, there is also the possibility of giving the audience what it is perceived to *need* rather than what they are perceived to *want*, but this option is mostly no longer on the table.

Diverse *funding-audience adjustment* strategies exist within and across nearly all ownership forms. The omnibus vs. elite distinction is evident in company media kits, where they try to entice advertisers in two ways: first, through the size of their audience; and second, through their audience "quality," as indicated by well above average levels of education and income. Of course, such broad demographic indicators do not come close to fully capturing how news organizations attempt to understand and respond to their audience. On a day-to-day basis, they take these broad demographics for granted and are focused in a much more granular way with which stories "succeed" and which stories "fail" to attract large audiences or new subscribers, as well as which stories prompt greater levels of engagement as indicated by time spent, comments, emails, or social media shares.[12]

Yet there is also a clustering of forms, funding, and audiences in such a way that we can point to distinct *ownership complexes*. Table 4.1 captures our sampled news outlet strategies in 2016: this year was chosen because it coincides with

Table 4.1 Funding-Audience Adjustment Strategy by Ownership Form and Subform: Percentage of Outlets

	Adv.-Elite*	Adv.-Omn.	Subscrip.-Elite	Subscrip.-Omn.	Philan.-Elite	Public-Omn.
SM-WH(8)	37.5 (3)	37.5 (3)	12.5 (1)	12.5 (1)	0.0	0.0
SM-DS (7)	28.6 (2)	28.6 (2)	28.6 (2)	14.3 (1)	0.0	0.0
Market (15)	33.3 (5)**	33.3 (5)	20.0 (3)	13.3 (2)	0.0	0.0
Private (16)	31.3 (5)	25.0 (4)	37.5 (6)	6.3 (1)	0.0	0.0
CivSoc (14)	0.0	7.1 (1)	21.4 (3)	28.6 (4)	42.9 (6)	0.0
Public (6)	0.0	0.0	0.0	0.0	33.3 (2)	66.7 (4)
Conglom. (12)	25.0 (3)	33.3 (4)	25.0 (3)	16.7 (2)	0.0	0.0
Journ. Control (15)	13.3 (2)	0.0	40.0 (6)	13.3 (2)	33.3 (5)	0.0
Religious (3)	0.0	0.0	33.3 (1)	33.3 (1)	33.3 (1)	0.0
Partisan-affil. (6)	0.0	16.7 (1)	16.7 (1)	50.0 (3)	16.7 (1)	0.0
Total Sample (51)	19.6 (10)	19.6 (10)	23.5 (12)	13.7 (7)	15.7 (8)	7.8 (4)

*Funding-Audience Adjustment Strategy categories are Advertising-Elite audience, Advertising-Omnibus audience, (Audience) Subscription-Elite audience, (Audience) Subscription-Omnibus audience, Philanthropy-Elite audience, and Public-Omnibus audience.

**Dominant funding-audience adjustment strategies for each of the four main ownership forms are highlighted.

the main sample year for our content analyses presented in Chapters 5, 6, and 7. Overall, as one moves from the most commercial to the least commercial ownership forms, there is a shift from advertising to subscriber to philanthropic and public funding. However, the pattern for audience types is more barbell-shaped, with the two ends (market and public) reaching a more even mix of omnibus and elite audiences, whereas private and civil society-owned media in the middle mostly target elite audiences. Current/legacy journalist-controlled media are the most exclusively elite-targeted of any ownership subform, relying mostly on subscriber or philanthropic funding. (For outlet-level primary funding and audience and owner characteristics, see Appendix Table A2.1).

In the remainder of this chapter, we build on Pierre Bourdieu's insight that cultural production is "homologous" with cultural reception by combining it with media management studies' focus on organizational practices.[13] We explore how this fit is achieved—or not achieved—in relation to the production of public service-oriented news as owners and their top managers and editors imagine their audiences and then adopt various strategies of form, content, and distribution to reach them while providing adequate funding for the enterprise. We consider, in turn, advertising funding for omnibus or elite audiences; subscriber funding for elite or omnibus audiences; philanthropy funding for elite audiences; and public funding for omnibus audiences.

As we will see, some types of funding, target audiences, and news content are more mutually synergistic than others.

Advertising Funding for Omnibus and Elite Audiences

Primary reliance on advertising funding—present at two-thirds of all stock market-traded outlets and over half of private media in our sample—shapes outlets' relationships with their audiences, which may vary depending on whether the audience is omnibus or elite. Omnibus audiences can be further distinguished between the *mass* omnibus audiences of legacy "broadcast" television news (*ABC* and *CBS* in the US, France's *TF1*, all stock market-traded), free print legacy newspapers like *Metro* (stock market-traded, except in the US), and regional private and civil society-owned Swedish newspapers (*Jönköpings-Posten* and *Norran*) versus the *segmented* omnibus model of youth-oriented free online outlets (such as privately held *BuzzFeed* and *Nyheter24*).

At France's *TF1*, news director Antoine Guélaud says that he is "obsessed with the audience, but in the good sense of the term": "I always felt that it was better to write for the greatest number, to speak to the greatest number, communicate to the greatest number rather than the smallest number . . . . It seems obvious to me." Guélaud says that *TF1* does not choose story topics based on audience "marketing" data about which topics are most popular because it would be counterproductive by undermining the channel's "legitimacy." Even so, "marketing" has a role to play in what Guélaud terms "the paradoxical superiority of form over substance": "We wonder whether we should create a logo for this or that thing . . . [or] choose a particular music. . . . We also try to make infographics [that are] very very thorough, and at the same time very simple, to help the audience understand the situation. We constantly ask ourselves about this question of form."[14]

In the US, commercial television news managers have stressed the need to be cautious so as not to alienate audiences or advertisers. According to Isaac Josephson, former *ABC News* vice president for product development, the "cardinal rule" is to "do no harm": "It's a totally lame cardinal rule. . . . The idea is you have to get your audience not to change the channel. The way you do that in broadcast media is to not do anything too outside the box, too strong or too offensive, because you've got to protect those so many million people a night that come watch you. And you kind of have not too strong a voice . . . a milquetoast voice." Commercial considerations—with civic consequences, not necessarily negative—shape the news mix and even particular news stories. On any given nightly news show, one or more stories may be created purely because they seem likely to attract an advertiser. According to Josephson, a multi-week series on the *ABC Evening News* called "Made in America," focused on "homegrown" US industries, was sustained so long in part because it had a major discount retail store as an advertising sponsor: effectively, a relatively pro-worker message was being conveyed with corporate support. In another instance, he recalled, in the lead up to the 2008 presidential election, *ABC News Online* interviewed Libertarian party candidate Ron Paul, perceiving that it was not only consistent with news values but also a way to attract his highly motivated millions of voters to the news website. Effectively, the extra traffic increased advertising revenues, but in the process also expanded the outlet's "internal pluralism" (see the analysis of pluralism in Chapter 5).[15] Beyond profits, there also remained a professional commitment to news "that we needed to cover, not because it was popular but because . . . this was a story that America should know about," according to Josephson.[16]

Metro embodies a unique "advertising only" free model of print press that had previously been mostly limited to so-called "shoppers" almost entirely filled with advertising or "alternative weeklies" targeted to young urban professionals and university students, often with a social movement activist bent.[17] In contrast, the Sweden-launched worldwide *Metro* franchise and its competitors, such as *20 Minutes* and *Direct Matin* in France, or *amNew York* in the US, have adhered more closely to traditional journalistic practices, but with an emphasis on accessibly written, short articles, many of them "aggregated"; that is, reprinted and slightly adapted from wire services or other media.[18] In France, *Metro* reportedly also initially ran a much leaner operation than *20 Minutes*, operating at half the cost as its main competitor.[19] *20 Minutes* is majority-owned by Groupe Sipa-Ouest France and, until 2016, was just under half-owned by the Norwegian Schibsted, when its minority share was purchased by the Belgian private Groupe Rossel.

At *20 Minutes*, former *Libération* managing editor Frédéric Filloux was able for a time to win the support of both rank-and-file journalists and profit-driven shareholders. One journalist fondly remembers the newsroom under Filloux: "With Frédéric, we had total editorial freedom . . . even investigations and even better, we had room to write! It was an 'open bar'. His only requirement was to make the best possible newspaper. . . . We were making a little *Libé*."[20] Filloux, for his part, felt he was doing something very different from *Libération*, for which he had little nostalgia: "Based on my experience at *Libération* when I became one of the editors of the paper I was really upset because at some point I asked maybe could we have some marketing studies to see who is reading us and people said, What? Marketing? Never!"[21] In contrast, at *20 Minutes*, he recalls:

> We ran some small readers' surveys . . . it is super useful. I think that I am kind of embarrassed for the profession of journalist, the younger generation might change this, but my generation is super reluctant to work with marketing data because they believe that if they get interested in marketing data it will automatically taint their editorial judgment. As if, if I have a glass of wine, I will automatically become an alcoholic . . . . As long as you have strong editorial management, it should not interfere with editorial choices which should also be based on what is best for the readers at one particular moment. The two are perfectly compatible. And I applied that at *20 Minutes* and it worked.[22]

It worked, in a sense, until it didn't. Filloux, in his recollection, had not been unreasonably opposed to working with the commercial side of the newspaper. But at the same time, he had drawn a line to insist that an investment in quality journalism was the best way to make money. Four years after he had helped to establish *20 Minutes*'s journalistic bona fides in a journalistic field overwhelmingly hostile to the free dailies, Schibsted brought in a new CEO who had no intention of attempting to directly control editorial content, but who did intend to adopt the *Metro* approach to dramatically increase revenues (by increasing the proportion of advertising from one-third of total content to an even fifty–fifty split with editorial) and lower costs (by cutting staff and making sure that the number of pages was driven by the amount of advertising). Filloux and the new CEO clashed, and within a year, Filloux left.[23] Under the new regime, *20 Minutes* moved toward shorter, more simply written articles; more breaking news, but not too much controversial content; and more of the upbeat lifestyle, consumer, and cultural news that provides the most favorable environment for ads.[24] The "idyllic" Filloux period of *20 Minutes* echoes that of John Paton at Digital First (in Chapter 3) or Jonah Peretti with *BuzzFeed News*: the early years of a start-up when even the most profit-driven owners may provide journalists with significant autonomy as they search for the winning commercial formula, a period that may produce strong public service-oriented journalism but that is destined not to last.

Does the advertising-only funded *online* media environment change the approach to public affairs news? During the early 2010s, at *ABC News*, Josephson thought so. In contrast to the cautious approach prevalent on legacy "broadcast" television, he said, "what resonates on the internet is a very, very strong voice and a very clear value proposition and a singular one at that."[25] This distinctive voice could be political, as we discuss in Chapter 6, but hard-edged political news is not a winning formula for advertising-only supported media on the web (see the discussion on *HuffPost* in this chapter): controversial content drives advertisers away, and readers of traditional political news tend to be older than the eighteen- to thirty-five-year old high consuming demographic most desired by advertisers.

SEO (search engine optimization) puts the onus on the media worker to create stories that are simple, sensational, and appealing to basic human emotions. Thus, advertising-driven digital-only media like *BuzzFeed* and *Nyheter24* constantly adjust their content to "generate traffic" from an audience that they understand both as a mass and as an array of people with specialized interests against which advertising can be sold (often in the form of soft news "verticals" like "Tech", "Food," and "Fashion"). Both *BuzzFeed* and *Nyheter24* have been targeted to young, majority female audiences.[26]

Outlets with this economic model are often called "traffic factories" for a reason: only low-paid journalists glued to their desks quickly repackaging other web content can produce enough content at a low enough cost to attract the volume of clicks necessary to generate profits. Even then, with Google, Facebook, and other large platforms collecting more than three-quarters of digital advertising revenues, it is increasingly not enough.[27]

The uncertainty of a digital payoff has meant that most online-only outlets have been launched not by large stock market-traded corporations but by small private start-ups backed by risk-taking venture capital. The incentives all point away from classic public service-oriented news and toward news that "you can use" or news that amuses. Even so, *BuzzFeed* founder and CEO Peretti sought for many years to create a commercial-public service "win-win."[28] The formula included three components: first, generate most of the revenues from non-political, soft content; second, define the political in a way that resonates with target audiences (i.e., identity politics); and third, invest in *BuzzFeed News*, initially a serious public affairs "vertical" on the website and eventually a separate website that was implicitly tasked with accruing symbolic capital more than economic capital.[29]

As Filloux, now a prominent media industry analyst, bluntly observes: "In *BuzzFeed* you have two products: the shitty one and the great one. The shitty one is making 90 percent of the audience, the cat videos, etc. The good one is *BuzzFeed News*, maybe makes 1 percent of the audience."[30] Upon the eve of *BuzzFeed*'s stock market public offering in fall 2021, *BuzzFeed News* employed more than one hundred journalists, many of whom were engaged in investigative reporting and had brought acclaim and good publicity to *BuzzFeed* as the recipient of a Pulitzer Prize and other professional awards. (Even so, *BuzzFeed*'s version of quality news often pushed the boundaries of style and decorum. For example, the headline of a serious investigative story about a large psychiatric hospital chain began: "What the fuck just happened?"[31]) Asked if it's a "prestige operation," Filloux replied, "Yes, but like any prestige operation their lifespan is not guaranteed. Someone will eventually pull the plug. I know the drill."[32]

Indeed, the day before the first quarterly earnings call with investors after *BuzzFeed* listed itself on the stock market in fall 2021, the company announced major cuts in the non-revenue generating news division. In a memo to employees, Peretti made clear that the old model of subsidizing news for prestige and civic goodwill was over: "I've made the decision that I want News to be break-even and eventually profitable. We won't put profits ahead of quality journalism and I'll never expect [*BuzzFeed News*] to be as profitable as our entertainment divisions. But we can't keep losing money,"[33] which reportedly amounted to more than a hundred million dollars since the News division's founding. In short, "quality" journalism would still be produced and celebrated under stock market ownership, but there would be less of it, or quality would be redefined to reflect lesser aspirations and expectations. Yet even this compromise was not enough for investors. After the listing, the stock price fell precipitously, eventually to less than one-tenth the value of the initial offering. Shareholders pressed Peretti to go further and shut down *BuzzFeed News* once and for all. In April 2023, he did.

* * *

Advertising funding can also be associated with more elite audiences, especially in the US, where through the early 2000s, most newspapers, even the elite *New York Times*, earned sixty-five to eighty percent of their revenues from advertising.[34] As of our news content sampling period of 2016, many stock market-traded newspapers with relatively elite audiences, such as the Tribune-owned *Los Angeles Times* and Gannett-owned *USA Today*, still earned the majority of their revenues from (combined print and digital) advertising.[35] To the extent that owners and managers perceive audiences as a distracted mass largely uninterested in public affairs news—even though this judgment is often based on little actual knowledge of their audiences[36]—this perception may create pressure to produce sensationalized, "dumbed down" news similar to that provided to omnibus audiences. Indeed, former *Los Angeles Times* editor-in-chief James O'Shea recounts in detail the numerous times Tribune executives insisted that a more consumer-focused approach to news was necessary to maximize shareholder profits. On one occasion, a "Chicago Tribune advertising executive dispatched to Los Angeles to revive the paper's sagging ad revenues" delivered the message that "the advertisers didn't like the weighty content in the *Times* . . . 'the dogs don't like the dog food.'"[37] Despite constant pressures to lighten up the news, and deep cuts to political and international reporting, the *Los Angeles Times* continued to experience a long-term pattern of yearly declines in print circulation and advertising, and little hope of replacing this revenue stream with meager digital advertising revenues. In recent years, under private ownership, the *Los Angeles Times* has been engaged in a long and so far unsuccessful effort to transition to a sustainable elite subscription-funded economic model.[38]

Likewise, the stock market traded and privately owned digital only outlets in our sample with advertising-elite audience models (*HuffPost US* and *HuffPost France*, *Slate US* and *Slate France*, *Rue89*, and *KIT*) have either been tentatively moving in the direction of digital audience subscription funding, or missed the opportunity to do so, as in the case of the now defunct *KIT*. An online-only outlet owned by Bonnier, *KIT* used *BuzzFeed*-style analytics to identify emerging topics and then write in-depth feature articles about them.[39] It was an interesting approach for producing accessible quality news but it was never able to attract large enough audiences to generate sufficient advertising to be even minimally profitable. Its newsroom was shut down in 2019 and the company decided to focus on content marketing instead.[40] Both *KIT* and *BuzzFeed* lost a major portion of their audiences when Facebook changed its algorithms to deprioritize the circulation of professionally produced news.[41]

Another problem online is that while advertisers want large, well-educated, and prosperous audiences, just as they do for more exclusive mediums like print, they also want "advertising-safe" news next to their ads (which is more difficult to control online with the use of automated advertising networks). This creates a contradiction that is difficult to resolve. Heavy news consumers tend to be more partisan than other audiences and, as a result, the best way to attract audiences to public affairs news is to give it a partisan spin, whether in the news or opinion articles, or both. Yet this same partisan spin can repel advertisers. In the words of former *BuzzFeed News* editor Ben Smith, advertisers' "allergy" to politics is "an old problem for hard news that would only intensify online."[42]

As a result, partisan news sites like *HuffPost* find themselves in a situation where they are unable to profitably monetize their massive audiences. The partisan orientation becomes a commercial handicap. According to a former *HuffPost* staffer, Verizon's managers urged *HuffPost* journalists to focus less on "hot" political controversies. The telecommunications conglomerate commissioned a redesign of the homepage to feature fewer "shouty" all-caps headlines, large images and font sizes, and controversial topics, in favor of more "ad-safe" or "ad-friendly" content, meaning less politically or culturally controversial. In the US, well-established *HuffPost* editors, long accustomed to the hard-edged partisan approach, largely ignored the redesign, keeping the distinctive all-caps headlines and political focus, and as noted previously, Verizon managers were too pre-occupied elsewhere to do anything about it. In France and other countries, however, *HuffPost* editors voluntarily made greater use of the new format, which arguably encouraged a more thoughtful and in-depth approach to public affairs, as well as more non-political topics.[43]

Such was the industry consensus for many years that only a "free" advertising-supported model could work on the internet that even the church-subsidized *Christian Science Monitor* sought for many years to make it work. Historically, the *Monitor* had survived on the annual $4 million to $5 million interest generated by a designated endowment fund plus an additional $3 million to $4 million in extra subsidies provided by the church, depending on need. As managing editor Marshall Ingwerson recalls, "In the old days, the church almost worked like the Ford Foundation . . . where you'd say, if we're going to do this then we're going to need this much money. Editorially, that was the game you were in and on the business side they tried to produce revenue the best they could but it was never a match for the expenses."[44] Around 2008, the church set upon a course to increase commercial revenues to reduce and eventually eliminate the extra subsidy. The *Monitor* closed its daily print newspaper, replacing it with a monthly magazine, and shifted the daily news operation online.

The unique challenge for the *Christian Science Monitor* was that it was attempting a very difficult balancing act. "In practical terms," Ingerwerson said, "the tension is that we are trying to grow page views which can tend to take you into the commodity zone without really building your brand but will bring in traffic and raise your throwaway. I think of that as sort of widening the mouth of the funnel. And on the other hand, there is the effort to bring people down the funnel, which is further into your community and their involvement with you as a brand . . . the value-added zone." For the *Monitor*, Ingwerson emphasized, this "valued-added" is its reputation for providing quality news along three dimensions: "the international focus, the constructive approach [focusing on solutions], and the context and explanation."

In the early 2010s, the *Christian Science Monitor*'s monetization strategy split the "brand" and "commodity" approaches across mediums: the in-depth approach continued to be the core of the subscriber-supported monthly magazine, while digital seemed by necessity to have to be more about commodity news. Online, because only five percent of readers came to the homepage, finding an audience required extensive promotion on social media (primarily Facebook), paying close attention to search engine optimization to raise the *Monitor*'s ranking on Google News, and in-kind "link" sharing agreements with exponentially larger outlets like *Yahoo News*. The *Christian Science Monitor* eventually reached twenty-five million monthly unique visitors, enough to put it among the top fifty US news sites.

For the *Christian Science Monito*r online, quality was thus largely redefined as "trending" topics that they could ride like "everyone else" while adding a unique *Christian Science Monitor* substantive spin. Ingwerson provided the example of the *Monitor's* heavy coverage of the popular television singing show "American Idol":

> This morning, if you look at our top 10 or 15 stories from yesterday for page views, there is a lot of American Idol on there. And that's not our main event, obviously. We're not a brand that's going to make a business based on American Idol. On the other hand, you read these stories . . . and they are good, solid pieces. One is a blogger who is a true Idol fan who has watched it minutely from the beginning and knows all sorts of stuff. It's like reading a really savvy theater or dance or movie reviewer, which I see as legitimate.

Conversely, according to Ingwerson, the *Christian Science Monitor* presented public affairs stories in a more entertaining, digestible manner, such as "the list story . . . 5 ways or 7 lessons or 10 most something [that] are very digestible, accessible, and appealing but you can do real explanatory or contextual work with that, in other words, 5 reasons Obama and Netanyahu don't see eye to eye."

In the end, though, the experiment never generated anywhere near enough revenues to reduce the need for a church subsidy. Starting in 2014, Ingwerson and the *Christian Science Monitor* pivoted, following the lead of the *New York Times*, to begin shifting toward a digital audience subscriber-funded model (which was fully instituted in 2017). The *Christian Science Monitor* rearticulated its core values both as an end in themselves and as a means of seeking a strong and loyal niche audience to support its operations.[45] We can see in this case that civil society ownership did not provide foolproof protection against the adoption of a commercial strategy at odds with the newspaper's historical definition of quality journalism; however, it does seem to have limited the duration of the experiment and prevented deep budget cuts. While the new strategy has failed to pay its own way commercially—the church endowment fund is still the *Christian Science Monitor's* largest single source of funding[46]—it did help herald across the US journalistic field (with a few exceptions) a new era of reserving quality news only for those willing to pay.

Two major privately owned US newspapers with elite audiences in our sample still relied on advertising as their primary revenue source during our content sample year of 2016—the *Washington Post* and the *Minneapolis Star Tribune*. In 2016 and 2017, both newspapers were in the process of dramatically increasing their digital subscriptions.[47] After its purchase by billionaire Jeff Bezos in 2013, the *Washington Post* immediately invested in technology, refocused its reporting from local to national, and jumped ahead of the *New York Times* in pageviews and social media. Once it became clear that online advertising could never provide adequate revenues, the *Washington Post* made digital subscriptions its top priority and, as of 2020, had attained around three million subscribers, jumping ahead of the *Wall Street Journal* to trail only the *New York Times*.[48] Increasing revenues from digital subscriptions (bolstered by the fact that Bezos declined any dividends and allowed all profits to be reinvested in the newsroom) helped the *Washington Post* increase its staff from 580 to one thousand and win ten Pulitzer Prizes.[49] In a 2019 interview published by the US Local Media Association, the *Washington Post*'s director of consumer marketing uses the language of marketing, but at no point does he suggest any conflict between the economic strategy and a quality journalistic mission:

> Our entire organization is focused on subscriber acquisition . . . . We are obsessed with the consumer experience. This obsession translates itself into top-notch journalism both in terms of investigative reporting, opinions and life-style content. It also means an investment in technology to ensure our stories load as fast as possible and it's easy to login to our site and apps . . . . We don't assume our subscribers will retain so throughout the organization we are always looking for reasons to appreciate and provide additional value to our subscribers—but it's mostly through providing an outstanding product.[50]

Since 2020, however, the *Washington Post* has lost forward momentum and has not yet achieved profitability under Bezos's ownership, in part because of a loss in digital subscriptions. It has struggled to find its niche in the face of strong competition from the *New York Times*, the British *Guardian*, and other would-be national general news outlets, as well as inherent limits in the total purchasing power of elite news consumers.[51]

The *Minneapolis Star Tribune* also benefited from having a supportive billionaire owner, but it had the additional advantage of operating in a less intensely competitive media market. With its strong regional leadership in public affairs and investigative reporting for Minneapolis and Minnesota, and paradoxically, policies that make it easier for readers to cancel their subscriptions, the *Minneapolis Star Tribune* gradually attained one hundred thousand digital subscriptions. As of 2018, combined print and digital subscription revenues have exceeded advertising revenues, and the newspaper has achieved consistent profitability.[52]

Subscription Funding for Elite and Omnibus Audiences

The alternative to advertising funding for media that do not have access to noncommercial support (public or philanthropic) is to ask the audience to pay, which in turn, generally means attracting regular and reliable subscribers. As the editor of *La Croix* remarked, "daily purchases don't matter much" both because subscribers bring in most of the revenues and because there is much more information available about subscribers.[53] While advertising funding encourages production of news that attracts both a large and financially "desirable" audience (even if the two are difficult to reconcile online, sustainably), subscriber funding pushes news organizations further toward the well-educated and well-off with less need for a massive audience.[54]

As discussed in the previous section, this realization that audiences could pay and are needed to pay directly for "quality" digital news came slowly but is quickly becoming the new common sense. In the early internet years, only the financial news outlets, like the *Wall Street Journal*, the *Financial Times*, and *Bloomberg*, bucked the conventional wisdom of free access: digital subscriptions immediately worked well for them because their professional audience of business executives and investors needed financial news to effectively do their jobs. Going beyond the financial press, in our three-country sample, we identify five broad types of *elite audience* news organizations that rely primarily on subscriptions for funding: first, digital-only subscription-funded outlets (only *Mediapart* in our sample); second, prestigious national newspapers, either owned privately or by a stock market dominant shareholder (with the exception of the widely held Schibsted-owned *Svenska Dagbladet*); third, private regional newspapers shifting to subscription revenues under great duress as the advertising market collapsed; fourth, civil society-owned or private partisan-affiliated or religious news outlets; and fifth, the possibly sui generis privately owned *Vice*, with its multiple niche-driven advertising-funded websites, but mostly funded at its peak by television licensing agreements and cable television subscription fees for its documentaries. In sum, as shown in Table 4.1, a plurality of elite audience outlets relying on audience subscription funding have private ownership, but this type of funding is also used by some civil society-owned and market-owned outlets.

Mediapart's "pure" model of generating all its revenues from its digital subscribers has been widely hailed as principled and courageous; the surprise, perhaps, is that it has also been so economically successful. The refusal of advertising as a sign and source of independence is a long French tradition, most famously embodied to this day by the satirical investigative weekly *Le Canard enchaîné*. As the weekly's CEO told us: "We know where our money comes from, there's no advertising, we're not depending on advertising, so, there's no connection to capitalism, or the money powers, call them what you will . . . [and] that allows us to write what we want."[55] Similarly, *Mediapart* journalist Jade Lindgaard recounts, "Very early on, [lead founder and former *Le Monde* editor] Edwy Plenel's vision was that we had to be independent economically, and that independence could only come from subscriptions."[56] Plenel himself puts it this way: "We fight for the value of information: only our readers can buy us."[57]

However, because readers may have political or cultural biases linked to their social properties, reader funding may not be as "pure" as these French journalists claim. *Le Monde* founder Beuve-Méry actually favored a mix of advertising and audience funding to ensure journalistic independence. In his memoirs, he noted that "if all the revenues are dependent on the circulation," then one must not "displease the clientele," which he saw as leading to a self-satisfied, "complacent" journalism.[58] In fact, *Mediapart* openly claims a distinct political identity on the left (although not associated with any political party). Its political commitments have helped strengthen its bond with its readers, who are encouraged to post comments and participate in live events hosted on the website.[59]

Still, "complacent" hardly seems the right term to describe *Mediapart*, which is best known for its investigative "scoops" that have exposed serious wrongdoing by French politicians on both the left and right. Plenel speaks of investigative journalism as a civic imperative given that most French media are owned by non-media industrial companies with close links to the state. "We want a return to democracy," he has said. "We want to fight against corruption. We are sort of like the Robin Hood of media."[60] At the same time, Plenel seamlessly links civic and marketing discourses, noting that the Robin Hood label is "sort of a brand that has taken hold and become widely accepted."[61] He portrays investigative journalism—"original information, surprises"—as a successful economic formula to attract audiences: indeed, *Mediapart*'s biggest climbs in subscribers have come immediately after its revelations of government corruption.[62]

The second group of elite audience-funded outlets consists of prestigious national news outlets: especially the *New York Times*, but also in recent years, *Le Monde*, *Dagens Nyheter*, *Le Figaro*, and *Svenska Dagbladet*. At the launching of the *New York Times*'s digital subscription plan in 2011, when dominant shareholder/publisher Arthur Sulzberger Jr. memorably defined "the math of journalism" as "quality journalism" that "attracts a quality audience," he still hastened to add "that we sell to quality advertisers."[63] Advertising continued to be an essential revenue generator. It included a mix of luxury brand ads in the magazine's Sunday "T" fashion magazine; other print advertising in soft news supplements; and digital advertising, including sponsored content produced in coordination with advertisers by the "T-Brand Studio"[64] inside the *New York Times*. The major shift since 2011 has been to gradually lessen this reliance on advertising. Now it is the "quality" subscribing audiences themselves who are expected to pay the majority of the cost for the quality journalism. By 2021, the *New York Times* drew on its more than eight million subscribers (more than ninety percent of them digital and which included two million subscriptions to online games, cooking recipes, and consumer product reviews) to dramatically expand its political and international reporting.[65]

In Sweden, Lars Truedson, former director of the Institute for Media Studies in Stockholm, says of *Dagens Nyheter*'s well-known Editor-in-Chief Peter Wolordarski, "He's poached the best writers in the Swedish media . . . people will be prepared to pay for a well-written, well-thought out story. So, you have to go up-market to get the reader funding."[66] In 2017, *Dagens Nyheter*'s CEO reported that "investments in journalistic quality" paid off as digital reader-generated revenues increased twenty-five percent during a year when print revenues fell four percent; by 2020, *Dagens Nyheter* had two hundred thousand digital-only subscribers and attained a fifteen percent profit, its highest since 2000.[67]

Le Monde has led the way in France in moving to a digital subscription strategy, reaching more than four hundred thousand digital subscribers in 2021.[68] A decade earlier, two years before the launch of its digital subscription plan, Le Monde Group CEO Louis Dreyfus told us that he had "two preoccupations: editorial requirements and the needs of one's audience, whether it's for print or internet." Implying that the two tasks were potentially at odds, he added, "And then, after: it's finding a balance."[69] By 2016, with the digital subscription strategy well underway, Dreyfus described to an audience of news media executives at the World News Media Congress in Cartagena, Colombia, a strategy that assumed a fundamental synergy between quality journalism and economic success, over the long-term: "Whatever the difficulties or losses are, people will buy our product . . . as long as we have exclusive content. We will survive and grow if we have the best journalists, and that is the first priority for us." Dreyfus also described a number of initiatives focused on leveraging *Le Monde*'s "high-end audience" for advertising, such as the launch of the "weekend glossy magazine called 'M, le magazine du Monde,'" which is "a natural for attracting a younger audience, especially women" and which has "proved just as attractive to advertisers and big brands"; the partnership with *The Huffington Post* to create *Le Huffington Post*; and the creation of video-oriented content for Snapchat Discover to reach younger audiences.[70]

Le Monde's trajectory shows that for outlets *not* engaged in "harvesting" any and all extra cash from operations, getting to the place of producing positive net revenues can be a means of deepening the commitment to public service news. Despite the financial difficulties it endured during most of the 2010s, *Le Monde*'s journalistic mission and need to maintain its prestige brand ensured that it would not abandon its strong public service orientation. But it was only in 2021, when the success of its digital subscription plan seemed assured, that its newly reelected director, Jérôme Fenoglio, pledged to expand *Le Monde*'s international reporting. This pledge was partly an acknowledgment of the newspaper's newfound stability, but just as crucially, it was a public service commitment backed up by a funding-audience adjustment strategy that seemed to have a good chance of success. *Le Monde*'s expansion of international reporting coincided with its push to increase international subscriptions, particularly in Francophone Africa.[71]

Svenska Dagbladet and *Le Figaro* have likewise pivoted in recent years to digital subscriptions, but with more limited success, reflecting a broader tendency for digital news subscribers (with the exception of financial news) to lean left in their political views.[72] As of 2016, *Svenska Dagbladet* had forty-five thousand digital subscribers, a total that had increased to eighty thousand by 2020.[73] *Svenska Dagbladet* showed a slight profit in 2020, with help from press subsidies.[74] Despite this financial precarity and the profit pressures that normally accompany stock market ownership, a former editor-in-chief of *Svenska Dagbladet* emphasized that a significant portion of the outlet's news is still based on professional judgments about audience "needs" rather than their "wants":

> We became rather good at understanding which type of article, which type of angle, which type of approach, which type of topic generates new subscribers or a high reading rate among current subscribers, so if we were to only speak of percentages . . . I'd say that fifty to sixty percent of daily production is pretty aware of and based on what we know about our readers and their interests. . . . [Then there is the] thirty or forty percent that we always publish since we consider it important news for everyone . . . whether they are super interested or not.[75]

Le Figaro has historically attracted a disproportionate share of French national advertising and circulation, but it has struggled in the shift to digital and has been only intermittently profitable during the past two decades. According to public records, from 2006 to 2019, it was profitable only one year—in 2016, when it managed to generate a net 8 million euros for a two percent profit—and in 2019 sustained a loss of 54 million euros.[76] Toward the end of this time period, *Le Figaro* sought to increase its online advertising revenues through maximization of its online traffic; development of diverse thematic verticals responding to advertiser demand along with a proprietary online advertising audience data-gathering and targeting platform (to directly compete with Facebook); and the purchase of a group of synergistic educational, travel, and lifestyle sites (CCM Benchmark).[77] Only in very recent years has it shifted toward a more singular focus on digital subscribers, reaching a total of 205,000 in 2020, about half of *Le Monde*'s total.[78]

The third grouping of elite audience subscription-funded media are a subset of our sample's regional newspapers, as of the time of our 2016 sampling only including the Swedish private Stampen chain-owned *Göteborgs-Posten*—although in more recent years, as noted, also the *Minneapolis Star Tribune* and the *Boston Globe*. *Göteborgs-Posten* earned a majority of its revenues from subscribers, although primarily for its print edition. If achieving sustainability from digital subscriptions has been difficult for national newspapers, it has been even more challenging for regional and local papers.[79] *Göteborgs-Posten* began its digital subscriber program in 2017 and, by 2021, had 109,000 subscribers (as part of the shared Stampen collection of newspapers offered to all digital subscribers).[80] Around the time that *Göteborgs-Posten* was starting its digital subscriptions, Hansson, CEO of the Stampen Media Group, told us that the key to boosting subscriber revenues at *Göteborgs-Posten* has been focusing on "local" news, whether it is local sports news or local in-depth investigative reporting. Investigative reporting, he explained, also has "economic value because it is original content close to home that no one else is offering."[81] Notably, despite its financial difficulties and need for digital subscription revenues, Hansson noted that *Göteborgs-Posten* maintained non-paywalled access to one part of its digital website—the "leader" or editorial sections—as a way of promoting the classical liberal ideology the newspaper was founded upon.

The fourth grouping of elite audience subscription-funded media are private or civil society-owned religious or openly politically left media outlets that rely heavily on public subsidies, effectively bridging commercial and noncommercial funding-audience adjustment strategies. In our sample, these include *Libération*, the religious newspaper *La Croix*, and the party-affiliated newspaper *L'Humanité*. Of the three, *La Croix*, as part of the Bayard (Catholic) publishing group, is the only one that has been even occasionally profitable, although it is also somewhat insulated from commercial pressures by its civil society religious owner.[82] Long deeply indebted, *L'Humanité* appears to have somewhat stabilized its finances in recent years. In 2016, it showed net revenues of 1.3 million euros, and after a few years of losses, had net revenues of 3.3 million euros in 2020.[83] Non-market press subsidies and voluntary donations are a key part of *L'Humanité*'s capacity to stay in the black: in 2016, after the sixty-one percent of revenues from reader subscriptions/daily purchases, thirteen percent came from government allocated press subsidies (see next section), thirteen percent from donations, and seven percent from advertising, plus six percent that was miscellaneous.[84]

At *Libération*, some critics, and indeed *Libération* co-founder Serge July himself, have argued that overly ambitious and ultimately disastrous management decisions contributed to the newspaper's desperate straits.[85] Long bankrolled by "friends of July" who had little to no expectation of profits but did not have an unlimited capacity for losses, this economic model reached its limits in 1994 with July's push for a new graphic design and expanded page format—"*Libé*

3"—devised during a period of rising paper costs to dramatically increase readership and advertising, but which did neither while incurring massive debts. In the wake of this disaster, *Libé*'s journalist union (CFDT) distributed a tract that proclaimed: "There is no pilot." July replied: "Communiqué from the pilot: Sin of pride, the specialty of journalist-managers."[86] In their defense, the financial difficulties of newspapers like *Libération* and *L'Humanité* could also be attributed to their uncompromising civic project to provide critical information and analysis from a left perspective—the kind of information rarely adequately funded by the market. Does this mean that the only choice is to abandon these projects or reimagine them in market-friendly terms that risk "losing one's soul," as journalists at some of France's "independent" media outlets have insisted?[87]

Around the same moment when telecommunications magnate Patrick Drahi became the controlling private shareholder of *Libération* in 2014, Johan Hufnagel, a former *Libération* journalist who had left to help edit the *20 Minutes* website and then to co-found *Slate.fr*, was invited back to become online editor-in-chief working alongside Joffrin. Hufnagel's mandate was to help *Libé* navigate the transition to digital. Upon arriving, Hufnagel was frustrated by the time wasted first on redesigning the print newspaper (yet another "new formula"), then on a marketing study likewise focused on the print audience.[88] This survey found that the average reader was older than sixty-five, faithfully read the columns of the most senior journalists (many of whom were about to depart with severance pay as part of one hundred layoffs), and was engaged on the left, although with a political imaginary frozen in time with an earlier era of social movements. *Libération*, in Hufnagel's view, unlike *Le Monde*, was "following its initial readership" and had not "rejuvenated itself with the [new] generations." From Hufnagel's perspective, to succeed commercially, *Libération* actually needed to go "further to the left" in order to "respond to the cultural demand of a more radical French youth" with different political engagements than those of previous generations. Separately, Hufnagel had become increasingly interested in video, inspired by *Slate* US's "smart, highly-curated" videos for YouTube as well as emerging social media driven video production. He imagined that *Libération* could provide left-leaning video content for cable or online that could occupy the same space as the US *MSNBC* between Vincent Bolloré's Fox-style *C-News* and Drahi's *CNN*-style breaking news, *BFMTV*. However, this was a non-starter because Drahi was already committed to *BFMTV* and did not have the bandwidth to create two cable channels. Hufnagel made limited progress in developing new online formats for investigation and fact-checking designed especially with younger readers in mind. After three years, he left to co-found another digital start-up (the short video news website *Loopsider*, modeled partly on *NowThis* and *Brut*). In retrospect, Hufnagel perceived that there had simply not yet been "the alignment of the planets" necessary to expand the newspaper's target audience and create the online-driven transformations he envisioned.

Instead, change at *Libération* moved in another direction, largely sticking with the existing audience, but finding new and better ways to monetize their loyalty. By 2020, around the same moment as telecommunications billionaire Drahi transferred ownership of the newspaper into a nonprofit trust (still effectively controlled by Drahi), Dov Alfon, former editor-in-chief of the left-leaning Israeli newspaper *Haaretz*, was put forward by the newspaper's board as a candidate to be the new director.[89] Alfon was presented as the person best equipped to implement a strategy to dramatically increase the newspaper's digital subscriptions. Under rules that provide *Libération*'s journalists with the right to elect the director, in 2020, ninety-one percent voted to approve Alfon's appointment.[90] Belatedly, and likely inspired by *Mediapart*, *Libération* has finally embraced a digital strategy, but one in which quality and independence are supposedly assured through reliance on the reader rather than advertising or public subsidies.[91] By 2021, *Libération* had attained forty thousand total subscriptions (including twenty thousand digital only), although it was still far from basic sustainability.[92]

The final elite audience/subscription-funded subcategory is represented by *Vice* (*Vice News*), both the US and French editions. While known for its advertising "branded content" on its websites, in the mid- to late-2010s, *Vice* had more in common in its funding model with cable channels like *CNN* and *Fox News* than with advertising-only websites like *BuzzFeed*, *HuffPost*, and *Nyheter24*. Like *CNN* and *Fox News*, *Vice* is a multimedia company that provides free access to its website and thus continues to use display or native advertising, but also relies heavily on subscription revenues generated by the legacy television/radio parts of the company.[93] At its peak, *Vice*'s largest source of revenues were from its highly regarded HBO internationally focused documentaries generously funded by subscriptions to HBO and other television channels around the world.[94]

To be clear, except for *Mediapart*, none of the elite audience outlets in our 2016 news content sample earned a majority of their revenues from *digital* subscriptions. For the US print legacy outlets, the shift at that time (still of historic significance) was to a majority of revenues generated by paying audiences, with the largest amount still from print. At the other end of the spectrum, French news outlets included in this category of elite audience-funded media were mostly continuing a longer legacy of majority (but not sole) reliance on direct audience funding but beginning to supplement print single issue sales (a tiny revenue source in the US) and subscriptions with digital subscriptions.[95]

* * *

Beyond their considerable economic and civic strengths, even the exemplars of subscriber-only funded *Mediapart* and the predominantly subscriber-funded *New York Times* share a similar civic weakness: their inaccessibility for much of the public. As we saw in Chapter 2, digital subscribers tend to have higher levels of education and income than the public at large (as well as print newspaper readers). At least some senior editors, with the support of owners, are concerned about accessibility. Brian McGrory, editor of the *Boston Globe*, said in an online forum in response to a question from one of the authors, that "we think about this all the time." McGrory pointed to the continued existence of *Boston.com*, an advertising-only, freely accessible website owned by the *Boston Globe* but separate from its main subscriber-funded website. *Philadelphia Inquirer* editor Gabriel Escobar said that the newspaper was in the process of developing "a free version of the *Inquirer* at all of Philadelphia's public libraries." At the *Seattle Times*, editor Michele Matassa Flores pointed to the increasing use of advertising-supported email newsletters as a "really important way to get our journalism out to all types of communities, including those that can't afford subscriptions." She noted that partly in response to younger subscribers who "are holding us accountable for reaching all types of readers" and for covering "social justice movements" and "reach[ing] out to underrepresented communities," the *Seattle Times* had started a weekly "equity newsletter" that highlighted the newspaper's "work around equity and underrepresented communities [and] social justice movements."[96] Accessibility (and finding a way to appeal to younger readers) has also been a concern at *Le Monde*, motivating efforts to create special content for young people on Snapchat Discovery, develop media literacy curriculum working with the public schools, and produce more content accessible outside paywalls.[97] These approaches, with the exception of the public schools and library initiatives, involve finding ways that advertising can supplement digital subscription strategies, simultaneously as an additional revenue source, a vehicle to increase the circulation of journalists' work, a form of branding that appeals to subscribers, and a way to fulfill civic obligations.

Is there any way that subscription funding can be directly compatible with broad, even if not free, access for omnibus audiences? The British *Guardian* represents a hybrid model, permitting free access to its website, while strongly encouraging donations and increasingly being supported by subscriptions that provide easier and more extensive access via its mobile app. Otherwise, in our three-country sample, we find two main subscription funding-*omnibus* audience adjustment strategies.

One model relies on the fees negotiated by news channels as their share of the revenues generated from millions of cable subscribers, which are not specific to the news outlet and can generate substantial sums. From the $3 per US cable subscriber fee that it receives, *Fox News* generated $1.48 billion in 2016 (for sixty percent of its total revenues); *CNN*, with a smaller per subscriber "carriage" or "license" fee, earned $837 million in 2016, also sixty percent of its total revenues.[98] Both *CNN* and *Fox News* have been extremely profitable: in 2020, profit margins (net revenues) were 62.1 percent for *Fox News* and 42.9 percent for *CNN*.[99] Advertising on the cable channels' websites is a smaller revenue source, but makes possible free public access. This funding model, as with *Vice*, means that there may be significant differences in the social profile and size of the funding audience (cable or streaming service subscribers) and the online audience. The profiles of both *Fox News* and *CNN* online audiences are omnibus, approximating closely the average educational and income levels of the national population (while being significantly older than average).

Otherwise, in our study, a handful of civil society-owned newspapers in Sweden and France, with variable degrees of economic sustainability, continue to reach and receive most of their funding from omnibus audiences. Foundation-owned newspapers *Barometern*, *Gefle Dagblad*, and *Ouest-France* all have effective regional monopolies, with at most limited competition from nearby papers, thus lessening pressures toward audience segmentation; as civil society-owned outlets, they are also motivated by pluralistic civic missions.[100] In Sweden, the possibility of reaching omnibus subscribing audiences is also facilitated by a much stronger and deeper culture of newspaper reading than exists in France and the US. As noted in Chapter 2, a higher percentage of Swedes across the class spectrum read daily newspapers. As for *Ouest-France*, according to former deputy editor Paul Goupil, the generally profitable newspaper is guided by the words of its long-time publisher Jean Paul-Hutin: "We are a popular newspaper of quality. We need to proceed seriously, but accessibly." The newspaper pursues a "double strategy" of appealing to well-educated readers with complex articles on the global economy and new technologies, while simultaneously attracting a broad, omnibus audience with very local news in the "local pages," special sections for each of the regions served by *Ouest-France*.[101]

The paying audiences for the partly church-owned *Dagen* and the partisan-affiliated *Dagens ETC* are not elite, but they *are* part of religious and political communities deeply connected to these newspapers. *Dagen* CEO/Editor-in-Chief Felicia Ferreira told us she experienced a real change in practice as the newspaper's website shifted from advertising-funded free access to digital subscriptions. In the free model, she said, "it was very click driven . . . and then, at least, my experience was that it was quite hard work to not let that affect the journalism, it was an extremely important and quite delicate balancing act." In contrast, with the digital subscription model, "you actually start with what the readers or the target group is willing to pay for and I can feel that it is easier to combine [that] with the ideals [of *Dagen*] . . . you have to trust that the target group has the same ideals."[102]

At the "Red-Green" *Dagens ETC*, editor-in-chief Andreas Gustavsson makes a further distinction between what is needed to attract new digital subscribers and what is needed to retain existing subscribers:

> We work in an extremely data driven manner. I know exactly what drives traffic but especially what lures a maximum number of people to sign off on a subscription [and] in this way the business aspect is present in journalistic discussions all the time . . . . The risk is obvious that, well, I know that I could create enormous conversion numbers by using a certain [news angle] in certain ways . . . but at the same time our existing subscribers expect a quality product that has a factual approach, that [is] in-depth, the kind of articles that perhaps do not reach new target groups [or] attract new subscribers.[103]

Of these omnibus audience subscription-funded newspapers, only *Ouest-France* earned a significant profit (just under fourteen percent) in 2016.[104] *Dagen* self-reported in 2019 that while the newspaper had lost about 14 million Swedish Kronor ($1.3 million at 2022 rates) in 1997, since that time it had steadily improved and that the newspaper had been making a "profit for a few years."[105] As print advertising declines and audiences move exclusively online, these omnibus newspapers risk facing a future similar to one that has already arrived in the US: greater consolidation and accompanying staff layoffs and budget cuts to achieve economies of scale, accompanied by an ongoing struggle to dramatically boost digital subscriptions. There is one key difference, however, in their situation compared to US regional newspapers—a difference that also holds for almost all commercial media in Sweden and France: many of them are beneficiaries of direct or indirect press subsidies from their governments, designed expressly to mitigate the civic damage produced by market failure. On that note, we turn now to non-market strategies to support public service-oriented news.

Philanthropic and Public Funding for Elite and Omnibus Audiences

Where there is market failure—commercial models that fail to meet the needs of democracy by providing public affairs news in sufficient quality, quantity, *and* accessibility, which is often the case—public funding-audience adjustment strategies offer an essential component of a civically vital media ecology.[106] We first consider the *partial* support provided by public subsidies to a wide range of print legacy and online media in Sweden and France. We then consider two types of funding that are the *primary* support for some media: tax-advantaged philanthropy (mainly in the US) and majority to total public funding for legacy public television and radio news (including their websites). Even though taxpayers universally underwrite all of these forms of public support, in all but the cases of French and Swedish public TV and radio, these funding formulas tend to enable diffusion to elite rather than omnibus audiences and thus fall short of normative civic expectations for news to be broadly inclusive and accessible.

In Sweden and France, direct and indirect press subsidies have long been justified to support news outlets that provide civic benefits (such as expanding pluralism of perspectives) but that cannot maintain themselves solely through market means. Subsidies have also provided crucial support for the press as a whole during difficult financial circumstances. One Pew Research Center study connected the presence of public subsidies and lesser dependence on advertising in western European countries to a less dramatic decline, at least initially, in newspaper revenues and staffing compared to the US.[107] To date, in the US, only a few states, such as New Jersey and California, have offered modest taxpayer-funded subsidies to support local journalism; no national-level direct press subsidies exist.[108]

About half of Sweden's newspapers receive some subsidies, which make up about two percent of total revenues (although the percentage may be significantly higher for some small outlets).[109] In our sample, the recipients of the largest press subsidies were the Schibsted-owned *Svenska Dagbladet* (as "second" newspaper in the Stockholm region elite newspaper market), the Christian *Dagen*, and the "Red-Green" *Dagens ETC*.[110]

According to *Dagen* CEO/editor-in-chief Ferreira, "the fact that we are very dependent on press subsidies . . . means that we are very dependent on the rules continuing to be such that we can fit in," such as requirements that outlets "contribute to diversity in society."[111] *Dagens ETC* made headlines when it announced in 2019 that it would no longer take advertisements from fossil fuel companies, a policy consistent with its long-standing environmentalism.[112] The refusal may have been facilitated by the fact that only two percent of its total revenues derive from advertising, with at most twenty percent of this amount coming from fossil fuel companies.[113] In contrast, thirty-seven percent of its total revenues come from government press subsidies, which editor-in-chief Gustavsson later described to us as "constitut[ing] such a large part of our basic security." However, out of concern that any government "with a strong element of the [populist right] Sweden Democrats" could dramatically change media policy and reduce press subsidies, Gustavsson stressed that *Dagens ETC* is continuing to deepen its relationship with its readers.[114] Subscribers and crowdfunders provide fifty-seven percent and four percent, respectively, of total revenues.[115]

In 2024, a new Swedish media subsidy law went into effect.[116] Media scholar Tobias Lindberg has suggested that the law will make it tougher for local "second" newspapers to survive, since "media diversity" will no longer be prioritized. Instead, the focus will be on ensuring that each locality has at least one newspaper.[117]

In France, press subsidies make up a larger share of total newspaper revenues than in Sweden, on average between ten to fifteen percent (again, significantly higher for some outlets).[118] Not included in this total are the generous government-subsidized severance payments available to employees who are laid off (not only journalists) or benefits only offered to journalists, such as "conscience clause" separation salary payments (often for up to two years) available to journalists who have the right to quit their job if their news organization changes its "editorial line" under a new owner. Many of the former *Libération* and *Le Monde* journalists who founded *Rue89* and *Les Jours* were able to work without pay during the early years of these start-ups because of these non-market payments.[119] Content-neutral assistance in support of "pluralism" is provided to general interest national newspapers with low circulations (less than one hundred thousand in print) and advertising revenues (less than one-third of total revenues): recipients of these grants over the past decade have included *La Croix*, *L'Humanité*, *Libération*, and the far right weekly *Présent*.[120]

Former *Libération* director Joffrin recounts the crucial importance of public subsidies needed to keep the newspaper afloat:

> The worst is the budgeting, because you have a budget plan, you know when the money comes in, when it goes out. And then, when you have a [budget] hole, well then you have a problem. Even more so because *Libération* didn't have any more credit. So, you have to always search . . . A lot of times, I said to myself: "But we don't have the money to finish the month." To meet the payroll, you know . . . So, you have to find the money, you go see the investors, you go see the State: "That subsidy that you were supposed to pay us in September, can you spin that for June?" . . . At the end of the day, you end up having to do a lot of things that you never learn about in the journalism schools.[121]

Subsidies make up the highest proportion of revenues for these smaller, more precarious news organizations, but significant awards—generally in support of "distribution" or "modernization"—also go to larger, more profitable outlets. In 2016, the single largest recipient of French direct press subsidies was *Ouest-France* (5.8 million euros, effectively two cents per copy at the time), followed by the aforementioned recipients of "pluralism" awards: *Libération* (4.9 million euros, twenty-seven cents per copy), *La Croix* (4.1 million euros, fourteen cents per copy), and *L'Humanité* (3.4 million euros, thirty-eight cents per copy).

Significant funding also went to *Le Figaro* (2.4 million euros, six cents per copy) and *Le Monde* (1.7 million euros, six cents per copy).[122] These totals do not include indirect subsidies, such as a value-added tax reduction on sales revenues and exemptions on the professional tax for newspaper distributors.

We will address in Chapter 6 the extent to which such subsidies contribute to lesser or greater criticism of the party in power. *Libération* director Joffrin, for his part, insisted that there is no direct pressure.[123] A former director of the French Press Institute, Pierre Albert, sees French press subsidies as the guarantor of a "positive" press freedom to achieve a civic obligation of "public service" and "pluralism" (in line with US legal scholar C. Edwin Baker's view):

> In France, with the tradition of Roman law, the press asks for the law to guarantee its freedom in the name of the necessary protection of pluralism against the eventual excesses of the powers of money; the media cannot be treated as ordinary products or goods for the simple reason that they perform a public service.... While certain State subsidies are, for us, considered as a natural contribution of the collectivity to safeguard the press' pluralism, they are... across the Atlantic considered as a soft-core form of corruption of the paper's independence.[124]

If press subsidies function as Albert hopes, those outlets receiving extra subsidies in support of pluralism should be incentivized to feature voices and viewpoints not heard elsewhere.

State tax-advantaged philanthropic donations from foundations and individuals provide another means to fund public service-oriented news made available—in principle—to everyone. Using this strategy, a growing number of US national and regional "nonprofits" have attained some level of economic sustainability. The *Christian Science Monitor*, discussed earlier, is a model in and of itself, recipient of dividends from a generous tax-advantaged church endowment that it supplements with revenues from audience subscriptions and advertising.

In the US, it is important to distinguish between the large national nonprofits, chiefly *ProPublica*, *CIR/Reveal* (*Center for Investigative Reporting*), and *CPI* (*Center for Public Integrity*), and the regional or local nonprofits like *MinnPost*, the *Texas Tribune*, or *Voice of San Diego*. The former rely primarily on large national foundation contributions and individual gifts for their funding, and their focus is almost entirely on "impact" as defined by themselves in dialogue with their foundation funders. They put their news stories on their websites but the primary way they reach audiences is through articles that they give (free of charge) to partner media, either public (*PBS*, *NPR*, or local affiliates) or commercial (*New York Times*, *Washington Post*, leading regional newspapers, or more specialized outlets). While the nonprofits' content is provided free of charge on their websites, their audiences tend to be much wealthier and more highly educated than the national population; many of their commercial distribution partners also target elite audiences and require subscriptions for full access. Foundations decide to support the national investigative nonprofits because they trust in the ability and judgment of the journalists in charge. As a result, the most important audience for these nonprofits is, in many ways, the foundation officials.

When asked how much he knows about his audience, a prominent nonprofit journalist such as Chuck Lewis, founder of the *Center for Public Integrity* (*CPI*) and current executive editor of the American University-based *Investigative Reporting Workshop* (*IRW*), is hard pressed to provide a specific answer. Lewis said that at both *CPI* and *IRW* he had "data about traffic and all that" but that ultimately it wasn't something he thought about much: "I'm not trying to be flip. I just want to investigate the bastards, whoever they are, and I want to do good stuff and I want it to win awards and I want funders to think it's cool and to support it."[125] At *ProPublica*, Senior Vice President for Development Ragan Rhyne emphasizes that foundation and other charitable funding creates an entirely different relationship between the news outlet and its audience: "Our goal is impact. Our goal is that our stories will change something. So it kind of doesn't matter how many people see, as long as they're the right people."[126] While *ProPublica* often shares its content with major national media with large audiences, in some cases it decides that the most appropriate venue is a much smaller outlet. Rhyne gives the example of a story that *ProPublica* did on "military veterans," that was ultimately published with the small audience military magazine *Stars and Stripes*, because it included "the right people who were in a position" to do something about the problem.[127]

While still relying primarily on philanthropic funding, regional nonprofits like *MinnPost* have a slightly different funding-audience adjustment model, closer to commercial audience-supported media. According to *MinnPost* cofounder (and former *Minneapolis Star Tribune* editor and publisher) Joel Kramer, *MinnPost* is a "destination site" funded by a mix of individual donations, local foundations, and local businesses who pay premium advertising rates, for a "target audience" of "highly engaged citizens who care about public policy and politics [and] our goal is to get them to keep coming back and reading stuff on the site." This economic model shapes the kind of news that *MinnPost* produces. "Generally speaking," Kramer explains, "you can build your site more and build more traffic and membership by doing analysis than by doing investigations. Investigations take a really long time and they produce relatively small amounts of copy infrequently. They don't work as a model for a destination site."[128] (This diagnosis might be a surprise for the editors of France's highly successful investigative news "destination site" *Mediapart*, but as noted, *Mediapart*'s formula also includes other kinds of content, including live video events and community forums, that keep subscribers coming back to the site.)

As reported in Chapter 2, France has no major general audience philanthropy funded media outlets. Sweden's left-leaning *Dagens Arena* is majority funded by the LO labor union (close to the Social Democratic Party), and is part of a larger organization, the Arena Group, a nonprofit organization that also generates commercial revenues from consulting and a think tank.[129] When editor-in-chief Nordling talks about *Dagens Arena*'s audience, it is primarily in terms of partisan identity. As noted in the Introduction, Editor-in-Chief Jonas Nordling sees *Dagens Arena* in strongly partisan terms, as "a kind of resistance movement in forgotten terrain, a bit like that." And this formula is not only consistent with Nordling's own views, but also one he believes is most likely to connect with readers and provide adequate funding. He adds: "I want us to have the self-image that we really are funded by readers and they should see us as partisan. Because it is also an important image when you are donation-funded media."[130] We will return to this link between audience subscription funding and partisan slanted news content in Chapter 6, a phenomenon that extends well beyond *Dagens Arena.*

A final non-commercial funding-audience adjustment strategy is full or substantial public funding for either elite (*PBS, NPR*) or omnibus (*SVT, SR, FranceTV,* and *France Info-radio*) audiences. "Public" television and radio in the US actually receive the majority of their funding from philanthropic sources: business sponsors, foundations, universities, and individual donors.[131] They are thus similar in many ways to other philanthropy-supported media in the US and increasingly have formed journalistic and distribution partnerships with other nonprofit media. Perhaps making a virtue of necessity, US public media executives and journalists, including legendary network and *PBS* journalist Bill Moyers, have praised the virtues of their heavy reliance on philanthropic funding. As Moyers wrote to one of the authors: "I've had to raise every penny for every production but with that challenge I've had far more freedom than I ever did at CBS and ABC."[132] Nevertheless, US public media's hybrid funding model—which also provides them with access to direct public funding—sets them apart from other nonprofit media. Public funding provides a base of relatively stable funding and serves as a magnet to help draw additional support.

David Fanning, founder and executive producer of *PBS*'s investigative news broadcast *Frontline*, has emphasized the crucial role of government funding in supporting *Frontline*'s investigative mission: "Seventy-five to 80 percent of the budget for Frontline comes from public [taxpayer supported] television. And we have never been able to get corporate sponsorship or the kind of large significant philanthropic support to do those kinds of things . . . there would be no Frontline without public broadcasting."[133] Despite the diversity of funding sources, US public media have been chronically underfunded compared to their counterparts in France and Sweden.

Paula Kerger, president and CEO of *PBS*, has clearly articulated a "market failure" justification for public media consistent with arguments made by Baker and Victor Pickard: "We were created with the recognition that there was market failure, that there was a whole range of conversation that was not happening, particularly in the public affairs space that public television could address." Kerger adds: "There is an obligation for the public broadcaster to continually look for ways to serve the public good in a deeper way than our commercial brethren."[134] The implication in this language is that the "public good" is something more than the sum of what the public itself chooses as good, that it is appropriate to give the public what they are perceived to "need" and not just what they "want." As it happens, it is also the news that certain publics *do* want, notably policymakers and business, political, and cultural elites who are highly motivated to follow the latest and most in-depth information on issues connected to their interests and concerns. The cultivation of these audiences is especially crucial for a "public" media system that is not fully funded by the entire citizenry. Despite the lack of paywalls, audiences for *PBS* and *NPR* are very similar in their "up-market" sociodemographics to the paying subscribers of the *New York Times* and other elite commercial news outlets. This less than universal audience does not invalidate the professionalism or civic commitment of public media journalists, who continue to write about communities and topics that have no obvious bottom-line return, but it does clearly indicate that US public media are not fully achieving their self-professed goal of serving the broad public. US public media's particular funding-audience adjustment strategy fosters this impasse.[135]

French public television relies on two main sources of funding: revenues from "license fees" levied on all French residents who own an electronic device capable of showing public television or radio or their online or mobile sites (changed to funding from a percentage of the Value Added Tax as of 2023), as well as commercial advertising.[136] In the wake of cuts to advertising mandated under the Sarkozy presidential administration in 2008 (ostensibly to allow public media to fulfill its public service mandate without commercial constraints, but also to relieve *TF1* of competition for advertising revenues), French public media have struggled financially given that government funding has not been increased to make up for the loss. An executive at *France Télévisions* complained of constant oversight on budgeting and pressures to keep costs down, with little autonomy and too little for investing over the long term.[137] Despite these challenges, several of our French interviewees singled out for praise public *France 2*'s news program *Cash Investigation* for its hard-hitting reports on sensitive topics, such as business tax evasion and corruption, and compared it to the longstanding US *CBS* television news program *60 Minutes*. These investigative programs have been not only a means of bolstering public television's symbolic capital but they have also provided a way to compete for audiences with the commercial channels.

Finally, Swedish *SVT* public television and *SR* public radio stand alone in our three-country sample of non-commercial media in their ability to stand apart from market pressures while also being well-resourced and reaching a large omnibus audience.[138] Swedish public service broadcasting had long been fully funded by a universal "license fee" levied on anyone with a television. As media consumption has moved increasingly to other devices, the TV license fee was changed (as of January 1, 2019) to an individual public service fee collected via the tax system, but in a "closed system" handled separately from the general government budget. It is calculated as one percent of taxable earned income up to a maximum of approximately $120 per person per year (which is half the amount of the previous household-based license fee). This fee can only be used to finance public service-oriented media (TV, radio, and online versions).[139]

Former *SVT* Commissioning Editor Johan Lindén sees the lack of advertising as crucial in securing Swedish public media's independence.[140] Lindén recounts an almost comical example that resulted in the station being fined for a violation of the rule against advertising:

> You know, in the newsroom, when the program is over, it used to be, not anymore, that the camera goes up in the ceiling and you get an overview of the studio. And [this one time], we had that last shoot and there was a studio worker walking across the studio with a Camel [cigarette] jacket, with a logo on the back, and we were fined 50,000 [Swedish] kronor [about $5,000] because that Camel jacket was not supposed to be there.... We are not allowed to make mistakes with commercial messages.[141]

Investigative reporting has been a major way for Swedish public media, especially television, to both attract audiences and reinforce its reputation for quality and independence. Lindén highlighted the public channel's investigative "magazine" shows, in particular *Uppdrag granskning* (*Mission: Investigation*). Truedson underlined the tough, independent reputation of *Uppdrag granskning*: "There's even a book published by a PR consultant where the title is 'If Janne Josefsson calls'—he's the face of this show—what to do if he calls . . . if he calls, you're in trouble."[142]

Because *SR* and *SVT* are not dependent on subscriptions or advertisers interested in only reaching certain audiences, they can—indeed this is their reason for being—aim for a broad public. Klas Wolf-Watz, *SR* editor-in-chief of the national radio news program Ekot, says: "We have an ambition in a way to reach everybody, we should just [provide] news for everybody who as citizens are in need of quality news . . . we don't really have that direct target group thinking."[143] *SVT* National News Editor-in-Chief Charlotta Friborg suggests along similar lines: "For a company like *SVT*, it's important that we have a large audience, and if one has a large audience then [one] has a pretty diverse audience. . . . We gather people with widely divergent values, and that's a great strength." Friborg conceded, however, that *SVT* has struggled to reach some members of the public, in particular, "people born outside of Europe" as well as younger people. To reach excluded groups, *SVT* does engage in some "target-group thinking," creating news exclusively for the online audience, or connecting to platforms where such audiences can be found, such as Facebook or Instagram.[144] Compared to their commercial legacy audio-visual competitors, audiences for both Swedish and French public TV and radio are marked by their slightly higher cultural capital (as indicated by prevalence of university degrees).[145] However, compared to most legacy print media, they still reach larger and more omnibus audiences, at least partially bridging the social and ideological divides that organize differences among the commercial legacy print and online-only media.

In sum, many of the leading news outlets in all three countries have developed partial or wholly non-commercial funding-audience adjustment strategies in support of some measure of economic stability and autonomous, public service-oriented journalism. Even though they face less or zero profit pressures, their chances of succeeding (even in their own terms) depend on an adequate and predictable provision of financial resources. Sweden's well-funded *SVT* and *SR*, with their legally protected "arms-length" relationship to government, provide a rare example of non-commercial media able to garner significant resources, focus their energies on journalistic excellence, and reach relatively broad and large publics. Even so, they—like most commercial media and their public media counterparts in France—may fall short in reaching marginalized and disadvantaged populations.

Conclusion

We began this chapter by noting the tendencies of funding-audience adjustment strategies to cluster with ownership forms, producing distinct ownership complexes.

As we moved from the most commercial (market) to less commercial (private, some civil society) and non-commercial (nonprofit civil society, and public) ownership forms, we saw a gradual shift from advertising to audience subscriber and ultimately philanthropic or public funding. Omnibus audience targeting is most prevalent, however, at the two ends of the spectrum: market and public. With the decline in advertising revenues, increasing numbers of news outlets are searching for financial sustainability from audience digital subscriptions. The result has been a shift toward the targeting of culturally and economically elite audiences, who are perceived to appreciate the kind of in-depth, public affairs reporting that professional journalists aspire to produce. The cost, however, has been to exclude an ever-greater share of the populace. Non-commercial philanthropic funding, focused on influencing policy-making elites, has to date only reinforced this tendency.

Even so, there are also exceptions and tensions within and across ownership complexes. There are gaps between strategies and the social positioning of outlets: both advertising and subscription funding are used to reach elite and omnibus audiences. Finding an audience and adequate funding is filled with risk, reflecting the difficulty of ascertaining which funding-audience adjustment strategies will work best to create sustainable news operations. Some combinations are more unstable than others. Advertising-funded media may seek elite audiences, but the public affairs and partisan content best suited to reach them is not perceived as optimal by advertisers. Outlets with omnibus audiences find it difficult to assemble large enough subscribing audiences to abandon advertising, even as advertising's ability to fund operations, especially for online-only outlets, is being progressively siphoned off by Google, Facebook, and other platforms.[146] Except for the most elite national outlets across all three countries, and, for the moment, Swedish public media, finding a sustainable funding-audience adjustment strategy has become a desperate struggle. For news organizations still committed to public service news, partial public subsidies play a key role in bridging the gap between aspirations and financial necessity.

Ultimately, the links between structures, strategies, and the actual production of news can only be established through systematic empirical analysis of news content across ownership forms and complexes. We turn now to this investigation, beginning in the next chapter with an examination of public service "information" and "pluralism" in news content.

5
Public Service Orientation in Action

Public service orientation is indelibly associated with journalism's principles and ideals, as articulated by journalists themselves or embodied in professional ethics codes and prizes.[1] These principles, in turn, are in conversation with longstanding debates in political, legal, and academic fields about the democratic normative purposes of journalism.[2] Public service may also be driven by commercial motives: there is a market for "quality" news.[3] But, what is public service orientation, concretely? In this chapter, we focus on two ideals that consistently emerge as central in professional, academic, and industry discussions: *information* (including holding the powerful to account) and *pluralism* (giving voice to a wide range of speakers and viewpoints).

Throughout this book, we are interested in the relationship between the structures and strategies of ownership on the one hand and the news that gets produced on the other. So far, we have mostly analyzed the political economy of media ownership, including funding and target audiences. In this chapter, we begin to make explicit connections between the political economy and the end product of the journalistic work process, the actual articles published on the websites of news outlets. We want to know if outlets with different forms of ownership—along with different funding models, audiences, and particular owners—will diverge in the amount and type of public service-oriented news that they publish. To answer these questions, we analyzed the informational and pluralist characteristics of articles published in late 2015 and early 2016 in fifty-one news outlets in the US, Sweden, and France that vary along these structural dimensions. This chapter thus provides new findings on how ownership forms and complexes matter in shaping the production of public service news.

Public Service Information

In this section, we measure the relative frequency of *four* dimensions of *public service information* (PSI). First, we analyze the proportion of articles focused on *public affairs*. Second, we document the subset of public affairs articles devoted to *international affairs/foreign policy*. Third, we identify the percentage of articles devoted to critical enterprise *investigative* reporting about government,

How Media Ownership Matters. Rodney Benson et al. Oxford University Press. © Rodney Benson, Mattias Hessérus, Timothy Neff, and Julie Sedel 2025. DOI: 10.1093/oso/9780199931293.003.0006

business, or other powerful institutions. Finally, we track the proportion of *in-depth* articles that go beyond breaking news to provide deeper context.

Rather than comparing the raw percentages that can vary substantially across countries, we create scales for public service information calculated in relation to national means. For each dimension, each outlet receives a 1 to 4 scale score that captures its news coverage pattern in relation to the *national* average, from well below the mean to well above the mean (see Methods Appendix). In other words, these scores are *relational* and tell us how outlets with distinct types of ownership, funding-audience adjustment strategies, and particular owner and audience political preferences are similar or different from one another *within* their own national fields. They allow us to focus our analysis on consistencies of news coverage patterns across three countries produced by ownership forms and complexes *within* fields, rather than the broad differences produced *by* these fields.[4]

Focus on public affairs is our first public service information dimension. We find that public affairs focus is most strongly associated with civil society ownership, especially the religious group ownership subform. It is also significantly linked, in rough order of strength, with press subsidies, philanthropy and audience subscription funding, current/legacy journalist control, elite audiences, and left-leaning owners and audiences. (To be clear, in relation to subsidies, we do not refer to all French and Swedish newspapers, only those that receive extra subsidies in support of press pluralism—*L'Humanité, La Croix, Libération, Svenska Dagbladet, Dagen*, and *Dagens ETC*.)

International affairs coverage is most strongly associated with religious ownership, along with press subsidies, audience subscription funding, current/legacy journalist control, and elite audiences.

Investigative reporting is highest at civil society-owned media, closely followed by public media, especially those with primarily public funding as in Sweden and France. Compared to other types of news, investigative reporting makes up only a very small percentage of articles in our sample: a finding that concurs with previous research.[5] The major exceptions, in this study, are US nonprofit websites *ProPublica* and *CIR/Reveal*, which are by design almost entirely dedicated to investigative reporting.

Finally, we find that in-depth analysis on average is highest at outlets with current/legacy journalist control and left-leaning audiences. (See Appendix Table A5.1 for PSI dimensions and overall mean scores by ownership forms and subforms, owner and audience characteristics, and funding, as well as Appendix Table A5.2 for outlet level data.)

To identify the overall patterns, we average the four distinct dimensions to create a total PSI or "information" mean score, again, ranging from 1 to 4 (see Figure 5.1). Of the four broad ownership forms, civil society ownership provides

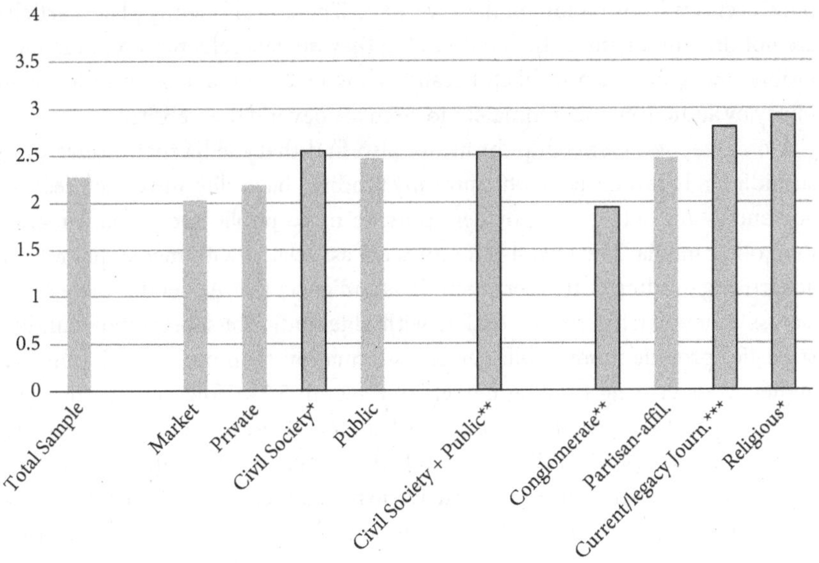

Figure 5.1 Public Service Information (PSI): Average Outlet 1–4 National Relational Scale* by Ownership Form and Subform

*1–4 Scale measures each outlet's PSI raw performance in relation to other outlets *in the same national field*. A score of 1 is more than 0.5 SD (standard deviation) under the national mean and a score of 4 is more than 0.5 SD above the national mean, while scores of 2 and 3 are within 0.5 SD below and above the mean, respectively. The same procedure is used for all figures or tables presenting national relational scale data.

Categories with statistically significant differences from all other outlets are outlined in bold:

*$p \leq .10$, **$p \leq .05$, ***$p < .005$

the highest levels of information, followed closely by public ownership; together, these two forms of non-commercial ownership provide significantly greater proportions of information than stock market-traded and privately owned media.[6] Figure 5.1 also shows the results for three subforms of ownership or control: conglomerate, religious, and current/legacy journalist control. Religious newspapers, a subset of civil society-owned media, provide the highest levels of public service information, followed closely by media with current/legacy journalist control. Conversely, conglomerates are the least oriented toward producing high quality public service information.

Our method does not capture the overall volume of news produced across various types of outlets. Commercial news media, including stock market-traded outlets, may produce more news articles (including on public affairs) each day than some of their civil society-owned or public counterparts. What we can say, from our research, is that civil society-owned media and public media are more likely than stock market-traded media and private media to highlight public service information on their websites. These prominently placed articles are not the sum of any outlet's output, but they do generally represent the most visible news content, more likely because of their placement to be accorded legitimacy by audiences and, ultimately, to circulate beyond the website.

Going beyond ownership forms, we also find that media that receive press subsidies, rely primarily on philanthropy funding, have elite and/or left-leaning audiences, and left-leaning owners provide more public service information than other media. The lowest PSI scores are associated with media that rely on advertising funding or that serve omnibus audiences (see Appendix Table A5.1). Across all ownership forms, outlets with elite audience-subscription funding strategies provide more public service information than outlets with omnibus audience-advertising funding models (see Figure 5.2). However, because they are governed to a greater extent by market incentives, these distinct strategies make more of a (statistically significant) difference in information production for stock market-traded and privately owned outlets than for civil society-owned and public media. With the exception of a single outlet with advertising funding and an omnibus audience (*Norran*), there is little difference in provision of public service information between the funding-audience models that make up civil society-owned and public media.[7] Thus, while the stock market-traded and private ownership forms do not prevent outlets with conducive

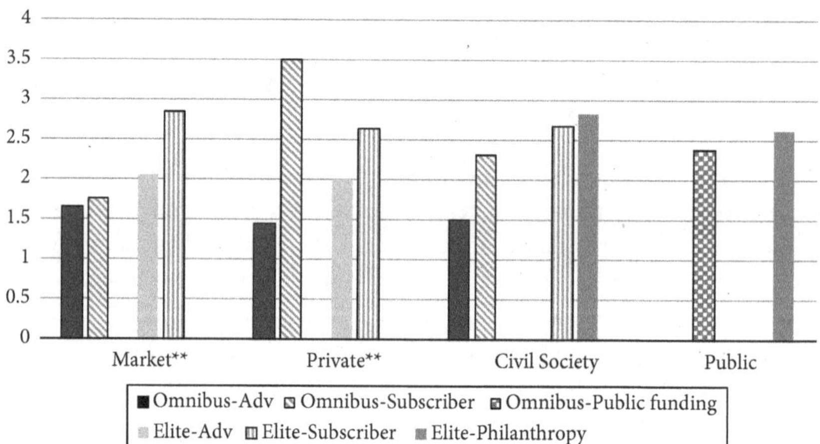

Figure 5.2 Public Service Information (PSI): Average Outlet 1–4 National Relational Scale by Ownership Funding-Audience Adjustment Complex

Funding-audience adjustment strategies are listed in the following order: Omnibus-Advertising, Omnibus-Subscriber Funding, Omnibus-Public Funding; Elite-Advertising, Elite-Subscriber Funding, and Elite-Philanthropy.

For differences across funding-audience adjustment strategies within each ownership form: $^{**}p \leq .05$
Differences across funding-audience adjustment strategies regardless of form are significant at $p < .001$.

funding-audience adjustment strategies from achieving high PSI scores (notably the *New York Times*, *Svenska Dagbladet*, *Dagens ETC*, *Le Monde*, *Vice France*, and *Libération*), it is the civil society-owned and public ownership forms that afford a consistently higher proportion of public service information.

To be clear, public media in our sample include both the omnibus Swedish and French public service broadcasters and the elite audience, majority philanthropy funded US *NPR* and *PBS* (*PBS NewsHour*). US public media thus function in many ways like civil society-owned media. The distinctiveness of French and especially Swedish omnibus public media as a unique combination of quality and accessibility becomes clearer when we compare them to other omnibus audience media. These public broadcasters have a mandate to be accessible to everyone and thus may dilute their public service content with entertaining content to achieve "universal service." However, unlike commercial omnibus media, they also are statutorily committed to a strong pedagogical and civic mission. Compared to all other omnibus media in our three-country sample, omnibus public media score twenty-one percent higher in public service information provision. When compared to omnibus legacy television/radio commercial media, however, omnibus public media score thirty-nine percent higher (see Figure 5.3). This pattern highlights how ownership form can matter in civically consequential ways. While audience demographics consistently shape news content, how much they do so can vary substantially depending on the dominant institutional logic of the ownership form. Holding constant for omnibus audiences, public media perform differently than their commercial counterparts.

As economist James Hamilton argues, to create news that will "sell," media outlets offer a mix of "serious" and "light" news.[8] Of course, public affairs news may be presented in an entertaining way, but broadly speaking, we can learn a lot about a media outlet's relative positioning in the field by identifying its mix of topics: of "serious" public affairs focused news (one of our four dimensions of public service information) versus "light/sensational news" (coverage focusing on celebrities, crime, or human interest).[9] Figure 5.4 shows the ratio of public affairs news to light/sensational news converted to a 1 to 4 relational scale for ownership, funding, and audience characteristics. On the left side of the figure, outlets with conglomerate ownership, relying on public funding or advertising, targeted to omnibus audiences, or with right-leaning owners (and audiences, not shown) are associated with the lowest ratio of public affairs to light/sensational topics; in other words, the highest proportion of light/sensational news. At the other end of the spectrum, with the greatest emphasis on public affairs over light/sensational topics, are outlets with any of the following characteristics: civil society and possibly religious ownership (the latter not statistically significant), current/legacy journalist control, primary funding by philanthropy, recipient of press subsidies, elite audience, and/or left-leaning owner.

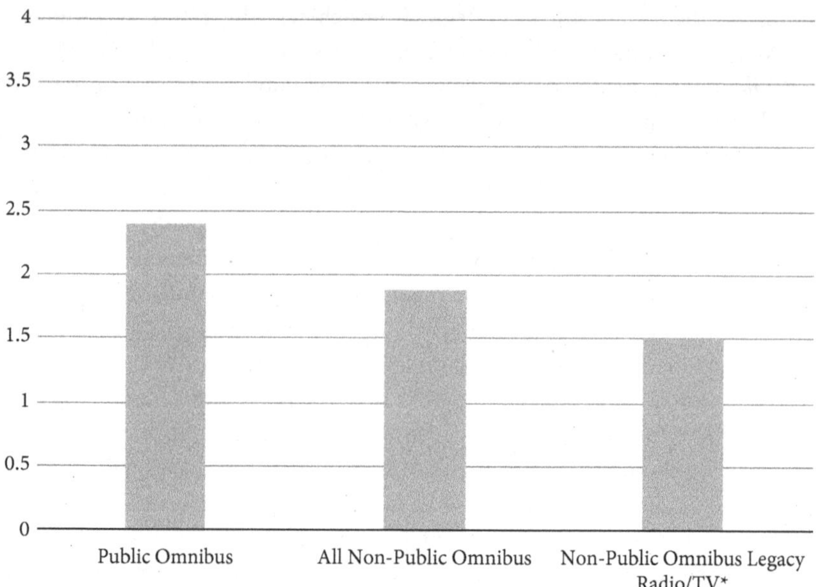

Figure 5.3 Public Service Information (PSI): Average Outlet 1–4 National Relational Scale for Public versus Non-Public Omnibus Audience Media

Public Omnibus (n = 4), All Non-Public Omnibus (n = 17), Non-Public Legacy Radio/TV Omnibus (n = 5)

*Difference from Public Omnibus Media, p < .10

These findings make clear that a focus on "serious" public affairs to the exclusion of "entertaining" light and sensationalist content tends to be the hallmark of the least commercial media consumed by elites likely to have the highest cultural capital. In consequence, such an exclusive focus is at the expense of accessibility. It is worth emphasizing that both stock market-traded and public media, and even more so advertising and publicly funded media, have in common a much higher proportion of light-sensational news than other media. Whether the reasons are entirely civic or a mix of civic and commercial goals, the results in the type of content (although there may still be differences in execution and style) are similar. It becomes a question of balance. *ABC*'s Isaac Josephson describes the thinking inside an advertising-funded stock market-traded media outlet: "People come for the veggies and they stay for the candy. . . . Everybody kind of comes to see the daily political news, or something that happened with an earthquake in Mexico. And the challenge is to get them to stay for one more click or two more clicks because you sell advertising against those clicks. And that's where you get the Lindsey Lohan slideshows . . . but you have to find the right mix of that, right? Because you don't want to completely ding your brand

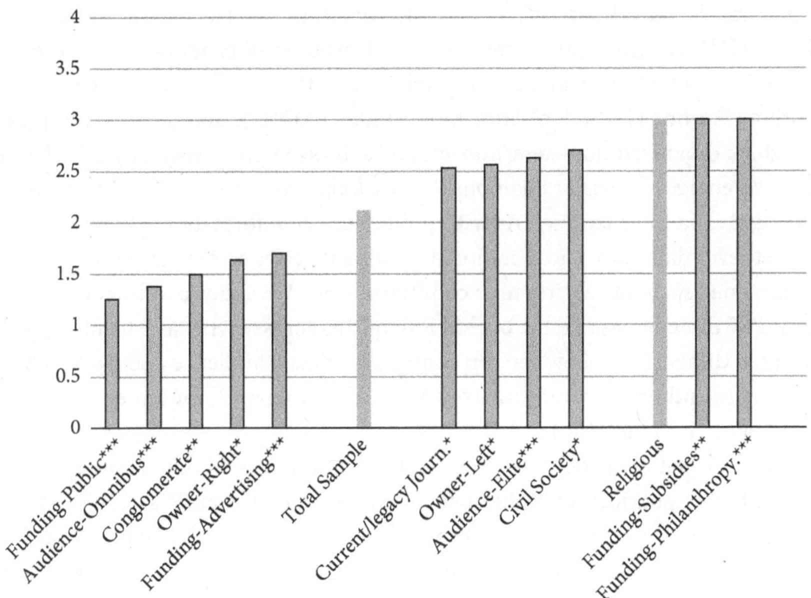

Figure 5.4 Public Affairs to Light/Sensational News Ratio: Average Outlet 1–4 National Relational Scale by Ownership Complex Dimension

Bars outlined in bold attain statistical significance. Funding, audience, and owner category differences are significant vis-à-vis each other; ownership form differences are significant vis-à-vis all other outlets: $^{*}p \leq .10$, $^{**}p \leq .05$, $^{***}p < .005$

equity by putting too much of the soft stuff on there. But you want to put enough so that you're going to get the extra clicks and the repeat visits."[10]

Public Service (Internal) Pluralism

Pluralism of voices and viewpoints in the news, as Daniel Hallin and Paolo Mancini have emphasized, can be either internal (diverse perspectives within a single outlet's news content) or external (diverse across the field, with each outlet offering a distinct perspective).[11] In this section, we present our findings for internal pluralism; in the next section, we analyze external pluralism. For our three-country sample, we measure *internal* public service pluralism (PSP) along four dimensions: first, the degree of even dispersion of *mentions of mainstream and marginal left and right political actors* (government, party, and social movement), through what we term a Political Herfindahl-Hirschman Index (PHHI); second, the degree of even dispersion of *mentions of institutionally and socially located actors* (government, various civil society, business, international, unaffiliated individuals, etc.), with an Institutional Herfindahl-Hirschman Index (IHHI); third, the degree of even dispersion of types of article *authors* according to institutional affiliation (similar to the IHHI for actor mentions), with an Author Herfindahl-Hirschman Index (AHHI); and fourth, the extent to which organized non-state/non-market actors are given voice, by calculating the percentage of all *actor mentions that are linked to civil society*, including both domestic and international. As with public service information, we convert the outlet-level data into 1 to 4 national relational scales to facilitate the simultaneous analysis of the entire three country sample. We analyze differences in the four PSP dimensions and the overall PSP means across ownership forms, as well as other dimensions of ownership complexes, chiefly audience and owner characteristics and primary funding (see Appendix Table A5.3; for outlet-level data, see Appendix Table A5.4).

We find that civil society-owned and partisan-affiliated outlets offer significantly higher political actor pluralism (PHHI) than other outlets: this is in most cases because they give greater voice to social movements and marginal parties than outlets that focus on the mainstream parties. Philanthropy funding is also associated with high political actor pluralism. To be clear, our indicator for political actor pluralism does not take into account valence (which we consider in the next chapter). For example, the left *Dagens Arena* mentions populist right parties twice as often as Swedish outlets on average, although much of this attention is critical.

Public media exhibit the highest institutional pluralism (IHHI). Press subsidies also contribute to greater institutional pluralism, while advertising funding and an online-only medium are associated with the lowest levels of institutional pluralism.

As for author pluralism (AHHI), the overwhelming majority of authors across all outlets are journalists, primarily on staff, but some are freelancers or journalists working for wire services or affiliated with other outlets. Because our sample of articles from each outlet includes labeled opinion or commentary articles and blogs (if present on the website), an opportunity is also provided for some non-journalists to "speak" in their own voice. In our combined three-country sample, no single ownership form stands out as significantly higher than the others in author pluralism; however, public media are substantially lower than the rest. The reason for lower author pluralism at public media seems mostly related to the genre of articles posted on their websites. Across our sample, most of the non-journalist authored articles are labeled as opinion or commentary, and most of the public media websites published very few labeled "opinion" articles. It is important to emphasize that our measures of pluralism refer only to authors (or actors) mentioned, and do not consider distinct viewpoints. Thus, for example, because the *New York Times* mostly publishes articles by journalists and academics in its opinion sections, its "author" pluralism is very low: an analysis of viewpoints, however, might reveal a greater degree of pluralism.

Finally, civil society actor mentions are not strongly associated with ownership forms, but audience subscriber funding is linked to the lowest levels of mentions. This is also one of the rare cases in our study where medium seems to be most influential. Online-only outlets mention civil society actors far more than both legacy print and TV/radio outlets. While some of these online-only outlets are civil society nonprofits, such as *CIR/Reveal*, *MinnPost*, and *ProPublica*, many are privately held pure players, such as *BuzzFeed*, *KIT*, *Nyheter24*, *Slate.fr*, and *Rue89*, which have in common their digital age participatory missions and youthful audiences.

When we combine the four dimensions into an average public service pluralism (PSP) scale, the differences across ownership forms become clearer (see Figure 5.5 and Appendix Table A5.3). Just as with public service information, in its level of pluralism civil society ownership is higher than the other main ownership forms.[12] Different from the pattern for information, journalist current/legacy control is *not* connected to greater pluralism, while the partisan-affiliated

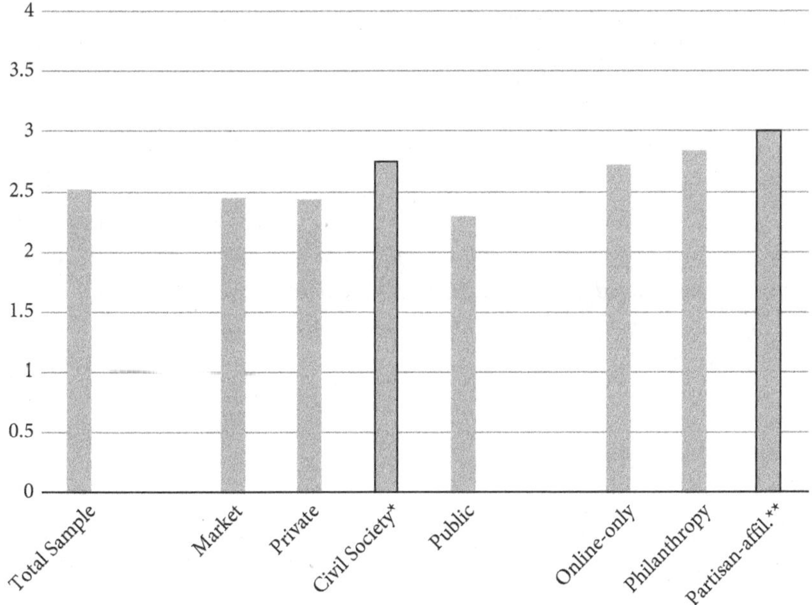

Figure 5.5 Public Service Pluralism (PSP): Average Outlet 1–4 National Relational Scale by Ownership Form and Subform, Primary Funding, and Medium

Bars outlined in bold indicate a statistically significant difference from all other outlets: $^{*}p \leq .10$, $^{**}p \leq .05$

ownership subform is most strongly linked to higher pluralism. Philanthropic funding and the online-only medium may contribute to higher pluralism, although our results fall just short of statistical significance.[13] Again, our analysis here does not examine *how* various actors are mentioned. Partisan-affiliated outlets may mention ideologically opposed actors mainly to strongly criticize them; this may be the case as well for some stock market-traded outlets with overtly ideological dominant shareholders. For example, *Fox News* and *Le Figaro* have higher than average PSP scores (although we find no consistent differences between outlets with left-leaning and right-leaning owners or audiences).

Also, unlike with public service information, outlets with omnibus audiences or advertising funding are not all that different in their level of pluralism from those with elite audiences or audience subscription funding. Whereas provision of public service information may require some commercial sacrifice (given that more light/sensational news may attract bigger audiences and revenues), pluralistic news coverage may offer more of a civic-commercial "win-win"—providing more opportunities for audiences to find themselves reflected in the news coverage or using a diversity of voices to make the news more interesting and entertaining. Such motivations may help account for possibly higher pluralism at online-only media that use blogging or other audience engagement initiatives to increase traffic to their websites. We can see how this process worked in reverse at *HuffPost*. In 2018, two years after former *New York Times* journalist Lydia Polgreen had taken over as *HuffPost*'s editor-in-chief, she announced the end of the blogging program. As one former staffer speculated, "She was motivated [to end blogging] by wanting to strengthen the legitimacy of *HuffPost* to really refine our content and to have greater control over the quality of the content on our website. I think the primary motivation was to be taken a bit more seriously."[14] Whether or not Polgreen intended to or was able to completely replace *HuffPost*'s pluralist approach, we see in this incident evidence of the importation of a journalistic professional sensibility, especially strong in the US, ultimately valuing information over pluralism.[15]

External pluralism

External pluralism, a national field-level property, is higher when some outlets focus their news coverage on particular topics, frames/angles, or speakers, increasing the differentiation among outlets. In this section, we search for these patterns and seek to answer the question: Do certain types of news outlets contribute significantly more attention to certain speakers (actor mentions) than other outlets in the same national field? (See Appendix Tables A5.5a–c for outlet-level data by national field.) We focus on a subset of speaker categories that are most crucially linked to a broadening of voice in the public sphere, beyond the traditional powers of governing parties, law enforcement, and business; further, we call attention only to the most distinctive outliers in each national field (in each instance signaling their ownership form), those with the highest percentage of mentions of a particular actor type.

Marginal left and right parties and social movements contribute perspectives often ignored by mainstream governing parties and politicians. In the US, political parties beyond Democrats and Republicans are completely absent in our news content sample, but of course the situation is different in multi-party parliamentary democracies like Sweden and France. In Sweden, marginal left parties are given the greatest attention by civil society-owned, partisan-affiliated *Dagens Arena*; marginal right parties are most often mentioned at the privately held newspaper *Jönköpings-Posten*; and left social movements appear most often in the private (but heavily state-subsidized) *Dagens ETC*. In France, news outlets that mention marginal voices often do so from an oppositional stance: the left-leaning *L'Humanité* and *Vice France* mention marginal right parties and social movements, respectively, most often; and the right-wing *Le Figaro* mentions left social movements most frequently. This pattern of coverage echoes Eugénie Saitta's discovery that the communist (PCF or PC) *L'Humanité* offered heavy coverage of the far right, but minimal, and generally critical, news coverage of other far left parties that potentially competed with the PCF for voters. As Saitta concluded, "This hierarchization of information corresponds to a perception of the political game where the 'enemies' of the PC, the right and the far right, are in fact easier to write about than the direct competitors, the Greens, LO-LCR [other French far left parties], and the Socialist party."[16] This tendency is not uniform, however: the center left-leaning *Le HuffPost*, for example, mentions marginal left parties most often.

Journalists have been criticized for paying too much attention to politicians and the political game and not enough to the workings of government bureaucracies, a form of hidden power. Thus, it is noteworthy that the US civil society nonprofit *CIR/Reveal* gives a disproportionate attention to bureaucratic actors, likely in support of its heavy emphasis on investigative reporting. However, we also find disproportionately high mentions of bureaucratic actors by the civil society foundation-owned *Barometern*, which had some investigative reporting but was not the highest in Sweden, and by the French stock market-traded *TF1*, which had no investigative reports.

Various civil society voices are highlighted most often by outlets with civil society or private ownership. Academic voices appear most often in the US *Texas Tribune*, Sweden's *KIT*, and *Slate.fr*. Labor union representatives are rare across all media, with the exception of substantial mentions by the Swedish civil society (and labor union supported) *Dagens Arena* and the French civil society leftist newspaper *L'Humanité*.[17] Mentions of actors belonging to our category of "other civil society," which includes religious and humanitarian associations, are perhaps not surprisingly highest in Sweden at the Christian *Dagen* and in France at the Catholic *La Croix*. Artists and entertainers, in turn, are mentioned most often at private online-only outlets *BuzzFeed* and the Swedish *Nyheter24*, along with the stock market-traded French *Metronews*. Unaffiliated individuals, the proverbial "person on the street" asked to provide their first-hand witness or perspectives on public issues, appear most often at *BuzzFeed*, the Swedish foundation-owned *Norran*, and the stock market-traded *TF1*. Finally, foreign governments are mentioned most often by the *Christian Science Monitor*, the French civil society-owned regional newspaper *Ouest-France*, and the Swedish public radio *SR*; international governmental organizations (UN, EU, etc.) are mentioned most often by the *Monitor*, the privately held *Vice France*, and the stock market-traded Swedish elite daily *Svenska Dagbladet*.

Amidst this complex portrait, we can recognize some media titles appearing more often than others, as well as the absence of some of the most prestigious legacy newspapers (e.g., *New York Times*, *Le Monde*, *Dagens Nyheter*). Media that bring marginal or frequently silenced voices into the public debate are themselves often relatively marginal. To further solidify the emerging patterns, we calculate the number of times that an outlet has actor mentions higher than one standard deviation above the national mean for each of the categories noted above: far left and far right parties, left and right social movements, bureaucracy, academia, entertainment/arts, labor, other civil society, unaffiliated individuals, foreign governments, and international governmental organizations. As it happens, in all three countries, there is a clear break between those outlets with three or more such occurrences (again, of mentioning any of the foregoing categories of actors one standard deviation or more above the mean) and the rest of the sample. In the US, these outlets are *MinnPost* (civil society), *Christian Science Monitor* (civil society), and *BuzzFeed* (private); in Sweden, they are *Dagens Arena* (civil society) and *Dagens ETC* (private); and in France, they are *L'Humanité* (civil society), *La Croix* (civil society), *Vice* (private), and *TF1* (market).

Overall, civil society-owned and private outlets (notably, newer digital outlets motivated to mark their difference in the field[18]) are the leading contributors to external pluralism. With a few exceptions, well-established stock market-traded and public media outlets tend to be weaker contributors to external pluralism.

Conclusion

This chapter has shown that informational and pluralistic news content vary systematically across ownership forms and complexes. Civil society ownership and, to a certain degree, philanthropy funding both contribute to greater amounts of public service-oriented information *and* pluralism. Outlets with civil society ownership are also most likely to give extra attention to marginal, expert, or international voices, thus adding to the external pluralism of a national field.

In other ways, however, patterns for information and pluralism differ. Outlets that are religious-affiliated and have current/legacy journalist control, elite audiences, left-leaning owners, and/or audience subscriber funding provide higher than average levels of public service information; conversely, outlets with conglomerate ownership, omnibus audiences, right-leaning owners, and/or advertising funding provide below average levels. Public media (especially compared to omnibus commercial media) also assure high levels of information. For pluralism, we see different tendencies. Pluralism tends to be higher at partisan-affiliated outlets, but the type of primary funding doesn't seem to make a difference. And current/legacy journalist control is *not* associated with relatively higher pluralism as it is with information—perhaps because information is more highly valued than pluralism by most professional journalists.

When it comes to the mix of public affairs versus light/sensational news, we see yet another slightly different configuration of ownership complexes. News outlets with religious affiliation, philanthropy funding, press subsidies, civil society ownership, and/or elite audiences have the highest ratios of public affairs to light/sensational news. In contrast, light/sensational news is emphasized most by media with omnibus audiences, public funding, and/or advertising funding. It may seem odd that both advertising and public funding are associated with more light/sensational news: it makes sense, however, given that both types of media are incentivized to provide accessible content for a broad public.

Ownership forms are deeply entangled with funding-audience adjustment strategies. Across all ownership forms, public service information provision tends to increase as one moves from omnibus to elite audiences and advertising to subscriber or philanthropic funding. However, the differences among outlets based on these audience and funding differences are less substantial for civil society and public ownership than for stock market-traded or private ownership: this pattern suggests that these less commercial ownership forms express institutional logics that shape journalistic production in ways that cannot be reduced to their funding or audiences.

In the next chapter, we turn to the second mode of power: political instrumentalism. As we will see, there are synergies as well as tensions between public service orientation and political instrumentalism.

6
Political Instrumentalism and Partisanship

The idea that the press can and ought to be a vehicle to promote political parties, causes, and ideas is as old as journalism itself.[1] In international surveys, journalists embrace the "interventionist role"—a "strong disposition . . . to pursue a particular mission and promote certain values," second only to the informational "monitorial" role.[2] Nevertheless, cross-national differences remain. In France and Sweden, direct control by parties has declined, but informal and openly admitted affiliations with political or ideological currents are still compatible with a "mainstream" journalistic identity. Less so in the US, where mainstream journalists still tend to vociferously refuse ideological labels.[3]

Paolo Mancini has argued for the need to distinguish between a civically constructive "political parallelism" of media outlets offering distinct political positions, enhancing the public sphere's "external pluralism," and a venal "instrumentalism" of owners using their media properties to promote their interests.[4] We partially preserve this dichotomy in separating political instrumentalism, discussed in this chapter, and economic instrumentalism, considered in the next. However, when analyzing a media outlet's tendency to praise or criticize various parties, politicians, and political ideas, we see no reason to make an a priori normative distinction between business and other types of owners. Distinguishing our use from Mancini's, by political instrumentalism we mean the intentional use, whether partial or total, of a media outlet to exercise political effects (promotion or criticism of political actors, movements, or policies) that may or may not coincide with the specific interests of the owner but always at least partially transcend them: for instance, regulatory, tax, or spending policies that could be plausibly justified, even if contested, as serving the common good. In this sense, political instrumentalism could be equally exercised (although with differential effects depending on many factors) by a large business owner, a trade union, a church, a nonprofit foundation or association, or even a collective of journalists.

Political instrumentalism, as an ideal type, is mission driven. Real world media owners, managers, and journalists will likely have mixed motives. A media outlet seeking to enlarge its audience may find that appealing to the audience's preconceptions, including political views, is a highly effective strategy. Knowing this, such a strategy may be pursued passionately if consistent with

How Media Ownership Matters. Rodney Benson et al. Oxford University Press. © Rodney Benson, Mattias Hessérus, Timothy Neff, and Julie Sedel 2025. DOI: 10.1093/oso/9780199931293.003.0007

one's professed values, and ambivalently if contradictory to them. Journalists may also produce news content that is more favorable to one side than another without any conscious intention to do so. Unbalanced coverage could be unintentionally produced by professional news gathering practices; for example, giving greater attention to some politicians over others, not because of support for their views but because of their perceived greater news value (more impactful or interesting).

In the analysis that follows, partisan slant or favorability refers to the unbalanced positive or negative tone in news coverage accorded to some political groups over others. Such patterns of coverage may or may not be the result of political instrumentalism and must be interpreted in context. Knowing both the partisan preferences of owners and audiences, we are in a position to potentially disentangle the two. However, as we will see, owner and audience partisan preferences tend to overlap.

While instrumentalism connotes intent, direct interventions by owners can be difficult to document due to their controversial character and confidentiality agreements that restrain top managers from fully revealing what they know. But political instrumentalism does not require direct owner intervention. It can be, and often is, a delegated power. As Hervé Kempf, a former editor at *Le Monde* and founder of environmental news website *Reporterre*, told us:

> There's something very simple that one must always remember. The main investor in a newspaper, in other words the newspaper's owner, names the editor-in-chief of a newspaper, who will be in ideological accord with [the owner]. This editor-in-chief will then hire the desk editors and the other journalists. It's important to always have that in mind, that's the ABCs of the functioning of the press.[5]

As in our analysis of public service orientation, we analyze the effects of ownership complexes (ownership forms, owner and audience characteristics, and primary funding) on the production of news, but with a tighter focus on coverage of political actors. We also consider two potentially countervailing constraints: journalistic professional standards—as expressed and enforced by prominent journalists or journalistic organizations—that may promote homogenization across the field; and contingent organizational legacies and circumstances that may increase variation within ownership forms and complexes.

In this chapter, we first draw on our interviews and other qualitative and quantitative data to explore the mechanisms linking these structural and social factors to practices of political instrumentalism. Drawing on a quantitative analysis of mentions of political actors, we then seek to answer the following questions, with a focus on variation across ownership complexes: Comparing the left and right, broadly defined, who gets the most attention? Who is mentioned most favorably? And how great is the imbalance in partisan favorability between left and right: in other words, how *intensely* partisan is the coverage?

Ownership Forms

Are some ownership forms more amenable than others to political instrumentalism? As programming director of Sweden's public television channel, *SVT* (at the time of our interview), as well as former editor-in-chief and CEO of the country's largest circulation newspaper, *Aftonbladet*, Jan Helin can answer the question based on direct experience. Both commercial and public media, he says, are "risk constructions." For Helin, the primary risk for commercial media is not so much about political instrumentalism, but rather that they will become too profit-driven, not invest as they need to in quality, and "sell out" (as discussed in Chapters 3 and 4). The "risk in public service [media]," he continues, "is of course that it is a political framework."[6]

On a global level, state-established and citizen-funded ownership is, in fact, the largest form of ownership for legacy television news, and it is often used in authoritarian societies to promote the interests of the party in power. For this reason, some scholars have dismissed this form of ownership as very politically instrumentalist on behalf of ruling elites.[7] This line of analysis ignores how state "rational-legal" authority—essentially, laws and regulations limiting partisan intervention—has been effectively deployed over decades in many countries to protect the "arms-length" autonomy of public media.[8] Nevertheless, Helin is of course correct to emphasize the risk of political influence. If adequate firewalls are not maintained, government "capture" is an ever-present danger. No government, whether left or right, is immune from the temptation to control the media to preserve its power. In recent years, this threat has become most evident in the rise of populist right parties in many countries (including many supposedly strong democracies) that have sought to weaken, abolish, or transform public media into a direct instrument for their partisan ends.[9]

It would seem that in Sweden, as Helin also emphasizes, this political risk for the moment has been largely forestalled. *SVT* has historically been protected by a right–left consensus on the importance of public media and by legal, administrative, and funding buffers that maintain this arms-length relationship between the public broadcaster and the political party in power at any given moment.[10] The norm, Helin said, is even against government ministers calling to complain about *SVT* news coverage, although in recent years some national populist Sweden Democrat party legislators have done so. Johan Lindén, a former *SVT* commissioning editor, likewise stresses the political consensus that has maintained strong support for Swedish public media. If that were to ever break down, he says, *SVT* and *SR* could be vulnerable. Parliament could at any time vote to abolish the public media. But this vulnerability has not induced greater "caution" on the part of public media journalists, Lindén says, at least not yet.[11]

In France and the US, for different reasons, public media are often subject to political pressures, especially through the appointment of directors and budgeting.[12] French public radio and television are "hyper-controlled" in their budgeting, a former CEO of *Radio France* relates, with every expense reviewed by a "state controller" installed inside the organization.[13] In addition, there is continual surveillance by legislative commissions, government ministries, and the regulative agency CSA (High Council for the Audiovisual; reconstituted as of 2022 as ARCOM, Regulatory Authority for Audiovisual and Digital Communication).[14] The government also retains the right to, at any time, suppress or reduce budget allocations, which opens the door to political pressure: this happened when *France 2* broadcast a documentary show on the government's controversial temporary work contract to encourage businesses to reduce unemployment among young people. The *France 2* show had used a supplementary budget that the channel had requested from the Budget ministry. As a former *France Télévisions* editor-in-chief recalls of the broadcast:

> It was very, very good, but they had decided it was totally hostile to the government. The Budget minister at that time, Nicolas Sarkozy, said to [the head of public *France Télévisions*]: "That was a great show, it was really great . . . but as for your budget extension, I'm sure you can make do without it!" So, that's it, it's more or less visible, more or less said.[15]

While President of the Republic (from 2007 to 2012), Sarkozy changed the law to allow direct presidential appointment of public media directors. When the *Radio France* director he hired subsequently fired a comic who had made political jokes at Sarkozy's expense, suspicions were raised that the director had acted in response to presidential pressure. The director has vigorously denied the accusation, but what is certain is that the shift to direct presidential appointment undermined public belief in the political independence of French public media.[16] After Sarkozy left office, the right to appoint directors of public media was restored to the CSA (now ARCOM). Subsequent directors of *France Télévisions* say that they have received political pressure from the president's office even as they minimize its threat to their "independence."[17]

Similarly, US public media—*PBS NewsHour* television and *NPR* legacy radio and their websites, the national faces of a highly decentralized system—are vulnerable to political pressure from the party in power. The Corporation for Public

Broadcasting (CPB), the quasi-governmental agency that distributes funds, is also charged with monitoring the "objectivity and balance of all programs or series of programs of a controversial nature."[18] Republican legislators have frequently used the annual budget appropriations process to complain about public media's "liberal" (left) bias. According to the *New York Times*, under George W. Bush's Republican administration from 2001 to 2009, the CPB chairperson "jokingly" told local members of the Association of Public Television Stations that their programming should "better reflect the Republican mandate," and he successfully pressured PBS to create a new public affairs program, *The Journal Editorial Report*, hosted by the editor of the *Wall Street Journal*'s conservative editorial pages.[19] Hostilities between the executive branch and public TV and radio resumed under the Trump administration from 2017 to 2021.[20]

According to the "indexing" hypothesis, news media as a whole will follow the lead of the party or parties in power in setting the news agenda.[21] However, indexing may vary across the journalistic field, depending on proximity to the state. Public media, therefore (even if protected by arms-length regulations), might feel subtly pressured to index their coverage (including the amount and valence of mentions) more closely to the party in power than other media. Some conservative and populist right critics accuse public media of having a left-leaning "bias," regardless of the party in power.[22] Alternatively, regulatory constraints requiring balanced treatment by public media of all political actors may tend to minimize strong political instrumentalism.[23] Perhaps because of such constraints, either regulatory or self-imposed, surveys have shown that public media are among those "most trusted" by the public.[24]

What of the "opposite" of public media described by Helin—commercial ownership? Is the main "risk construction" for commercial media only that they will turn away from politics in favor of crime and celebrity news? Before this question can be answered, it is important to distinguish between market and private ownership forms. While an earlier wave of research emphasized how the profit-maximizing impulse of stock market-traded media led them to ignore politics in favor of entertaining or sensational fare (partially confirmed by our research, as reported in Chapter 5),[25] in recent years the profit potential of "opinion" journalism and new formats and styles of analysis that tread the border between news and commentary has become increasingly apparent.[26] Thus, under market ownership, profit pressures may also contribute to partisan imbalance, especially in patterns of attention to the politicians who are the most extreme and provocative.

Private ownership by families or individuals, along with the stock market dominant shareholder subform, brings to the fore the "amenity potential" of either replacing or supplementing a profit-maximizing orientation with other goals, such as promoting a particular ideology, party, or politician. Most owners are reluctant to admit using a media property for such purposes, but a few have done little to hide their intentions. In addition to Vincent Bolloré (as mentioned in the Introduction), notable examples include Rupert Murdoch and the late Serge Dassault.

Murdoch's penchant for using his media properties to advance his political interests was evident from the moment he entered the US market, most notably when he purchased the *New York Post* in 1976 and immediately transformed its editorial line from moderate-liberal to hard-core conservative, as well as making it substantially more sensational in its use of headlines and images.[27] Coordination between *Fox News* and Republican President Trump and top administration officials—especially on the news commentary shows—has been well documented.[28] One historian insists that Murdoch's News Corporation is sui generis in its willingness to privilege politics over business concerns (such as at the *New York Post*, which has lost more than $100 million).[29] During his early years in the US, however, Murdoch also owned the *Village Voice*, and ultimately was convinced that "the paper's radical views were essential to its success" and "did not seek to impose a conservative editor."[30] At *Fox News*, Murdoch has been able to combine political instrumentalism and profit maximization: he and his lieutenants (for many years, led by former Republican political consultant Roger Ailes) have developed increasingly sophisticated "data-driven" strategies to provide the entertaining and ideologically reinforcing news and views that will "build and hold" their conservative audience.[31]

Upon assuming ownership of *Le Figaro* in 2004, Serge Dassault, the dominant shareholder of the stock market conglomerate Dassault, made his conservative partisan views and intentions for the newspaper abundantly clear: "For me, it's important to own a newspaper to express my opinion as well as to be able to respond to certain [critical] journalists."[32] In another interview with a radio station, Dassault said that "newspapers should diffuse sane ideas . . . ideas that work. The ideas of the left are not sane ideas."[33] Former *Le Figaro* editor-in-chief Nicolas Beytout recalls Dassault as "a politically engaged actor": "He did not intervene in the daily editorial line and in the daily treatment of news, but he himself defined the editorial line. It's easy enough, because of his political activity, this line was easily seen. He is a UMP [conservative party] senator."[34] Indeed, according to Beytout, Dassault took care not to physically visit or even call the newsroom. However, every week he summoned a group of editors and managers to his corporate office for an hour-long meeting that included discussion of both commercial and editorial matters, including how to handle specific topics.[35]

For Dassault and Murdoch, the stock market dominant shareholder ownership subform provides flexibility to use news outlets as an "instrument for personal expression."[36] While the direction of partisan slant of such outlets may vary

(*Fox News* and *Le Figaro* toward the right, the *New York Times* toward the left, etc.), we might expect that partisan *intensity* will be higher under "concentrated" stock market dominant shareholder (or private) ownership than at "dispersed" widely held stock market-traded or public media ownership forms in which either the search for profit or the adherence to civic missions will be paramount.[37]

Archival research of the letters of *New York Times* publisher/owner Arthur H. Sulzberger during the late 1950s and early 1960s offers strong evidence of owner political interventions: Sulzberger communicated frequently with his editor-in-chief to impose a political slant (both liberal and conservative) on news and opinion articles.[38] This kind of owner micromanaging of content decisions may be less common today, although ultimately the only persons who know for sure are the owners themselves and the highest-level managers and editors. Long-time *Washington Post* editor Len Downie relates that publisher/dominant shareholder Donald Graham made clear on multiple occasions that the editor was free to make journalistic decisions as he saw fit, even if Graham disagreed, and Downie did in fact occasionally diverge from the publisher's wishes.[39] Similarly, former *Washington Post* editor-in-chief Marty Baron has insisted on multiple occasions that current owner Jeff Bezos was never involved in news decision-making.[40]

Civil society-owned media, especially in Sweden and France, are generally more forthright about their political purposes. Rather than serving as the partially concealed amenity potential for a commercial owner, political instrumentalism for civil society-owned media is often openly mission-driven.

Sweden has a long tradition of party-controlled or affiliated newspapers, which has somewhat continued through foundation ownership. Why do foundations historically linked to the Liberal party own newspapers? The same answer was repeated by many of our interviewees: to ensure the "everlasting publication" of a newspaper that will promote "liberal" values and causes.[41] As Swedish media analyst Olle Lidbom puts it, all the liberal foundations have an ideological goal, and the goal is to "keep a liberal debate alive."[42]

Nevertheless, liberal foundation-owned papers often stress their "independence" from the party. Editor-in-chief of the liberal foundation-owned newspaper *Gefle Dagblad*, Anna Gullberg, identifies the paper's identity as "independent liberal" with a "liberal perspective of the world." But she acknowledges there can be tensions when you have an owner who is "closely tied to the [Liberal] party" with foundation board members who are or have been active politicians. "It easily happens in such circumstances," she says, "that situations arise where there are expectations on the newspaper to adopt a certain position for a party rather than to have a more independent view . . . there is a conflict between expectations and independence."[43]

Foundation boards have a great deal of discretion, however, to interpret the meaning of party values, as well as additional policy issues central to the foundation when it was originally formed. For *Norran*, anti-alcohol temperance had long been a major cause, but in recent years the foundation has re-interpreted it in a way that broadens the scope to accommodate both changing public mores and the economic need to take grocery store advertisements that include alcohol. As former *Norran* CEO Anders Westermark explains:

> We used to be very strict, there were to be no alcohol [ads] at all. We've eased up on that a bit. If we are to have grocery ads we have to be able to combine them with ads for alcohol. . . . The document of origin stipulates that we are to take a sobriety-friendly stance. This has been revised, and today we focus on protecting the public health in a broad way.[44]

In a follow-up interview, Westermark offered another illustration of *Norran*'s new approach to temperance, "Sober October initiatives": "We go out in the local society and say, try to be sober for October. Only, not because we . . . like to point a finger at you but because we think it's healthy for you to reflect on your relationship with alcohol. That's a very typical *Norran* thing."[45] On other local issues "important to the region," such as an initiative to build a railway connecting the city to other regions, Westermark says that *Norran* "takes a clear stand" and even "runs campaigns in different ways."[46] As a civil society-owned commercial newspaper, *Norran* thus continually seeks to articulate its ideological and civic preoccupations with the search for profitability.

Even when there is direct party involvement, as with the French Communist Party (PCF)'s dominant shareholder influence over *L'Humanité*, there may be intense internal debates about political positioning. After the fall of communism in eastern Europe and the Soviet Union, beginning in 1989, the newspaper struggled financially. Thus, in the wake of France's widespread social protests of 1995, *L'Humanité* Director Pierre Zarka sought to broaden the paper's appeal to include readers affiliated with other parties and trade unions on the left. Around the same time, the newspaper began allowing the hiring of journalists without ties to the communist party.[47] While these measures helped increase circulation, they ultimately brought about Zarka's firing in 2000. As Zarka recalls, the PCF considered that it was the "depository of communism, and thus, anything situated outside of itself, was by definition, not communism; the party felt that *L'Humanité* should be its megaphone" and that he thus had to be fired because his editorial approach would "lead to [the party's] political ruin."[48] In the years since, as the PCF's collapse as a significant party has become seemingly permanent, *L'Humanité* has actually continued in the path that Zarka initiated, becoming an important "opinion newspaper" of the left, even as relations to the PCF remain close.[49]

Each national journalistic field also has at least one major religious news outlet: the *Christian Science Monitor* in the US, *La Croix* in France, and *Dagen* in Sweden. There seem to be important similarities across countries among the church-owned news outlets, both in a spiritually motivated concern with humanitarian issues and in a restrained, non-sensationalist approach to the news. As Clay Jones, the *Christian Science Monitor*'s chief editorial writer, summarized: "We consider ourselves a publication for the [family] home," connoting a socially conservative or at least cautious approach to the news. Top editors of the newspaper are typically members of the Christian Science church, and while the church does not tell the journalists what to write, a member of the Church's board must pre-approve all editorials and editorial cartoons before they are published.[50]

At *La Croix* (*The Cross*), ownership by the Catholic Assumptionist Order-controlled Bayard company manifests itself in a Catholic perspective on certain sensitive topics, such as abortion, euthanasia, bioethics, or same-sex partnerships, and through a commitment to prioritizing news about religion, especially Catholicism, with some room, however, for critical views. Just as important as any particular position, the newspaper emphasizes—both in its news coverage and its internal culture—a "spirit of The Cross" marked by humility and the search for consensus.[51] Asked about the newspaper's political line, Director Dominique Quinio stressed a general focus on social problems, and said that the newspaper had distanced itself from any particular "vision of politics" in response to a perception that its readers had become less politically engaged than they were in the past.[52]

Sweden's *Dagen*, owned by the Norwegian Mentor Medier company (whose major shareholders include evangelical or "Free" churches) and founded by the same person (Lewi Pethrus) who co-founded Sweden's conservative Christian Democrats party, focuses on news with relevance to "Christian values" or that can be given a "Christian" angle.[53] Felicia Ferreira, *Dagen*'s editor in-chief since 2013, argues that *Dagen* works hard to avoid "benefitting any particular party."[54] According to *Dagen* former digital editor (2007–2009) Emanuel Karlsten, however, the newspaper did not in his view always live up to the journalistic ideals he embraced. Karlsten joined *Dagen* because he "admired the courage of the newspaper, doing journalism about the church, investigating the things that the church couldn't investigate themselves." He left after three years, he said, when it seemed clear to him that he had unwittingly become "part of the opposite thing, putting a lid on things that should be open [and] it was a few more of those kinds of things that made me say 'I can't be a part of this.'"[55]

As noted in Chapter 2, US philanthropy-supported nonprofit outlets tend to avoid any overt partisanship due to regulations governing eligibility for 501(c)(3) association status, which allows a nonprofit news organization owned by such an association to avoid paying taxes if it can show that it essentially performs an "educational" role. As Joel Kramer, co-founder and CEO/editor of *MinnPost*, stressed, "We don't have institutional positions that represent the views of *MinnPost* at all. We do [publish] opinion pieces, but they don't represent *MinnPost*."[56] At *Voice of San Diego*, Editor Andrew Donohue articulated a political engagement for the outlet that likewise avoids clear partisan identities: "I don't think we have an overarching political ideal but an overwhelming sense of justice of going after whatever needs to be investigated . . . [of course] people will see [our projects] through their political constructs. We have a bias but it's more just about, we think things can get better. So we push, but it's not going to happen from a right wing/left wing perspective."[57]

In the journalistic content produced by civil society-owned outlets, we should expect variation depending on the specific institutional logics that predominate, notably religious, journalistic professional, or partisan-community. As we saw, Swedish foundation-owned newspapers exist to promote a political line. Likewise, historic party-affiliated newspapers, like France's *L'Humanité*, or trade union-funded outlets, like Sweden's *Dagens Arena*, openly express a strong political instrumentalist purpose. It seems likely that such foundation-, party-, or trade union-connected outlets will exhibit a strong partisan content slant. US nonprofits established by former legacy journalists well-practiced in the conventions of "objective" reporting and further constrained by the 501(c)(3) restrictions on political endorsements may be expected to avoid any impression of political slant.

Situating News Outlets in the Political Space

How does the variation in partisan preferences of journalists, audiences, and owners relate to the direction and intensity of partisan slant in the news?

Survey data has shown that journalists, like most other cultural professionals, tend to lean toward the center-left politically.[58] At *TF1*, widely perceived to be on the right, former Director Patrick Le Lay dismissed accusations that *TF1* had a right-wing bias by insisting that "the vast majority of [our] journalists lean left."[59] But if journalists are mostly left-leaning, such relatively uniform attitudes can do little to help explain variation across ownership forms or particular news outlets.

A more robust scholarly debate concerns the relative influence of owners versus audiences. This research has attempted to juxtapose data on partisan preferences of audiences (or potential audiences) versus owners' publicly stated partisan preferences or donations. A number of surveys have identified differences in the partisan preferences of audiences across a range of media outlets (see Methods Appendix and Online Appendix Tables, Series 2.2 and 2.4). Even if owners do not expressly state that they control the political slant of the outlets they control—as was the case with *Le Figaro*'s dominant shareholder Dassault—we can reasonably assume that they will nevertheless exercise indirect political influence through their selection of top editors. Audience partisan preference may correlate with the partisan slant of news both because audiences will tend to seek out news that confirms their pre-existing beliefs and because media outlets generate revenues by appealing to their audience's beliefs.[60] Commentators and editorial writers may also seek to achieve accordance between owner and audience views through the persuasive power of their writing. But research suggests that even the most overtly partisan media tend to reinforce and intensify rather than fundamentally change audience partisan attitudes.[61]

Economists Matthew Gentzkow and Jesse M. Shapiro conducted a study of news articles in 433 newspapers with regional monopolies representing seventy-four percent of total US daily newspaper circulation. They found that consumer partisan preferences (as measured by voting records by postal code in each newspaper's geographic circulation area) accounted for about twenty percent of the measured political slant in newspaper content, as opposed to only four percent attributable to owners' political ideology, as proxied by their political campaign donations.[62] The study's value for understanding ownership and audiences in the contemporary nationalized digital media environment, however, is limited by the authors' exclusion of digital-only outlets operating across geographic regions, their reliance on local population statistics as proxies for audience data rather than actual audience data, and their lack of consideration of funding models established by owners, a factor that did not vary significantly in their sample (given the overwhelming dominance of advertising during the early 2000s) but does today.

Another hypothesis of how audience political leanings shape news coverage is offered by Harvard legal scholar Yochai Benkler and colleagues. In their book *Network Propaganda*, they suggest that media in the US with left-leaning audiences will be less partisan overall than media with right-leaning audiences. They argue that media outlets with left-leaning audiences (disproportionately composed of highly educated professionals) still adhere to professional norms of fact-based reporting and balance and are sensitive to audience criticisms of any violation of such norms. In contrast, media outlets catering to conservatives—led by *Fox News* and its more radical offshoots—provide readers information that confirms their pre-existing partisan biases, reject the separation of news versus opinion, and compete with other media not by calling out errors of factual truth but rather deviance from information that is identity confirming.[63] Their analysis does not question that there may be partisan tendencies in media with left-leaning audiences, but it suggests that the partisan "intensity" (the degree of one-sidedness) may be higher at media with right-leaning audiences.

Funding-Audience Adjustment Strategies

Just as funding-audience adjustment strategies can shape public service orientation, they can also have direct or indirect associations with political instrumentalism and partisanship.

Media executives and editors that most sharply deny any political instrumentalism or partisanship often work for mass audience media whose economic model requires them to reach across partisan lines. As Étienne Mougeotte, *TF1*'s former programming director, told us:

> You can't cut yourself off from a big part [of the audience]. The left is 50 percent. When things are better for them, it's 52, when things are bad it's 43 or 45. Well, well . . . maybe the left will even get 53 percent [and win the election]. So you can't produce a program, which is addressed to the greatest number, by taking strong political positions.[64]

Similarly, at *ABC News*, as noted in Chapter 4, the "cardinal rule" is to adopt a "milquetoast voice" and to avoid any strong political positioning that could lead some audience members to "change the channel."[65] For similar cautious reasons, the large audience national news daily *USA Today*, owned by the stock market-traded Gannett chain, has long declined to make presidential endorsements.[66] Large scale omnibus public media, such as *France 2* and Sweden's *SVT*, are doubly determined to adopt a nonpartisan approach by both their public service missions and their mass audience aspirations,[67] and for this reason should resemble in this aspect other omnibus media, even profit-maximizing stock market-traded media.

Beyond these legacy national mass media—and some regional outlets that embrace a more neutral approach (such as most Swedish regional newspapers,[68] *Ouest-France*, etc.)—heightened partisanship has become an important way for news outlets to differentiate themselves in the highly competitive cable, online, and social media environment. As political scientist Markus Prior has powerfully demonstrated, in high choice media environments, many people choose not to consume news at all and the news consumers who remain tend to be highly partisan and seek out news that affirms their pre-existing views.[69] In US cable news, *Fox News* was the first to carve out a strong partisan identity. Stock market conglomerate-owned *CNN* and *MSNBC* maintained for a while a more neutral positioning, steadily losing audience share to *Fox News*. Gradually, their corporate owners realized that liberal-left counterprogramming provided the most effective commercial response to *Fox News*'s dominance.[70]

Partisanship for some news outlets can thus serve not only a non-financial amenity potential but also be a savvy strategy to increase audiences and profits. We see this strategic approach to making the most of a media outlets' partisan reputation at the Swedish liberal-conservative newspaper *Svenska Dagbladet*, owned by the stock market-traded Schibsted company. As former Editor-in-Chief Fredric Karén analyzed the newspaper's "bourgeois" (close to the Moderate Party) partisan reputation:

> I always maintained throughout my years as editor-in-chief that I saw it as an advantage—from a marketing perspective, as there are an abundance of liberal newspapers in Sweden. And our biggest competitor *Dagens Nyheter* is liberal. . . . The incredibly competitive situation that exists in this market means that you have to be conspicuous, it needs to be [a] conspicuous, "value proposition in the market" as they say in English.[71]

Digital native news websites, like *KIT* or *BuzzFeed*, may also adopt partisan identities, in their cases that sync with the young audiences they seek to reach. Their politics, congruent with their youthful audiences, are often identical to their commercial strategies (see the discussion in Chapter 4). *KIT*, according to former News Editor Martin Schori, sought to create a "modern media product" for "a highly educated and modern target audience," with a clear partisan stance on topics such as climate change, racism, and the populist right Sweden Democrats.[72]

Likewise, for *BuzzFeed* founder Jonah Peretti, "Content is about identity."[73] After conducting research about its eighteen- to thirty-five-year-old audience, *BuzzFeed News* not only decided to invest heavily in reporting on LGBTQ rights, gay marriage, and other gender and sexuality issues, but also to take "a side and [come] out slugging," abandoning any notions of "equivalency and objectivity."[74] This partisan content strategy (never fully pursued because of editor Ben Smith's resistance) might have been commercially successful if *BuzzFeed* had been able to continue to grow digital advertising revenues. This path was blocked as the platforms (Google and Facebook) driving traffic effectively cornered more than three-quarters of the online advertising market and changed the algorithms in ways that disadvantaged *BuzzFeed*'s content.[75] Another limitation for the mass audience strategy is that even though partisanship may generate large audiences, cautious advertisers often make it clear that they do not want to be associated with such content, thus serving as a brake on the most extreme or intense partisanship.[76] As discussed in Chapter 4, *HuffPost*'s brand of left-leaning party politics has always sat uneasily with its commercial aspirations for profitability.

In contrast, as many elite media outlets come to rely more and more on subscribing audiences, they will face incentives to make their news content more partisan as one important means to attract and keep audiences who are paying, in part, for news that confirms rather than challenges their biases. Thus, media funded entirely (*Mediapart*) or mostly by subscribing audiences (such as *Svenska Dagbladet*) or activist-linked donations (*Dagens Arena*) may have significantly higher partisan intensity than media funded entirely or mostly by advertising. *Dagens Arena*'s funding model, heavily reliant on donations from the trade union LO along with other activists, tends to reinforce partisan journalism. These donations push *Dagens Arena* to be more partisan, to take strong "progressive, radical, independent" stances on its leader page, according to Editor-in-Chief Jonas Nordling. Such economic incentives for partisanship, however, are fully in sync with Nordling's own partisan self-identity and his sense of *Dagens Arena*'s mission.[77]

Nonprofit media have been shown to use audience metrics to make "editorial decisions" less often than market-driven commercial media.[78] A key variable for the leading US nonprofits, which are in almost all cases effectively journalist-controlled, is the extent of their reliance on large-scale funding from local and national/international philanthropic foundations. What kind of political agenda do these funders have? One major foundation staffer said, "The truth is really boring . . . Our only agenda is to support journalism." Yet this same foundation official said that "some foundations do have a point of view."[79] In fact, a survey conducted by the American Press Institute found that fifty-two percent of US foundation funders of news organizations offered grants for reporting on issues in which they also had policy stances; and, while forty-three percent of foundations said they were motivated to "strengthen a free press," one out of three said that their main objective was to "advance a larger strategic agenda."[80] A subsequent Harvard/Northeastern University study found that between 2010 and 2015, only three percent of foundation funding for national news nonprofits went to explicitly conservative/right-wing news outlets, and six percent went to explicitly liberal/left-wing news outlets: the highest proportions of funding went to investigative/public affairs news outlets, thirty-nine percent; foreign/international coverage, fourteen percent; and topic-specific niche news outlets, sixteen percent.[81] Funding to encourage a certain newsworthy topic of reporting is not what we would label political instrumentalism; however, whether it ventures into this territory depends in large part on how the funding agreement is structured and what protections are set in place to ensure journalistic autonomy.

Indeed, some nonprofit news leaders are extremely sensitive to accusations of partisanship or externally influenced bias and take steps to avoid any hint of scandal, even at the risk of losing significant funding.[82] For example, while directing the *Center for Public Integrity* (*CPI*), Chuck Lewis felt that the funding the Center was receiving from the Open Society Foundations was tainted by George Soros's highly visible and substantial support for the Democratic candidate in the 2004 presidential election. Even though Soros had never attempted to steer *CPI* toward critical political reporting of the Republicans, Lewis, who recalled his childhood experience as a "Boy Scout," was sensitive to any hint of guilt by association:

> [Soros] was so focused on the election with his money and massive amounts of it, I just felt it was incongruous with me also receiving a few hundred thousand from that [source]. I just felt, given that the name of our organization, it was and is the *Center for Public Integrity*, it just didn't feel right to me. I was polite. I just said, thank you so much. You've always been so supportive. I think we're going to pass this year and I tried to be gentle. Well, that didn't go over well.... Soros was apoplectic. I mean, absolutely livid.... And then from that day on, he never spoke to me. It was painful and we didn't get several hundred grand that would have been helpful, but I sort of thought it was the right thing to do, but it's, those are hard decisions, really hard.[83]

After *CPI* declined Open Society's money, according to Lewis, the foundation did not contribute to the news organization for many years, but in recent years has resumed some funding.[84] Lewis's ability to give back a funder's money was strengthened by the fact that *CPI* had a large number of funders. In fact, the Holcomb-led Pew Research Center study of nonprofits mentioned earlier concluded that what set apart the most *non*partisan nonprofit outlets—*ProPublica*, *California Watch* (a *CIR/Reveal* partner), *MinnPost*, *Texas Tribune*, and *CT Voice*—was their greater number of funders and types of funding (reader subscriptions, advertising, events, as well as large foundation donors).[85]

Countervailing Factors: Professionalism and Organizational Contingencies

To be clear, for most commercial media outlets, political instrumentalism is exercised with some caution. Even in Sweden and France, where the mixing of politics and journalism is less taboo, restraint is generally the watchword for news organizations that want to be respected by their peers.

To operate a successful, or at least sustainable, news organization, owners need to hire reputable, competent journalists. These journalists have internalized a set of professional standards that include the need to separate news from opinion and the obligation to balance opposing voices and viewpoints. These standards have become global, with national and organizational inflections, and at no legitimate news organization can they be entirely flouted. Owners who hope to exploit the political instrumentalist amenity potential of their media outlets must be careful not to overstep these boundaries. As journalism scholar John Soloski perceptively observes, "As long as [the owner's] news policy does not force journalists to violate the norms of news professionalism, there is no reason to assume that journalists will see [organizational] news policy as a constraint on their work."[86] The question remains whether we might nevertheless see some differences across outlets in the degree of professional acceptance or resistance to political instrumentalism—related to factors such as the separation of news and opinion sections, journalistic collective action or negotiated internal agreements, and organizational legacies that owners may be hesitant to modify or else risk damaging the brand.

Political instrumentalism is most readily accepted as a practice confined to the opinion or editorial sections. In the words of American political scientist Benjamin Page, "It would be surprising if owners' and managers' values and preferences had no effect upon the overall shape of what they printed on their editorial and op-ed pages."[87] As political scientist Timothy Groseclose and economist Jeffrey Milyo concede, "there is little controversy over the slant of editorial pages; e.g., few would disagree that *Wall Street Journal* editorials are conservative, while *New York Times* editorials are liberal."[88] While owners have the final word on the hiring of all top editors, they will take a special interest in ensuring the ideological fit of the editorial page editor's views and their own. An ideological slant in editorials, consistent with the owner's views (whether that be an individual, a company, or an association) is thus generally expected and not considered professionally or civically problematic.

At the *Washington Post*, for example, a high-level editor had this to say about owner Jeff Bezos's involvement: "I think it's fair to say that he was more engaged with the editorial page [than with news]. In general, he was more engaged with what was going on in the editorial page."[89] During the 2010s, *New York Times* publisher and dominant shareholder Arthur Sulzberger Jr., was reported to rarely attend editorial page meetings except for major political endorsements and the occasional controversial issue. This did not mean that his influence, however, wasn't felt. As one *New York Times* editorial page sub-editor wryly confided, "The publisher's views are well-known."[90]

At foundation-owned *Norran*, which is openly committed to a "Liberal" political agenda, CEO Westermark clarifies that the political part of the newspaper is primarily found on the "editor's page" or "leader page" (what would be known as the editorial or opinion pages in the US).[91] In addition, the expression of political views in the "cultural" pages has long been common at many newspapers in Sweden.[92] At newspapers with a liberal tradition, there is an expectation from the foundation board that the editorial page editors "are liberal," adds Anders Frostell, chair of two Liberal party associated foundations.[93] But in cases where a liberal foundation owns newspapers with different party traditions, as Mittmedia did in 2016, he added, there would not be that expectation: "Mittmedia also owns papers with a social democratic or center [party] background. We don't care about them, but we care about the editors responsible for the liberal papers."[94] For the foundation-owned *Barometern*, according to Editor-in-Chief Anders Enström, it is the conservative foundation owner itself that insists on a strict separation of type of journalism within the newsroom: "It is [on the leader page] and nowhere else that we conduct advocacy journalism. For the rest of the newspaper, it's important that we don't express political opinions or partisanship or prejudice against any political party. Rather, we try to work as impartially and objectively and as fairly as possible."[95] Likewise, *Norran* CEO Westermark insists that "regular news" continues to abide by "classic journalistic values."[96]

However, there is evidence that the views on the opinion pages may be reflected in the news pages even without any self-conscious coordination. Page, in a comprehensive analysis of multiple outlets' coverage of the Los Angeles riots of 1991, discovered a tendency of "editorial stands to spill over into news stories," notably at the *New York Times*, the *Washington Post*, and the *Washington Times* (a seemingly much more overtly partisan outlet than the other two), in which newspapers "treated news stories in ways that conveyed a clear evaluative thrust, usually a thrust consistent with their editorial point of view."[97] Only at the (pre-Murdoch) *Wall Street Journal* did Page find a "sharp discrepancy between its editorial pages and news pages," which accords with the *Journal*'s long-standing reputation of preserving a strict separation between its conservative opinion section and its professionally edited news sections.[98]

To be clear, even if a partisan slant is somehow limited to the opinion and possibly the cultural pages that does not mean it is necessarily less impactful. Especially with the greater prominence and mixing of opinion and news in online news websites, and media outlets' promotion of opinion articles (not always clearly labeled as such) on social media, the prominence and potential influence of opinion journalism is arguably greater than ever.[99] At the *Christian Science Monitor*, for example, Chief Editorial Writer Clay Jones sees the "firewall" between news and commentary breaking down online: "That firewall isn't really evident on the web. People look at a home page and they can't tell what's objective and what's commentary, you know." The *Christian Science Monitor* has even attempted to link information and commentary more closely. Jones described "a little feature we're starting": "We have a news story and then we have a little box, 'Which way forward?' and it's about how readers say ok, we've read the analysis and the news but where is this going? So, our commentary team puts a little box together about which way forward, what might be a solution depending on how you look at it."[100]

Most "mainstream" journalists, as well as many journalists working for openly partisan outlets, value balance and fairness.[101] If one point of view is presented, opposing perspectives should be as well; if the governing party is criticized, the opposition should also be criticized. In the US, with its two-party system, journalists often speak of presenting "both sides." In France or Sweden, shaped by their multiparty parliamentary systems, journalists may embrace an ideal of "polyphony" or pluralism similar to Herbert Gans's ideal of multi-perspectival news.[102]

When owners overstep and blatantly violate norms against the politicization of news content and the need for balance, journalists may protest. In the US, given the lack of worker rights and job security, protests tend to be individual rather than collective. Sometimes they succeed, but just as often they do not, depending on the owner, the journalists, and their alignment of values and incentives. At *BuzzFeed News*, according to former Editor-in-Chief Ben Smith, founder Peretti "saw that the energy was on the militant left, and that our staff's sympathies—and his own—mostly leaned the same way. But our journalistic scruples, the impulse toward fairness and away from propaganda, sometimes handcuffed our drive for traffic." Peretti supported Smith's insistence on upholding mainstream professional standards, but the refusal to go all in politically may have played a role in *BuzzFeed News*'s ultimate shuttering.[103] In its own calculations of the proper balance between commercially successful partisanship and journalistic professional standards, *Fox News* has tended to favor the former, making it difficult for some journalists to feel at home at the news organization. Reflecting on his decision to leave *Fox News*, long-time news presenter Shepard Smith said he stayed for as long as he did in order to provide a factual counterpoint to the "mis- or disinformation" of many opinion shows. "At some point," he said, "I realized I've reached a point of diminishing returns, and I left."[104]

In France, where most national newspapers openly embrace political identities, there may nevertheless be journalistic resistance when political instrumentalism is perceived to be too manifest. In response to Étienne Mougeotte's outspoken conservative direction of *Le Figaro*, the newspaper's société de journalistes (journalists' professional association) spoke out publicly in dissent, arguing that a newspaper should "not be the political advertisement for any party, government, or President of the Republic [at that time, the conservative Nicolas Sarkozy, seeking re-election]." Mougeotte reportedly urged those journalists who were complaining to apply for a job at the left-leaning *Libération*, implicitly referencing the "conscience clause" that allows French journalists to leave (with government-paid unemployment benefits) if they find themselves ideologically marginalized by new management. Reflecting the countervailing ethos of non-ideological professionalism, the journalists responded that they were "proud of this paper which they are a part of" and "don't see themselves looking elsewhere to feel comfortable in their profession."[105] These kinds of professional protests against perceived transgressions of journalistic norms may not happen often, but when they do it seems to be at dominant shareholder or privately held outlets where owners and their appointed editors have the greatest discretion to act as they wish, even at the risk of public controversy.

While rare in the US, structural remedies may also be put in place to protect journalists from owner attempts to shape coverage (either from general ideological or self-interested economic motives). Legal and contractual protections of journalist control seem most common in France, growing out of the strongly anti-commercial thrust of post-World War II legislation that sought to correct the corruption and ethical violations that marked the country's pre-war and Vichy Occupation commercial media. These include internal journalists' or editors' professional associations, which provide journalists with a collective voice to monitor and expose owner misconduct;[106] the just-mentioned conscience clause providing state aid to journalists who wish to leave an outlet when a new owner changes its political line;[107] and ethical, not necessarily legally binding, charters according journalists independence from owner interference and the right of approval for appointment of director or sale to a new owner.[108] In the wake of the 2023 journalist strike at *Le Journal du Dimanche* to protest the owner's imposition of an editor associated with the far-right, French legislators introduced a bill designed to "protect the editorial liberty of all media soliciting state assistance": in particular, the bill would establish "the right of approval by journalists over the nomination of their editor-in-chief."[109] In Sweden, the legally instituted role of ansvarig utgivare (legally "responsible *publisher*," sometimes translated as *editor*)—generally held by the journalist editor-in-chief—provides a measure of independence from owner interference: if an owner asks the responsible publisher to do something that might result in a lawsuit, the publisher would be on firm legal grounds to refuse or resign, creating considerable public embarrassment, at the very least, for the owner.[110]

In some cases, government or voluntary company policies may be enacted to restrain both journalists and owners from political bias or any suspicion of political bias. In France, reforms in the early 2000s strengthened the autonomy of the broadcast regulator CSA (now ARCOM) to ensure that television and radio news, both public and commercial, maintain a "political equilibrium," especially during election periods.[111] In Sweden, a similar role is held by Granskningsnämnden för radio och TV (GRN).[112] Schibsted-owned *Svenska*

Dagbladet has voluntarily kept track of its own election coverage to ensure balance. As *Svenska Dagbladet* Editor-in-Chief Karén reports, "When an election campaign was in full swing, we had a large Excel sheet where we entered how much we had written about the Social Democrats, how much we had written about the left-wing, [and the other parties], and tried to put that in to proportion to their representation in parliament . . . to try to be as fair as possible." Karén added that the paper had nevertheless been criticized for being too negative in its news coverage of the "liberal-conservative" Moderate party when the prime minister was a member of that party, but explained that this was "natural" given the tendency to adopt a "slightly more critical attitude toward those parties that are actually in the government, as they are in power and are more severely scrutinized as a consequence."[113]

In the US, long before Murdoch bought the *Wall Street Journal*, policies were established (and continue) at the newspaper to prevent and protect reporters from engaging openly in politics or being perceived as partisan, including a ban on participation in social movements, protest marches, petitions, and the like. In addition, as a condition of the sale to Murdoch, the Bancroft family negotiated a clause in the contract establishing an "independent committee" composed of journalists and Bancroft family members that would serve as an internal watchdog to ensure the maintenance of a strict wall between the "opinion" and "news" pages and that would need to be consulted before any change in the news or editorial page editor positions. Within a few years after the sale, questions were raised whether this "editorial integrity committee" exerted any real constraining power.[114] However, according to the *Columbia Journalism Review*, *Wall Street Journal* journalists believed that the committee played a role in Editor-in-Chief Gerard Baker's moving in 2018 to "become an editor at large" after reporter complaints that under his watch there had been a blurring of the newspaper's long-standing policy of separating news and opinion. In the aftermath, a committee member neither affirmed nor denied such a role, saying only, "We operate more or less behind the scenes.".[115]

A final factor restraining owners from changing the political line or intensifying an already existing political slant is organizational legacy. Swedish Stampen newspaper group CEO Johan Hansson stresses that owners "hire, and that's where they set the agenda." But "the agenda is often set a long, long time ago. I think the *New York Times* has probably been a liberal paper for a very long time, and it's very similar here, we've been a liberal paper since a very long time back."[116] Prospective owners are aware of a media outlets' reputation, tradition, and audience, and will likely be reluctant to make fundamental changes, unless necessary to ensure economic survival or revival.

In this understanding, the tradition of the paper is an important factor in determining what the French refer to as its "editorial line." When Schibsted purchased the Swedish *Aftonbladet* and *Svenska Dagbladet* newspapers, it preserved the social democratic line at the former and the liberal-conservative (Moderate Party) line at the latter. According to former *Aftonbladet* Editor-in-Chief (and legally responsible publisher) Helin, the company was thus responding to "a very strong tradition" at these papers. At *Aftonbladet*, even after it had obtained absolute majority control of shares, Schibsted allowed the now minority shareholder, social democratic trade union LO, to retain a veto power over the appointment of the editor of the editorial page (who in turn oversees the editor of the cultural pages).[117] Thus, even though now part of a stock market-traded conglomerate, *Aftonbladet*'s organizational tradition has exerted a kind of inertial force to maintain a social democratic slant in the editorial/opinion and cultural sections of the newspaper.

In France, former *Libération* Director Laurent Joffrin also referred to the importance of organizational legacies in limiting owner interventions. "Every newspaper has its history," he said. Long after *Libération*'s "employees had lost their shares in the capital and their voting rights," the newspaper's tradition of "employee self-management" inhibited outside investors from exerting any influence. This situation changed at the level of commercial management when Edouard de Rothschild became the majority shareholder in 2006, but even then, according to Joffrin, despite the fact that de Rothschild's personal views were conservative, he ultimately resisted external political pressures to make the long-time left-leaning newspaper cover conservative president Sarkozy more positively.[118]

Later, when the French–Israeli telecommunications entrepreneur Patrick Drahi became the dominant shareholder, former *Libération* Online Editor-in-Chief Johan Hufnagel recalls that, in his experience, Drahi "never made a single remark about the content of the newspaper." Hufnagel then recounted two exceptions. One, suggesting that the owner was more concerned with business than with politics, was when Drahi complained about an error in an "infographic" comparing numbers of subscribers to his SFR telecom company with those of a competitor. Drahi thought that SFR's numbers had been understated, but later he admitted that he was the one who was wrong. Hufnagel also recounted a trip in which a part of *Libération*'s editorial leadership went to visit Drahi in Israel:

> At that moment, we clearly understood that the editorial line of *Libération* on what was happening between Israel and Palestine was not aligned with what Patrick thought, but there were never other remarks [or] a demand for a change in the line. He knew, he knew that when he bought *Libération*, it was a newspaper of the left with very particular positions on Israel.[119]

Even so, some owners do radically change the political lines of their news outlet acquisitions. Bolloré and Murdoch are prime examples. In both cases, however, the changes tend to be most dramatic at their less elite properties, whether tabloid newspapers (Murdoch's *New York Post*) or cable TV channels (*Fox News* for Murdoch; *I-Télé*, transformed into *C-News* for Bolloré).

***

We have now taken into consideration several dimensions of ownership complexes that may shape the direction and intensity of political instrumentalism and partisan slant: ownership form, partisan preferences of owners and audiences, and funding-audience adjustment strategies. Alternatively, we have also identified countervailing factors that may minimize partisan slant across the field (regulatory constraints, journalistic professional standards) or in contingent ways depending on the news organization (reputation, individual or collective resistance, and other "local" organizational legacies and circumstances).

With these factors in mind, we now present the findings on news outlets' partisan favorability from our content analysis of fifty-one news outlets in the US, Sweden, and France.

For our analysis of slant in partisan attention and valence, we draw on the total sample of articles used for most of our public service orientation content analysis. We gathered general news, business news, and opinion articles from each news outlet's website from a "constructed business week" of five non-contiguous days, spread over a seven-month period from December 2015 to June 2016. This was a time period in which the cross-national political climates differed substantially, although left-of-center parties held national executive power in all three countries at the time. The differences, however, can help strengthen our claims. To the extent that we find consistent patterns in three national fields with distinct historical and structural characteristics, we can have greater confidence in the generalizability of our findings.

For our analysis in this chapter, we focus on mentions and valences of those mentions (positive, negative, neutral, or mixed) of a subset of actors appearing in articles: domestic political actors, including politicians, parties, and social movements specific to the US, Swedish, and French domestic political spheres and clearly identifiable as having left or right ideological affiliations in each of these national contexts. Our method thus focuses on two of the elements of political slant or "favorability" identified by political scientist Benjamin Page: selection of certain sources (actors) over others, and overtly evaluative words used to describe these sources.[120]

We examine three dimensions of partisan favorability: first, imbalances in the relative *mentions* of left or right actors; second, the *degree of favorability of right and left* actor mentions and whether on balance mentions are more favorable to the left or the right; and third, the *intensity of slant*, the degree of imbalance in favorability *regardless of the ideological direction*. For analysis of our combined three-country sample, we primarily present nationally contextualized relational indicators (based on 1–4 scales) rather than raw numbers or percentages, which may differ widely depending on the particular circumstances of each national political field at the time. As such, cross-national differences in circumstances should not cloud our analysis because our characterizations of outlets' partisan favorability will always be in relation to other outlets in the same field, responding to the same set of political field dynamics.[121]

As in the previous chapter, we parse the results by differences in ownership forms, funding-audience adjustment strategies (primary funding and audience demographics), and individual/organizational owner or audience partisan preference. We categorized audiences and owners as either leaning left, balanced, or leaning right, all relative to what left and right mean in each national field. Ownership partisan preference is coded based on any public information about the individual or ownership group's political affinities (whether financial contributions, party membership, public remarks, or mission statements); audience partisan preference is documented through audience survey and social media sharing data (see Methods Appendix for sources, and Online Appendix Tables, Series 2.2 and 2.4 for documentation).

Attention Imbalances in the Age of Trump: Political Sensationalism or Public Service?

Frequent mentions of some political actors over others can have partisan effects, even if there is no imbalance in positive or negative valence, and even if there is no political instrumentalist motivation on the part of owners or journalists. In Sweden and France, across all ownership forms, left political actors are mentioned more than right actors: nearly three times as often in Sweden (eight percent versus three percent of all actors mentioned), and twice as often in France (ten percent versus five percent). It is likely that this imbalance has much to do with the fact that left party governments were in power in both countries during our sample period of December 2015 through June 2016. Left-of-center officials were thus the "primary definers" of the news and media outlets tended to "index" news coverage to their pronouncements and agenda.[122] In this context, such an attention imbalance in favor of the left is seen as legitimate by journalists even at well-known liberal-conservative newspapers, such as Sweden's *Svenska Dagbladet*. As a former "Svenskan" publisher told us, "It's reasonable to write more about the Social Democrats and the Green Party for example, in combination, as they are presently in power."[123]

In the US, however, despite the fact that a "left" Democratic administration was still in power, right political actors dominated total coverage (making up fourteen percent of all actor mentions versus eight percent for left political actors). During the spring of 2016, US primary elections for both major party presidential nominees for the fall's general election were being held, but it was the Republican primary with the surprise success of non-politician Donald Trump's candidacy that spurred the most news interest. Was attention to this sensationalistic and divisive political figure driven by political, commercial, or even public service incentives?

Our sample of news during this highly polarized and dramatic presidential campaign primary season provides a natural case study to examine how various types of US media deemed which politicians were most "newsworthy": for this reason, we provide a deeper analysis of attention patterns only for the US case.[124] (A similar analysis could be carried out for news coverage of the populist right presidential candidate Eric Zemmour during the French presidential campaign of spring 2022).

Across all of our US outlets, mentions of Donald Trump dramatically outstripped those of all other major candidates: 685 mentions of Donald Trump, compared to 139 mentions of Hillary Clinton, 128 mentions of Ted Cruz, ninety mentions of Bernie Sanders, and sixty-three mentions of Marco Rubio.[125] This dramatic difference in attention, whether or not politically motivated, had significant political effects. As an article in the nonprofit news outlet *The Intercept* argued the spring after the election, "The media industry arguably helped Trump enormously in the early presidential campaign with extensive coverage that drowned out his competitors and left little room for discussion of the substantive policy issues facing voters."[126] What has been little discussed, however, is the extent to which news outlets varied in their focus on Trump depending on their structural characteristics.

In our sample, US stock market-traded media far exceeded all other ownership forms in mentions of Donald Trump: on average, nearly fifty mentions per news outlet, versus thirty-one per privately held outlet, ten per civil society-owned outlet, and nineteen per public media outlet (see Appendix Tables A6.1 and A6.2). We did not find a significant difference between widely held stock market-traded outlets (such as *CNN*) and those with a dominant shareholder (like the *New York Times* or *Fox News*). Some private outlets, notably the *Washington Post*, also had high Trump mentions. Journalistic practices prevalent across the US journalistic field certainly played a role in shaping news coverage. As Matt Carlson, Sue Robinson, and Seth Lewis argue, outsized coverage of Trump compared to other candidates (and news topics) can be partly attributed to "journalists' penchant for the unexpected." The ideal news story is not only important but also interesting, as political scientist Timothy Cook emphasized, and Trump "kept journalists interested."[127] Even so, CBS President Leslie Moonves's famous remark about Trump's rise—"It may not be good for America, but it's damn good for CBS"[128]—unambiguously highlights owners' awareness of the profit-generating effects of their Trump coverage. One could argue that this was simply a case where professional news judgments and audience maximizing profits coincided, and indeed it is difficult to disentangle the two. However, the tendency of profit-maximizing stock market-traded media to especially maximize attention to Trump underlines the value-added influence of economic factors.

In contrast, at the civil society-owned *Christian Science Monitor*, Donald Trump was still a big name in the news, but one among many. Civil society-owned outlets demonstrated a greater autonomy to make their own mission-driven choices in the mix of political actors mentioned: this autonomy was facilitated in some cases by religious owners eager to give voice to particular actors closer to their concerns, in other cases by journalists' sense of their audience's interests or from their negotiations with philanthropic funders who explicitly encouraged them to write about topics that involve more than the "usual suspects."

As always, other dimensions of ownership complexes must also be taken into account (see Appendix Table A6.1). We do not find any systematic or statistically significant differences in attention to Trump, or to right or left political actors in general, between media with owners or audiences with different partisan preferences. However, media outlets reliant on audience subscriber funding mentioned Trump more often than media reliant on other types of funding: forty-nine mentions on average versus forty for majority advertising-funded and thirteen for philanthropy-funded outlets. News organizations funded primarily by subscribing audiences probably felt the most intense pressure—again, reinforced and sublimated by professional practices—to provide their "political junkie" audiences with the most exciting and interesting political story of the moment.

In sum, in this particular US case study, imbalanced partisan attention to political actors seems to be driven most by commercial and professional logics rather than *strictly* partisan logics. However, in the contemporary online attention economy in which P. T. Barnum's classic dictum that "all publicity is good publicity" seems more accurate than ever, such imbalances may nevertheless have partisan effects. Criticism or praise are far from irrelevant, though, and in the next sections we turn to ownership and other mechanisms shaping the *valence* (leaning left or right) of partisan favorability and its intensity.

Partisan Favorability and Intensity

To assess favorability for left and right political actors, we first coded each mention as negative (–1), neutral (0), or positive (+1). The net balance of mentions for each outlet produces both left and right favorability scores ranging from –1, indicating that all mentions are negative, to +1, in which case all mentions are positive.[129] We then converted these negative and positive scores into 0 to 2 scales to make it easier to assess the relative balance in valence between left and right actors. Partisan favorability ratio scores were created by dividing the right favorability score by the left favorability score. Scores below 1.00 indicate a net left favorability and scores above 1.00 indicate a net right favorability. For example, the Swedish conservative foundation-owned *Barometern* has a 1.20 right favorability score and a 0.89 left favorability score: when the latter is divided into the former, the newspaper is shown to have a partisan favorability right–left ratio score of 1.35. Conversely, with a right favorability score of 0.55 and a left favorability score of 0.97 (indicating that coverage is net negative for both left and right political actors, only more so for right actors), *L'Humanité* has a partisan favorability right–left ratio score of 0.57, showing that it is significantly to the left of *Barometern*. On average, outlets are slightly more favorable to left actors than right actors. The mean partisan favorability right–left ratio score for the fifty-one-outlet sample is 0.95, with the US at 0.90, France at 0.95, thus both slightly to the left, and Sweden at 1.04, slightly to the right.

It is also useful to have a more direct comparison of the *intensity* (or degree of imbalance) of partisan favorability regardless of the direction.[130] For each outlet, we standardize the partisan favorability scores to facilitate such a comparison by dividing the lower of the right or left favorability scores into the higher. Because *Barometern*'s partisan favorability ratio score of 1.35 is above 1 (like all outlets with a net right favorability), its partisan intensity ratio score is identical to its partisan favorability ratio score. For *L'Humanité*, however, to create a comparable partisan intensity score, we need to divide its lower right favorability score of 0.55 into its higher left favorability score of 0.97, thus producing a partisan intensity ratio score of 1.75. In other words, from the partisan favorability ratio scores, we learn that *L'Humanité* is significantly to the left of *Barometern*; from the partisan intensity ratio scores, we see that *L'Humanité* is also more intensely partisan than *Barometern* (more imbalanced, regardless of the specific partisan direction).

The ratio scores reported above are based on combined news and opinion articles, consistent with audiences' typical reading habits and frequent unawareness of the distinction. Nevertheless, in deference to those journalists—and audiences—who find the difference across these genres meaningful, we report findings relevant to these distinctions. The ideological slant of news and opinion articles tends to be positively correlated and thus they lean in the same direction. If an outlet's news is favorable to the right, its opinion articles tend to be as well; the same is true, conversely, with outlets leaning left. However, opinion articles tend to be more intensely partisan than news articles: in other words, regardless of the direction of ideological slant, opinion articles at most outlets were

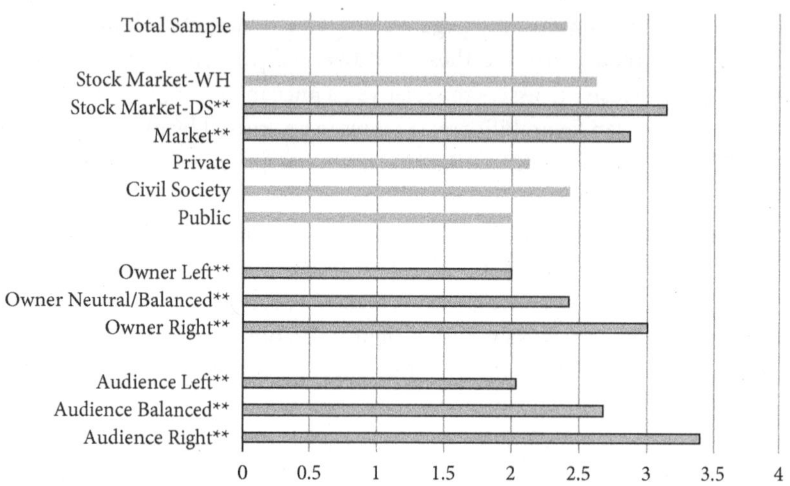

Figure 6.1 Partisan Favorability: Average Outlet 1–4 National Relational Scale by Ownership Form, and Owner and Audience Partisan Preference

A *longer bar indicates a relatively* (not absolutely) *stronger right-leaning content favorability*, while a shorter bar indicates a relatively stronger left-leaning content slant. Bars outlined in bold attain statistical significance. Ownership form differences are significant vis-à-vis all other outlets; owner and audience category differences are significant vis-à-vis each other: $^*p \leq .10$, $^{**}p \leq .05$, $^{***}p < .005$.

more imbalanced than news articles, favoring one side more lopsidedly than the other.[131]

As in our analysis of public service news, we transform these raw favorability and intensity scores into national relational scales: for each outlet, a nationally standardized 1–4 point scale indexed to standard deviations below and above the national mean. Such a scale shows how a media outlet differs from all other news outlets in the same national field, thus avoiding distortion in our combined three-country findings due to contingent national differences in partisan politics during a particular time period. In Figures 6.1 and 6.2, we present the results for the national relational scales: partisan favorability (i.e., direction, with lower scores more left leaning and higher scores more right leaning) and partisan intensity regardless of direction. The bars are organized by four dimensions of ownership complexes: ownership forms, owner partisan preference, audience partisan preference, and primary funding.

In Figure 6.1, a longer bar indicates a *relatively* (not absolutely) stronger right-leaning content favorability, while a shorter bar indicates a relatively stronger left-leaning content slant. Outlets with scores of 2 or 3 may have relatively balanced left-right valence ratios: the closer the mean scores get to the extremes of 1 and 4, the greater the certainty of distinct partisan slants.

The only ownership form that is significantly associated with a more right-leaning favorability is market ownership, especially with a stock market dominant shareholder (SM-DS). This slight right-leaning favorability cannot be easily explained by a consistent "amenity potential" exercised by right-leaning dominant shareholders: in our sample, stock market dominant shareholders are evenly split between left-leaning (2), neutral/balanced (3), and right-leaning (2). It might, however, be due to a cautiously right orientation of market ownership, with its greater tendency to rely on advertising: indeed, advertising primary funding is linked to higher right-leaning favorability, although the difference with other types of funding is not statistically significant (see Appendix Tables A6.1 and A6.2).

Do owners or audiences shape the direction of partisan favorability more? We find that owner and audience partisan preferences move parallel to one another: partisan favorability in content moves from left to right as both owners and audiences move from left to right. Both are statistically significant at similar levels ($p < .05$), although the gap between left and right favorability produced by differences in audience partisan preferences is slightly larger than for differences in owner preferences. No type of funding is associated with statistically significant differences in the direction of partisan favorability. However, there is a link between primary funding, audience partisan preference, and partisan favorability that demonstrates the shaping role of ownership. As Chapter 4 showed, owners and their appointed managers play an important role in deciding whether and how to appeal to particular audiences, for either commercial or mission-driven ideological purposes. In fact, funding-audience adjustment strategy plays an important role in shaping how *much* audience partisan preference is associated with outlet partisan favorability. At outlets where owners/managers have chosen an audience subscription funding strategy, the differences in partisan favorability between outlets with left, neutral, or right-leaning audiences is substantially greater than at outlets with other types of funding (advertising, philanthropy, or public).[132]

Does government support via public funding or partial subsidies lead media that receive such support to be less critical of the government, which during our sample period was left-leaning in all three countries? In fact, public media, along with public funding and philanthropic funding, are associated with more left-leaning favorability scores, but the differences with all other media are not statistically significant. *NPR* is evenly balanced and Swedish public radio *SR* leans slightly right, while *PBS*, *SVT*, and both French public radio and TV lean slightly left. Newspapers that receive significant public subsidies have scores nearly identical to the overall sample mean.

Favorability toward business actors in the entire sample partially parallels media treatment of right political actors.[133] Market and religious ownership are most favorable toward business. Business favorability is higher for media outlets with right-leaning owners (and to a slightly lesser extent with right-leaning audiences) than for balanced or left-leaning owners (and audiences): in other words, while the patterns for partisan slant and pro-business slant are similar, owners seem to have a relatively stronger influence (compared to audiences) on business coverage than they do on political coverage. Current/legacy journalist-controlled and partisan-affiliated outlets, along with those that receive press subsidies, are the least favorable toward business (see Appendix Tables A6.1 and A6.2).

In our explanations of the *particular* ideological direction of partisan slant of outlets, it makes sense as we have shown that individual owner or audience partisan preference often play the greatest role in shaping journalistic content. But what factors shape the *intensity* of partisan imbalance, regardless of its particular direction? To review, four major claims have been offered for partisan intensity: *amenity potential* (thus highest at stock market dominant shareholder, privately held, or civil society-owned outlets, where owners have the greatest discretion); *profit focus* (profit incentives to pander to partisan audiences, thus highest with market ownership); *audience partisan preferences* (higher at media appealing to right-leaning than left-leaning audiences because of a lesser concordance between political and journalistic neutral professional values on the right than on the liberal/left), and *funding model* (higher at media directly funded by audiences than at those with other primary funding).

Looking at Figure 6.2, we find some support for the amenity potential over the profit maximization hypothesis. Stock market-traded media (especially those

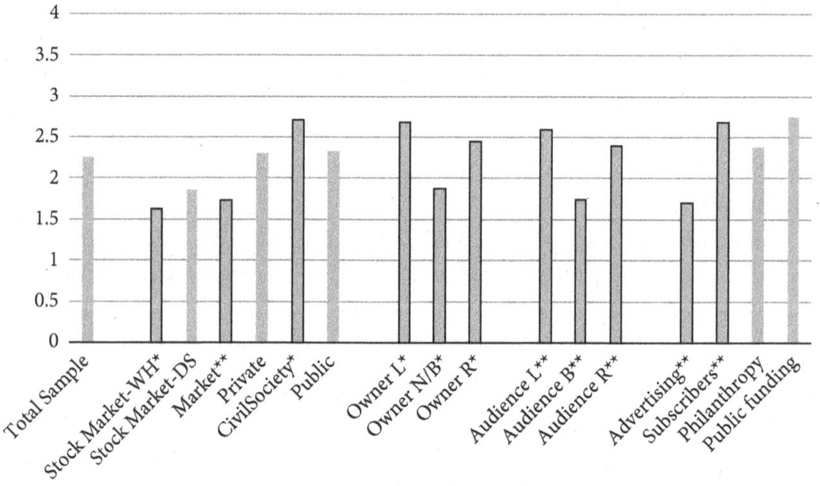

Figure 6.2 Partisan Intensity: Average Outlet 1–4 National Relational Scale by Ownership Form, Owner and Audience Partisan Preference, and Primary Funding

Partisan intensity refers to the degree of imbalance in partisan favorability *regardless of the ideological direction*. Bars outlined in bold attain statistical significance. Ownership form differences are significant vis-à-vis all other outlets; owner, audience, and primary funding category differences are significant vis-à-vis each other: $^{*}p \leq .10$, $^{**}p \leq .05$, $^{***}p < .005$.

that are widely held) have the lowest partisan intensity. Civil society-owned media, driven by non-economic motivations, including political influence in some cases, have the highest partisan intensity. However, while privately held and stock market dominant shareholder-owned media also offer amenity potential affordances, they are not significantly different in their partisan intensity from other ownership forms or the overall average. Similar to the particular left or right slant, partisan intensity is significantly associated with both owner and audience partisan preferences. However, for intensity, the main difference is not between left and right, but rather between audiences or owners with *any* partisan preference versus those who are neutral or balanced. In other words, owners or audiences with partisan preferences of any direction are associated with outlets that are more intensely partisan; when owners or audiences do not express a clear partisan preference, their associated media outlets likewise are likely to be more neutral or balanced. This finding partially counters Benkler and colleagues' expectation that right-leaning media will be more intensely partisan than left-leaning media.[134] Finally, funding model is strongly associated with partisan intensity. News outlets primarily reliant on audience subscription funding have significantly higher partisan intensity than outlets mostly reliant on advertising. (Public funding for Swedish and French public media is also associated with higher-than-average levels of partisan intensity, but the difference with all other outlets is not statistically significant.)

Conclusion

In this chapter, we explored the practices of political instrumentalism as they vary across ownership forms and funding-audience adjustment strategies. We documented how owners have exploited the amenity potential of media outlets to influence political news coverage either directly or indirectly. We also showed how considerations of funding and target audiences provide economic incentives to politically slant the news. Conversely, we discovered ways in which political instrumentalism may be constrained. Professional journalistic resistance, either formal or informal, as well as organizational legacies and branding provide countervailing forces to overly one-sided political coverage.

As a driver of attention to political actors, ownership form and funding models, at least in the US, both seem to play a crucial role. In the midst of a sensationalized party primary, US media with profit-maximizing stock market ownership and/or reliant on audience subscription funding were the most likely to highlight controversial Republican candidate Donald Trump.

The extent to which a news outlet's content is more favorable to the right or left is also partially related to ownership form: outlets with stock market dominant shareholder ownership were more right-leaning than other outlets. Owner and audience partisan preferences, however, were a stronger predictor of left or right favorability. Unlike previous studies that have identified audience preferences as being a significantly stronger predictor of partisan slant, we found little difference between the two: as both owner and audience partisan preference moved from left to right, journalistic content moved in parallel. Reliance on audience subscription funding, a strategy related to ownership power, strengthened the association between audience partisan preference and partisan favorability.

Partisan intensity, the degree of imbalance in relative favorability whether left or right, in contrast, is highest at outlets with civil society ownership and lowest at stock market-traded outlets (especially widely held), suggesting that amenity potential rather than profit maximization is the stronger driving factor. Audience subscription funding is associated with partisan intensity to a much greater degree than advertising. As with favorability, intensity is associated with both owner and audience partisan preferences, in this case differentiating owners and audiences with both left or right partisan preferences from those with balanced or neutral views.

We now turn to the question of economic instrumentalism.

7

Economic Instrumentalism: The Ultimate Taboo

Regardless of ownership form, economic considerations are fundamental for the media. All news organizations need financial resources to survive and thrive, as well as efficient management to channel resources in support of a professional or civic mission. In this chapter, however, we are focused on economic gain as an end in itself. We ask the question: how are ownership forms and particular owners oriented to maximize economic gain, either short-term or long-term, for any associated economic interests they may have?

In this chapter, we consider two dimensions of economic instrumentalism: *promotion* and *suppression.* (A third, profit maximization, was analyzed in Chapter 3 on harvesting profits versus investing). Promotion and suppression are economically instrumentalist rewards that economists would say offer amenity potential—benefits that may not directly and immediately generate money, but in the long-term may improve the owner's capacity to make more money.[1] Promotion refers to owners' use of news outlets to publicize or praise their "ownership interests": major shareholders, investors, donors, or associated companies or brands. Suppression refers to an owner's attempts to suppress negative news of these economic interests. Both promotion and suppression—or the implicit threat to engage in such economically instrumentalist actions—can also be used to help create a policy and market environment that is more amenable to the interests of an owner's business portfolio, including but not limited to any news properties.

Economic instrumentalism raises concerns that the public is not being provided with complete or accurate information about the interests that may be influencing journalistic content. The potential civic threat is substantial given that many news media owners have stakes in industries whose actions have financial, health, or safety consequences for the public; news media outlets may fail to expose abuses of power, corruption, and illegal competitive practices in companies associated with their owners. News outlets may also provide more positive or neutral coverage of their owners' economic interests than would be merited by an autonomous professional journalism oriented toward the

How Media Ownership Matters. Rodney Benson et al. Oxford University Press. © Rodney Benson, Mattias Hessérus, Timothy Neff, and Julie Sedel 2025. DOI: 10.1093/oso/9780199931293.003.0008

democratic ideal of "public accountability."[2] Thus, instead of investigative, public affairs-focused "watchdog" reporting that holds the powerful to account, including an outlet's ownership interests, articles labeled as news may serve as self-interested promotional marketing. Seemingly benign celebrations of popular companies like Disney, now the owner of the *ABC* television news network, may help create "myths" that protect such owners from "critical scrutiny" of their history, contemporary business and workplace practices, product safety, and non-news programming.[3]

In this chapter, we focus first on promotion and attempt to measure it across ownership forms through mentions in news coverage of owners and associated interests. We then consider public scandals about news outlets accused of engaging in either promotion or suppression. We conclude with a discussion of the challenges of obtaining complete information about economic instrumentalism and the extent to which owners may achieve economic instrumentalist goals without having to (or only very rarely) engaging in promotion or suppression.

What Contributes to More or Less Promotion?

Previous research suggests that ownership form, owner characteristics, and audience demographics may contribute to more or less economic instrumentalist promotion.

At vertically integrated conglomerates, shareholders and managers have openly touted "the coordination of parts of a company so that the whole actually turns out to be worth more than the sum of its parts acting alone."[4] Such public enthusiasm by owners about synergies can distort news coverage. For example, "an editor might now worry about alienating a powerful executive in another branch of the organization or hurting shareholder equity through inappropriate coverage or non-coverage of a story relating to the corporation's interests."[5] Media companies that most obviously have such conflicts of interests are those owned directly by non-news media conglomerates (e.g., Disney's ownership of *ABC News*, Dassault's ownership of *Le Figaro*) or by individuals who simultaneously are dominant shareholders in non-news media companies (e.g., Amazon founder Jeff Bezos's ownership of the *Washington Post*).[6]

Do characteristics of individual owners or audiences affect owner willingness to engage in economic instrumentalism? At some outlets, owners or top editors may speak or act in ways that suggest a certain distancing from classic journalistic standards or that serving audiences is more important than abiding by journalists' professional demands. Such distancing could be imputed to Rupert Murdoch from his open ambivalence toward the Pulitzer Prizes, highly valued by owners and journalists alike at center-left mainstream outlets like the *New York Times* or the *Washington Post*.[7]

According to scholar Jonathan Hardy, Murdoch reported to the UK House of Lords Select Committee for Communications in 2007 that there "was no cross-promotion between his different businesses" and that his "own papers often give poor reviews of his programmes."[8] In separate studies of Murdoch-owned media carried out in 1998 and 2009 to 2011, Hardy found that cross-promotion in news coverage was minimal to non-existent at the elite "quality" papers and in the main news sections, but that it was more frequent at the popular tabloids and in the sports and entertainment sections.[9] Hardy's finding thus suggests that audience demographics (elite versus popular or omnibus audiences) as well as the topical focus of coverage can influence the amount of promotion that an owner will encourage or allow.

What about less commercialized or non-commercial ownership forms? Foundation- or trust-owned outlets engage in commercial activity but are required to reinvest all profits back into the organization. If they are involved in diversified non-news media activities, they could have conflicts of interest. *Norran*, with investments in real estate and other businesses, has such potential conflicts. *La Croix*, part of the Bayard Press Group, might be used to help publicize other non-news media subsidiaries of the group, such as children's books and religious devotional publications. *Dagens ETC* is close to the ETC-företagen (The ETC Companies), which holds companies with a climate focus.[10] *Mediapart*'s initial large investors included Xavier Niel, the telecommunications entrepreneur who also is the largest investor in the Le Monde Group (including *Le Monde*, *Rue89*, and *HuffPost*).

While it is self-evident that philanthropy supported nonprofits have no shareholders to enrich or placate, is it possible for them to engage in economically instrumentalist promotion? Media scholars Kate Wright, Martin Scott, and Mel Bunce have argued that the answer is "yes."[11] They conducted an in-depth study of the international humanitarian news website IRIN in 2015, during a period when it was partially funded by the Hong Kong-based Jynwel Foundation, which in turn received its funds from the Malaysian billionaire Taek Jho Low. Wright, Scott, and Bunce discovered no change in the news content of IRIN during this period that could be linked to more favorable treatment of Low, his business interests, or the Jynwel Foundation, or that adopted a less critical approach in general to the international aid industry.[12] However, during the time period in which IRIN received $2 million from the Jynwel Foundation, Low was embroiled in a legal investigation accusing him of misappropriating funds from a Malaysian Development bank. Wright and colleagues argue that the timing of the donation from the Jynwel Foundation, personally directed by Low, suggests that Low was using his association with IRIN to gain "reputational benefits," "social capital," and "moral window-dressing."[13] Indeed, at the urging of Low's foundation staff, IRIN managers explored creating a "celebrity advisory committee" that would have allowed Low to burnish his reputation through association with people like Amal Clooney and Arianna Huffington. In the end, as news coverage of Low's legal troubles mounted, it was the fear of reputation damage through association with Low that led IRIN's other funders and board members to demand an end to IRIN's relationship with the Jynwel Foundation.[14] Similar concerns could be raised for any news organization that takes money from a foundation associated with an individual with ongoing business interests. How much a given nonprofit news outlet relies on these kinds of foundations can vary.

ProPublica, the investigative news nonprofit, initially had just one funder: it was launched with a three-year investment of $30 million by Herbert and Marion Sandler, billionaires who had made their money in the savings and loan industry. The Sandlers sold their savings and loan business for a hefty profit in 2006, just two years before the industry crashed and produced the nationwide financial crisis of 2008. There have been charges, including an investigative report by the *New York Times*, that the Sandlers engaged in lending practices that contributed to the crisis.[15] However, a lengthy investigation in 2010 by the *Columbia Journalism Review* concluded that the charges had been overstated and unfair.[16] Distinct from Low, the Sandlers' philanthropic support of journalism followed, rather than coincided, with their active years in business; moreover, from the beginning, they worked with *ProPublica* to lessen its reliance on them as sole donors. As of 2016, Ragan Rhyne, *ProPublica* senior vice president for development, told us that *ProPublica* receives about fifty percent of its funding from "foundations from living donors," which she said are "technically" foundations but essentially individual gifts, twenty-five percent from individuals making large or small donations out of their personal accounts, and twenty-five percent from "professional" foundations (such as Ford, Carnegie, MacArthur, etc., whose founders are no longer living) with "professionals that are doling it out."[17] The Sandlers remained among *ProPublica*'s largest "living foundation" donors, but by 2016, their contribution made up less than ten percent of total revenues. *ProPublica* holds that its independence is secured by the fact that no single foundation—living or professional—constitutes such a large proportion of its funding that they cannot afford to turn down the money if need be.[18] This tendency toward reliance on a wide range of donors is now a widespread practice for US news nonprofits and may indeed partially offset pressures for promotion or suppression.

US public media's reliance on philanthropy (including small donors) for more than half of their funding subjects them to the same potential conflicts of interest as civil society-owned nonprofit media. *PBS NewsHour* has also relied extensively on "corporate underwriting," essentially direct sponsorship of particular programs, from companies including Dow Chemical and the Lockheed Martin arms manufacturer.[19] French public media have not faced this problem, but concerns were raised when it was revealed that the CEO of *France Télévisions* also served on the board of directors of a competitor to a company that was the focus of a public television investigative journalism program.[20] Swedish public media, fully funded by taxpayers and legally shielded from any external pressures, would seem to be well protected against such economic conflicts of interest.

Ownership Interests in the News

To assess levels of promotion, we measure the frequency and valence of ownership interest mentions across a wide range of outlets with varying degrees and types of conflicts of interest and different forms of ownership. Our main sample is from the US, including some news outlets not included in our public service-oriented and partisan news samples.[21] We added a purposive sample of major Swedish and French outlets incorporating variation in ownership forms and other structural dimensions to create a combined sample of twenty-eight news outlets (see Appendix Table A7.1 for a complete list).

For each of these outlets, we identified the most prominent (up to ten) ownership interests: individual owners, shareholders/investors, donors, and, in some cases, other businesses or organizations affiliated with the company or with the main owner.[22] All mentions of each outlet's ownership interests (in the outlet's respective news and opinion content produced during twenty to twenty-one month periods between 2015 and 2019) were gathered from the databases Factiva, ProQuest, Nexis Uni, and Mediearkivet Retriever.

To calculate frequency, we measured the amount of ownership interest mentions for each outlet out of the total word count for each outlet's items: a higher Ownership Mention Index (OMI) indicates a higher relative frequency of ownership interest mentions (as a proportion of total coverage controlled for word length, multiplied by one million for ease of interpretation).

Coding of valence (positive, negative, or neutral) is based on a subsample of mentions for each outlet (see Methods Appendix for more information). In contrast to the chapters on public service orientation and partisan favorability, in this chapter we analyze and present the raw scores and percentages rather than primarily national relational scales.

Frequency and valence of ownership interest mentions

Across the three countries, ownership interest mentions are lowest at public (the US hybrid version with significant corporate and philanthropic funding) and civil society-owned media, somewhat higher at privately held and stock market dominant shareholder-owned outlets, and highest at widely held stock market-traded and conglomerate media. (See Figure 7.1 for OMI averages for ownership forms and subforms across the three-country sample and OMI scores for selected outlets; see also Appendix Table A7.1 for OMI and

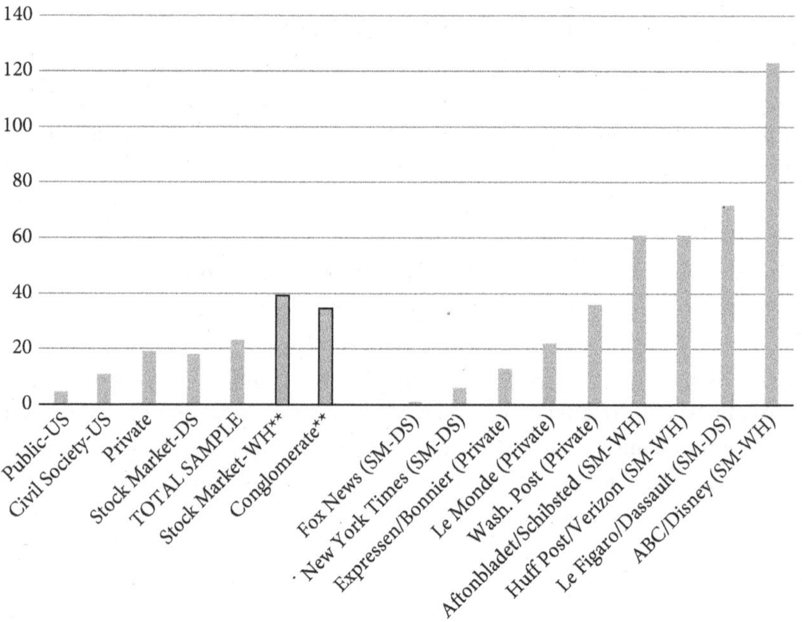

Figure 7.1 Ownership Mention Index (OMI) by Ownership Form* and for Selected Outlets

Means from multi-country purposive sample, n = 28.

Bars outlined in bold indicate a statistically significant difference from all other outlets: $^{**}p \leq .05$. See Appendix Table A7.1 for complete OMI outlet data. OMI index is based on the percentage of words in the entire corpus of each outlet's news coverage over the sampled twenty to twenty-one month periods, multiplied by one million for ease of interpretation.

ownership interest favorability scores for all sampled outlets.) OMI scores are highest at stock market-traded widely held conglomerate-owned *ABC News* (Disney), *HuffPost* (Verizon), and *Aftonbladet* (Schibsted), as well as at stock market-traded dominant shareholder conglomerate-owned *Le Figaro* (Dassault).[23]

To put these results in context, however, even *ABC News*' relatively high OMI suggests that mentions of ownership interests make up only an estimated 0.0123 percent of its total news coverage, scarcely 1 mention for every 10,000 words of coverage.

Outlets with omnibus audiences tend to mention ownership interests more than elite audience outlets, but the difference is not statistically significant.[24] Owners' or audiences' political preferences are not associated with any differences in ownership interest mentions.

Overall, in our three-country sample of twenty-eight outlets, mentions of ownership interests are on balance positive. When we calculate favorability (as we initially did in Chapter 6 for political and business actors) on a spectrum of –1.0 to 1.0, ownership interest mentions have a positive average favorability score of +0.018. (For outlet-level data, see Appendix Table A7.1.) Unlike the frequency of mentions, favorability is *not* higher at widely held stock market-traded and conglomerate media than at other ownership forms. Instead, ownership interest mentions are most positive at (US) philanthropy funded public media, followed by US civil society-owned media, and then dominant shareholder stock market-traded media and privately-held media; only at widely held stock market-traded media are mentions more often negative than positive (all differences statistically significant at p=.10). This finding must be placed in the context of far fewer ownership interest mentions by public and civil society-owned media than at commercial media. Nevertheless, it shows that when donors *are* mentioned at philanthropy reliant outlets, such as *NPR*, *MinnPost*, and *ProPublica*, they tend to be more often positive than negative.

Valence varies widely within the private, stock market-traded, and conglomerate forms. Stock market-traded *ABC News*/Disney and *Le Figaro*/Dassault, as well as the privately held *Washington Post*, have more positive than negative ownership interest mentions, while *Aftonbladet*/Schibsted and *HuffPost*/Verizon are on balance negative. The US *HuffPost*'s particularly high percentage of negative mentions (a favorability score of –0.205) is largely due to a non-staff blogger who stands out in our samples as a singularly consistent critic of owner Verizon, producing posts such as "Verizon's $300 Million Shell Game in Boston and Cross-subsidizing Wireless."[25] In this case, a non-staff, non-paid blogger provided critical reporting about the owner that was largely absent in the paid staff's coverage.[26] Ironically, as reported in Chapter 5, in the name of professionalization, reforms undertaken at *HuffPost* subsequently entirely eliminated the blogging program and hence made any future independent oversight *on* the website of the website's owners even less likely.[27]

Similar to the frequency of mentions, we did not find systematic differences in the favorability of ownership interest mentions based on owner or audience partisan preferences. Likewise, while outlets with omnibus audiences tended to have more favorable ownership interest mentions, the differences were once again not large enough to be statistically significant.[28]

We must emphasize that neutral or mixed mentions made up on average almost ninety percent of all ownership interest mentions. While neutral mentions are probably not as promotionally beneficial to owners as positive mentions, they, too, likely serve a promotional function. Taking that into account, the fact that at no outlet do negative mentions outnumber neutral and positive mentions combined suggests that there are potentially some promotional benefits from mentions at all the news outlets in our study.

Ownership interest mentions in the context of other business news

Is our finding that ownership interest mentions are more positive than negative specific to coverage of ownership interests or is it characteristic of business news in general? In other words, is a promotional orientation toward ownership interests simply a by-product of an overall pro-capitalist, pro-business ideology in mainstream journalism? There is reason to believe that coverage of business overall will be positive, or at least more positive than political coverage, given generally pro-business sensibilities of commercial owners and boards of directors and media reliance on businesses for advertising revenues.[29]

Studies have shown that the visibility of business and labor in the news are far from equal, and that when business interests and worker interests conflict, commercial media tend to slant coverage in favor of business interests.[30] How does coverage of ownership compare to general business news? Communications scholar Adam Saffer and colleagues analyzed how news organizations covered their board members and the organizations they were affiliated with, and similar to our study of ownership interests, found relatively low levels of coverage and critical scrutiny. Saffer et al. suggested that their findings could serve as a baseline for future studies of "business news generally."[31] We are able to make such a comparison.

To measure the valence of all business mentions, we return to the same December 2015–June 2016 news sample we used to measure public service orientation and partisanship in Chapters 5 and 6. This time period overlaps significantly with our US ownership interest mention sample (a twenty-one-month time period from 2015 through 2016) and is relatively close to the time period for the Swedish and French ownership interest mention samples drawn in 2018 and 2019.

To assure comparability, we present here the data only on the twenty-two news outlets that appear in both the general news (with business mentions) and ownership interest mentions samples (thus, *not* including the *Des Moines Register*, *Chicago Tribune*, *Boston Globe*, *Aftonbladet*, *Expressen*, and *Le Parisien*). Here is what we discovered: When an outlet mentions its own ownership interests, eighty-nine percent of mentions are neutral; when it mentions other businesses, a slightly lower amount, eighty-four percent, are neutral. Of the non-neutral mentions, we see a clear difference in the direction of valence. Again, using a favorability index (from −1.0 to 1.0) that takes into account the mix of neutral, positive, and negative mentions, business mentions overall are on balance negative (−0.039) while ownership interest mentions are positive (+0.027), and the differences are statistically significant. This direct comparison makes clear that, on average, news outlets that are offering critical coverage of business in general are offering positive coverage of their ownership interests: thus, ownership economic interests are treated more favorably in journalistic coverage than other businesses (see Figure 7.2).

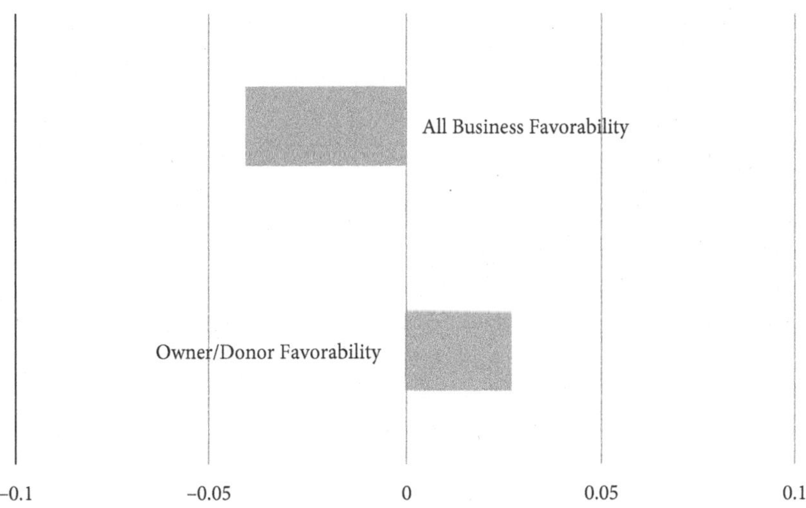

Figure 7.2 Favorability Index (−1.0 to 1.0) for Outlet Mentions of All Businesses versus Mentions of Ownership Interests

Note: Mentions are from the overlapping sample of twenty-two outlets included in both the 2015–2016 constructed week of general news and the 2015–2019 sample of ownership mentions. Differences in positive, negative, and neutral/mixed mentions are significant at $p < .001$, chi-square test (2, n=5,772) = 90.1939.

From this comparison of ownership interest and business mentions, we see that promotional coverage tends not to be a feature of business news in general. Instead, it is specific to the awkward situation journalists may find themselves in relation to their owners, donors, and associated businesses and organizations, leading them to write about them in a cautious way that they would not otherwise adopt. Even if such ownership interest coverage is only a small subset of all business coverage, it is no small matter. Special treatment of any ownership interest is problematic. Further, many of these entities and individuals are connected to major industries whose operations extend across multiple sectors of national and international economies. Ownership of major media by conglomerates and other owners with conflicts of interest thus risks putting too much of the economy "off-limits" to normal critical journalistic scrutiny.

There are limitations to what a purely quantitative approach can tell us. While this method captured major ownership interests, it surely did not capture all of them, including all outside investments by the dominant shareholder or companies or properties owned by colleagues or friends. Further, it does not permit us to draw out the important distinctions between casual ownership interest mentions and sustained campaigns to promote or protect the owner. In the next section, we thus turn to a more qualitative method to broaden our inquiry into promotion and to examine suppression.

When Economic Instrumentalism Becomes Public: Promotion and Suppression Scandals

In this section, we use the public record as an additional indicator of where and how promotion and suppression may be taking place. We use "public scandals" over ownership interest promotion and suppression as a way to qualitatively assess not only where such economic instrumentalist actions may be occurring but also how they are constructed and contested as a problem in the public sphere. For the US, Sweden, and France, we searched leading media and journalistic professional and trade magazines and websites for any mentions of suppression or promotion (using standardized search words adapted and translated for each country), generally between 2010 and 2021 (see Methods Appendix for more information about sampling and search terms). More than just noting the number of scandals that occur, we pay close attention to the particulars of the accusations leveled at the news organizations and the discourses that circulated around the controversies. It is important to note that the accusations are almost always contested and hard to verify. We focus primarily on the outlets included in our content analysis samples, while referring the reader to additional information on the other cases that emerged from this research.

Promotion scandals

In the US, promotion scandals at major news media have been rare. The one incident that emerged from our search of media professional and trade press coverage involved the owner of the *Los Angeles Times*, biotech billionaire entrepreneur Patrick Soon-Shiong. In the early months of the COVID-19 crisis, Soon-Shiong created a series of YouTube videos about the science behind the virus, with his title of Executive Chairman, *Los Angeles Times*, prominently visible on screen. The videos were produced for the *LA Times Today* local cable show and were publicized to readers from a *Los Angeles Times* email account. The videos were offered as a public service, but as *NiemanLab* director Joshua Benton noted, Soon-Shiong also owns companies that are developing coronavirus and other vaccines. Acknowledging that he may have missed it, Benton wrote that he "didn't see any sort of disclosure or disclaimer of this potential conflict of interest." Benton concluded: "For the most part (Adelson [to be discussed below] being a very big exception), I think the billionaire buyers have generally done okay at recognizing their civic duty and not abusing their new toys as tools for their other interests. But the concern is a legitimate one."[32]

In France, the same news outlet with the highest number of promotional mentions in the French quantitative sample—*Le Figaro*—was also most often the focus of promotion accusations, chiefly from the media criticism website *Acrimed*. At Dassault-owned *Le Figaro*, announcements that Dassault had secured a new sale of Rafale military jets, while legitimate news, were perceived by some critics as being fawning and promotional. In 2014, *Le Figaro* reported the official decision by the French government to spend a billion euros to develop the Rafale jet for its military operations. Underneath a neutral headline, "The State Orders the New Rafale," the language is arguably effusive: "Afghanistan, Libya, Mali, Central Africa . . . In the heat of fire, the Rafale has proven its operational qualities and its omni-role character—it was designed to replace seven types of previous generation combat aircraft—in the theaters of operations where France is involved. In operation, it has shown the decisive advantage it gives, underlined [the] Defense Minister."[33] The praise was even more ebullient, according to critics, a year later when Dassault completed a sale of twenty-four Rafale jets to Egypt, its first contract with a foreign nation-state. In this instance, the amount of coverage was also abundant: sixteen articles over the course of ten days.[34]

Le Parisien's dominant shareholder, Bernard Arnault of LVMH, was publicly criticized by his own journalists for excessive self-promotion. "Bernard Arnault invites himself too often to the pages of *Le Parisien*," proclaimed the newspaper's journalists' association in an email to its top editors. The journalists' association pointed in particular to the newspaper's coverage of the department store Carrefour, of which Arnault is also a shareholder: on the same day that Carrefour announced 4,500 job layoffs, *Le Parisien* scarcely mentioned it and headlined the front page "The Man Who Wants to Revolutionize Retail," with a flowery portrait of the Carrefour CEO's plans to invest in the internet.[35] In December 2020, Arnault's LVMH was again accused of promotion when his son, Antoine, appeared on LVMH-owned *Radio Classique* to discuss the company's pro-environmental actions; according to critics, the journalist-interviewer did not challenge him, except to laconically note at the end of the interview, "It's marketing, but not only, we got it."[36]

At *Libération*, an attentive media critic noted "an excess of zeal" in a *Libération* journalist who wrote an analytical article about the Italian telecommunications market that seemed to closely accord with the business interests of *Libération*'s owner, Patrick Drahi, the dominant shareholder in the French stock market-traded telecommunications company Altice/SFR. The *Libération* journalist identified the many benefits achieved by concentration to just three companies in the Italian communications market, such as increased profit margins for the companies and stable prices for consumers, while ignoring any negative effects, such as employee layoffs. In an allusion to Drahi's recent failed attempt to buy out a competitor, which would have likewise reduced France's telecommunications sector to just three companies, the author reportedly concluded in a vein likely to please Drahi: "Certain observers notice that the capitalist structure [for French telecoms] makes mergers of operators much more complicated in France."[37]

At *Le Monde*, a journalist was criticized for writing a review of a book about dominant private shareholder Xavier Niel that accentuated the positive aspects and played down the criticisms that also appeared in the book.[38] Although not otherwise part of our sampled outlets, it is worth noting that two other French media owners appeared in promotional scandals over the past decade: Vincent Bolloré, dominant shareholder of stock market-traded Vivendi, which is the owner of the cable channel *I-Télé* (renamed *C-News*); and Credit Mutuel, a cooperative-owned bank that owns a chain of local newspapers.[39]

Just as with the US, in Sweden promotional scandals appear to be rare. No Swedish promotional scandals emerged from our searches. Questions have been raised periodically about whether Bonnier uses its newspaper book reviews to unfairly promote the books that it publishes. Leading media economist Karl-Erik Gustafsson, in a 2008 *Nordicom Review* article noting the significant financial losses at Bonnier's tabloid *Expressen* at the time, speculated about the motives that might lead Bonnier to hold on to *Expressen* despite these losses. Imagining an economic instrumentalist rationale, he asked: "How important are the cultural pages of *Expressen* for promoting the book publishing business of Bonnier?" However, he did not attempt to answer this question.[40]

Suppression scandals

In the US, suppression scandals emerged at widely held stock market-traded *NBC News* (via General Electric); dominant shareholder stock market-traded *Fox Business* (News Corporation) and the *New York Times*; and the privately held *Washington Post*, *Bloomberg*, and *Las Vegas Review-Journal*.

News of a study that several major corporations had paid no federal taxes in 2010, including General Electric, then a co-owner of NBC, was not reported by *NBC News*. The *Washington Post*'s media reporter, Paul Farhi, wrote that NBC's silence looked like something "between a lapse and a coverup." An NBC spokesperson dismissed the criticisms, saying that NBC's ignoring the story "was a straightforward editorial decision, the kind we make daily around here."[41]

Around the same period, *Fox Business* was accused of extensively and one-sidedly covering California's Proposition 24 ballot measure, which sought to repeal $1.7 billion in corporate tax breaks, without disclosing that the group promoting the measure had received a $1.3 million contribution from News Corporation, *Fox Business*'s owner. A *Fox Business* executive said he did not know about News Corporation's contribution. *CBS News* and *NBC News*, whose parent companies (CBS corporation and General Electric, respectively) contributed to the campaign, also covered the proposition without revealing their owners' corporate contributions, but, according to the *New York Times*, "no news outlet has covered the issue as aggressively as *Fox Business*."[42]

The *New York Times*, in turn, was accused of not being transparent about its own conflicts of interest. In 2011, the *New York Times* published several articles about conflict of interest at *TechCrunch*, where blogger Michael Arrington started the venture capital fund CrunchFund, "that invests in start-ups like those that *TechCrunch* covers." However, the *New York Times* articles did not reveal that the New York Times Company invested in the venture capital firm True Ventures, which had invested in another technology blog competing with *TechCrunch*, *GigaOM*, and that the founder of *GigaOm* had been a partner in the venture capital firm True Ventures. In other words, the New York Times Company was doing exactly what its reporters accused Arrington of doing. The company responded that they have many outside investments and that they sometimes report such investments and sometimes do not, given that the company policy is to provide a disclosure only when the New York Times company has a "significant financial connection." The *New York Times* associate managing editor for standards, Phil Corbett, said that the "real safeguard" is that different people make the investments and write the stories, and they don't interact.[43]

Around the time of Jeff Bezos's purchase of the *Washington Post*, concerns were raised about Amazon securing a $600 million contract to provide cloud computing services to the CIA. The activist group RootsAction circulated a petition demanding that any *Washington Post* coverage of the CIA "should include full disclosure that the sole owner of the *Post* is also the main owner of Amazon—and Amazon is now gaining huge profits directly from the CIA." Editor Marty Baron rejected this demand, but insisted that the *Post* "has among the strictest ethics policies in the field of journalism," that the newspaper has "routinely disclosed corporate conflicts when they were directly relevant to our coverage," and that "neither Amazon nor Jeff Bezos was involved, nor ever will be involved, in our coverage of the intelligence community."[44] Concerns were also raised about two news outlets that were otherwise not part of our study. *Bloomberg*, the business news magazine, came under scrutiny in 2013 for alleged suppression of investigative reports on top Chinese officials and their families due to fears of "the possibility of *Bloomberg's* [news operations] being evicted from China," according to reporting by the *New York Times.* Bloomberg company also sells financial terminals to the Chinese market, but the top editor's decision, according to the *Times'* account, was not about "protecting company revenues."[45] In 2016, concerns were raised about the *Las Vegas Review-Journal* after its change of ownership to Sheldon Adelson, the casino owner and Republican mega-donor. The *New York Times* reported several incidents of interference in *Las Vegas Review-Journal* news stories by top editors that could not be directly linked to Adelson but could be seen to be aligned with his business interests.[46]

In France, three "industrial" dominant shareholders in stock market-traded companies were mentioned in relation to supposed cases of suppression. Defense aviation magnate Serge Dassault of the Dassault Group (*Le Figaro*); Bernard Arnault of the LVMH luxury and fashion goods company (*Les Echos*, *Le Parisien*, *Europe 1*); and SFR/Altice telecommunications conglomerate founder Patrick Drahi (*Libération*, BFMTV). Charges of suppression were also leveled against the privately held *Le Monde* and the cooperative bank Credit Mutuel, owner of many regional newspapers.

From 2013 until his death in 2018, Serge Dassault was continually in the news for judicial accusations of buying votes to secure the election of his successor as mayor in the Paris suburb of Corbeil-Essonnes. While linked to Serge Dassault's political activities, these negative stories were also damaging to the Dassault corporate "brand." In contrast to most of the rest of the French media, *Le Figaro* was accused of ignoring or downplaying the charges of corruption.[47] Even *Le Figaro*'s minimal level of coverage was reportedly the result of a complaint from the members of the newspaper's internal journalists' association, who felt that they were the laughing stock of the French press: they conceded that they could not demand the right to conduct independent investigations of their owner or "to get out in front of the others," but insisted on their right to "cover the news" that other media were already talking about.[48]

Accusations were also made that Dassault had distorted international news coverage to protect his business interests, particularly the sales of his Rafale jets to foreign governments. In the summer of 2010, famed *Le Figaro* foreign correspondent Georges Malbrunot wrote in his blog that the Arab Emirates were using Israeli technology to secure their borders and their oil wells, news that deeply embarrassed the Emirates, with whom the Dassault company was in negotiations to sell jets. Early in 2011, *Le Figaro* Director Francis Morel resigned. Morel had previously been on good terms with Serge Dassault, and Morel had been praised for his successes in strengthening the financial standing of the company. *Le Monde* reported that Morel's absolute refusal to fire Malbrunot at Dassault's urging was the spark that led to a rapid deterioration in his relations with the owner.[49] When we spoke with Francis Morel shortly after his departure, he told us that *Le Monde*'s reporting of the reason for his resignation was "pure fantasy," but declined to reveal other reasons.[50] French media reporters Amaury de Rochegonde (*Stratégies*) and Richard Sénéjoux (*Télérama*) document other *Le Figaro* international news articles and editorials that have allegedly aligned with the owner's business interests, such as reports that gave summary treatment to human rights violations in Egypt, a crucial client state for Dassault.[51]

As noted in the Introduction, *Le Parisien* owner Bernard Arnault (LVMH) came under fire when it was claimed that the newspaper's cultural reporters had been prohibited from writing about a documentary film (*Thanks Boss!*) critical of Arnault. The editor in charge took full responsibility for the decision, justifying it journalistically as not worthy of coverage because it was a small film only released in a few theaters; however, even after the film achieved record sales for a documentary, Arnault-owned media did not cover it.[52] Media critics were also alarmed when the top editor of Arnault-controlled *Les Echos* participated in a Europe 1 radio show where he attacked a judicial decision regarding a real estate development—without revealing that the interested party in the case was Arnault's LVMH.[53]

Regarding *Libération*, there has been some discussion concerning the motives that originally led telecommunications billionaire Patrick Drahi to purchase the newspaper. Drahi testified at a hearing of France's Assemblée nationale (Parliament) that he was convinced to buy the struggling left-leaning daily by a *Libé* journalist who was interviewing him for an article about his purchase of the telecommunications company SFR: "But Mr. Drahi, you are going to spend 14 billion [euros] to buy SFR, at *Libération*, we only need 14 million for you to save us."[54] Insiders suggested an additional reason for Drahi's purchase. Around the same time of the Drahi SFR purchase in 2014, President François Hollande was reported to have related his concern to Drahi about *Libération*'s financial difficulties. The telecoms magnate no doubt wanted to ensure warm relations with the party in power.[55] Whatever his motivations, saving *Libération* would allow Drahi to present himself as a defender of press pluralism, even as he also bolstered his status and influence.[56] Shortly after Drahi's initial investment in *Libération*, a portion of the regular column by journalist Pierre Marcelle that included a slightly negative reference to Drahi was reportedly cut before publication.[57]

At *Le Monde*, owners Pierre Bergé and Matthieu Pigasse (but not Niel) publicly criticized the newspaper's participation in the SwissLeaks investigation that exposed wealthy French possible tax avoiders. *Le Monde* journalists publicly responded that the shareholders' public statements would not prevent them from "working serenely in total independence and responsibility."[58]

Finally, when the French news wire *Agence France-Presse* reported that confidential customer banking information had inadvertently been made accessible to journalists working for Credit Mutuel's EBRA chain of nine daily newspapers in Eastern France, the majority of the EBRA newspapers reportedly did not publish the AFP report. Credit Mutuel's alleged information suppression prompted a public reprimand from France's Syndicat National des Journalistes (SNJ, or National Union of Journalists).[59]

In Sweden, *Svenska Dagbladet* media columnist Malin Ekman prompted a lively debate in 2014 about the potential conflicts of interest that could arise as media companies, such as Schibsted, Bonnier, and the foundation-owned Mittmedia group, branched out into other business ventures to supplement declining news media revenues. Ekman raised the specter of newspapers owned by either Schibsted or Bonnier hesitating to investigate companies affiliated with their owner. CEOs of the companies were asked to respond, and all of them insisted that any such conflict of interest could not arise in Sweden. As Bonnier CEO Thomas Franzén said, "Editorial independence is as always the key principle, and I don't see this being threatened."[60]

One notable series of reported incidents demonstrated the possibility—although not the ultimate success—of a Swedish owner wanting to influence news coverage in relation to business interests. In 2010, a bank co-owned by investor Mats Qviberg, HQ Bank, had its banking license revoked because it was accused of inflating the value of its actual trading portfolio. Qviberg and other bank executives were later exonerated of criminal charges.[61] In 2016, Qviberg began investing in Swedish media outlets (via the Custos company), notably the business news website *Realtid*, which had previously reported extensively on the HQ Bank scandal. In an article in *Svenska Dagbladet* in which Qviberg was asked whether he would influence *Realtid*'s content, Qviberg responded: "Of course I want to influence, and I also want to secure its quality." Asked to define the latter, Qviberg said, "I believe that there have been many untrue articles during the seven years of HQ's activities. In my opinion it can be offensive."[62] In 2017, Qviberg and an associate (via Custos) purchased *Metro* Sweden and hired as CEO the former CEO of HQ Bank. They also hired a journalist who had co-written a book – *HQ-Gate* – that criticized journalistic reporting about the HQ bank scandal.[63]

What ultimately ended Qviberg's involvement with *Realtid* and *Metro*, however, were his flirtations with the populist right. In an interview with the right-wing populist website *Nyheter Idag*, Qviberg and his associate revealed that they would like to make *Metro* less "politically correct" and develop collaborations between *Metro* and *Nyheter Idag*.[64] Following the interview, several *Metro* journalists resigned. Local politicians also threatened to revoke *Metro*'s distribution rights in the public transport system and the Bonnier-owned *TV4* chose to end a collaboration with *Metro*.[65] Within days, Qviberg sold his shares in the media outlets, having lost more than 70 million Swedish kronor [approximately $8.2 million in 2017 average exchange rate] in less than six months.[66]

Making Sense of an Elusive Mode of Power

What have we discovered in this chapter about economic instrumentalism? And how do we explain our findings?

Quantitative analysis of everyday news coverage over twenty-to-twenty-one-month periods revealed that ownership interests are mentioned infrequently—accounting for at most an estimated one-hundredth of one percent of coverage. When such interests are mentioned, it is most often at outlets traded on the stock market or controlled by conglomerates.[67] Most mentions of ownership interests are neutral, but of those with any valence, mentions tend to be more positive than negative. Donors at US nonprofits are mentioned less often than owners and associated interests at commercial media, but when they are mentioned, they tend to be more positive. This overall net positive tendency of ownership interest mentions stands in contrast to mentions of other businesses, which, like reporting about political actors, tend to be on balance negative. Thus, even if ownership interest coverage is not strongly positive, the fact that it is positive at all shows that owners and their associated interests are being treated differently than other businesses.

In our review of public reports, likewise, we discovered only a small number of economic instrumentalist scandals: less than thirty altogether across three countries and a decade or more. Suppression scandals have been more frequent than promotion scandals. This does not necessarily mean that suppression happens more frequently than promotion. It may reflect a greater taboo associated with "censorship" than with self-promotion. Given the increasing blurring of lines between advertising (native or traditional), public relations, and news, promotion (except in the most egregious cases) may be perceived as not ideal, but not exactly a scandal either. In contrast, even the slightest hint of suppression, if discovered, is likely to provoke fierce criticism. Overall, both suppression and promotion scandals are linked most often to stock market-traded dominant shareholder and privately owned media. We also find cross-national differences, with the number of scandals higher in France and the US than in Sweden.

Broadly speaking, we imagine two possible responses to our overall finding that instances of economically instrumentalist suppression and promotion are relatively infrequent. The first is to doubt the findings and insist that promotion and suppression are *not* in fact infrequent, just difficult, and perhaps even impossible, to fully capture empirically. The second is to trust our findings but to probe further as to why suppression and promotion are relatively rare, for reasons such as professional resistance and reputational disincentives—or simply the fact that the implicit threat of taking such action, rather than the action itself, is sufficient to achieve owners' economic instrumentalist aims.

Let us first consider any methodological reservations about our findings. What reasons are there to suppose that economic instrumentalist suppression or promotion occurs more often than our research has shown? Only a few "scandals" emerged in the professional and trade publications, but given their limited "carrying capacity,"[68] and the need to report other kinds of news, they only have enough time and space to mention the arguably most egregious cases involving the most well-known or prestigious media. Thus, the accusations that emerged may not be a full indicator of the actual extent of suppression or promotion across a national journalistic field.

Another challenge is fully identifying economic interests. In our qualitative and quantitative searches, we focused on direct ownership or significant shareholdings (such as Disney's ownership of the *ABC* network, or Bezos's significant shares in Amazon). If not for the *Poynter* article accusing the *New York Times* of not being transparent about its investments in small technology companies, thus turning these interests into a public scandal, we would not have captured these less visible economic interests in our account. (A thorough search through every year's annual report of stock market-traded companies could have revealed such investments, but this information would generally not be available from privately held companies.) If we broaden the analysis to include personal investments, as well as companies owned or run by colleagues, family, or personal friends of owners and their top managers and editors, the challenges in documenting the full range of potential economic interests, and thus conflicts of interest, are only increased exponentially.

The other interpretation of our findings is that they are accurate: that, indeed, actual promotion and suppression are rare. Should we automatically dismiss the fact that virtually all owners insist that they do not engage in or allow such practices? Testifying at the Leveson Inquiry prompted by the privacy intrusions of Murdoch-owned *News of the World*, Murdoch insisted, "I take a particularly strong pride in the fact that we have never pushed our commercial interests in our newspapers" and "I certainly do not tell journalists to promote our TV channels or our TV shows or our films."[69] Similar denials were frequently heard during French Senate interviews of leading media owners, including Arnault, Drahi, Niel, and Bolloré, held in 2021.[70]

If ideals are not enough, in a more calculating mode, owner attempts—both direct and indirect—may be rare because the potential costs simply outweigh the benefits. Reticence to intervene may be driven by the nature of the relationship to a professionalized staff, which closely guards its autonomy. In many newsrooms, staff have established ethical charters precisely to prevent abuses of owner power. Publicly exposed promotion or suppression could make it more difficult to attract and keep good journalists. Further, the publicity could damage the reputation and credibility of the brand, which could drive away audiences and reduce revenues and profits. In such cases, owners may feel that the cost of intervention is too risky and that therefore the wisest business policy is not to try to hide the interference (working through trusted intermediaries) but to simply not interfere.[71] Owners might also perceive that not only does a strong ethical charter make it more difficult for them to intervene, but that as a compensation its mere existence also provides positive publicity and status recognition to their news property. As LVMH executive Nicolas Bazire once proudly proclaimed, the guarantees of editorial independence for *Les Echos* (expressly prohibiting the owner from pressuring the newsroom) go beyond what "any other press group in the world has agreed to."[72]

In Sweden, journalistic resistance may be especially effective when exercised given that the top editor at each outlet tends to have the status of "responsible publisher," which makes the editor legally responsible for whatever is published. It is no small matter for an owner to try to override the editor/publisher's decision. Marie Johansson Flyckt, responsible publisher and editor-in-chief of Hallpressen (later Hall Media) of which *Jönköpings-Posten* is part, relates that the question of ownership interests "is not really simple when you are family-owned, by an owner who is also present in the building, and who works very close and who is regarded as a representative for the publication." In such situations, she emphasizes, "that question is very, very hot."[73] Until 2020, when it was bought by Bonnier and Amedia, the media group Hallpressen/Hall Media was owned or effectively controlled by the Hamrin family. Under Hamrin family control, according to Flyckt, whenever journalists planned to write a story that touched on the family's ownership, "we usually inform them that we are writing about this and sometimes you had to ask them." Flyckt adds:

> I was myself involved in a conflict once when I — as [responsible] publisher— when I said that if you want it that way, you will have to change publisher because I cannot stand for it. So, in a sense, they wanted to put their own interests before what we considered to be newsworthy, but it ended up being published the way I wanted.[74]

In some cases, however, direct or even indirect interventions may be rare because they are simply not necessary to achieve the owner's aims. If the aim is to lessen critical coverage of the owner, the mere fact of investing in an outlet (even without a dominant position) may exert a chilling effect. Indeed, in a moment of seeming candor, one owner generally regarded as non-interfering said that he sees his media properties as affording him a certain level of insurance or protection against journalistic criticism. Xavier Niel has invested in many French digital start-ups (but never more than one-third of the capital), including *Mediapart*, *Causeur*, *Bakchich*, *Atlantico*, and *Marsactu*. According to journalist Odile Benyahia-Kouider, Niel was very frank about his reasons: "When journalists piss me off, I invest in their newspaper, and then they leave me alone." (Niel did not expressly say that this strategy worked for his dominant shareholding stake in *Le Monde*, and he maintains that his remark was a "joke" [boutade].)[75]

In such cases, the organization of the newsroom and routine news practices may help ensure that news content is not overly critical of the owner. A Pew Research Center study found that thirty-five percent of surveyed journalists at local and national outlets in the US said they had not pursued stories because of potential conflicts with the financial interests of ownership, compared to twenty-nine percent reporting the same because of potential conflicts with advertisers. These omissions in coverage most often stem from "signals from [journalists'] bosses" or anticipation of "how [journalists] think their bosses would react."[76] As the representative of the société de journalistes (Journalists' Association) at the French newspaper *Le Parisien* noted, after its purchase by the luxury brands giant LVMH: "The biggest danger comes less from a telephone call from the owner than from the self-censorship that perniciously operates at the level of desk editors."[77] Perhaps even without conscious awareness that they are engaging in self-censorship, just choosing to avoid "trouble" and delay, desk editors who make day-to-day decisions on assignments and placement of stories are in a crucial position to make sure sensitive stories do not rise to the attention of the editor-in-chief or the owner. A story that broaches a sensitive topic touching on the owner's political views or economic interests can be rejected, delayed, shortened, or buried deep inside the newspaper or at the bottom of the home page, denied any proactive social media promotion. All of these micro-decisions can be justified in relation to limited time, space, or resources, or the competition with other news stories judged more important or urgent in any given news cycle.[78] Sensitive stories may indeed be published, but not entirely coincidentally at a time when they will cause the least damage to the owner, such as after other outlets have already made the issue public, or when it no longer matters to the owner—that is, *after* any linked public policy decisions affecting the owner's economic interests have already been favorably rendered.[79]

For an owner, self-censorship functions so that even if the journalists at an outlet one owns may occasionally write critical stories, it is likely that they will not lead the charge in scrutinizing one's business interests. The benefit is especially great if the outlet one owns is prominent and respected: for Bezos and Amazon, the *Washington Post*; for Niel and his telecommunications company Free, *Le Monde*; for the Bonnier family and their publishing and entertainment companies, the top national daily *Dagens Nyheter*; and for Arnault, dominant shareholder of LVMH, the French business newspaper *La Tribune*. In an interview, the Arnault-hired CEO said that he made sure the journalists understood that the owner would not intervene in coverage of any other businesses, but that they were to "treat correctly, objectively, and factually" Arnault and LVMH—maybe a euphemism for getting softer coverage.[80] Our quantitative finding—that most news outlets on balance are negative in their mentions of other businesses but positive in their mentions of their owners—gains resonance in these remarks.

Finally, promotion or suppression in news content may be rare because they are not the most effective ways to leverage media ownership to increase owners' prestige, access to political power, and ultimately influence over regulatory policies affecting their business interests. Owners may accrue symbolic and economic benefits from ownership even if there is no self-interested change in news coverage, simply due to a widespread *belief* in their power: the assumption that owners can exert influence over their media properties and in turn that these media influence the public. Both beliefs may exaggerate the actual likely degree of influence, but this doesn't matter, because "presumed influence" also exerts influence.[81] As such, the presumed power and the status conferred by ownership of prestige titles like *Le Monde* pays dividends in access to policy makers. Niel has reportedly confided that his access to government officials noticeably improved after his purchase of *Le Monde*.[82] He viewed such entrée as crucial for his telecommunications company to seriously compete for government licenses and contracts against competitors like the Bouygues Group, which also had major news media properties (*TF1*).[83] Rupert Murdoch's purchases of the *Wall Street Journal* and other news outlets have also reportedly been driven by the desire to exert influence over government regulations necessary for the expansion of his media holdings.[84]

In sum, it seems most likely that economic instrumentalist promotion and suppression are relatively rare, as we find. While successful acts of suppression or promotion might be good for business, public revelations complicate the relationship with the newsroom and the ability to recruit top-notch talent. They tarnish the brand. Many of the benefits of ownership—status, presumed influence, access—can be achieved without attempting to distort news coverage. If and when owners intervene, they will likely do so informally, with plausible deniability, and infrequently, although perhaps just often enough to achieve their goals.

Conclusion: How Media Ownership Matters

In this concluding chapter, we take stock of our investigations into media ownership in three western democracies: the US, Sweden, and France. We revisit the book's theoretical approach, summarize key findings and situate them in their national contexts, and show how our framework can provide a useful heuristic for organizing past and future research on media ownership.

Theorizing Ownership

How Media Ownership Matters develops and puts to work an original theoretical framework for the analysis of media ownership. We first called for going beyond previous approaches that emphasized market concentration and moguls, which, while important, are insufficient for fully understanding ownership power. Instead, we argued that more attention needs to be paid to the distinct institutional "forms" of ownership, an approach heralded by James Curran, C. Edwin Baker, Robert Picard, and others, but until now underdeveloped conceptually and empirically. We have improved on previous efforts by theoretically specifying categories of forms relevant for the analysis of ownership in democratic polities: *market*, *private*, *civil society*, and *public*. We also identified the subforms of *religious*, *partisan-affiliated*, and *conglomerate* ownership (by a major company with control over significant non-news media holdings) and the non-ownership mechanism of *current/legacy journalist control*. These categories capture clusters of *institutional logics* that specify standards and values and organize journalistic action in distinctive ways.

We then took up the call to situate ownership in context but brought attention to the ways in which relevant factors are not independent from but rather intertwined with ownership. As such, we identified *ownership complexes* of forms, funding, and target audiences. Building on Pierre Bourdieu's field theory and media management studies, we argued that one of the main ways that owners and their appointed managers implement their allocative and operational power is through their development of *funding-audience adjustment strategies*, each of which has distinct affordances for news production.

How Media Ownership Matters. Rodney Benson et al. Oxford University Press. © Rodney Benson, Mattias Hessérus, Timothy Neff, and Julie Sedel 2025. DOI: 10.1093/oso/9780199931293.003.0009

Finally, we argued that ownership power is not only about domination but also is productive: in Steven Lukes's terms, it is a "power to" as well as a "power over."[1] We emphasized that such power and its effects are worthy of our attention because of journalism's normative civic importance. We thus analyzed performance of ownership forms and complexes in relation to outcomes—*modes of power*—that are civically consequential: public service orientation, political instrumentalism and partisanship, and economic instrumentalism.

Our approach thus combines in a new way diverse currents of thought in the sociology of news, institutional logics, and field theory to build a powerful, relatively parsimonious framework for the study of media ownership. It acknowledges contingency and complexity while nevertheless identifying consistent patterns in the content of journalistic production linked to ownership forms and complexes. We demonstrated the utility of this framework through a multi-methodological, multi-country research design. What did we find?

What Matters?

What are the differences in ownership forms and complexes that make a difference? How do they shape journalistic performance in relation to public service orientation, political instrumentalism and partisanship, and economic instrumentalism?

Investing in public affairs news is both an economic and professional project, driven by the need to achieve economic sustainability, aspirations for prestige, and professional and civic ideals. It varies systematically across our four broad forms of ownership. Investing, as a proportion of revenues, tends to be highest at (mostly US) civil society-owned nonprofit media funded by philanthropy. Unlike large commercial news outlets that seek to entertain as well as inform, these small and lean operations are laser-focused on providing high quality public affairs news. Public media with relatively generous and secure long-term public funding, such as in Sweden, are able to concentrate on public affairs news on a much larger scale. In Sweden and France, many newspapers and online outlets are also provided partial subsidies in acknowledgment of journalism's civic importance. These subsidies are content neutral—they support right-leaning as well as left-leaning media—and they incentivize the production of news that broadens and deepens the public debate.

Market ownership prioritizes short-term profit above all else, which tends to reduce the proportional investment in news. In recent years, stock market-traded companies and hedge fund/private equity firms have shifted toward "harvesting" the maximum profits from what they perceive to be a dying industry, through progressively deeper cuts in newsroom budgets. Even so, significant investment in news by media with market ownership may be possible under certain conditions: for example, in the shadow of a large conglomerate distracted by the management of more profitable divisions, as we saw at *HuffPost* under Verizon, or during the brief period of experimentation before the surest path to maximum profitability is found, as at Alden Capital-owned Digital First media in the early 2010s. When a stock market-traded company has a controlling dominant shareholder, this shareholder can choose to forgo dividends and allow stock values to drop to pursue long-term investments: we saw this strategy at the *New York Times* as it shifted to a digital subscription model that gradually restored the profits lost from falling advertising and print circulation.

Private ownership provides the greatest discretion to invest or not invest over the short-term or long-term, and in some cases, the investment may be substantial, equaling or surpassing what public or civil society ownership forms can support. This ownership form includes private individuals such as Jeff Bezos, the Bonnier family of Sweden, and entrepreneur/founders Arianna Huffington, Jonah Peretti, and Shane Smith and their venture capital investor partners. Some owners who invest even in the face of low profits or losses are motivated by the pursuit of non-financial *amenity potential*, such as a civic or partisan mission, favorable news coverage of their business interests, or the search for status and policy influence. (With this context, we can see that the position of "mogul" arises out of particular forms of ownership—often private but also stock market-dominant shareholder—that provide the legal and material conditions for the personal realization of ownership's amenity potentials.)

Others, such as entrepreneurs backed by venture capital, are strongly profit-motivated but are willing to endure losses in the short term in the hopes of achieving an even higher long-term gain. Even if these start-ups ultimately fail to become economically sustainable, let alone reliably profitable—as has been the case with *BuzzFeed*, *Vice*, *Rue89*, *KIT*, *Slate*, and many others—in the interim, they may make important and unique journalistic contributions to the public sphere. We should thus not minimize the civic value of commercial *failures*, whether ephemeral or sustained over the long-term by partial public funding.

Ownership forms also tend to be associated with particular missions, funding, and audiences. Market-driven missions are highest for stock market-traded media. Information, pluralism, and democracy missions are emphasized most in public media. Private and especially civil society-owned media feature the widest range of missions, including partisan and religious. Funding models tend to cluster together in particular ownership forms: advertising for stock market-traded media, audience subscription funding for privately held media, a mix of subscription and philanthropic funding for civil society-owned media, and public funding for public media. When we also consider audience characteristics, we find two major structuring oppositions. The first is between stock market-traded and public ownership, where two visions of "universal" outreach confront one another: one, driven by profit and audience maximization, the other by public service obligations. The second opposition pits mostly elite civil society-owned media and private media against mostly omnibus stock market-traded and public media: at stake here is the extent to which "quality" news is reserved for elites, especially those willing to pay, or whether it should be accessible to all.

When we examine the news content of fifty-one news outlets across the three countries, we are able to sort out more clearly how ownership complexes interact to reinforce certain tendencies. Among the four broad ownership forms, we find that public service information makes up the highest proportion of news content at civil society-owned outlets; it is even higher at news outlets with the subforms of religious ownership or current/legacy journalist control. Public service information makes up the lowest proportion of news under stock market-traded and conglomerate ownership. Although some dominant shareholder-controlled outlets, such as the *New York Times*, provide exceptionally high-quality public service information, others do not: we do not find a strong or consistent difference between dominant shareholder and widely held stock market-traded outlets. In addition, we find that public service information provision is highest at outlets with left-leaning owners and left-leaning elite audiences, that rely primarily on philanthropy funding, and/or receive press subsidies. Conversely, advertising funding and omnibus audiences are associated with the lowest proportions of public service information provision.

Indeed, the mass omnibus Swedish and French public media provide lesser proportions of public service information than most elite audience outlets. However, they exhibit the strongest commitment to public service information among all omnibus audience media. This finding calls attention to the crucial mediating role played by ownership form—in this case civic mission-driven public ownership versus commercial ownership forms—as well as the indispensability of public media to ensure that non-elites also have access to quality public service information.

When we examine the proportion of public affairs to light/sensational content, we are able to make finer distinctions between ownership complexes: civil society-owned outlets with philanthropy funding and elite audiences differ from other outlets supported by elite subscribing audiences not only in their overall focus on public affairs, but especially in their more *exclusive* focus on such news.

Pluralism in news content is measured by the range of voices mentioned in articles. Pluralism is the highest at outlets with civil society ownership, and particularly at (mostly civil society-owned) partisan-affiliated outlets like the French *L'Humanité* and the Swedish *Dagens Arena*. To be clear, pluralistic coverage does not mean a news outlet is neutral in its treatment of everyone it mentions.

Partisan outlets may give ample voice to their ideological opponents the better to criticize them.

What of sociologist Jeffrey Alexander's claim that the "cultural power of the [journalistic] profession" can ensure the news media's commitment to public service news?[2] It is true that journalistic professional values help ensure a minimum of public service news at even the most market-driven outlets, as many journalists themselves contend. We find, however, that the profession's power to shape practice is strongest when it is backed by owners whose missions and economic models are aligned with, rather than in tension with, these ideals.

Our analysis complicates the Bourdieusian emphasis on autonomous versus heteronomous actors in fields. To be sure, Bourdieu helps us make sense of our finding that outlets with autonomous current/legacy journalist control provide the greatest proportion of public service information and that outlets with heteronomous stock market-traded or conglomerate ownership provide the lowest proportion. However, various civil society ownership subforms—religious, political party, trade union, foundation, or nonprofit association—are heteronomous to the journalistic field and yet also facilitate among the highest levels of information and pluralism, including giving voice to actors rarely heard at other outlets. This suggests that ownership forms cannot be entirely reduced to their field position, but also must be considered for their particular institutional logic. As opposed to Bourdieu's field theory, which stresses how a field *refracts* or shapes external influences according to the logic of the field (in this case journalistic), the *institutional logics* approach allows us to focus our attention on the unique incentives and affordances *introduced into the field* by non-journalist owners.

Turning to political instrumentalism and partisanship, we called attention to the natural experiment of US media coverage during the fall of 2015 and spring of 2016. Whereas Swedish and French news outlets engaged in the typical "indexing" of coverage to the party of the government in power, most US media outlets, in the midst of presidential primary elections, mentioned right-leaning political actors more often than left-leaning political actors. In the attention it accorded to populist right candidate Donald Trump, US coverage was driven not by a partisan political logic but by an audience-maximizing audience logic. Our research shows that US stock market-traded media outlets, regardless of the partisan leaning of their owners or audiences, accorded much greater attention to Donald Trump than media with other ownership forms.

Across our sampled news outlets, a right-leaning partisan favorability is associated with stock market dominant shareholder ownership. Otherwise, partisan favorability, whether left or right, is not significantly associated with any ownership form. Instead, we find that the relative favorability toward the right or left moves in parallel and almost equal strength to both owner and audience political preferences. Owners and their management teams, however, determine how *much* audience views will be taken into account: the decision to rely on audience subscription funding magnifies the degree to which audience partisan preferences correlate with an outlet's partisan slant in news content. Partisan intensity—a measure of the magnitude of favorability, whether left or right—is most strongly linked to civil society-owned and partisan-affiliated ownership, audience subscriber funding, and partisan audiences and owners (whether left or right). Intensity is lowest for news outlets with stock market-traded ownership (especially widely held), advertising funding, and politically neutral or balanced owners and audiences. Thus, we find support for the "amenity potential" argument that owners driven by motives other than profits will be the most partisan. Going beyond the US, our investigations partially counter Yochai Benkler and colleagues' argument that right-leaning owners and audiences foster more intensely partisan news content than left-leaning owners and audiences.[3]

Finally, we explored the professionally and ethically taboo world of economic instrumentalist promotion and suppression. In our quantitative analysis, we found that ownership interests are only rarely mentioned, but when they are mentioned, it is most often at stock market-traded widely held outlets and conglomerates. Most mentions are neutral, but those mentions with any valence tend to be positive more often than negative. This tendency is specific to coverage of ownership interests and suggests special treatment: in contrast, business mentions overall (like those of political actors) are more negative than positive. In our qualitative analysis of economic instrumentalist scandals, we found that accusations of suppression surfaced more often than those of promotion. Most of the scandals were tied to outlets with conglomerate, stock market dominant shareholder, or private ownership.

Unique contingencies of history and place are part of the story of every news organization, and thus not every outlet fits neatly into consistent patterns of ownership forms or complexes. If we want to fully explain the behavior of any *particular* news organization, we need to take into account in each case a localized, unique array of factors and circumstances.[4] However, ownership forms and complexes also matter. They foster distinct sets of organizational incentives and disincentives that operate across multiple individual outlets and thus influence those outlets to function in similar ways. We do not need to choose whether institutional structural regularities of ownership complexes or local contingencies shape the news. Clearly, both processes are at work.

What Differences do Nation-States Make?

To fully understand how ownership shapes the news, we must also consider variations across national fields.

The US field is the most bifurcated, with a large market ownership sector, historically heavily reliant on advertising, countered by a relatively small public and civil society-owned sector, mostly reliant on philanthropic donations. The Swedish field has historically been more equally balanced between a few major stock market-traded and private (or foundation) owners and a large and prestigious public broadcaster. Sweden also has among the highest levels of media trust and readership levels, historically supporting a relatively prosperous and politically partisan regional press, with a strong tendency to reach omnibus rather than only elite audiences across all ownership forms. In France, private ownership is dominant in audience reach and professional prestige, although often financially precarious and subject to widespread public distrust; most media rely on a mix of advertising, paying audiences, and public subsidies, so there is not the clear divide that one finds in the US between commercial and noncommercial ownership forms and funding. In recent years, an increasing proportion of France's national media has been purchased by stock market-traded conglomerates with control over significant non-news media holdings, creating potential conflicts of interest. Partly in response to these developments, but also as part of a longer French tradition of journalistic collective action, strong legal and professional movements have developed to install formal guarantees of journalistic autonomy against owner interference.

These field-level environmental differences have been crucial in generating unique ownership forms and subforms in each of the three countries. We should add that some aspects of these national patterns are not unique to journalism but are also related to differences in the amount and type of state support for a range of sectors, from education and medicine to other realms of cultural production like film, music, book publishing, and the performing arts.[5]

In the US, stock market-traded family dominant shareholders, like the Sulzbergers at the *New York Times*, have played a key role in maintaining a commitment to high journalistic standards: either through investment in new business models, or when necessary, in sacrificing short-term profits. US public media (*PBS*, *NPR*) are a hybrid of public and civil society ownership. They were founded with a mission to correct for the "market failure" of a hyper-commercialized media system that had abandoned historic public service obligations. Chronically starved of adequate public funding, they have turned to charitable donations from large foundations, business sponsors, and small donors to make up the difference. A growing civil society-owned online-only nonprofit sector—including *ProPublica*, *CIR/Reveal*, *Texas Tribune*, and *MinnPost* in our study—builds on the US multi-funding source "public media" model, minus the direct public funding (but benefiting from their non-taxable status for donations or revenues).

France's long and troubled history of corrupt "industrial" ownership of commercial media, countered by periodic attempts to launch "independent" alternatives, partly accounts for its unique mix of mission-driven private and civil society-owned outlets, old and new—*L'Humanité, Le Monde, Libération, Rue89*, and *Mediapart*, among others. *Mediapart* successfully pioneered a digital audience subscription-only model at a time when most media owners still believed the mantra that "information wants to be free," while *Rue89* fostered a loyal online community of co-contributors but failed to become financially viable. Elite legacy media and increasingly digital news start-ups are partly sustained by direct and indirect state subsidies.[6]

In Sweden, the continuing strength of public TV and radio—*SVT* and *SR*—is an outgrowth of the country's long-standing ambition to ensure that all citizens have access to comprehensive and independent information. Private family ownership—especially by the Bonniers, who have expanded their newspaper holdings in recent years—is more extensive than stock market-traded ownership. Political party/partisan-linked foundations are the most prevalent subform of civil society owner. The trade union LO remains a minority shareholder in the largest daily newspaper, *Aftonbladet*, and the largest funder of the left-activist online-only outlet *Dagens Arena*.

We also see these historical and policy differences reflected in national patterns of public service-oriented, partisan slanted, and economic instrumentalist news. For example, while civil society-owned media devote the highest proportion of their news coverage to public service information in all three countries, this tendency is strongest in the US. This finding accords with the sharp distinction in mission (more exclusively civic) and funding (philanthropic) at US civil society-owned (and public) media in comparison to their stock market-traded and private counterparts. It is important to note the degree of difference. For example, at national investigative news nonprofit outlets *ProPublica* and *CIR/Reveal*, investigative reporting made up forty-one and sixty-three percent, respectively, of their sampled articles, compared to five percent at *HuffPost*, the next highest US outlet. This is a much larger difference, for example, than the gap in investigative reporting in France between *Mediapart* (seven percent) and the next highest outlet, *Le Monde* (four percent). In Sweden, overall provision of public service information was highest for public media, while in France, it was highest for privately held media. These differences suggest which ownership forms exert symbolic leadership in each field.

Of the three national fields, public media are least oriented toward public service information in France. In contrast to the US, where public media have carved out an elite audience niche, and Sweden, where public media have maintained the dominant mass omnibus audience position, French public media occupy a secondary market position vis-à-vis the stock market-traded *TF1* (the former public channel #1). As such, to compete for audience share, French public media—particularly the *France 2* television channel—are often forced to partially emulate many of *TF1*'s informational strategies.[7] In an earlier report on public service news, we found that cross-ownership form differences were less pronounced in Sweden than in France and the US.[8] This finding suggests that journalistic practices across the field may be more homogeneous when there is a strong public service broadcaster.

Whether commercial pressures or non-commercial amenity potential most drive partisan favorability and intensity varies cross-nationally. In the bifurcated US field, non-commercial, nonprofit media have been explicitly established to correct for the market failure of commercial media. As such, they embrace the journalistic professional ideals of neutrality and non-partisanship. In contrast, civil society ownership in Sweden and France builds on their countries' long traditions of a partisan political press. In the US, partisan intensity functions largely as a sensationalistic means of attracting audiences and is highest at privately owned media; in France and especially Sweden, it tends to be higher at mission-driven civil society-owned media.

Economic instrumentalism tends to be concentrated at conglomerates. These ownership subforms are more prevalent in the US and France than in Sweden, and in fact, we found the least evidence of economic instrumentalist promotion and suppression in Sweden. While there are strong professional and ethical traditions against self-serving promotion or suppression in all three countries—and our data suggest that they are relatively low in all three countries—Sweden's cultural and legal norms and high levels of trust in media may both contribute to and reflect a particularly strong rejection of economic instrumentalism.

A Unified Framework for a Fragmented Field

At the end of the last century, a handful of scholars compared US corporate "chain"-owned and "independent" newspapers and declared the results "inconclusive." Their findings, based on a single portion of the media landscape in one country at a particular moment, were long cited by many as a definitive judgment about the supposedly minimal effects of media ownership.[9] That assessment can no longer stand, if it ever could. Elsewhere in the world, comparisons between public and commercial broadcasters have long established that media ownership matters.[10] And as nonprofit and other civil society forms proliferate in the wake of the breakdown of commercial models—just as much or more in the US as elsewhere—even the casual observer can see that previous ownership differences are being transformed and new ones are emerging.

Today, a growing body of research is showing the multitude of ways that ownership matters in shaping journalistic practice and news content. But the conclusions of this scholarship are difficult to trace because of the research's dispersion across a range of disciplines (sociology, political science, economics, journalism studies, and media management), journals and book publishers, national case studies, and time periods, not to mention languages of publishing. Even though these researchers are asking many of the same questions about media ownership, in any given place or time only a small portion of this scholarly universe is speaking directly to one another. To deepen our understanding of media ownership, we need to find a way to bring these and other research schools and individual studies into closer contact.

We believe that the theories and methods developed in this book offer such a way, a lingua franca to help facilitate dialogue and the advancement of knowledge and critical insight. To wit, we offer this book's conceptual framework of ownership forms and modes of ownership power as a heuristic capable of both organizing previous research and orienting future research. This framework seeks to make explicit a set of crucial questions that are often left implicit, and as a result, lost in the shuffle: what are the relationships between varieties of ownership (ownership forms linked to institutional logics), related structural dimensions (funding-audience adjustment strategies), and civically meaningful outcomes (modes of power)?

In this section of the Conclusion, we thus attempt to model what such an organization of the research might look like, although we make no claim to its comprehensiveness. We review and, where relevant, situate our empirical findings to this broad but dispersed literature in relation to (a) the three distinct modes of power of public service, political instrumentalism/partisanship, and economic instrumentalism; and (b) ownership forms and complexes, including primary funding, audience social characteristics (high education/income versus low education/income), and both owner and audience political preferences. We focus primarily on studies conducted after 2000 that link ownership and funding-audience adjustment to news/opinion content. This review can confirm the extent to which our findings (based on a limited time period and number of countries and media outlets) hold for other news organizations, places, and times. More broadly, our hope is that this framing of the research—both in what it includes and what it inevitably fails to include—will help generate a richer and more generative dialogue among media ownership researchers across the globe.

We begin with the *information* dimension of *public service orientation.* One of the most consistent findings of this research is the civic superiority of public television and radio (often referred to by its European moniker of public service broadcasting) compared to commercial audio-visual media. For example, a widely cited study comparing publicly and commercially owned television news in the US, the UK, Denmark, and Finland by Curran and colleagues shows that "public service television gives greater attention to public affairs and international news, and thereby fosters greater [public] knowledge in these areas, than the market model."[11] In a study of political election news in Sweden and the US, Daniela Dimitrova and Jesper Strömbäck found that the public *SVT* had more substantive "issue" framing (as opposed to the strategic "political game" framing) than commercial *TV4*, and that *TV4* in turn was very similar to US commercial channels *ABC*, *CBS*, and *NBC*.[12]

The same public versus commercial audio-visual differences seem to hold for the content of their websites. In their multi-country study of political news, Claes H. de Vreese, Frank Esser, and David Nicolas Hopmann, leading a distinguished international team of scholars, show that public broadcasters compared to commercial media (both online and offline) provide more "hard" issue-based news coverage and less "soft" news (similar to our "light/sensational" news).[13] British media scholar Stephen Cushion compared online *BBC* news to online commercial outlets including legacy elite as well as popular newspaper sites and online-only outlets *BuzzFeed* and *HuffPost*: he found that the *BBC*'s online news focused more on public affairs while the commercial outlets featured a higher proportion of celebrity and entertainment articles.[14] In her comparative study of online news in the US, France, the UK, Germany, and Switzerland, Edda Humprecht showed that across all these countries public media provided, on average, more "hard news" (defined partially as news with "political relevance" and focus on "societal versus individual relevance") than commercial media. This tendency was especially marked in those countries in her sample with well-funded, autonomous public broadcasting (Great Britain, Germany, Switzerland) and less so in the US, France, and Italy. She found that "analytical depth" (measured in terms of inclusion of historical context, multiple perspectives, and discussion of causes and significance of events) was substantially higher at public *France 2* than at stock market-traded *TF1*.[15]

In this book, we also find that public service orientation is strong at online public media. But because our approach considers funding and audiences, we can nuance and qualify what public media can and cannot do. As noted, we found that public media directed to omnibus audiences and wholly or mostly publicly funded—as in Sweden and France—are less purely focused on public affairs news than are many elite commercial outlets. Rather than automatically condemning public media for compromising on "quality," however, we should acknowledge their need to provide a mix of "hard" and "soft" news to achieve their civic mission of reaching a wide public. Compared to commercial *omnibus* media, these public media provide more public affairs information. As such, public media can overcome the opposition that tends to structure the commercial space between high quality public service-oriented news for elites and lower quality news for everyone else. Public media offer a unique means of combining quality *and* accessibility.

Conversely, while research suggests that the most market-driven media will produce the lowest proportion of public affairs news,[16] the clarity and usefulness of these findings have sometimes been undermined by the use of the imprecise category of "corporate" ownership, blurring the important distinction between privately owned and stock market-traded companies. With this caveat, the weight of the evidence does seem to point to a progressive abandonment of public affairs news at US stock market-traded media outlets as the "shareholder value" governance model has been widely adopted. Over the last decades of the twentieth century, US stock market-traded national television network evening news shows increased their production of "soft news tales" and decreased their coverage of "votes on major congressional legislation."[17] Likewise, after the widely held stock market-traded Gannett Corporation purchased the privately held *Louisville Courier-Journal*, the proportion of public affairs "hard news" decreased, as did that of originally produced news, while the proportion of wire-service to staff-written articles increased.[18] Other studies confirm that both stock market-traded newspapers and television stations, because they tend to cut costs by reducing the number of political reporters, provide less substantive issue coverage of politics than privately held newspapers.[19] Humprecht's six-country study highlights a significant difference between stock market-traded and private media, with a greater public service orientation in the latter.[20]

Research is just emerging about hedge fund-owned outlets. A comparison of the 2016 election news coverage of three "investment company"-owned (hedge fund/private equity) newspapers with two *non*-investment company-owned newspapers found that the latter "tend to cover local [political] races in greater detail than their investment-owned peers, dedicating more space to staff-written articles about state and local elections" and starting their coverage earlier, thus providing crucial information for mail-in and other early voters.[21] In a large scale study of 1,600 newspapers, scholars found that when a newspaper's ownership shifted to private equity, the "number of reporters and editors falls," news composition "shifts away from local governance," and citizen "participation in local elections declines."[22]

For journalism scholar Gavin Ellis, family-controlled newspapers like the *New York Times*, even if stock market-traded, can constitute a type of "trust" providing "structural protections" to support a commitment to good journalism in the public interest. Indeed, as we showed in Chapter 2, among those commercial news outlets that have recently won journalistic professional prizes, the highest proportion have had stock market dominant shareholder ownership (in the US) or private (family or individual) ownership (in all three countries). This pattern was also borne out by separate studies conducted by James Hamilton and Steve Waldman on the awarding of US journalism prizes.[23] Yet Ellis also notes that when dominant shareholder-controlled companies own secondary papers, as the *Times* did with the *Boston Globe* until 2013, the protections and commitment may not extend to these additional newspapers in the same way.[24] Moreover, the stock market dominant shareholder subform is not reserved only for high prestige companies like the *New York Times*. As Gilbert Cranberg and colleagues showed in their 2001 study, many other US newspaper companies traded on the stock market at that time had dominant shareholders, but not all of them were particularly noted for their journalistic excellence.[25] In our content analysis, we also find that the *New York Times* provides more public service information than most other outlets, but *Fox News*, *CBS*, and *Slate*, which have the same ownership subform as the *Times*, do not. Conversely, *Svenska Dagbladet*, owned by Schibsted (a widely held stock market-traded company), also produces high levels of public service information. In sum, we need more research to clarify when and why stock market-traded news outlets with a dominant shareholder are more or less public service-oriented than their widely held peers.

Given the relative youth of most civil society media, systematic research is only beginning to emerge about this ownership form. Our framework identifies both the general tendencies across the broad civil society ownership form as well as the most salient lines of difference. As reported in Chapter 3, nonprofits invest a substantially higher proportion of their revenues than commercial legacy media in investigative and other types of public affairs reporting.[26] A study of local news provision in the Philadelphia regional media system found that nonprofits and public media tended to devote a higher proportion of their coverage to community impacts of the COVID-19 pandemic than did their commercial counterparts, which tended to lean more toward attention-grabbing coverage of breaking crime news.[27] Other case studies comparing local nonprofit and commercial legacy newspapers have found that the nonprofits provide more in-depth, interpretive and explanatory news, and less sensationalist news.[28] And when commercial newspapers are forced to cut back or close, the public affairs and investigative reporting provided by nonprofits (despite their often small size) have been shown to play an "important, supplemental role in shoring up governmental accountability that can help mitigate the impact of the declines of local newspapers."[29]

Not all research on public service orientation, however, discovers a clear-cut civic superiority of civil society media. Journalism scholar Magda Konieczna compared the nonprofit *MinnPost* and the privately held *Minneapolis Star Tribune* (both included in our study) during a period when the Minnesota state legislature "shut down." She found that *MinnPost* published far less content, hosted less citizen discussion, and reposted (or aggregated) far more news content than the *Star Tribune*. Konieczna attributes this difference to fewer overall resources at *MinnPost*, a reliance on foundation project-based funding that made it impossible to reallocate reporters to breaking news, and a strategic management model that emphasized appealing to high education/income elites over ordinary citizens. Nevertheless, *MinnPost*'s mission to supplement, rather than replicate, commercial media offerings led the outlet to commission a survey of citizen opinions of the shutdown when it became clear no other outlet would be doing so.[30]

To re-emphasize, as our framework shows, the civil society ownership form, while bringing together all outlets situated between the market and the state, is actually a constellation of institutional logics. While evidence is growing that philanthropy-supported nonprofits focus more exclusively on public service information than their commercial or even public counterparts, research on other types of civil society-owned outlets—religious, party-affiliated, and foundation/trust-owned outside of the US 501(c)(3) form—is still scarce. Scholars have argued that Swedish foundation-owned newspapers are more focused on investing in their operations than on maximizing profitability,[31] and we found support for this thesis in our interviews, but until now it has not been clear how that might translate into any actual difference in public service news provision. Confirming Jonas Ohlsson's view that the "distinctive features of foundation ownership compared to the more traditional, profit-oriented private ownership" have become "less prominent" over time, we found that the Swedish foundation-owned newspapers in our study (*Barometern*, *Gefle Dagblad*, and *Norran*) are *not* significantly different from other Swedish news outlets in their production of public service news.[32] The same can be said in our study for the French foundation-owned but commercially operated newspaper *Ouest-France*, confirming Humprecht's finding of average or below average public service performance by outlets with this ownership subform—both *Ouest-France* and the US *Tampa Bay Times* in her study.[33] In other words, these ownership forms may help maintain an important level of basic investment in public service news but they do not stand out as providing substantially more public service information than other outlets.

We are not aware of systematic research beyond ours showing that religious organization-owned media tend to provide a higher proportion of public service information than other outlets. More research is needed to pursue our finding that outlets with current/legacy journalist ownership control, a subform most often associated with private or civil society ownership, also tend to have among the highest levels of public service information.

Our framework, however, also highlights the importance of funding-audience adjustment strategies and how they interact with ownership forms.

Public funding is an integral part of what makes public media "public," and it is facilitated by governments with the explicit intent that this funding (either from dedicated fees or general tax revenues) be used to produce the crucial information about government and public affairs that citizens need to exercise their civic rights and obligations. This book and other comparative studies have shown that publicly funded public media tend to provide this kind of news more often than most of their commercial peers with omnibus audiences. In our research, even partial public funding, in the form of subsidies to newspapers or digital outlets, contributes to greater provision of public service information. Other studies confirm this finding. For example, a comparison of publicly subsidized and unsubsidized newspapers in Norway discovered that the subsidized papers actually produced "far more original news stories" than the non-subsidized papers.[34]

Other forms of funding also can have a powerful effect on the kind of news that is produced. Philanthropic funding, largely associated with civil society ownership, is overtly motivated by a desire to generate measurable "impact" on urgent social issues. Previous research has documented how philanthropy supports the kind of in-depth or investigative reporting valued most highly by journalists (even if this support can sometimes come with a hidden or not-so-hidden agenda);[35] our research, however, is among the first large-scale content analyses to demonstrate the strength of this connection. In contrast, primary reliance on advertising funding, most often linked to stock market-traded ownership, is associated with the lowest proportions of public service information in our research. This finding confirms the long-standing political economy critiques of Baker and others.[36]

As advertising declines as a source of revenue, the question is how much difference will commercial alternatives like audience subscription funding make? Helle Sjøvaag's study of Norwegian newspapers showed that "paywalled" content only available to subscribers tends to feature more "resource-demanding journalistic production," whereas the free, advertising-supported content is mostly from wire services, breaking news, and stories that are "highly traffic-generating."[37] Indeed, our journalist and managerial interviewees often stressed the quality-enhancing aspects of the shift to subscription funding. In our content analyses, we likewise found that audience subscription funding contributed to a higher amount of public service information than advertising funding, but not as much as philanthropy.

However, as our framework emphasizes, the other half of funding-audience adjustment—the class and political characteristics of the audience—is just as if not more important. In connection to public service information, this connection has been investigated much less systematically.[38] In our study, outlets with elite or left-leaning audiences tend to produce more public service information than outlets with omnibus, neutral/balanced, or right-leaning audiences. Additional carefully structured research is needed, especially as the widespread use of audience metrics makes audiences (or at least the journalistic perception of audiences) a force within the field that is likely to grow.

Public service or public affairs journalism is colloquially understood as a singular phenomenon, but our framework emphasizes its multiple, potentially cross-cutting dimensions. In this sense our approach is similar to the news or role performance research projects led by Claes de Vreese and Claudia Mellado, respectively.[39] The outlets that emphasize production of public service information may or may not also provide the widest range of voices and viewpoints. In her six-country study of news outlets, Humprecht showed that "independent" (which included some civil society-owned) media had the highest levels of topic diversity, followed by media with public and "corporate" ownership (in her study, a close proxy of stock market) grouped together: this finding (echoing ours) suggests less of an opposition between public and commercial media for pluralism than for information provision.[40] In contrast, we discover that outlets with the partisan-affiliated subform—even though they are not distinctive in their production of public service information—offer the most pluralistic coverage.

Just as we found, other scholars have shown that relatively new entrants in the field, such as the privately held (until 2021) online-only *BuzzFeed* and the digital/cable *Vice*, may invest in pluralism as a way to generate both large audiences and peer respect. Research comparing *UK BuzzFeed* and *UK Vice* to the *Guardian* and *BBC* showed that the two digital start-ups cited fewer political elite sources, slightly more civil society sources (at *BuzzFeed*), and substantially more ordinary citizens.[41]

This distinction between two elements of public service orientation—information and pluralism—can further nuance how ownership forms and associated funding-audience adjustment strategies shape news production. For example, we find that philanthropy funding is just as supportive of pluralism as it is of information. However, public funding—which is nearly equal to philanthropy in its support of information—is associated with the lowest levels of pluralism. This finding, subject to further research, tempers our understanding of what public media can and cannot best accomplish. While public media may be well incentivized to provide crucial information underproduced by the market, they may be less well equipped (or even disincentivized due to political pressures) to provide a wide range of voices and viewpoints, particularly from marginal party or social movement actors.

Moving on to the second mode of power—political instrumentalism/partisanship—our framework highlights the need to reach beyond the sociology of news and journalism studies to engage with the important research being conducted by political scientists and economists. Few previous political communication studies of partisan slant have focused on ownership form differences, but some case studies may include findings on a range of outlets that could be re-interpreted in light of our framework.[42]

Likewise, the results of large sample studies by economists can be re-interpreted with a greater focus on ownership form. In a comprehensive US study of media "bias" that included most of the leading US national mainstream media, economists Timothy Groseclose and Jeffrey Milyo compared each media outlet's citations of major think tanks with the think tank citation pattern in the speeches of US Senators (as documented in the *Congressional Record*), whose voting records have been independently rated as more or less "liberal" (left). Media outlets whose citation patterns are closer to Senators rated as more left-leaning thus receive higher left-biased scores.[43] Groseclose and Milyo found that most US mainstream media outlets leaned left of center. They did not analyze ownership form directly, but the outlets they identified with the strongest left bias in their news pages almost uniformly had stock market dominant shareholder ownership (with the notable exception of *Fox News*, which was among the furthest to the right): the *Wall Street Journal* (under Bancroft family control), the *New York Times*, *CBS*, and the *Washington Post*.[44] This finding may be at least partly US-specific. In our three-country sample, relative to other ownership forms, we found an association between stock market dominant shareholder ownership and a slightly higher favorability toward the *right*, not the left.

While not offering a comparison with other ownership forms, a study of Swedish public media coverage of elections and referenda between 1979 and 2010 found that the amount of coverage of all political parties by *SVT* news (Rapport and Aktuellt) was roughly in proportion to their vote share, while the large parties, whether liberal-conservative (Moderate Party) or left (Social Democratic Party), tended to get the most negative coverage. Overall, Rapport and Aktuellt provided slightly more positive coverage of the right than the left parties, while Ekot (*SR* radio news) covered left parties more favorably by a narrow margin. Swedish media scholar Kent Asp concluded: "Public service [media], in a total and long-term perspective, has been fair—in so far as no party or opinion has unduly and systematically been favored or unfavored."[45]

In contrast to economists Matthew Gentzkow and Jesse M. Shapiro's oft-repeated finding that audiences matter more than owners in shaping US media outlets' partisan content slant, we find that owners and audience preferences are roughly comparable in their effects.[46] A recent study by Marcel Garz and Jonna Rickardsson analyzes 127 Swedish newspapers with forty distinct owners, many of them part of chains with the same owner circulating across regions differing sharply in their party loyalties. Analyzing eight "ideologies" linked to the major Swedish political parties, the authors find that newspapers with the same owners tend to have "the same mix of slant, rather than aligning their bias with consumer preferences in their area of circulation": this tendency tends to be even stronger during time periods directly before elections, "when the political returns to persuasion are high."[47] Indeed, it may be that the inclination or ability of owners to shape news content independent of audience preferences varies cross-nationally. When we break out our findings by national field, we find that while all three countries follow the same patterns, the association between owner political preferences and partisan slant is stronger in France and Sweden (and strongest in the latter) than in the US; conversely, audience political preferences are linked to partisan slant in all three countries, but most strongly in the US. Nevertheless, even in the US some owners, such as the Sinclair local television channel chain, have produced ideologically slanted news content (in this case, right-leaning) out of sync with audience preferences.[48] Deep-pocketed private owners and investors have long played a role in supporting unprofitable partisan media on the right and the left, with varying levels of impact.

Our framework also enables us to shed light on the understudied phenomenon of partisan *intensity*; that is, the magnitude of favorability independent of the direction. Without using the term, some studies of partisan slant also examine intensity. For example, the Groseclose and Milyo study that emphasized a left-leaning bias in US mainstream media also presented outlets in relation to their "distance from center" (whether from the right or left). Their data show that the single outlet closest to the center was the public television *PBS NewsHour*.[49] In the research for this book, we find a statistically significant opposition between stock market-traded ownership, with the lowest partisan intensity, and civil society ownership, with the highest. However, this finding is substantially shaped by the inclusion of openly partisan civil society Swedish and French newspapers in our sample. Conversely, our finding that philanthropy contributes less than audience funding to partisan intensity may also be contextually limited. A Pew Research Center study of thirty-nine US nonprofits found that US Institute for Nonprofit News (INN) members *ProPublica*, *Texas Tribune*, *MinnPost*, *California Watch* (a project of *CIR/Reveal*), and the *Connecticut Mirror*, were "non-ideological," based on their high level of balanced treatment of left and right actors and viewpoints. However, the Pew study also revealed that a number of small nonprofits, generally reliant on a single left- or right-leaning foundation, did exhibit strong partisan slant in their news coverage.[50] This research allows us to see that it may not be philanthropic funding per se that shapes political slant, but rather the type and number of philanthropic funders. Few other studies to our knowledge have attempted to analyze the links between the full range of funding types and partisan intensity. Further research is needed to test our finding that media outlets with audience subscription funding have the highest partisan intensity, while media with advertising funding have the lowest. As digital subscriptions become a major funding source for news media across the globe, more research is needed on this important factor that may be contributing to increased political polarization.

Finally, *economic instrumentalism* provides a useful umbrella term to organize the wide-ranging research focused on owner attempts to either promote positive information or suppress negative information related to their business interests. Overt promotion, as we measure it here, has been found to be relatively rare across a range of media. Our findings accord with Dmitri Williams's research that US commercial TV morning news shows mentioned their ownership interests in less than four percent of all stories.[51] Similarly, Adam Saffer and colleagues analyzed how news organizations covered their owning company board members and the organizations they were affiliated with: their research also found relatively low levels of coverage.[52] As for the valence associated with these mentions, Williams found that the TV shows treated products and services linked to owners "more favorably than others"; Saffer and colleagues found only small amounts of "critical scrutiny" of ownership interests.[53] But is such treatment a byproduct of overall uncritical business coverage? Our research expands on previous studies by showing that coverage of ownership interests *is* exceptional: it is positive on average, while mentions of other businesses are on balance negative. More research is needed, however, on how economic instrumentalism varies across ownership forms.

The important research of British media scholar Jonathan Hardy links to our claim that funding-audience adjustment strategies may also shape media performance. Hardy found that cross-promotion was higher at Murdoch's News Corporation popular tabloids than at his elite "quality" newspapers, as well as being higher in the newspapers' entertainment and sports sections than in general news.[54] While we only found modest support for this thesis in our quantitative content analysis, this argument does align with economic instrumentalist public scandals we discovered that revealed the divergent experiences of journalists at elite and popular newspapers with the same dominant shareholder.

One aspect of economic instrumentalism we did not examine, and which deserves much greater research attention, is self-interested media policy coverage. An exemplar of this type of research is Martin Gilens and Craig Hertzman's study of coverage of the 1996 Telecommunications Act. They compared US newspapers owned by companies also owning substantial numbers of television stations (and thus likely to be favorably impacted by passage of the legislation) with newspapers owned by companies without television station properties. The authors found both promotion and suppression effects. In their news coverage of the legislation, newspapers with substantial television properties were more likely than other newspapers to promote potential positive impacts and to suppress potential negative consequences.[55]

In sum, our framework of four ownership forms and three modes of ownership power provides a useful heuristic to organize and focus ownership research. It provides a way to analyze ownership forms in context, as part of complexes of inter-related dimensions, especially primary funding and audience characteristics. Further, each time that ownership is identified as worthy of research, it encourages the researcher to clarify which "mode" of ownership power will be examined. The framework, however, should not be taken as a static end product, but rather as a historically situated intervention that can and must evolve as news media and the broader hybrid media system continue to change.[56]

New Directions

Of course, this book does not exhaust all possible important dimensions of ownership power. We focus on mainstream media, making room for national differences in how the mainstream is defined. More research is needed on the ownership of media at the margins of the journalistic field, such as growing sectors of highly partisan far right media that may not be fully accepted by professional journalists but which increasingly attract large audiences.[57] We would expect that most of these marginal media would be small-scale private (individual or family privately held) or civil society-owned, but research will need to confirm this hypothesis. Systematic research is also needed on funding-audience adjustment strategies that may be unique to extremist hyper-partisan media: for example, some journalistic investigations have suggested that this sector is marked by a lack of transparency about its investors and donors, who often directly shape news coverage.[58]

This book has been focused on the decade from the early 2010s to the early 2020s, a period of rapid transformation across the news industry and profession. As such, we capture an "unsettled" period in which news organizations struggled to find new economic models that would replace the old ones that were no longer working. New research in the decade to come *might* capture a more "settled" period marked by less experimentation and a more constrained set of practices—but just as likely, it will have to contend with a new set of disruptions, whether from artificial intelligence, the rise of populist right political parties, or other technological, political, and economic changes as yet unforeseen.

Future research could go beyond the content analysis indicators we developed to measure other aspects of news relevant to the three modes of power. Scholars could build on our focus on the proportion of prominent articles devoted to public service information by also calculating the total volume of public service-oriented coverage. To fully measure impact and reach, they might also analyze news sharing partnerships that have been common at many US nonprofits.[59] At some nonprofit outlets, the number of individual articles produced per day may be small compared to large commercial news outlets; however, the volume of re-publications and social media shares of the nonprofit articles may be significantly larger.

In addition to institutional and ideological pluralism of voices and viewpoints, research could examine the diversity of identities (class, gender, sexuality, race/ethnicity, age) of individuals appearing in news coverage. Studies could construct larger samples of subforms explored in this study, such as religious or partisan-affiliated, or various types of foundations, cooperatives, or nonprofit associations, to fill out an understanding of the range of possibilities within the civil society-owned and private ownership forms. Quantitative research could be supplemented by more qualitative case studies, preferably comparative across two or more outlets, to reveal in-depth the functioning of distinct ownership forms or subforms.[60] Scholars could also probe more deeply into emerging hybrid ownership forms, such as mergers in the US of public media and digital nonprofit outlets, with an eye toward any changes that are being produced in newsroom practices and news content and form.[61] Types of funding not examined in this book, such as advertising-funded email newsletters or podcasts, or negotiated payments to media outlets by large digital platforms analyzed by Benedetta Brevini, also deserve systematic study for their relation to ownership forms and journalistic practice.[62]

Research could explore the effect of more or less democratic investment and governance procedures inside news organizations, in line with economist Julia Cagé's call for reforms: do such procedures, where they exist, lessen economic instrumentalist promotion or suppression?[63] Similarly, do news outlets where journalists exercise the right to elect their publisher or top editor (either directly, or through a veto, such as at *Le Monde* or *Libération*) differ in the kind of news they produce from those where journalists do not have such rights? We know from this study that *Le Monde* and *Libération* highlight public service information more than most other news outlets, but more case studies and larger samples of similar outlets are needed to understand precisely how this kind of journalist control shapes the news.

Our sample countries are limited to North America and western Europe. Our findings can be aligned with the growing body of ownership research in other parts of the world. In their study of journalistic role perceptions in eighteen developing and developed countries, Zvi Reich and Thomas Hanitzch find that ownership factors are perceived to be influential by professional journalists and do seem to be objectively influential in the case of state-owned media; Mellado and colleagues conclude in their study of nine European, Asian, and Latin American countries that ownership, editorial policies, and audience orientation together begin to explain gaps between journalists' role perceptions and performance.[64] Our findings about the amenity potential offered by media ownership—particularly for wealthy private owners—are echoed by research in Central and Eastern European countries and in India. Indian regional press "proprietor-editors" seem particularly apt to politically instrumentalize their media holdings. As in our research, inclinations and capacities to advance partisan causes or business interests are shaped by national and regional media market and field contexts.[65]

Audience metrics have been adopted at media organizations around the world, potentially reshaping news to be in closer accord with audience preferences. Our research shows the use of web metrics in audience adjustment strategies across ownership forms in the US, France, and Sweden. Similarly, despite the absence of commercial ownership pressures, Nikki Usher discovered that journalists at the non-commercial, Qatari royal family-funded *Al Jazeera* were keen to know how many viewers their content was gathering.[66] More research is needed to analyze these and other technological tools across ownership forms, types of states, and global regions.

International research has also found configurations of institutional logics, ownership complexes, and national field effects that underscore the need for more historically and geographically situated research. For example, commercial and state logics are mixed in China's socialist market economy and in Oceania countries where governments own shares in media through private investment companies.[67] Likewise, in some African countries non-journalistic actors, such as international NGOs, comedians, bloggers, and musicians, are entwined with ownership influences.[68] Ownership may also be linked to complex transnational networks, as in the case of "pan-Arab media."[69] Further, various African countries have seen the emergence of foundation-funded and other nonprofit organizations like those analyzed in this book that pursue deep investigations of government malfeasance and corruption.[70] This book's framework can help guide research across a wide range of geographically specific contexts even as we expect that it will need to be modified to make sense of forms and strategies not present in our three countries.

To conclude, research on media ownership—ours and others—presents a complex, multifaceted, but far from inconclusive portrait of contemporary journalism. Our understanding of the patterned and consequential ways in which ownership forms differ has steadily increased. It is true, however, that no single ownership form or funding-audience adjustment strategy will be the magic bullet to solve all of journalism's or democracy's problems. Each has its civic and economic strengths and weaknesses, which owners and managers, journalists, policymakers, and citizens should become aware of to develop new and better organizational strategies, professional practices, and supportive media public policies. We hope this book will be a useful resource for these important and urgent projects.

Acknowledgments

This book grew out of an invitation from Mattias Hessérus to Rodney Benson, on behalf of the Swedish Axel and Margaret Ax:son Johnson Foundation for Public Benefit and its project on Journalism and Democracy, to join in researching and writing a book on media ownership. In initial conversations with Hessérus, Benson agreed that the topic was important and interesting, but suggested that instead of the typical focus on concentration, the book could systematically analyze differences in ownership forms across multiple countries. Once the two had settled on conducting a US–Sweden–France comparison, Benson suggested that Julie Sedel be brought on as a French collaborator, and she accepted the invitation. Subsequently, Timothy Neff joined as co-author to help coordinate the quantitative news content coding and analyses. It has been a long journey, simultaneously stimulating and demanding given the complexity of the research questions, the challenges of gaining access to elite informants and organizational data, and the vagaries of coordinating synchronous collaboration given other professional and personal responsibilities. At one point, we discussed separate chapters for each country; we concluded that a thematic organization would be more dynamic and was better suited to the book's theoretical aims. This organization necessitated a particular division of labor. The lead author assumed the main responsibility in organizing the research and in writing, with input from co-authors (listed in alphabetical order on the book's title page).

As lead author, Benson conceptualized the organization of the book as a whole and wrote the first drafts of all chapters, as well as the penultimate and final versions of the entire manuscript. Benson also developed the theoretical framework outlined in Chapter 1 and the news content indicators presented in Chapters 5 and 6; conducted interviews in the US, France, and Sweden; and gathered (or supervised the gathering of) the US, Swedish, and French statistical data and much of the US and French literature review. Hessérus contributed interviews and an internally shared paper on Swedish media ownership history, and he worked with Benson to coordinate research by Swedish research assistants. Neff developed the original content indicators of ownership mentions and valence presented in Chapter 7; carried out research on US outlet funding, audiences, and owner characteristics; and worked closely with Benson on the statistical analysis and literature review. Sedel conducted interviews and wrote internally shared papers providing portraits of French news outlets and synthesizing French media ownership history. Hessérus and Sedel shared their country-specific expertise and confirmed factual accuracy of descriptions of the Swedish and French media. Hessérus, Neff, and Sedel also participated in the editing and proofing of multiple chapter and manuscript drafts, offering comments and contributing references and language.

Many other people made important contributions throughout the research process.

Carl Ritter conducted interviews; carried out research on Swedish media owners, funders, and audiences; and compiled an annotated bibliography of the relevant Swedish research. His contributions, including helping to supervise research assistants, were invaluable to the book's successful completion.

We are grateful to the news organization founders, executives, editors, and reporters who took the time to share their experiences and insights with us.

In addition to interviews conducted by Benson, Sedel, Hessérus, and Ritter, interviews (and other research) were also conducted by Swedish research assistants Erik Thyselius and Marcus Nilsen.

Shuanghao Tang and Jacopo Angeloni provided meticulous research on Swedish media and overall fact-checking. Additional valuable research assistance was provided by Ella Shoshan, Elly Hanauer, Laura Bullon-Cassis, Hyo Jung Kim, Tim Wood, Patrick Stancil, Rodrigo Ferreira, Zhuoru Deng, Danny Solomon, Gabriel Lagerström, Astrid Viktorsson, Thomas Benson, and Najate Zouggari. Tyler Leeds and Sarah Mastrocola meticulously and expertly proofed the final manuscript.

We received helpful comments on presentations of earlier iterations of the project or chapter drafts from the Ax:son Johnson Foundation conference in Stockholm; the Reuters Institute conference on media ownership at Oxford; Boston University and Rutgers University Departments of Sociology; the University of Zurich media and communication research group, led by Frank Esser; the Toulouse Institute d'Études Politiques; the Assises du Journalisme in Lille, France; the University of Roskilde (Denmark) Department of Communication; the International Journal of Press/Politics Oxford conference; the Centro de Estudios de Conflicto y Cohesión at the University of Chile, Santiago; University of Stockholm Department of Media Studies; the (virtual version of the) International Media Management Conference in Stockholm; and annual conferences of the International Communication Association, American Sociological Association, and Association française de science politique.

Dan Hallin and Olle Lidbom read versions of the entire book and offered insightful and generative comments. Michael Schudson, Victor Pickard, and Matthew Powers read chapter drafts and provided very helpful advice. Sigurd Allern, Jonas Ohlsson, Henrik Örnebring, Kristina Riegert, Jesper Strömbäck, and Lars Truedson helped fill out our portrait of contemporary Swedish media.

In addition, we received useful and generous information, comments, and diverse forms of helpful feedback, suggestions, support, and encouragement from Leona Achtenhagen, C. W. Anderson, Olivier Baisnée, Pablo Boczkowski, Henrik Bødker, danah boyd, Benedetta Brevini, Mel Bunce, Julia Cagé, Ned Crowley, Peter M. Dahlgren, Eric Darras, Giovanna Dell'Orto, Paul DiMaggio, Martin Eide, Des Freedman, James Graff, Laura Grindstaff, Jonathan Groves, Serge Halimi, Mark Hannah, Alfred Hermida, David Hesmondhalgh, Richard John, Jeff Manza, Phil Napoli, Erik Neveu, Rasmus Kleis Nielsen, Jérémie Nollet, Johanna Ollevik, Étienne Ollion, Robert Picard, Steve Reese, Claire Richard, Pierre Rimbert, Guy Rolnick, Anya Schiffrin, Martin Scott, Marco Solaroli, Sergio Splendore, David Swartz, Nikki Usher, Elise Vincent, Philippe Wallez, Kimberly Wear, Oscar Westlund, Ida Willig, Kate Wright, and Mary Lynn Young.

We also wish to thank Oxford University Press's anonymous reviewers, who provided immensely useful comments both on the initial proposal and the completed manuscript. While we seriously engaged with all the excellent suggestions provided by our colleagues, any remaining shortcomings in the book of course are the responsibility of the authors alone.

James Cook was the ideal editor in every way—patient, diplomatic, reachable, encouraging—to shepherd this project to completion. Alexcee Bechthold, Nirenjena Joseph, and Lavanya Nithya provided expert guidance throughout the final production process. Ken High offered valuable design suggestions that further improved an already strong cover design.

We gratefully acknowledge the financial support provided for this research from the Axel and Margaret Ax:son Johnson Foundation for Public Benefit, the NYU University Research Challenge Fund, and the NYU Steinhardt Dean's Grant.

APPENDIX I

Tables

Table AI.1 Sampled Media Organizations by National Journalistic Field, Ownership Form, and Specific Owner (as of 2016; any major changes through 2022)

Ownership Form/ Subform and dominant Institutional Logics	United States	Sweden	France
Market: Stock market-widely held (market)	***ABC News*** (Disney) ***CNN*** (Time Warner; AT&T 2018; Discovery 2022) ***HuffPost*** (Verizon; BuzzFeed Inc. SM-DS 2021) ***Los Angeles Times*** (Tribune; Patrick Soon-Shiong-Private 2018) ***USA Today*** (Gannett) ***Chicago Tribune**** (Tribune; Alden Global Capital 2021) ***Des Moines Register**** (Gannett)	***Svenska Dagbladet*** (Schibsted) ***Aftonbladet**** (Schibsted)	***TF1#*** (Bouygues) ***Metronews#*** (TF1/Bouygues)
Market: Stock market-dominant shareholder (market, family)	***CBS News*** (Viacom/ National Amusements—Sumner and Sheri Redstone) ***Fox News*** (21st C. Fox; Fox Corp. 2019/Murdoch family) ***New York Times*** (New York Times Co./Sulzberger family) ***Slate#*** (Graham Holdings/ Donald Graham)	***Metro#*** (Kinnevik/Stenbeck family; Custos-Private 2017; closed 2019)	***Le HuffPost#*** (Verizon, Le Monde Group-Niel, Bergé, Pigasse, and Matthieu Pigasse private holding co.; BuzzFeed Inc. purchases Verizon share 2021) ***Le Figaro*** (Dassault) ***Le Parisien**** (LVMH/Bernard Arnault)
Private (family, market)	***Metro#*** (Pelle Törnberg) ***BuzzFeed#*** (Jonah Peretti and VC; BuzzFeed, Inc./ Peretti SM-DS 2021) ***Minneapolis Star Tribune*** (Glen Taylor) ***Washington Post*** (Jeff Bezos) ***Vice#*** (Shane Smith and VC) ***Boston Globe**** (John Henry)	***Dagens Nyheter*** (Bonnier) ***Dagens ETC#*** (Johan Jenny Ehrenberg; foundation Stiftelsen ETC CS ≈2020) ***Göteborgs-Posten*** (Stampen group/ Hjörne family; Polaris Media with NWT and VK Media 51% 2019, ≈100% 2021 SM-WH) ***KIT#*** (Bonnier; closed as news outlet 2019) ***Jönköpings-Posten#*** (Hallpressen/ Hamrin family/Herenco; Hamrin Foundation CS 2018; Bonnier and minority partner(s) Private 2020) ***Nyheter24#*** (24 Media Network, with VC; Life of Svea 2019) ***Expressen**** (Bonnier)	***Le Monde*** (Niel, Bergé, Pigasse) ***Rue89#*** (Niel, Bergé, Pigasse) ***Slate.fr#*** (former *Le Monde* director Jean-Marie Colombani, former *Le Monde* journalists Eric Le Boucher and Eric Leser, former *Libération* journalist Johan Hufnagel, and economist Jacques Attali; Benjamin and Ariane de Rothschild 2017) ***Libération**** ** (Drahi; Altice/SFR/ Drahi SM-DS Aug. 2016–2019; Drahi-controlled Foundation CS 2020)

(*continued*)

Table AI.1 Continued

Ownership Form/ Subform and dominant Institutional Logics	United States	Sweden	France
Civil Society (professional, religious, partisan/ community)	***Christian Science Monitor*** (Church of Christ, Scientist) ***CIR/Reveal#*** (501(c)(3)) ***MinnPost*** (501(c)(3)) ***ProPublica*** (501(c)(3)) ***Texas Tribune*** (501(c)(3))	***Dagen#*** (Mentor Medier/Christian churches, organizations, investors) ***Barometern#*** (Gota Media/ foundations Stiftelsen Barometern and Tore G Wärenstams stiftelse) ***Dagens Arena*** (nonprofit association Arenagruppen)# ***Gefle Dagblad#*** (Mittmedia group/ foundations Stiftelsen Pressorganisation and Nya Stiftelsen Gefle Dagblad; Bonnier and minority partner(s) Private 2019) ***Norran#*** (foundation Stiftelsen Skelleftepress; foundation-owned NTM 2019)	***La Croix#*** (Bayard Presse/ Catholic Assumptionist Order) ***L'Humanité*** (Communist Party affil. individuals and nonprofit 1901 associations) ***Mediapart#*** (former *Le Monde* editor-in-chief Edwy Plenel, former *Le Monde* journalists François Bonnet and Laurent Mauduit, and former business executive Marie-Hélène Smiejan-Wanneroy; nonprofit Fund for a Free Press 2019) ***Ouest-France#*** (1901 Association, overseen by founding Hutin family)
Public (democratic state)	***NPR*** (501(c)(3) created by US Congress, overseen by NPR Board of Directors: partially elected by NPR member stations) ***PBS*** (501(c)(3) created by US Congress, overseen by PBS Board: elected by PBS member stations)	***SR#*** (Independent foundation: Förvaltningsstiftelsen; board members appointed by government with Parliament advice) ***SVT#*** (Independent foundation: Förvaltningsstiftelsen; board members appointed by government with Parliament advice)	***Radio France (France info)*** (Overseen by Board of Directors; Regulatory agency Conseil superieur de l'audiovisuel/CSA appoints director; Arcom 2022)# ***France Télévisions (Francetvinfo)#*** (Overseen by Board of Directors ; Regulatory agency Conseil superieur de l'audiovisuel/CSA: appoints director; Arcom 2022)

#Analyzed only in Chapter 5 (public service) and Chapter 6 (political instrumentalism), drawing on a December 2015 to June 2016 sample; *Analyzed only in Chapter 7 on economic instrumentalism, April 2015 to November 2019 samples; **Due to ownership change in August 2016, *Libération* is analyzed as "stock market dominant shareholder" for the economic instrumentalism content analysis, based on a 2018–2019 sample.

SM-WH, SM-DS, Private, or CS listed after a post-2016 owner indicates a change in ownership form. VC refers to venture capital.

Note: Given the frequency of ownership changes, some information may not be current at the time of this book's publication.

Outlet Abbreviation Key (for Tables A2.1, A5.2, A5.4, A5.5a-c, and A6.2):

US: ABC (*ABC News*), CNN (*CNN*), HuffPo (*HuffPost*), LAT (*Los Angeles Times*), USAT (*USA Today*), CBS (*CBS News*), Fox (*Fox News*), NYT (*New York Times*), SlateUS (*Slate*), MetroUS (*Metro*), BuzzF (*BuzzFeed*), MinnST (*Minneapolis Star Tribune*), WPost (*Washington Post*), ViceUS (*Vice*), CSMon (*Christian Science Monitor*), CIR/R (*Center for Investigative Reporting/Reveal*), MinnP (*MinnPost*), ProPub (*ProPublica*), TexTrib (*Texas Tribune*), NPR (*NPR*), PBS (*PBS NewsHour*)
Sweden: SvD (*Svenska Dagbladet*), MetroSW (*Metro*), DagNyh (*Dagens Nyheter*), DagETC (*Dagens ETC*), GPosten (*Göteborgs-Posten*), KIT (*KIT*), JPosten (*Jönköpings-Posten*), N24 (*Nyheter24*), Dagen (*Dagen*), Barom (*Barometern*), DagAren (*Dagens Arena*), GefleDag (*Gefle Dagblad*), Norran (*Norran*), SR (*SR*), SVT (*SVT*)
France: TF1 (*TF1*), Metnews (*Metronews*), LHPo (*Le HuffPost*), LeFigaro (*Le Figaro*), LeMonde (*Le Monde*), Rue89 (*Rue89*), Slate.fr (*Slate.fr*), ViceFr (*Vice France*), Libé (*Libération*), LaCroix (*La Croix*), L'Huma (*L'Humanité*), Mediapt (*Mediapart*), OuestFr (*Ouest-France*), FrInfo (*France Info*), FrTV (*France Télévisions*)

Table A2.1 Ownership Complex Structural Dimensions by Outlet: Ownership Form and Subforms, Primary Funding, Public Subsidies, Audience Demographics (Omnibus/Elite), and Audience and Owner Partisan Preference (~2016 data)

Outlet*	Ownership Form	Subform#	Primary Funding##/ Press Subsidies**	Omnibus/ Elite Audience	Audience Partisanship***	Owner Partisanship***
ABC	SM-WH	Conglom.	Adv.	Omnibus	Bal.	Left
CNN	SM-WH	Conglom.	Subscrip.	Omnibus	Left	Bal.
HuffPo	SM-WH	Conglom.	Adv.	Elite	Left	Bal.
LAT	SM-WH	—	Adv.	Elite	Left	Bal.
USAT	SM-WH	—	Adv.	Elite	Bal.	Bal.
CBS	SM-DS	Conglom.	Adv.	Omnibus	Bal.	Bal.
Fox	SM-DS	Conglom.	Subscrip.	Omnibus	Right	Right
NYT	SM-DS	Journ.	Subscrip.	Elite	Left	Left
SlateUS	SM-DS	—	Adv.	Elite	Left	Left
MetroUS	Private	—	Adv.	Omnibus	Bal.	Bal.
BuzzF	Private	—	Adv.	Omnibus	Left	Left
MinnST	Private	—	Adv.	Elite	Left	Right
WPost	Private	—	Adv.	Elite	Left	Bal.
ViceUS	Private	Journ.	Subscrip.	Elite	Left	Left
CSMon	CS	Religious	Philan.	Elite	Bal.	Bal.
CIR/R	CS	Journ.	Philan.	Elite	Left	Left
MinnP	CS	Journ.	Philan.	Elite	Left	Left
ProPub	CS	Journ.	Philan.	Elite	Left	Left
TexTrib	CS	Journ.	Philan.	Elite	Left	Left
NPR	Public	—	Philan.	Elite	Left	Bal.
PBS	Public	—	Philan.	Elite	Left	Bal.
SvD	SM-WH	Conglom.	Subscrip. + Subsidies	Elite	Right	Bal.
MetroSw	SM-DS	—	Adv.	Omnibus	Bal.	Bal.
DagNyh	Private	Conglom.	Subscrip.	Elite	Bal.	Bal.
DagETC	Private	Journ.; Part.-affil.;	Subscrip. + Subsidies	Omnibus	Left	Left
GPosten	Private	—	Subscrip.	Elite	Bal.	Right
KIT	Private	Conglom.	Adv.	Elite	Left	Bal.
JPosten	Private	—	Adv.	Omnibus	Bal.	Right
N24	Private	—	Adv.	Omnibus	Bal.	Bal.
Dagen	CS	Religious	Subscrip. + Subsidies	Omnibus	Right	Right
Barom	CS	Part.-affil.; Sw. Found.	Subscrip.	Omnibus	Bal.	Right

(continued)

Table A2.1 Continued

Outlet*	Ownership Form	Subform#	Primary Funding##/ Press Subsidies**	Omnibus/ Elite Audience	Audience Partisanship***	Owner Partisanship***
DagAren	CS	Journ.; Part.-affil.	Philan.	Elite	Left	Left
GefleDag	CS	Part.-affil.; Sw. Found.	Subscrip.	Omnibus	Bal.	Right
Norran	CS	Part.-affil.; Sw. Found.	Adv.	Omnibus	Bal.	Right
SR	Public	—	Public	Omnibus	Bal.	Bal.
SVT	Public	—	Public	Omnibus	Bal.	Bal.
TF1	SM-WH	Conglom.	Adv.	Omnibus	Right	Right
Metnews	SM-WH	Conglom.	Adv.	Omnibus	Bal.	Right
LeHPo	SM-DS	Conglom.	Adv.	Elite	Left	Bal.
LeFigaro	SM-DS	Conglom.	Subscrip.	Elite	Right	Right
LeMonde	Private	Journ.	Subscrip.	Elite	Left	Left
Rue89	Private	Journ.	Adv.	Elite	Left	Left
Slate.fr	Private	Journ.	Adv.	Elite	Left	Bal.
ViceFr	Private	Journ.	Subscrip.	Elite	Left	Left
Libé	Private	Journ.	Subscrip. + Subsidies	Elite	Left	Bal.
LaCroix	CS	Religious	Subscrip. +Subsidies	Elite	Bal.	Bal.
L'Huma	CS	Part.-affil.	Subscrip. +Subsidies	Elite	Left	Left
Mediapt	CS	Journ.	Subscrip.	Elite	Left	Left
OuestFr	CS	Journ.; Found.	Subscrip.	Omnibus	Bal.	Bal.
Fr Info	Public	—	Public	Omnibus	Bal.	Bal.
FrTV	Public	—	Public	Omnibus	Left	Bal.

#Subform categories are: Conglomerate; Current/legacy Journalist control; Partisan-affiliated; Swedish Foundation; and Foundation. An outlet may have more than one subform.

##Primary Funding categories are: Advertising; (Audience) Subscriptions (including cable TV fees); Philanthropy; and Public (taxpayer) funding.

*Most outlets' names are abbreviated. For a key to abbreviations, see Table AI.1. The same abbreviations are used in all appendix tables, except for A7.1, which uses complete names.

**Most French and Swedish legacy newspapers receive some subsidies. Press subsidies in this instance refer only to outlets that receive targeted extra subsidies not available to all media to preserve press pluralism beyond what the market will support.

***Balanced (Bal.) refers to a relatively even "mix" of right- and left-leaning owners (when an outlet has multiple dominant shareholders or governance by a board of directors) and audiences. Balanced should be understood as "Neutral" in those cases where owners do not publicly reveal or explicitly disavow any partisan preferences.

Sources: For supporting data for this table, see Online Appendix Tables, Series 2.1 – 2.4, available via Oxford Academic Digital Books or at https://rodneybenson.org/publications/how-media-ownership-matters/online-appendix.

Table A5.1 Public Service Information (PSI): Average Outlet 1–4 National Relational Scale by Ownership Complex Dimension

Ownership Complex Dimension (N)	Public Affairs Focus	International	Investigative	In-Depth	PSI Mean	Public Affairs/Light-Sensational Ratio
Total Sample (51)	**2.65**	**2.25**	**1.92**	**2.27**	**2.27**	**2.12**
SM-WH (8)	2.13*	1.88	2.00*	2.13	2.03	1.75*
SM-DS (7)	2.86*	2.29	1.14*	1.86	2.04	2.43*
Market (15)	2.47	2.07	1.60*	2.00	2.03	2.07*
Private (16)	2.38*	2.38	1.56*	2.44	2.19	1.75*
CivSoc (14)	3.36*	2.21	2.50*	2.14	2.55*	2.71*
Public (6)	2.17*	2.50	2.33*	2.83	2.46	1.83*
CS+Public	3.00*	2.30	2.45**	2.35	2.53**	2.45*
Conglom. (12)	2.08*	2.00	1.50	2.17	1.94**	1.50**
Partisan-affil. (6)	3.00	2.17	2.67*	2.00	2.46	2.50
Journ. Control (15)	3.27**	2.73*	2.33*	2.87*	2.80***	2.53*
Religious (3)	4.00**	4.00**	1.67	2.00	2.92*	3.00
Owner Left (16)	3.19*	2.44	2.19	2.75	2.64**	2.56*
Owner Bal. (24)	2.37*	2.42	1.75	2.21	2.19**	2.04*
Owner Right (11)	2.45*	1.64	1.91	1.73	1.93**	1.64*
Aud. Left (27)	2.96*	2.37	2.04	2.63*	2.50**	2.44*
Aud. Bal. (19)	2.16*	1.95	1.95	1.89*	1.99**	1.74*
Aud. Right (5)	2.80*	2.80	1.20	1.80*	2.15**	1.80*
Aud. Omnibus (21)	1.95***	1.76**	1.95	2.19	1.96***	1.38***
Aud. Elite (30)	3.13***	2.60**	1.90	2.33	2.49***	2.63***
Adv. (20)	1.95***	1.60**	1.45*	2.15	1.79***	1.70***
Subscrip. (19)	3.21***	2.89**	2.05*	2.05	2.55***	2.37***
Philan. (8)	3.50***	2.50**	2.25*	2.88	2.78***	3.00***
Public (4)	1.75***	2.00**	3.00*	2.75	2.38***	1.25***
Press Subsidies (6)	3.83**	3.67***	2.00	2.33	2.96**	3.00**

$^{*}p \leq .10$, $^{**}p \leq .05$, $^{***}p < .005$. Note: For the four main ownership forms, owner partisan preference, audience partisan preference, audience omnibus/elite, and primary funding, when all sub-categories have the same significance levels, differences are measured across the entire group; when only one sub-category is starred, the significance level refers to comparison with all other outlets. For all other dimensions (ownership subforms, CS+Public, and Press Subsidies), significance level refers to comparison with all other outlets.

Table A5.2 Public Service Information (PSI): Outlet-level Data and 1–4 National Relational Scales

Outlet (N Articles)	Public Affairs Focus % /	Public Affairs Focus Scale	Intern./ Foreign Affairs Focus %	Intern / Foreign Affairs Focus Scale	Investi-gative (%)	Investi-gative Scale	In-Depth Genres (%)	In-Depth Genres	PSI Mean	Public Affairs/ Light-Sensational News Ratio	Public Affairs/ Light-Sensational News Ratio Scale
ABC (60)	20.0	1	1.7	1	0	1	15.0	2	1.25	0.7	1
CNN (75)	38.7	2	5.3	2	1.3	2	17.3	2	2.00	1.0	1
HuffPo (75)	45.3	3	6.7	2	5.3	2	14.7	2	2.25	2.1	2
LAT (67)	46.3	3	1.5	1	3.0	2	14.9	2	2.00	3.9	4
USAT (75)	41.3	2	8.0	3	2.7	2	10.7	1	2.00	1.7	2
CBS (55)	32.7	1	3.6	2	0	1	23.6	3	1.75	1.4	1
Fox (75)	37.3	2	6.7	2	0	1	2.7	1	1.50	1.1	1
NYT (75)	57.4	4	9.3	3	2.7	2	30.7	4	3.25	5.4	4
SlateUS (72)	55.6	4	4.2	2	0	1	13.9	2	2.25	4.0	4
MetroUS (50)	16.0	1	2.0	1	0	1	16.0	2	1.25	0.4	1
BuzzF (69)	15.9	1	1.4	1	2.9	2	21.7	3	1.75	0.3	1
MinnST (75)	38.7	2	2.7	1	1.3	2	4.0	1	1.50	1.2	1
WPost (75)	53.3	4	9.3	3	4.0	2	13.3	1	2.50	2.5	3
ViceUS (75)	40.0	2	17.3	4	0	1	17.3	2	2.25	1.0	1
CSMon (75)	53.3	4	30.7	4	0	1	17.3	2	2.75	3.1	3
CIR/R (51)	54.9	4	2.0	1	62.7	4	60.8	4	3.25	2.2	2
MinnP (74)	50.0	3	5.4	2	2.7	2	27.0	4	2.75	2.5	3
ProPub (44)	45.4	3	2.3	1	40.9	4	34.1	4	3.00	2.0	2
TexTrib (74)	77.0	4	0.0	1	0	1	12.2	1	1.75	6.3	4
NPR (50)	46.0	3	12.0	4	0	1	30.0	4	3.00	1.9	2
PBS (60)	46.7	3	8.3	3	0	1	18.3	2	2.25	3.7	4
US Total	**Mean: 43.4 SD (.5): 7.2**		**Mean: 6.7 SD (.5): 3.5**		**Mean: 6.2 SD (.5): 7.8**		**Mean: 19.8 SD (.5): 6.2**			**Mean: 2.3 SD (.5): 0.8**	

Table A5.2 Continued

Outlet (N Articles)	Public Affairs Focus % /	Public Affairs Focus Scale	Intern./ Foreign Affairs Focus %	Intern / Foreign Affairs Focus Scale	Investigative (%)	Investigative Scale	In-Depth Genres (%)	In-Depth Genres	PSI Mean	Public Affairs/ Light-Sensational News Ratio	Public Affairs/ Light-Sensational News Ratio Scale
SvD (75)	44.0	3	20.0	4	1.3	2	12.0	3	3.00	2.5	2
MetroSw (75)	40.0	2	12.0	2	0	1	2.7	1	1.50	1.0	2
DagNyh (75)	38.6	2	10.7	2	0	1	6.7	2	1.75	1.3	2
DagETC (75)	53.3	4	25.3	4	1.3	2	22.7	4	3.50	2.1	2
GPosten (75)	48.0	3	10.7	2	0	1	4.0	2	2.00	2.2	2
KIT (75)	20.0	1	9.3	2	0	1	62.7	4	2.00	0.3	1
JPosten (75)	46.7	3	2.7	1	0	1	2.7	1	1.50	1.8	2
N24 (75)	16.0	1	2.7	1	0	1	5.3	2	1.25	0.2	1
Dagen (75)	49.3	4	21.3	4	0	1	12.0	3	3.00	1.1	2
Barom (75)	46.7	3	4.0	1	2.7	4	0	1	2.25	1.3	2
DagAren (75)	70.7	4	18.7	4	4	4	4.0	2	3.50	26.2	4
GefleDag (75)	28.0	1	5.3	1	2.7	4	8.0	2	2.00	0.6	1
Norran (75)	41.3	2	4.0	1	0	1	4.0	2	1.50	1.6	2
SR (75)	56.0	4	29.3	4	4.0	4	5.3	2	3.50	2.5	2
SVT (75)	33.3	1	9.3	2	2.7	4	8.0	2	2.25	0.9	1
Sweden Total	**Mean: 42.1 SD (.5) 7.0**		**Mean: 12.4 SD (.5): 4.3**		**Mean: 1.3 SD (.5): 0.8**		**Mean: 10.7 SD (.5): 7.7**			**Mean: 3.0 SD (.5): 3.2***	

(continued)

Table A5.2 Continued

Outlet (N Articles)	Public Affairs Focus % /	Public Affairs Focus Scale	Intern./ Foreign Affairs Focus %	Intern / Foreign Affairs Focus Scale	Investigative (%)	Investigative Scale	In-Depth Genres (%)	In-Depth Genres	PSI Mean	Public Affairs/ Light-Sensational News Ratio	Public Affairs/ Light-Sensational News Ratio Scale
TF1 (43)	18.7	1	4.7	1	0	1	7.0	1	1.00	0.5	1
Metnews (44)	34.1	2	4.5	1	2.3	4	22.7	4	2.75	0.7	1
LeHPo (73)	41.0	3	9.6	2	0	1	1.4	1	1.75	1.6	2
LeFigaro (75)	51.4	4	14.9	3	0	1	5.4	1	2.25	3.2	3
LeMonde (73)	46.5	4	19.2	4	4.1	4	8.2	1	3.25	3.1	3
Rue89 (57)	29.9	1	14.0	3	0	1	17.5	4	2.25	0.9	1
Slate.fr (68)	30.9	1	4.4	1	0	1	32.4	4	1.75	1.2	1
ViceFr (36)	50.0	4	30.6	4	0	1	19.4	4	3.25	1.5	2
Libé (72)	54.2	4	20.8	4	1.4	3	9.7	2	3.25	3.5	4
LaCroix (64)	46.9	4	28.1	4	1.6	3	6.3	1	3.00	4.3	4
L'Huma (74)	52.7	4	10.8	2	0	1	8.1	1	2.00	7.8	4
Mediapt (73)	47.9	4	12.3	2	6.8	4	11.0	2	3.00	2.5	3
OuestFr (76)	42.1	3	14.5	3	0	1	5.3	1	2.00	2.3	2
FrInfo (49)	22.4	1	6.1	1	0	1	14.3	3	1.50	0.9	1
FrTV (50)	24.0	1	4.0	1	2.0	3	18.0	4	2.25	0.5	1
France Total	**Mean: 39.5 SD (.5): 6.0**		**Mean: 13.2 SD (.5): 4.2**		**Mean: 1.2 SD (.5): 1.0**		**Mean: 12.4 SD (.5): 4.1**			**Mean: 2.3 SD (.5): 1.0**	

* Modified: Any ratio less than 1.0 coded as 1.

Table A5.3 Public Service Pluralism (PSP): Average Outlet 1–4 National Relational Scale by Ownership Complex Dimension

Ownership Complex Dimension (N)	Political HHI	Institutional HHI	Author HHI	Civic Society Voices	PSP Mean
Total Sample (51)	**2.45**	**2.69**	**2.61**	**2.29**	**2.51**
SM-WH (8)	1.88**	2.75	2.38	2.13	2.28
SM-DS (7)	2.57**	3.14	3.00	1.86	2.64
Market (15)	2.20**	2.93	2.67	2.00	2.45
Private (16)	2.25**	2.19	2.81	2.50	2.44
CivSoc (14)	3.29**	2.64	2.64	2.43	2.75*
Public (6)	1.67**	3.50*	1.83*	2.17	2.29
Conglom. (12)	2.58	2.83	2.58	2.17	2.54
Partisan-affil. (6)	3.50**	2.83	3.17	2.50	3.00**
Journ. Control (15)	2.67	2.60	2.73	2.60	2.65
Religious (3)	3.33	3.00	2.00	2.33	2.67
Owner Left (16)	2.63	2.56	2.56	2.75	2.63
Owner Bal. (24)	2.13	3.04	2.63	2.13	2.48
Owner Right (11)	2.91	2.09	2.64	2.00	2.41
Aud. Left (27)	2.52	2.67	2.67	2.56	2.60
Aud. Bal. (19)	2.32	2.74	2.58	1.95	2.39
Aud. Right (5)	2.60	2.60	2.40	2.20	2.45
Aud. Omnibus (21)	2.38	2.38	2.57	2.24	2.39
Aud. Elite (30)	2.50	2.90	2.63	2.33	2.59
Adv. (20)	2.35*	2.15**	2.75	2.50	2.44
Subscrip. (19)	2.47*	3.00	2.79	1.89*	2.54
Philan. (8)	3.25*	3.00	2.25	2.88	2.84
Public (4)	1.25*	3.25	1.75	2.00	2.06
Press Subsidies (6)	2.5	3.50*	2.67	2.67	2.83
Legacy print (24)	2.38	2.83	2.75	1.92**	2.47
Legacy TV-radio (11)	2.00	3.18	2.09	1.91	2.30
Online-only (16)	2.88*	2.13**	2.75	3.12***	2.72

*p ≤ .10, **p ≤ .05, ***p < .005; Note: When all sub-categories have the same significance levels, differences are measured across entire group; when only one sub-category is starred, the significance level refers to comparison with all other outlets.

Table A5.4 Public Service Pluralism (PSP): Outlet-level Data and 1–4 National Relational Scales

	PHHI: Political HHI (N Domestic Political Actors)*	PHHI Scale	IHHI: Institutional HHI (N Institutional Actors)*	IHHI Scale	AHHI: Author HHI (N articles: see Table A5.2)*	AHHI Scale	% of Civil Society Voices (N All Actors: see Table A6.2)	Civil Society Voices Scale	PSP Mean
ABC	5853 (84)	1	1162 (282)	3	8172	2	19.2	2	2.0
CNN	6313 (143)	1	1232 (411)	3	6679	4	16.8	1	2.25
HuffPo	5794 (154)	1	1317 (396)	2	5534	4	23.2	3	2.50
LAT	4866 (142)	3	1220 (385)	3	8062	2	13.5	1	2.25
USAT	5670 (132)	1	1112 (423)	4	6092	4	21.9	2	2.75
CBS	4986 (83)	3	1078 (272)	4	8955	1	18	1	2.25
Fox	4493 (130)	4	1143 (410)	3	6078	4	15.5	1	3.00
NYT	5088 (221)	2	1606 (424)	1	8528	1	13.9	1	1.25
SlateUS	5033 (180)	2	1310 (421)	2	7519	3	23.3	3	2.50
MetroUS	5536 (28)	1	1643 (237)	1	10000	1	22.2	2	1.25
BuzzF	5096 (50)	2	1776 (388)	1	7635	3	26.6	4	2.50
MinnST	5498 (89)	1	1059 (427)	4	6939	3	15.4	1	2.25
WPost	6051 (185)	1	1306 (470)	2	7806	2	16.3	1	1.50
ViceUS	3974 (65)	4	1087 (415)	4	7568	3	22.3	3	3.50
CSMon	4435 (82)	4	1053 (444)	4	7813	2	19.5	2	3.00
CIR/R	3554 (11)	4	1445 (189)	1	10000	1	31.3	4	2.50
MinnP	3897 (88)	4	870 (387)	4	5102	4	35.5	4	4.00
ProPub	3264 (45)	4	1475 (225)	1	10000	1	42.5	4	2.50
TexTrib	6329 (142)	1	1344 (418)	2	4576	4	16.6	1	2.00
NPR	4349 (41)	4	941 (219)	4	10000	1	17.8	1	2.50

Table A5.4 Continued

	PHHI: Political HHI (N Domestic Political Actors)*	PHHI Scale	IHHI: Institutional HHI (N Institutional Actors)*	IHHI Scale	AHHI: Author HHI (N articles: see Table A5.2)*	AHHI Scale	% of Civil Society Voices (N All Actors: see Table A6.2)	Civil Society Voices Scale	PSP Mean
PBS	5495 (81)	1	1070 (315)	4	7572	3	35.9	4	3.00
US Total	**Mean: 5027 SD (.5): 441**		**Mean: 1250 SD (.5): 118**		**Mean: 7649 SD (.5): 805**		**Mean: 22.2 SD (.5): 4.0**		
SvD	6566 (109)	1	990 (468)	4	8244	1	18.5	1	1.75
MetroSw	6017 (60)	1	1094 (610)	4	5168	4	32.6	3	3.00
DagNyh	4875 (62)	3	1145 (454)	3	5936	4	26.8	2	3.00
DagETC	4845 (63)	3	1056 (582)	4	6932	3	31.5	3	3.25
GPosten	7274 (43)	1	1340 (430)	2	8482	1	12.5	1	1.25
KIT	3771 (44)	4	1477 (517)	1	9737	1	34.7	4	2.50
JPosten	3805 (125)	4	1397 (524)	1	6690	3	12.5	1	2.25
N24	4432 (56)	3	1364 (618)	1	5495	4	39.9	4	3.00
Dagen	4922 (48)	3	1581 (618)	1	7568	2	54.6	4	2.50
Barom	4282 (46)	4	1363 (579)	2	6476	3	15.8	1	2.50
DagAren	2562 (124)	4	987 (595)	4	7554	2	32.5	3	3.25
GefleDag	4622 (47)	3	1360 (640)	2	6939	3	28.9	3	2.75
Norran	4841 (42)	3	1606 (427)	1	6309	4	17.1	1	2.25
SR	7622 (81)	1	1009 (675)	4	10000	1	24.1	2	2.00
SVT	6043 (77)	1	1028 (556)	4	5481	4	25.0	2	2.75
Sweden Total	**Mean: 5099 SD (.5): 687**		**Mean: 1253 SD (.5): 110**		**Mean: 7134 SD (.5): 738**		**Mean: 27.1 SD (.5): 5.7**		

(continued)

Table A5.4 Continued

	PHHI: Political HHI (N Domestic Political Actors)*	PHHI Scale	IHHI: Institutional HHI (N Institutional Actors)*	IHHI Scale	AHHI: Author HHI (N articles: see Table A5.2)*	AHHI Scale	% of Civil Society Voices (N All Actors: see Table A6.2)	Civil Society Voices Scale	PSP Mean
TF1	3772 (34)	3	1269 (209)	1	10000	1	29.7	3	2.00
Metnews	2798 (74)	4	1072 (329)	2	10000	1	41.6	4	2.75
LeHPo	2672 (128)	4	792 (353)	4	5767	4	27.8	2	3.50
LeFigaro	4065 (132)	2	880 (393)	4	5672	4	26.5	2	3.00
LeMonde	4018 (68)	2	865 (376)	4	6453	4	23.8	1	2.75
Rue89	5675 (34)	1	1365 (330)	1	6928	4	34.6	4	2.50
Slate.fr	3034 (89)	4	1331 (284)	1	6730	4	37.8	4	3.25
ViceFr	4756 (15)	1	1139 (252)	1	10000	1	25.6	2	1.25
Libé	4406 (81)	1	831 (386)	4	7141	4	31.7	3	3.00
LaCroix	3763 (40)	3	873 (263)	4	8813	2	19.3	1	2.50
L'Huma	2831 (120)	4	813 (360)	4	6892	4	35.1	4	4.00
Mediapt	3658 (85)	3	767 (451)	4	10000	1	20.3	1	2.25
OuestFr	3871 (69)	2	917 (299)	3	6627	4	18.2	1	2.50
FrInfo	4290 (26)	1	976 (195)	3	10000	1	26.5	2	1.75
FrTV	4081 (44)	2	1066 (222)	2	10000	1	28.0	2	1.75
France Total	**Mean: 3846 SD (.5): 402**		**Mean: 997 SD (.5): 100**		**Mean: 8068 SD (.5): 886**		**Mean: 28.4 SD (.5): 3.4**		

*Lower HHI scores are more pluralist.

Table A5.5a Public Service Pluralism (PSP): US Outlet-level Mentions of Actors (% of all Actors Mentioned)

	N Actor Men-tions	Gov. Main Left	Gov. Main Right	Gov. Mar-ginal Left	Gov. Mar-ginal Right	Move-ment Left Foreign + Domestic	Move-ment Right Foreign + Domestic	Gov. General Domes-tic	Bureau-cracy Domes-tic	Legal Foreign + Domes-tic	Law Enforce-ment Foreign + Domestic	Media Foreign + Domes-tic	Acad. Foreign + Domes-tic	Ent /Arts /Sports Foreign + Domestic	Labor Foreign + Domes-tic	Civil Soc Other Foreign + Domestic	Business Foreign + Domes-tic	Unaffil. Indiv. Foreign + Domestic	Foreign Gov.	Interna-tional Org.
ABC	282	8.2	21.3	0.0	0.0	0.4	0.0	1.4	3.5	0.4	8.5	12.1	4.3	6.7	0.7	3.2	11.7	13.8	2.5	1.4
CNN	411	7.8	26.5	0.0	0.0	0.7	0.7	2.4	3.4	8.0	5.8	6.3	3.2	7.3	0.0	0.7	8.0	12.4	1.5	5.1
HuffPo	396	7.6	28.5	0.0	0.0	0.8	2.0	2.5	2.5	3.5	2.3	10.6	2.3	7.8	0.5	1.0	7.6	11.4	3.5	5.6
LAT	385	18.7	17.7	0.0	0.0	0.0	0.5	5.7	3.9	9.6	4.9	4.4	5.5	0.5	0.5	3.1	7.5	16.6	0.0	0.8
USAT	423	7.6	22.2	0.0	0.0	0.5	2.8	2.4	4.7	2.1	4.0	10.9	3.5	6.4	0.0	4.5	3.1	16.1	5.7	3.5
CBS	272	12.9	17.3	0.0	0.0	0.0	0.4	2.9	3.3	4.8	5.9	10.3	1.8	4.4	0.0	1.5	10.7	16.2	3.3	4.4
Fox	410	15.1	14.9	0.0	0.0	1.0	2.0	2.0	4.6	5.9	9.5	7.3	2.4	2.0	0.0	2.4	2.4	20.7	2.7	5.1
NYT	424	17.0	33.0	0.0	0.0	0.5	2.8	6.1	3.8	2.1	2.6	3.1	3.5	5.7	0.0	0.5	6.4	6.1	3.8	3.1
SlateUS	421	13.1	27.3	0.0	0.0	0.7	1.7	2.9	2.1	5.0	2.1	7.8	5.2	9.7	0.0	0.7	8.8	8.8	1.4	2.6
MetroUS	237	1.3	8.4	0.0	0.0	2.1	0.0	0.0	2.1	5.1	15.6	8.9	0.0	7.2	0.0	4.2	10.5	32.1	2.1	0.4
BuzzF	388	2.3	8.8	0.0	0.0	0.3	2.6	1.3	0.5	4.4	4.9	8.0	3.6	13.4	0.0	2.6	8.5	36.1	1.0	1.8
MinnST	427	5.9	14.3	0.0	0.0	0.0	1.6	4.7	11.9	4.9	9.1	2.8	3.0	5.6	1.4	3.5	8.0	20.4	1.4	1.4
WPost	470	10.0	28.9	0.0	0.0	0.0	0.4	3.4	2.6	3.2	2.3	8.5	4.9	3.6	0.0	4.0	7.9	9.1	6.6	4.5
ViceUS	415	6.5	7.2	0.0	0.0	5.5	0.7	0.0	5.5	1.7	8.2	9.9	0.7	7.2	0.2	0.7	6.7	22.7	11.1	5.3
CSMon	444	8.3	9.0	0.0	0.0	2.0	2.3	3.2	3.2	0.7	2.5	5.2	4.1	2.5	0.0	4.7	4.5	16.2	17.8	14.0
CIR/R	189	1.6	2.6	0.0	0.0	1.6	0.0	2.1	24.9	2.6	9.0	18.0	1.1	5.3	0.0	7.9	4.2	16.9	1.1	1.1
MinnP	387	10.3	9.3	0.0	0.0	2.8	0.3	6.5	11.4	3.6	1.8	10.9	11.6	3.9	0.8	8.3	4.7	10.9	1.3	1.8
ProPub	225	8.4	6.2	0.0	0.0	4.4	1.3	1.3	10.2	4.4	2.7	27.1	0.0	1.8	0.0	8.0	2.2	20.0	1.8	0.0
TexTrib	418	4.5	26.6	0.0	0.0	1.9	1.0	6.5	6.0	10.0	0.7	2.9	12.9	0.2	0.0	5.3	10.5	11.0	0.0	0.0
NPR	219	8.7	8.7	0.0	0.0	1.4	0.5	6.4	7.8	3.2	4.6	9.6	2.3	0.0	0.0	7.3	14.6	14.6	8.7	1.8
PBS	315	7.6	17.5	0.0	0.0	0.6	0.0	3.5	4.8	3.2	0.6	14.6	8.6	7.9	0.0	6.3	8.6	14.0	1.6	0.6
AVG		8.7	17.0	0.0	0.0	1.3	1.1	3.2	5.8	4.2	5.1	9.5	4.0	5.2	0.2	3.8	7.5	16.5	3.8	3.1
SD		4.6	9.0	0.0	0.0	1.5	1.0	2.1	5.3	2.6	3.7	5.6	3.4	3.4	0.4	2.6	3.2	7.3	4.3	3.1

Note: Highlights in the table indicate that the outlet's percentage of mentions were at least one standard deviation above the national mean for the actor category. Percentages are of all actors included in the IHHI analysis, which excludes business section articles (see Methods Appendix).

Table A5.5b Public Service Pluralism (PSP): Sweden Outlet-level Mentions of Actors (% of All Actors Mentioned)

	N Actor Mentions	Gov. Main Left	Gov. Main Right	Gov. Marginal Left	Gov. Marginal Right	Movement Left Foreign + Domestic	Movement Right Foreign + Domestic	Gov. General Domestic	Bureaucracy Domestic	Legal Foreign + Domestic	Law Enforcement Foreign + Domestic	Media Foreign + Domestic	Acad. Foreign + Domestic	Ent / Arts / Sports Foreign + Domestic	Labor Foreign + Domestic	Civil Soc Other Foreign + Domestic	Business Foreign + Domestic	Unaffil. Indiv. Foreign + Domestic	Foreign Gov.	International Org.
SvD	468	18.2	5.1	0.0	0.0	1.5	1.1	1.3	5.6	3.0	7.7	10.0	2.4	4.3	0.0	0.4	7.9	12.6	8.3	10.7
MetroSW	610	7.5	0.5	0.0	0.7	2.3	1.0	2.5	6.7	0.5	4.3	14.1	3.8	6.6	3.1	3.3	14.8	20.8	5.1	2.6
DagNyh	454	8.8	3.3	1.5	0.0	0.0	0.2	1.1	7.3	4.0	5.9	8.8	5.3	4.4	0.9	6.8	5.3	26.4	5.5	4.4
DagETC	582	7.2	0.2	0.0	1.2	3.8	1.0	1.0	8.2	0.3	1.4	12.4	8.1	3.6	0.9	4.3	12.4	20.4	7.9	5.7
GPosten	430	8.4	1.6	0.0	0.0	0.0	0.0	0.2	20.9	0.9	4.2	6.5	4.2	1.9	1.2	2.3	20.0	16.7	4.9	6.0
KIT	517	4.3	2.7	1.4	0.0	0.4	0.0	1.0	4.1	0.4	2.3	19.3	10.1	4.8	1.0	1.2	18.4	24.0	3.3	1.5
JPosten	524	9.9	10.3	0.2	3.4	0.0	0.0	0.6	22.3	1.5	1.3	4.4	0.6	3.6	3.1	2.1	20.0	15.1	0.2	1.3
N24	618	5.7	1.6	0.0	0.6	0.2	1.1	0.2	3.6	1.9	3.7	16.0	3.6	14.9	1.1	3.9	17.2	22.2	2.1	0.5
Dagen	618	4.7	2.8	0.0	0.3	0.0	0.0	0.5	1.9	0.2	1.6	11.8	7.0	8.6	0.2	30.7	2.9	16.7	4.9	5.3
Barom	579	4.8	1.6	1.0	0.2	0.3	0.0	1.7	23.5	3.6	5.5	4.8	3.5	3.5	2.1	2.1	16.8	19.5	1.2	4.3
DagAren	595	8.1	5.2	3.5	2.2	1.3	0.7	0.3	18.5	0.2	0.7	11.6	4.7	0.5	10.9	3.2	10.6	10.3	4.2	3.4
GefleDag	640	4.5	1.9	0.0	0.0	0.9	0.0	0.6	12.2	0.5	3.6	8.4	5.6	9.7	0.0	5.3	16.6	25.8	2.0	2.3
Norran	427	5.9	3.5	0.0	0.0	0.5	0.0	1.4	20.8	1.6	4.0	5.2	2.8	4.2	0.5	6.1	7.7	30.7	2.3	2.8
SR	675	10.4	1.5	0.1	0.0	0.6	0.1	0.6	10.4	3.0	6.2	11.9	3.4	5.6	1.2	1.8	11.3	12.9	15.9	3.3
SVT	556	10.6	1.4	0.4	0.9	0.5	0.0	0.9	6.5	3.1	6.7	8.8	3.1	11.0	2.3	1.6	13.8	19.1	3.8	5.6
AVG		7.9	2.9	0.5	0.6	0.8	0.4	0.9	11.5	1.6	3.9	10.3	4.5	5.8	1.9	5.0	13.0	19.5	4.8	4.0
SD		3.6	2.5	1.0	1.0	1.1	0.5	0.6	7.6	1.4	2.2	4.3	2.4	3.8	2.7	7.4	5.3	5.7	3.8	2.5

Note: Highlights in the table indicate that the outlet's percentage of mentions were at least one standard deviation above the national mean for the actor category. Percentages are of all actors included in the IHHI analysis, which excludes business section articles (see Methods Appendix).

Table A5.5c Public Service Pluralism (PSP): France Outlet-level Mentions of Actors (% of All Actors Mentioned)

	N Actor Mentions	Gov. Main Left	Gov. Main Right	Gov. Marginal Left	Gov. Marginal Right	Movement Left Foreign + Domestic	Movement Right Foreign + Domestic	Gov. General Foreign + Domestic	Bureaucracy Foreign + Domestic	Legal Foreign + Domestic	Law Enforcement Foreign + Domestic	Media Foreign + Domestic	Acad. Foreign + Domestic	Ent / Artist Sports Foreign + Domestic	Labor Foreign + Domestic	Civil Soc Other Foreign + Domestic	Business Foreign + Domestic	Unaffil. Indiv. Foreign + Domestic	Foreign Gov	International Org
TF1	209	9.1	2.4	2.4	0.0	2.4	0.0	0.0	8.6	0.5	9.1	19.6	2.4	3.3	7.7	1.4	6.2	22.5	0.0	2.4
Metnews	329	8.5	6.7	4.3	2.4	0.6	0.0	1.5	0.3	1.2	6.4	12.8	4.0	20.7	2.1	1.5	6.4	14.6	2.4	3.6
LeHPo	353	13.0	9.6	6.5	6.8	0.3	0.0	2.0	1.1	5.9	5.1	11.6	3.4	1.4	4.0	3.4	4.0	8.5	3.4	9.9
LeFigaro	393	19.6	7.6	3.1	2.5	4.6	0.3	0.0	2.8	4.6	2.3	8.4	6.9	2.3	4.6	3.3	3.8	7.4	5.3	10.7
LeMonde	376	10.6	3.2	1.9	2.1	1.6	0.0	1.6	2.7	1.9	3.5	10.6	11.2	5.9	2.4	1.3	6.4	10.9	14.1	8.2
Rue89	330	7.6	0.6	0.0	1.5	0.3	0.3	0.6	0.3	0.6	4.5	23.9	8.2	7.0	0.6	4.2	14.5	18.5	2.7	3.9
Slate.fr	284	14.4	6.3	1.8	6.3	4.2	0.0	0.0	1.1	0.7	2.8	13.4	25.7	11.3	0.0	1.1	2.1	6.0	1.4	1.4
ViceFr	252	3.6	0.4	0.0	0.0	2.0	3.2	1.2	4.8	3.2	14.7	10.7	3.2	0.0	2.0	4.0	8.3	17.5	3.2	18.3
Libé	386	12.4	1.8	0.8	6.0	1.0	0.5	0.0	2.8	3.6	6.0	7.3	13.5	7.8	3.6	5.2	3.1	12.7	7.0	4.9
LaCroix	263	8.0	4.2	0.8	2.3	1.5	0.4	0.0	2.3	5.3	2.7	4.2	10.6	1.5	3.8	5.7	8.4	12.9	13.3	12.2
L'Huma	360	13.6	4.2	6.1	8.6	1.7	0.3	0.0	1.4	1.1	4.4	7.8	10.3	3.1	13.1	5.6	6.9	3.6	3.6	4.7
Mediapt	451	10.0	4.4	0.0	2.9	1.6	0.7	0.0	7.5	6.9	5.1	6.9	3.5	2.0	4.7	5.1	9.8	13.1	8.6	7.3
OuestFr	299	13.4	3.7	2.7	2.3	1.0	0.0	1.3	5.7	2.0	4.7	5.7	3.7	4.0	7.0	2.0	7.7	12.4	17.7	3.0
FrInfo	195	6.2	0.0	6.2	0.5	0.0	0.5	0.5	1.5	11.3	8.7	8.7	0.0	15.9	1.0	3.6	8.2	12.3	10.8	4.1
FrTV	222	11.7	3.6	2.3	2.3	0.0	0.0	3.2	3.2	3.6	10.8	21.2	1.4	12.2	0.9	1.8	3.2	8.1	2.3	8.6
AVG	—	10.8	3.9	2.6	3.1	1.5	0.4	0.8	3.1	3.5	6.0	11.5	7.2	6.5	3.8	3.3	6.6	12.1	6.4	6.9
SD	—	3.9	2.8	2.3	2.6	1.4	0.8	1.0	2.5	3.0	3.4	5.8	6.5	6.0	3.4	1.7	3.2	5.0	5.3	4.5

Note: Highlights in the table indicate that the outlet's percentage of mentions were at least one standard deviation above the national mean for the actor category. Percentages are of all actors included in the IHHI analysis, which excludes business section articles (see Methods Appendix).

Table A6.1 Partisan Attention, Business and Partisan Favorability, and Partisan Intensity: Average Outlet Trump Mentions (US only) and 1–4 National Relational Scale by Ownership Complex Dimension

Ownership Complex Dimension (N)	Mean Trump Mentions (US-only outlet N)	Business Favorability (1–4 Pro-Business)	Partisan Favorability (1–4 from Left to Right)	Partisan Intensity (1–4 Imbalance of Favorability, whether Pro-Right or Pro-Left)
Total Sample (21 US only; 51 three-country combined)	32.6 (21)	2.65	2.41	2.25
SM-WH (8)	48.0* (5)	3.00	2.63	1.63*
SM-DS (7)	50.8* (4)	3.14	3.14**	1.86
Market (15)	49.2** (9)#	3.07**	2.87**	1.73**
Private (16)	30.8** (5)	2.31*	2.13	2.31
CivSoc (14)	10.0** (5)	2.50	2.43	2.71*
Public (6)	19.0** (2)	2.83	2.00	2.33
Conglom.(12)	40.8 (5)	3.00	2.75	1.67**
Partisan-affil. (6)	—	2.00*	2.17	3.33**
Journ. Control (15)	20.7 (6)	2.00***	2.20	2.67*
Religious (3)	14.0 (1)	3.67*	3.00	2.33
Owner Left (16)	26.4 (9)	2.00***	2.00**	2.69*
Owner Bal.(24)	38.7 (10)	2.83***	2.42**	1.88*
Owner Right (11)	30.0 (2)	3.18***	3.00**	2.45*
Aud. Left (27)	34.9 (15)	2.37*	2.04**	2.59**
Aud. Bal. (19)	26.2 (5)	2.89*	2.68**	1.74**
Aud. Right (5)	31.0 (1)	3.20*	3.40**	2.40**
Aud. Omnibus (21)	31.7 (6)	2.81	2.57	2.43
Aud. Elite (30)	33.0 (15)	2.53	2.30	2.13
Adv. (20)	40.1**(10)	2.85	2.60	1.70***
Subscrip. (19)	49.0** (4)	2.63	2.53	2.68**
Philan. (8)	12.6** (7)	2.25	2.00	2.38
Public (4)	—	2.50	1.75	2.75
Press Subsidies (6)	—	2.00*	2.33	2.83

* $p \leq .10$, ** $p \leq .05$, *** $p < .005$

When only one item is starred within a related group, statistical significance test refers to the particular category against all other outlets (e.g., Market versus all other ownership forms). Note: For Trump mentions, differences between US Market, Private, CS, and Public forms are significant at $p < .05$; differences between US SM-WH, SM-DS, Private, CS, and Public forms are significant at $p < .10$.

Table A6.2 Partisan Mentions (US only), Business and Partisan Favorability, and Partisan Intensity: Outlet-level Data and 1–4 National Relational Scales

Outlet (All Actor Mentions)	Trump Mentions (US only)	Business Favorability (−1 to +1) (N mentions)	Business Favorability 1–4 Scale (Neg. to Pos.)	Left Favorability (0–2) 1 is evenly balanced (N mentions)	Right Favorability (0–2) (N mentions)	Partisan Favorability Right/Left Proportion	Partisan Favorability 1–4 Scale (L to R)	Partisan Intensity Standardized Valence Proportion	Partisan Intensity 1–4 Scale
ABC (442)	30	−0.050 (120)	3	0.97 (29)	0.97 (61)	1.00	3	1.00	1
CNN (606)	77	−0.009 (108)	3	1.03 (35)	0.77 (123)	0.75	1	1.33	4
HuffPo (607)	39	−0.051 (118)	3	0.77 (53)	0.77 (128)	0.99	3	1.01	1
LAT (572)	44	−0.015 (135)	3	0.85 (74)	0.74 (73)	0.87	2	1.15	2
USAT (661)	50	+0.055 (145)	4	0.86 (37)	0.90 (98)	1.04	4	1.04	1
CBS (449)	27	−0.031 (127)	3	0.91 (45)	0.84 (51)	0.93	3	1.08	1
Fox (631)	31	+0.017 (119)	4	0.66 (68)	1.03 (75)	1.55	4	1.55	4
NYT (648)	76	0.000 (107)	3	0.90 (83)	0.72 (150)	0.80	2	1.26	3
SlateUS (674)	69	−0.055 (164)	3	0.89 (75)	0.89 (145)	1.00	3	1.00	1
MetroUS (424)	10	−0.061 (132)	3	1.00 (13)	1.20 (20)	1.20	4	1.20	2
BuzzF (627)	15	−0.210 (167)	1	1.06 (16)	0.85 (40)	0.80	2	1.25	3
MinnST (636)	29	−0.018 (163)	3	0.89 (28)	0.54 (63)	0.61	1	1.65	4
WPost (687)	88	−0.055 (128)	3	0.97 (72)	0.69 (150)	0.71	1	1.40	4
ViceUS (640)	12	−0.032 (94)	3	1.10 (39)	0.76 (33)	0.69	1	1.46	4
CSMon (620)	14	+0.128 (94)	4	0.98 (41)	0.92 (51)	0.94	3	1.06	1
CIR/R (396)	1	−0.500 (60)	1	1.00 (27)	0.83 (6)	0.83	2	1.20	2
MinnP (606)	8	−0.073 (96)	2	0.98 (65)	0.82 (44)	0.83	2	1.20	2
ProPub (386)	6	−0.425 (40)	1	0.98 (51)	0.80 (25)	0.82	2	1.23	3
TexTrib (627)	21	−0.087 (115)	2	1.29 (38)	0.89 (168)	0.69	1	1.44	4

(continued)

Table A6.2 Continued

Outlet (All Actor Mentions)	Trump Mentions (US only)	Business Favorability (−1 to +1) (N mentions)	Business Favorability 1–4 Scale (Neg. to Pos.)	Left Favorability (0–2) 1 is evenly balanced (N mentions)	Right Favorability (0–2) (N mentions)	Partisan Favorability Right/Left Proportion	Partisan Favorability 1–4 Scale (L to R)	Partisan Intensity Standardized Valence Proportion	Partisan Intensity 1–4 Scale
NPR (443)	15	−0.041 (121)	3	1.00 (35)	1.00 (34)	1.00	3	1.00	1
PBS (499)	23	+0.019 (52)	4	1.07 (46)	0.89 (70)	0.83	2	1.20	2
US Mean (.5 SD)	**33 (13)**	**−0.071 (.073)**	**2.81**	**0.96**	**0.85**	**0.90 (.10)**		**1.22 (.10)**	
SvD (710)	—	−0.086 (162)	2	0.97 (88)	1.00 (24)	1.04	2	1.04	1
MetroSw (639)	—	−0.029 (69)	3	0.94 (50)	1.00 (10)	1.06	3	1.06	1
DagNyh (653)	—	−0.071 (56)	2	0.98 (50)	1.00 (19)	1.02	2	1.02	1
DagETC (664)	—	−0.264 (72)	1	0.83 (54)	0.42 (12)	0.50	1	2.00	4
GPosten (609)	—	+0.014 (148)	3	0.82 (39)	0.86 (7)	1.04	2	1.04	1
KIT (547)	—	+0.043 (70)	4	0.93 (30)	0.93 (14)	0.99	2	1.01	1
JPosten (593)	—	+0.028 (145)	3	0.90 (51)	0.84 (69)	0.93	2	1.07	1
N24 (631)	—	−0.075 (53)	2	0.86 (35)	0.76 (21)	0.89	1	1.13	2
Dagen (659)	—	+0.143 (14)	4	0.69 (29)	1.05 (19)	1.53	4	1.53	4
Barom (603)	—	−0.139 (101)	2	0.89 (36)	1.20 (10)	1.35	4	1.35	3
DagAren (603)	—	−0.421 (57)	1	0.95 (75)	0.58 (45)	0.61	1	1.64	4
Gefle Dag (664)	—	−0.022 (91)	3	0.77 (35)	1.17 (12)	1.51	4	1.51	4
Norran (624)	—	+0.200 (140)	4	0.91 (34)	0.93 (15)	1.02	2	1.02	1
SR (688)	—	−0.030 (66)	3	0.89 (71)	1.00 (10)	1.13	3	1.13	2
SVT (660)	—	−0.214 (84)	1	1.02 (64)	0.92 (13)	0.91	2	1.10	2
Sweden Mean (.5 SD)		**−0.062 (.078)**	**2.53**	**0.89**	**0.91**	**1.04 (.14)**		**1.24 (.15)**	

Table A6.2 Continued

Outlet (All Actor Mentions)	Trump Mentions (US only)	Business Favorability (-1 to +1) (N mentions)	Business Favorability 1-4 Scale (Neg. to Pos.)	Left Favorability (0-2) 1 is evenly balanced (N mentions)	Right Favorability (0-2) (N mentions)	Partisan Favorability Right/Left Proportion	Partisan Favorability 1-4 Scale (L to R)	Partisan Intensity Standardized Valence Proportion	Partisan Intensity 1-4 Scale
TF1 (380)	—	0.000 (41)	3	1.00 (29)	1.00 (5)	1.00	3	1.00	1
Metnews (356)	—	0.000 (17)	3	0.98 (46)	1.00 (30)	1.02	3	1.02	2
LeHPo (580)	—	+0.018 (57)	3	0.91 (77)	0.90 (58)	0.99	3	1.01	1
LeFigaro (634)	—	0.000 (56)	3	0.78 (93)	0.83 (40)	1.05	4	1.05	2
LeMonde (622)	—	−0.033 (61)	2	0.93 (54)	0.80 (20)	0.86	1	1.16	3
Rue89 (500)	—	−0.032 (31)	2	0.92 (26)	1.00 (10)	1.08	4	1.08	2
Slate.fr (563)	—	−0.083 (12)	1	0.98 (65)	1.00 (36)	1.02	3	1.02	2
ViceFr (289)	—	0.000 (10)	3	1.00 (15)	1.00 (1)	1.00	3	1.00	1
Libé (628)	—	−0.049 (41)	1	0.86 (59)	0.94 (36)	1.09	4	1.09	2
LaCroix (429)	—	0.000 (113)	3	1.00 (27)	0.94 (17)	0.94	2	1.06	2
L'Huma (610)	—	−0.080 (75)	1	.97 (90)	0.55 (47)	0.57	1	1.75	4
Mediapt (718)	—	−0.008 (133)	3	0.98 (61)	1.00 (33)	1.02	3	1.02	2
OuestFr (517)	—	+0.020 (147)	4	0.98 (51)	0.94 (18)	0.96	3	1.04	2
FrTV (397)	—	+0.036 (83)	4	0.97 (36)	0.80 (15)	0.82	1	1.22	4
FrInfo (396)	—	−0.033 (91)	2	1.00 (34)	0.83 (12)	0.83	1	1.20	3
France Mean (.5 SD)		**−0.016 (.018)**	**2.53**	**0.95**	**0.90**	**0.95 (.07)**		**1.11 (.09)**	

Table A7.1 OMI, Owner Favorability Score, and General Business Favorability Score by Sampled Outlets

			Ownership Mention Index (OMI)	Owner Favorability (−1.0 to + 1.0)	Business Favorability* (−1.0 to +1.0)
US	Stock Market-WH	*ABC News*	123	+0.176	−0.050
		CNN	33	0.000	−0.009
		HuffPost	61	−0.205	−0.051
		Los Angeles Times	15	−0.076	−0.015
		USA Today	20	−0.007	+0.055
		Chicago Tribune	15	-0.043	—
		Des Moines Register	13	+0.029	—
	Stock Market-DS	*CBS News*	3	0.000	−0.031
		Fox News	1	+0.107	+0.017
		New York Times	6	−0.049	0.000
	Private	*Minneapolis Star Tribune*	15	+0.039	−0.018
		Washington Post	36	+0.072	−0.055
		Boston Globe	15	-0.011	—
	Civil Society	*Christian Science Monitor*	5	+0.038	+0.128
		MinnPost	25	+0.124	−0.073
		ProPublica	11	+0.067	−0.425
		Texas Tribune	2	0.000	−0.087
	Public	*NPR*	2	+0.222	−0.041
		PBS NewsHour	7	+0.034	+0.019
Sweden	Stock Market-WH	*Svenska Dagbladet*	11	−0.038	−0.086
		Aftonbladet	61	-0.091	—
	Private	*Dagens Nyheter*	12	+0.010	−0.071
		Göteborgs-Posten	20	+0.020	+0.014
		Expressen	13	-0.034	—
France	Stock Market-DS	*Le Figaro*	72	+0.046	0.000
		Le Parisien	9	+0.045	—
		Libération	16	+0.005	−0.049
	Private	*Le Monde*	22	+0.014	−0.033

*Business favorability cannot be calculated for outlets not part of the 2015–2016 news sample.

APPENDIX II

Methods

This book draws on a multitude of primary and secondary source materials to shed new light on how media ownership matters: (1) semi-structured, in-depth interviews with current or former owners, founders, top executives and editors, supplemented by informal personal communications; (2) systematic review of trade and professional journals, biographies, and memoirs, supplemented by field notes of remarks by relevant actors at public events; (3) gathering and analysis of data from professional, industry, research institute, and academic sources to create original data sets on news outlets' audiences (primarily education, income, and political leaning), owners (political preferences), primary funding, organizational mission or "about" statements, and receipt of professional prizes; and (4) quantitative content analysis of news and opinion articles. These diverse sources were used to analyze journalistic practices and meta-discourses, possession of economic and symbolic capital, structural characteristics of news outlets indicative of ownership forms and funding-audience adjustment strategies, and news performance indicative of modes of power (public service orientation, political instrumentalism/partisanship, and economic instrumentalism). Data sources were used throughout the book, unless otherwise indicated by a specific reference to a chapter.

Journalistic Discourses about Practices and Values

We began the project by conducting interviews and continued to conduct interviews almost up to the time of this book's publication. All told, between 2010 and 2023, we conducted more than one hundred in-depth, semi-structured interviews with current and former founders, publishers, editors, and reporters, across a range of types of news organizations in the three national fields (with a roughly equivalent number in each country). Only a portion of these interviews are quoted in this book but all of them informed our analysis. Interviews focused on respondents' direct observations and experiences relevant to the three modes of ownership power. We were cognizant of the difficulty of using interviews—especially with public relations-savvy elites—to gather reliable information about practices that our respondents may have had ample reason to conceal. In some cases, we drew on overlapping social networks to help facilitate access and trust. We also sought to express our genuine interest in the work that our respondents were doing and thus to facilitate a conversational atmosphere in which they felt comfortable talking candidly about their career trajectories, interactions with other stakeholders, ideals, and day-to-day practices.[1] Some interviewees asked for anonymity or that some comments be considered off the record; most of those we spoke with are identified by name and title at the time of the interview and spoke to us on the record. While we did not interview someone at every news organization included in our news content samples, we were able to reach the majority and made sure that each ownership form in each country (including outlets not included in our content samples) was well represented in our interviews.

All interviews were transcribed and coded in relation to the three modes of power: public service orientation, political instrumentalism/partisanship (sometimes referred to as "partisan favorability"), and economic instrumentalism. At least one author and one research assistant read through each interview to ensure that all relevant passages were appropriately coded. We erred on the side of generosity: whether a quote belonged in one category or another was less important than the fact that it had been identified as important. Subthemes and patterns of similarities or differences across ownership forms or national fields were identified through an "iterative and reflexive process."[2] We wanted to make sure anything even marginally relevant was readily available for review, guiding future interviews and analysis, as well as for possible inclusion in the book. In subsequent review, we would often return to the transcripts to ensure that we were using any summaries or specific quotes accurately and in context.

Rodney Benson's interviews with Swedish executives and journalists were all conducted in English; his interviews with French respondents were conducted in various mixes of French and English, and then were transcribed but not translated. Passages from transcribed French interviews conducted by Julie Sedel or Benson presented in the book were translated into English by Benson or Patrick Stancil. With the exceptions of Swedish-language interviews conducted by Carl Ritter, which he translated himself (interviews with Klas Wolf-Watz, Charlotta Friborg, Andreas Gustavsson, and Martin Schori) and some early interviews translated by research assistants, Swedish-language transcribed interviews were translated into English by the professional translation firm AdHoc Translations. Mattias Hessérus and Ritter reviewed any excerpted translations used in the book for accuracy. Where necessary for comprehension or readability, quotes have been lightly edited for style and clarity.

In addition, we observed numerous in-person or online news industry or association events in the US and France involving executives and editors at news outlets included in our study: such remarks provide an additional source of information about journalistic practice self-reports and meta-discourses. These events also facilitated introductions that led to informal communications or formal in-depth interviews.[3]

Our source materials for journalistic practices and discourses also included trade and professional review articles and published interviews, and scholarly and journalistic biographies and memoirs. We conducted periodic searches of individuals and outlets in the Nexis Uni, Factiva, ProQuest, and Mediearkivet Retriever databases, supplemented by Google searches to capture the most recent materials. We also monitored and signed up for email updates from media information and watchdog news websites, including *NiemanLab*, American Press Institute, Poynter Institute, *Columbia Journalism Review*, *Acrimed* (Action-Critique-Médias), *La Lettre A*, and Nordicom. As French sociologist Jean G. Padioleau has remarked, journalistic investigations and first-hand accounts can provide very useful source materials for media scholars. Even though these works may not adhere to standards of social scientific rigor, they provide rare access to closely guarded information about the inner workings of media power.[4] They also represent "public stories" that shareholders, managers, and editors tell about themselves.[5] Even if they are not always accurate, they provide useful information about how these media elites wish to be perceived.

Finally, we analyzed the official mission or "about" (or "about us") statements provided on news outlet websites (Chapter 2). Language in these statements served as an indicator of the value-laden institutional logics officially embraced and promoted by the news organizations. Efrat Nechushtai and Lior Zalmanson use a similar method, analyzing newspaper appeals to readers (to persuade them to subscribe) for their "informational, social, and normative elements" and as expressions of "their strategies and their relationships with the communities they serve."[6] Coding of the mission statements involved an iterative process of developing and revising categories related to institutional logics while also remaining open to aspects that emerged inductively. Most mission statements quoted in Chapter 2 were current as of December 2021/January 2022; earlier mission statements from 2015 to 2016 were recovered, if available, especially if the media outlet had changed ownership since 2016 when we conducted our public service orientation content analysis.

News Organization Data

To gather structural data for news organizations, we relied on multiple academic, research institute, and industry sources, both proprietary and public. When conducting cross-national research, given differences in industry and government conventions, it is often impossible to obtain data that uses the exact same categories. We used multiple sources in an attempt to approximate as best as possible comparable indicators. We gathered data for the following characteristics of news organizations: journalistic prizes; audience size, social characteristics (education, income), and political preferences; owner political preferences; and primary funding.

As reported in Chapter 2, we re-analyzed publicly available information on journalistic prize winners in each country to identify the distribution of awards across ownership forms and subforms. For the US, we analyzed Pulitzer Prizes (newspaper and some online-only news outlets, for public service, investigative, and explanatory awards, from 2005 to 2020, https://www.pulitzer.org/prize-winners-by-year) and Peabody Awards (any awards to US news organizations, primarily television/radio and some print or online-only producing audio/visual content, from 2005 to 2019, https://peabodyawards.com/awards/search/). Our Pulitzer Prize calculations included all national and major regional news outlets but excluded small community newspapers. For France, we analyzed the Albert Londres prizes (separate prizes for print and audiovisual journalism, from 2000 to 2019), as identified by Gatien (2012, 367, 370–371), and supplemented by https://fr.wikipedia.org/wiki/Prix_Albert-Londres, for the years 2013 to 2019. (Note: The French *Wikipedia* list was identical to Gatien's for the period from 2000 to 2012.) For Sweden, we analyzed the "Stora Journalistpriset" (prizes for "investigation," "storytell[ing]", "innovator of the year," and "grand journalism prize," from 2002 through 2020, equally available to print, audiovisual, or online-only news outlets), at the official homepage of Stora Journalistpriset: https://www.storajournalistpriset.se/.

Audience size by ownership form (Chapter 2) is based on survey data of non-mutually exclusive "weekly use" produced by the Reuters Institute for the Study of Journalism at Oxford University. We calculated the accumulated percentages of audience weekly use for all named news outlets, aggregating totals by ownership forms (as current at the time of the survey). Additional measures of audience size by outlet with source documentation are provided in Online Appendix Tables, Series 2.3.

Categorization of audiences as either omnibus or elite are based, in most cases, on summative assessments of multiple data sources for education and income. We used or created parity index scores that compared a media outlet's audience composition (percentage with a relatively high level of education or income) with the national mean. Based on the distribution of index scores in each national field and contextually appropriate breaking points, we classified average scores of 125–130 or below (no more than twenty-five to thirty percent above the national mean percentage for that amount of education or income) as "omnibus," and average scores above 125–130 as "elite." Very few of the outlets included in our study had parity indexes for elite audiences below 100, or conversely, parity indexes (when such data was available) over-representing popular or working-class audiences. As supplementary data and to classify outlets not included in the surveys discussed below, we relied on estimates provided by our interviewees, public remarks of managers or editors, "marketing kits" publicly available online, or journalistic and trade journal reports.

For the US, we created average index scores of education (four years of college or above) and household income (above $75,000) from surveys conducted by the Pew Research Center (2012; Grieco 2020), supplemented by industry data that could be converted into parity indexes using census data (e.g., Nielsen, news organization media kits, Scarborough Research for the Audit Bureau of Circulations). For Sweden, our primary sources of audience social data were (1) a proprietary Orvesto Konsument [Orvesto consumer] 2020 survey (conducted by Kantar Sifo, https://www.kantarsifo.se/rapporter-undersokningar/rackviddsmatningar/orvesto-konsument) of online and legacy media audiences and (2) a 2017 SOM (Samhälle, Opinion, Medier [Society, Opinion, Media]) national survey of media use (conducted annually by the SOM Institute at Gothenburg University, https://www.gu.se/en/som-institute/the-som-surveys/about-the-som-surveys). The Orvesto survey provided percentages for both media outlet audiences and the national population as a whole, allowing us to construct parity index scores. We used the Orvesto survey results for higher education (two or more years of college) and income (42,000 SEK [around $4,500/month or $54,000/year] or higher). The SOM survey, extracted and processed expressly for this book by Peter M. Dahlgren (https://peterdahlgren.com), provided data on audiences' education (college degree or higher) and income (45,000 SEK [around $4,900/month or $59,000/year] or higher): we received online audience data for national newspapers *Dagens Nyheter* and *Svenska Dagbladet*, and legacy audience data for all other newspapers and public broadcasters.

French parity indexes are constructed based on proprietary data generously given to us by the leading French audience research firms ACPM (L'Alliance pour les chiffres de la presse et des médias) and Médiamétrie: we express our gratitude to Solenne Zlatanovic of ACPM, and Nils Savoye and Valéry Rochard of Médiamétrie. We received data, already constructed as parity indexes, for higher education and occupation (but not income) from 2016 and 2020 surveys: "Bac" [successful passage of high school exam] plus five years of college, from Médiamétrie; Bac plus four, from ACPM; professional-managerial occupation, from ACPM; and CSP+ (catégorie socio-professionelle plus, or "higher social-professional category," from Médiamétrie), the primary broad category used in marketing to capture elite audiences. We primarily used the education data because it was most comparable to our US and Swedish sources but consulted the occupational data to make finer distinctions as necessary.

For data on audience partisan preferences, we coded news outlets as either leaning left, balanced, or leaning right: "balanced" is used as shorthand in the book for measures sometimes termed mixed or balanced in the surveys cited in Online Appendix Tables Series 2.2a-c. We made this assessment through consultation with multiple sources identifying the percentage of audience members leaning left or right (or supporting relatively left or right political parties) compared to the national population as a whole.

In cases where we had sufficient data, we calculated the ratio between left-leaning and right-leaning audiences to identify outlets with right-leaning, balanced, or left-leaning audiences: in the US, we used sources comparing "liberals" and "conservatives" or "Democrats" and "Republicans"; for Sweden and France, we had multi-party data and compared clusters of left versus center/right parties. In other cases, we drew on whatever reliable data was available, including news outlet self-reports, trade press articles, and academic studies (Hamilton 2016), to make our best estimates. For the US, we drew primarily on surveys by the Pew Research Center (Pew Research Center 2014, Grieco 2020) and the Reuters Institute (Fletcher et al. 2020); we supplemented these sources with data provided by media outlet internal reports, Alexa (2017 data) and Similarweb (2022 data) websites, primary circulation area presidential election voting data, and visual partisan audience mapping data from Benkler et al. (2018). (Nelson and Webster [2017], however, suggest that the degree of audience political polarization across US news websites has been overstated.) For Sweden, we used the Orvesto 2020:1 survey (except for *Dagen*, which was only available from the Orvesto 2017:1 survey) and SOM 2017 data to construct parity indexes, and supplemented this mostly complete data with Pew Research Center (2018), Alexa 2017 similar websites, and data obtained from the trade press or interviews. For France, we primarily used two public surveys conducted by the French survey organization IFOP (*Institut français d'opinion publique*) of media usage of a range of news outlets by 2012 presidential and 2014 municipal election voters (IFOP 2012, 2014). We supplemented this nearly complete data with Pew Research Center (2019), Fletcher et al. (2020), and a visual mapping of outlets' positioning vis-à-vis one another based on Twitter audiences in Institut Montaigne (2019, 26).

To classify the partisan leaning of owners—as either left, neutral/balanced, or right—we searched for public records of political donations to candidates or parties (readily available in the US, through the "donor lookup" on the website www.opensecrets.org) or public statements by individual owners and dominant shareholders, or board members (in the case of stock market widely held, civil society, or public media outlets). Where such information was not publicly available, we sought to elicit it from our interviewees or consulted secondary sources. Due to legal restrictions in Sweden on internet research on the political views of individuals (even public figures), for our Swedish sample we generally relied on organizational statements of political stances.[7] In all three countries, we classified public media as having neutral/balanced owners given the legal and administrative barriers designed to create an arm's length relationship to the party in power; our analysis of their boards of directors also showed a rough balance between right, left, and nonpartisan members.

Primary funding for outlets was identified through exhaustive research in public records, including outlet self-reports or media marketing kits available online, company annual reports or other public reports (e.g., US nonprofit required 990 reports), industry trade press articles, insider accounts in the press or books, academic or reputable research institute (e.g., Pew) studies, and data released to us by our interviewees. More detailed information about data sources, as well as all outlet-specific data, is available in the book's Online Appendix.

News Content Analysis

Content analysis, when conducted in isolation from theory and other data, can be criticized for being limited to description or for improperly imputing causation from correlations to structural factors. Our approach, supplemented by interviews and other documentation to reveal news outlet mechanisms of control and practice as discussed above, seeks to overcome such limitations. As such, our stance toward content analysis is similar to that of Raymond Williams, who remarked in his book *The Sociology of Culture*: "Content analysis is often criticized for its 'merely quantitative' findings, but its data, while often needing further interpretation, are essential to any developed sociology of culture, not only in modern communications systems, where the large numbers of works make it inevitable, but also in more traditional kinds of work."[8] We conducted quantitative content analysis of original samples of online articles produced by a diverse array of news organizations in the US, Sweden, and France (see Appendix Table AI.1). We used distinct samples of outlets (partially overlapping) and articles for public service orientation, partisan favorability and intensity, and economic instrumentalist promotion.

Throughout this book, we often convert raw percentages or frequencies into national field relational 1–4 scales. A score of 1 represents an amount 0.51 standard deviations or more below the national mean, 2 represents an amount between 0.50 SD below the mean and the mean, 3 represents an amount between .01 and 0.50 SD above the mean, and 4 represents an amount of 0.51 SD and higher above the mean. As a result, similar figures (percentages, frequencies, Herfindahl-Hirschman index levels, etc.) in different national fields may have very different relational scores. Relational scales highlight how news outlets with similar or different characteristics are similar or different in their content from other outlets within the same national field (the historical, structural, and contemporary dynamic political-ideological context in which they function): as noted in Chapter 5, relational scales facilitate an analysis on patterns of news coverage produced by ownership forms and complexes *within* fields, rather than the broad differences produced *by* these fields.

Public service orientation and partisan favorability

Our public service orientation and partisan favorability samples of news outlets are broadly representative of the largest and most prestigious general information news organizations in our three countries: twenty-one in the US, and fifteen each in Sweden and France. Our samples include on average about sixty-seven percent of the outlets, with significant cross-national variation, listed as "most-read" in the 2016 *Reuters Institute Digital News Report.* The overlaps between our samples and the Reuters Institute's large survey-based lists of largest audience outlets are as follows: "online" overlap of nine out of ten for the US (ninety percent), eight out of thirteen for France (sixty-two percent), and seven out of twelve for Sweden (fifty-eight percent); "offline" overlap of nine out of ten for the US (ninety percent), seven out of fourteen for France (fifty percent), and six out of twelve for Sweden (fifty percent). The Reuters Institute's listings are based on national surveys asking respondents which outlets they used during the previous week. We did not include in the N for the Reuters samples in each country any news aggregators, foreign-based media, or non-specified local media. A significant proportion of our sampled outlets had won at least one of the major national journalistic prizes analyzed in our study (see Chapter 2): thirteen out of twenty-one for the US (sixty-two percent), five out of fifteen for Sweden (thirty-three percent), and five out of fifteen for France (thirty-three percent).

Our samples also included a "purposive" element: we strategically included outlets that contributed variation in structural features (ownership forms, funding, audiences) that we considered theoretically significant.[9] As explained in the Introduction, our sample of news outlets represent four broad ownership forms: market, private, civil society, and public. Ownership form refers to the ultimate holding company or individual(s). Some outlets bridge ownership types: keeping in mind national context, we sought to locate the outlet in relation to its dominant ownership logic. Given that legacy media (TV, print) now compete and cooperate online alongside digital native websites, both legacy and digital-only outlets were included to ensure the constitution of comprehensive samples. For ease of identification, all outlets, regardless of original medium, are italicized in this book.

PDFs of news items from each news outlet were gathered for a "constructed business week" of five non-contiguous days, spread over seven months: Friday, December 11, 2015; Wednesday, February 24, 2016; Thursday, March 31, 2016; Monday, May 9, 2016; and Tuesday, June 14, 2016. The five days were randomly selected and coincided with a broad range of news events: political campaigns, proposed legislation, protests, crimes, scandals, and new business offerings and products, just to name a few. No single news event comprised more than ten percent of the articles gathered on a single day for any of the national samples (French, Swedish, US), with the exception of the June 14, 2016, US coverage, in which twenty-eight percent of coverage was devoted to the Pulse nightclub shootings in Orlando, Florida. Swedish and French media also covered this shooting, although not as much. The sample was drawn during the period of US political party primaries, but only one of the sample dates was taken the day after a primary election (Nevada Republican caucus, February 24, 2016). Political party news was also common in Sweden and France during our sample period.

On each day, the sample included the most prominent (based on placement, headline size, and photo accompaniment) items from general news, business, and opinion sections, with the goal of drawing five items from each of these three categories. However, some outlets produced few or no business or opinion articles, in which case additional news articles if available may have been drawn to round out the sample. Therefore, the overall samples broadly reflect the differential production of general news, business news, and opinion from outlet to outlet and cross-nationally. All three national samples had roughly similar percentages of opinion articles (Sweden, thirty percent; US, twenty-six percent; and France, twenty-one percent). The Swedish sample had far more general than business news (sixty percent versus ten percent), whereas the US (thirty-eight percent versus thirty-seven percent) and French samples (forty-six percent versus thirty-three percent) were more evenly balanced between the two. This Swedish difference in sample composition does not appear to have substantially biased the findings. Historically, business news has tended to be less oriented toward investigative reporting than political reporting,[10] and yet the US and French samples with their greater proportions of business news contain as many or more investigative articles as the Swedish sample. More "general" over "business" news could conceivably contribute to more public affairs-focused articles or a greater proportion of civil society speakers, yet the Swedish sample is not the highest of the three national samples in these indicators of public service orientation. Such national differences are also less important for our analysis than in traditional cross-national studies, given that we primarily use nationally specific "relational indicators" (as discussed in the previous section) that hold constant for national context, rather than raw totals or percentages, for our analysis.

This process resulted in the selection of a maximum of seventy-five pieces of content for each news outlet. The final sample included 1,401 US articles; 1,125 Swedish articles; and 926 French articles. For all outlets, only online news textual content was analyzed.

The content analysis includes the first five paragraphs and the last two paragraphs of each item. Research shows that most readers do not read the entirety of news stories, particularly in an age in which content is quickly accessed and scanned online.[11]

We coded each article for topical focus, genre, author, and actors mentioned. We defined an actor as any mention of a particular person or organization. Excluded were vague mentions of categories or groups without any reference to a specific person or organization. Each actor was coded for its closest approximation to one of nineteen institutional categories, which in turn were coded as either domestic or non-domestic. We also coded each actor according to whether the reference to the actor is negative, positive, neutral, or mixed, as indicated by the manifest meaning of a specific word or phrase. Valenced references may be either in the authorial voice (journalist or other author) or embedded in a quote or paraphrase attributed to a source.

After the coding, aggregate categories were sometimes created to capture larger groupings of actors relevant to the analysis. We coded a total of 11,881 actors mentioned in US media; 7,619 actors in French media; and 9,547 actors in the Swedish media.

A person either native to the country or fluent in that nation-state's main language coded the appropriate sample: content coding was conducted by Timothy Neff (US), Ella Shoshan (Sweden), and Elly Hanauer (France). Coders participated in multiple pre-tests to clarify coding rules and establish adequate inter-coder reliability; coders also consulted with one another and with lead author Benson throughout the process. After the coding was completed, coders carried out a post-coding reliability test of ten percent of the US sample: Holsti's coding reliability scores (average of three two-way comparisons) for topical focus, genre, author, and actor variables used to calculate public service information and pluralism averaged 0.87; Holsti's scores for valence of actor mentions, used for analysis of partisan favorability and intensity, averaged 0.86.

Throughout the book, the primary unit of analysis is the news outlet, subsequently grouped together with other outlets according to ownership form, primary funding, or owner or audience characteristics.

For each outlet, Public Service Information (PSI) was calculated using four measures: public affairs focus, international focus, investigative reporting, and in-depth genre. An article was focused on public affairs when its primary focus concerned one or more of the following topics: national domestic politics/policy, local or regional politics/policy, national foreign politics/policy, international affairs (distinguished from national foreign politics/policy by the absence of a connection to the home nation-state of the media outlet), and political scandals (findings are generally similar with and without inclusion of scandals). We also measured international affairs/foreign policy focus as a separate category that combines international affairs and national foreign politics/policy. Investigative reporting included any article that involved journalistic initiative to hold government, business, or the nonprofit world to account for its words or deeds (e.g., from the December 2015 sample: "Small-scale violations of medical privacy often cause the most harm," *ProPublica*). In-depth genre included the following types of articles: news analysis (labeled), background article (historical context), feature article (no breaking news peg), and portrait/profile.

Public Service Pluralism (PSP) was calculated using four measures: civil society actor mentions, both domestic and international (as a percentage of all actor mentions); and pluralism indexes for partisan actors, institutional/individual actors, and authors. Civil society actor mentions include labor unions, social movements (right or left), academics, media (when cited within an article), entertainers, artists or sports figures or organizations, and other (religious organizations, and other voluntary associations, both domestic and foreign). The pluralism indexes are based on the Herfindahl-Hirschman Index (HHI), which is a measure of market concentration: in our use, it measures the extent to which various actor categories are concentrated or dispersed. The index is calculated by squaring the percentage that each actor type makes up of a given media outlet's total actor mentions and then summing the total. As such, the highest possible score is 10,000 (indicating that only a single type of actor appears in the coverage). The lowest possible score depends on the number of categories in the model: the more categories, the lower the bottom threshold; the lower the score, the higher the degree of pluralism (relatively even distribution across many voices as opposed to concentration of a few).

PHHI (Political HHI) is calculated based on the degree of even dispersion of six ideologically marked domestic categories: mainstream left party (or politician), far left party, left political movement, mainstream right party, far right party, and right political movement.

To calculate institutional actor pluralism (IHHI), we used our nineteen actor categories, which overlapped with but extended the author categories (and also allowed us to distinguish or combine domestic and foreign actors): government (category "government" includes political candidates) mainstream left domestic, government mainstream right domestic, government marginal left domestic, government marginal right domestic, government general (includes non-partisan local officials) domestic, bureaucracy domestic, social movement left foreign + domestic, social movement right foreign + domestic, legal foreign + domestic, law enforcement foreign + domestic, media foreign + domestic, academic foreign + domestic, entertainment/arts/sports foreign + domestic, labor unions foreign + domestic, business foreign + domestic, civil society other foreign + domestic, unaffiliated individuals foreign + domestic, foreign governments, and international governmental organizations.

For author pluralism (AHHI), we calculated for each outlet the level of even distribution across articles of fourteen categories of authors: journalist (whether staff or non-staff), mainstream left party/politician, mainstream right party/politician, marginal left party/politician, marginal right party/politician, left political social movement organization, right social movement organization, government agency, law enforcement, academic/think tank/writer, artist/entertainer, other civil society group, business, and non-affiliated individual. When an article had multiple authors, authorship was based on dominant institutional affiliation (first if two authors; most frequent if three or more).

Business articles likely oversampled business actors, which would skew measures of homogenization based on distribution of types of actors. We therefore excluded business section articles for the IHHI sample of institutional actors; business section articles were also excluded for the PHHI sample of domestic political actors. Author HHI scores are based on the full sample of articles. Civil society actor mentions are calculated as a percentage of all actor mentions in all articles.

For Chapter 6's content analysis of partisan favorability, we drew on the same subset of actor categories used to construct the Political HHI (PHHI), but given that we were not measuring homogenization, from the larger sample that includes business section articles. Instead of analyzing the degree of even dispersion of mentions across the six categories as in the PHHI, we identified the degree to which right (whether from major or marginal parties or social movements) or left (likewise) actors were mentioned more often at each outlet. Our classifications of right and left were sensitive to each national context. We then analyzed the data for valence, produced as explained above, to assess the proportion of left and right political actor mentions that were positive, negative, and neutral. This content data was in turn used to generate outlet-level partisan favorability and intensity ratios. Actor valence coding was also used to assess the ratio of positive to negative mentions of business actors at each outlet (Chapter 7).

Economic instrumentalism: promotion mentions and valence, and public scandals

We constructed a purposive sample of twenty-eight US, Swedish, and French media outlets that incorporates variation in our four main ownership forms (market, with both stock market widely held and dominant shareholder variants, private, civil society, and public), as well as the conglomerate subform, a commercial stock market-traded or private owner with control over significant non-news media holdings.

For each outlet in the sample, we verified up to ten of the largest "ownership interests" (owners, investors, and donors—based on percentage of shares held or amount of donations—and in some cases affiliated businesses/organizations) at the time of our economic instrumentalism content analysis (2016 for the US, 2019 for France and Sweden). We conducted searches of multiple reputable sources, including: company annual reports (when available), Yahoo! Finance, MarketWatch, CrunchBase, Vault.com, government tax documents, and authoritative articles in media trade or professional publications (e.g., *Columbia Journalism Review, Stratégies, Dagens Media, Resumé*), general business media (*Bloomberg, Forbes, Wall Street Journal, Dagens Industri*), business sections of major media (*Los Angeles Times, New York Times, Le Monde, Le Nouvel Observateur, Mediapart*), and blogs (Mondaynote.com). US nonprofit outlet donors were gathered online from GuideStar and Foundation Center.

We did not include all associated businesses, but to the extent that keywords for searches inclusive of associated interests would not introduce a great deal of noise or skew results, we sought to include major outside holdings such as *Washington Post* owner Jeff Bezos's substantial stake in the company he founded, Amazon. Similarly, for Bonnier, we included its ownership of Adlibris, Sweden's largest online bookstore. However, the Boston Red Sox, also owned by *Boston Globe* owner John Henry, and the Minnesota Timberwolves, also owned by *Minneapolis Star Tribune* owner Glen Taylor, were not included in the sample. In these cases, we judged that mentions of such outside "interests" would be difficult to separate from normal local sports coverage and would distort the sample.

Subsequently, we searched for mentions of the major ownership interest names appearing in each of the outlets during the following time periods: for the US outlets, between April 1, 2015, and December 31, 2016; for the Swedish and French outlets, from January 1, 2018 to September 1, 2019 (except, because of different database availability, for *Libération*, drawn from April 1, 2018 to November 30, 2019). This time span is long enough so that individual news events should not skew results. We used ProQuest and Factiva for the US sample, commercial databases widely used in content analyses that have been found to deliver roughly commensurable results (Driedger and Weimer 2015). ProQuest was used for fifteen of our sampled US outlets, and Factiva was used for four outlets not available at the time of our research in ProQuest: *ABC Network, Fox News, National Public Radio*, and *PBS NewsHour*. We used ProQuest and Nexus Uni for our French sample and the media archive Mediearkivet Retriever for our Swedish sample.

To account for frequency of ownership mentions relative to all news coverage during this time period, we used two methods. First, we did a simple search for items (articles or broadcasts) including at least one mention of any of the ownership terms for each outlet. The resulting percentages do not allow for the possibility of multiple mentions in a single news item, nor do they control for variation in item length (especially between the lengthy transcripts of *Fox News* and *PBS* news shows versus all other outlets). Second, to take into account all mentions and news item length, we engaged in a second, multi-stage process to calculate an estimated Ownership Mention Index (OMI) score. We started by drawing a randomized subsample of one hundred items from each outlet and averaging these articles' word counts. We multiplied this average word count by the total number of items on all topics during our sample period to provide an estimate of the overall word counts in the databases for this time period. We then drew a (separate) random subsample (every Nth, chronologically ordered) of up to one hundred items per outlet with at least one ownership mention to estimate the average number of mentions per item. (In cases where the outlet produced fewer than one hundred items, we gathered the total corpus. Our search terms surfaced some mentions not part of news content—such as email addresses, photo credits, and bylines—or coincidental with ownership terms, but these were relatively rare, making up just six percent of the sample used to calculate OMIs.) We multiplied this sample average number of mentions per item times the actual total number of items mentioning owners to generate an estimate of total mentions. This number, divided by the overall estimated number of words produced by each outlet, produced a very small percentage that we multiplied by 1,000,000 to generate an easily readable OMI score. A higher OMI indicates a higher relative frequency of ownership mentions (as a proportion of total coverage controlled for word length).

To make this concrete, the *Washington Post* has a total of 129,042 articles in the database during our search period for the US: April 1, 2015, to December 31, 2016. A random selection of one hundred of these articles shows that the average word count is 785.63. Multiplying the total number of articles by this average word count yields an estimated total word count of 101,379,266.5. This number becomes our denominator. There are a total of 1,559 *Washington Post* articles in this database that mention ownership interests. A random sample of these articles show that on average, ownership interests are mentioned 2.33 times per article. Multiplying the total number of ownership-related articles by the average number of ownership interest mentions per article yields an estimated 3,632.5 ownership mentions in the overall database. This number becomes our numerator. Dividing total estimated ownership mentions by the total estimated word count yields the very small proportion of 0.0000358. Multiplying this number by 1 million yields a final rounded OMI of 36 for the *Washington Post.*

To code for valence (positive, negative, mixed, or neutral mentions of owners), we returned to the second subsample used to estimate average ownership mentions per item. We coded the ownership mentions in the subsampled items for valence (through the first five mentions in each item). For our analysis in Chapter 7, we combined the small number of mentions with mixed (both positive and negative) valence with our neutral mentions into a single category labeled neutral. (See Neff and Benson 2021 for additional information on coding procedures.) Our analysis of economic instrumentalist promotion relies on raw scores and percentages rather than only nationally relational scales. We take this approach in Chapter 7 not only because we are working with less than complete national samples, but also because economic instrumentalism is arguably more outlet-specific and should not be shaped to the same extent as public service orientation or partisan favorability/intensity by nationally contingent political circumstances during our sample period. Nevertheless, our assessments of ownership form effects should thus be interpreted with reference to national contexts; additional research is needed with more countries and larger national samples to confirm our findings.

Intercoder reliability scores using Holsti's method were 0.84 for valence; using Gwet's AC_1 (which compensates for difficulties encountered when measuring reliability in largely homogenous samples, as our samples are due to their high levels of neutral mentions), the score was 0.83 for valence (see Gwet 2008). Due to non-normal distributions for OMIs, with some large outliers in our results, we use Kruskal-Wallis tests of significance across ownership forms (Kruskal and Wallis 1952); we also use Kruskal-Wallis tests to measure significance of differences in valence across ownership forms. We use chi-square tests of significance for direct comparisons of valence between two outlets or ownership forms (Gill 2017).

For our qualitative analysis of public scandals in each country, we searched a mix of the leading trade and business magazines, media criticism websites, major news media outlets with media beats, journalistic professional reviews, and ethics agencies. We searched similar but not exactly overlapping time periods and adapted search terms to the national context. For the US, we searched in the *Columbia Journalism Review*, *Editor & Publisher*, the *New York Times* through the ProQuest database, and the websites of Harvard *NiemanLab*, American Press Institute, Poynter Institute, and Pew Research Center, from January 2010 to December 2021. We used the following English search terms for the US search: ownership interest, scandal, self-promotion, self-censorship, cross-media promotion, cross-promotion, owner pressure or influence, ownership pressure, or conflict of interest.

For France, we searched in the Nexis Uni database for articles appearing from January 2010 through February 2022 in *La Correspondence de la Presse*, *La Lettre A*, *Challenges*, and *Stratégies*. We conducted additional searches on the websites of *Mediapart* and *Acrimed* (Action-Critique-Médias) and in the book *Médias: Les Nouveaux Empires* (2017), which compiled and extended media reporting by journalists Amaury de Rochegonde (*Stratégies*) and Richard Sénéjoux (*Télérama*). For France, in line with the public debate on the issue, we focused our search on the trade publications in Nexis Uni and on the *Mediapart* website for articles containing the broad terms: conflit d'intérêt (conflict of interest), indépendance (independence), or ingérence (interference), combined with actionnaire (shareholder), actionnariat (shareholders), proprietaire (owner), or journalis*. On the *Acrimed* website, we searched for articles on media ownership under their section headings "En Bref" (In Brief) and "Indépendance? Pressions, censures et collusions" (Independence? Pressures, censorship and collusions). Note: *Acrimed* is an independent association supported by individual donations. It situates its "radical" and "political" (but "not partisan") criticism in its interpretation of economic analysis and the sociology of media. Its frequent posts not only present its own stated "left of the left" positions but also often relay or link to reporting and critiques by a range of news outlets, journalistic unions and professional associations, and university researchers who may or may not share *Acrimed*'s views: For these reasons, we included it in our French sample alongside more mainstream journalistic professional reviews. See: *Acrimed*, "Quelle critique des médias?", February 22, 2018, https://www.acrimed.org/Quelle-critique-des-medias-5683.

Given the dearth of scandals surfaced by our Sweden searches, we extended the time period a decade to encompass 2000 to 2021 and expanded our databases and search terms to be sure of our results. Multiple searches were conducted, both in the main publications covering media and journalism (*Dagens Media*, *Resumé*, and *Journalisten*), and in articles about news and journalism accessed through Mediearkivet Retriever (Media

Archive Retriever, a broad database of all Nordic media, https://www.retrievergroup.com/sv/product-mediearkivet). These searches used combinations of the closest equivalents to the US English search words: ägarintresse (ownership interest), skandal ägare (scandal owner), skandal (scandal), ägarinflytande (owner influence), självcensur (self-censorship), ägarpåtryckningar (ownership pressure), and påtryckningar från ägare (pressure from owners), and also the less used modern anglicism självpromotion (self-promotion). The Swedish term uppdragsjournalistik (journalism for hire) was added as a search term because it emerged as an established way of describing economically instrumentalist news practice. Additional searches included Bonnier and Schibsted as search terms, given the prominence of these conglomerates in the Swedish media market. As an additional measure, we searched for evidence of cases of economic instrumentalism in the 763 decisions between 2002 and 2021 published online by Medieombudsmannen (The Media Ombudsman) and Mediernas Etiknämnd (The Media Ethics Committee), previously known as Pressombudsmannen (The Press Ombudsman) and Pressens Opinionsnämnd (The Press Opinion Committee).

Notes

Introduction

1. "ProPublica Wins Two Scripps Howard Awards," *ProPublica*, June 13, 2022, https://www.propublica.org/atpropublica/propublica-wins-two-scripps-howard-awards-2. For the sake of consistency and ease of identifying unfamiliar names as media, we italicize the names of all media outlets mentioned in this book, including digital native outlets and the names of television channels referred to as shorthand for their news websites.
2. Johan Lindén, former *SVT* senior advisor and commissioning editor, interview with Rodney Benson, October 2016, Stockholm. See also TT/SVT, "Bakgrund: Telias skandaler i Öst" [Background: The Scandals of Telia in the East], *Aftonbladet*, May, 27, 2015, https://www.aftonbladet.se/nyheter/a/KvaMde/bakgrund-telias-skandaler-i-ost.
3. Leslie Kaufman, "The Sock Puppet That Roared: Internet Synergy or a Conflict of Interest?" *New York Times*, March 27, 2000, https://www.nytimes.com/2000/03/27/business/media-the-sock-puppet-that-roared-internet-synergy-or-a-conflict-of-interest.html.
4. de Rochegonde and Sénéjoux (2017, 235–237).
5. Agence France-Presse, "French Newspaper 'Stunned' as Far-Right Editor Named," *France24*, June 27, 2023, https://www.france24.com/en/live-news/20230627-french-newspaper-stunned-as-far-right-editor-named; named; Tribune Collectif, " 'Le JDD ne peut devenir un journal au service des idées d'extrême droite,' dénoncent 400 personnalités," *Le Monde*, June 27, 2023, https://www.lemonde.fr/idees/article/2023/06/27/le-jdd-ne-peut-devenir-un-journal-au-service-des-idees-d-extreme-droite_6179372_3232.html; Giorgio Leali and Laura Kayali, " 'French Murdoch' sparks fears of far-right lurch at iconic paper," *Politico*, June 29, 2023, https://www.politico.eu/article/french-media-tycoon-sparks-outrage-after-far-right-top-editor-appointment//.
6. Jonas Nordling, *Dagens Arena* editor-in-chief, telephone interview with Erik Thyselius, August 2020.
7. Usher and Kim-Leffingwell (2023).
8. Levendusky (2013).
9. Gilens and Hertzman (2000) and Neff and Benson (2021).
10. Thornton et al. (2012, 2, 73).
11. Bourdieu (1984, 2005).
12. Lahire (2001).
13. Gitlin (2000).
14. Ownership rights are mediated through whatever governance mechanisms have been established through a given juridical structure (e.g., the US "Inc.," the French "SAS," etc.). As such, a dominant shareholder (whether in a stock market-traded or private company) is not an "owner" in the same sense as individual ownership outside of any organizational structure. See the discussion in Dudouet (2019) and Sedel (2022, 87–93).
15. Murdock (1982).
16. Madhulika Sikka, *PBS* Public Editor, posted February 6, 2018, last modified on July 6, 2020, https://www.pbs.org/publiceditor/blogs/pbs-public-editor/dear-youtube/.
17. Williams (1974), Hall et al. (1978), Hall (1982), and Curran and Seaton (2009).
18. Zelizer (2004), Schudson (2011), Reese and Shoemaker (2016), Esser et al. (2016), Neveu (2019), and Reese (2021).
19. Hallin and Mancini (2004). Brüggemann et al. (2014) and Nechushtai (2018) provide compelling evidence for reclassifications, while keeping intact the differentiation of the US, Sweden, and France as representatives of different models.
20. In this book, we do not attempt to determine whether ownership form and other "media types" matter more than national fields in shaping news production, as in Cornia et al. (2019); however, see Benson et al. (2018) for an earlier version of this book's public service news analysis that presents both ownership form and national field differences.

Chapter 1

1. Compaine (1995, 757); see also Hardy (2014, 80). For an earlier version of this discussion of the limits of the concentration paradigm, see Benson (2019).

2. Bagdikian (1983; 2004). But see Horwitz (2005), Baker (2007), and Freedman (2008), for attempts to take seriously both ownership concentration and form.
3. Bagdikian (2004, 1).
4. Bagdikian (1983, 226).
5. Curran et al. (2009), Aalberg and Curran (2011), Cushion (2012), and Aalberg et al. (2013).
6. Bagdikian (2004, 27).
7. Callum Borchers, "The Loophole that Enables Sinclair to Own So Many TV Stations," *Washington Post*, April 4, 2018, https://www.washingtonpost.com/news/the-fix/wp/2018/04/04/the-loophole-that-enables-sinclair-to-own-so-many-tv-stations/.
8. For national circulation levels achieved by Hearst, see Emery and Emery (1988, 627). To calculate the percentage of total national newspaper circulation controlled by Gannett, we divided the 2.95 million circulation of Gannett/Gatehouse's 260 daily newspapers (as of June 2019, see https://www.bizjournals.com/boston/news/2019/11/22/most-gannett-papers-are-losing-print-circulation.html) into the total US daily weekday newspaper circulation of 28.6 million (as of 2018, https://www.journalism.org/fact-sheet/newspapers/). In Noam and Mutter (2016, 502, Table 18-1: Daily Newspapers—Market Shares by Circulation), Gannett's share of US daily newspaper circulation was eleven percent in 2000, but had fallen to 9.6 percent in 2013.
9. Noam et al. (2016).
10. Noam (2016a, 7). See Compaine (1995) and Bagdikian (2004). For a thoughtful critical analysis that refuses this binary, Winseck (2008).
11. Most of Noam's ownership concentration data is derived from 2011 to 2013. Noam (2016b, 1017) explains that these thirty countries were chosen "on the basis of their importance in the media world, their GDP, and population size." Half of the sample is derived from Western Europe (Belgium, Finland, France, Germany, Ireland, Italy, Netherlands, Poland, Portugal, Spain, Sweden, Switzerland, and United Kingdom) and North America (Canada, the US), and the remainder captures many of the most populous and/or largest economies around the world (Argentina, Chile, and Mexico; the "emerging BRICS" countries of Brazil, Russia, India, China, and South Africa; Egypt, Israel, and Turkey; Australia, Japan, South Korea, and Taiwan).
12. For *all* media (content and platform), the US is also the least concentrated, with France ranked third and Sweden ranked ninth (Noam 2016c, 1316, Table 38-7).
13. See RSF-Reporters without Borders, 2013 Report, https://rsf.org/en/index?year=2013, accessed October 5, 2023. For analysis of the methodologies used by RSF, Freedom House, and other press "freedom" ranking systems, see Becker et al. (2007).
14. Rankings of top news websites can change from month to month. Rankings captured in 2019 and 2020 are provided for illustrative purposes, highlighting moments in time that illustrate how concentration (of audience attention) distributed across ownership forms may vary across national journalistic fields.
15. Coulson and Lacy (1996, 359).
16. Becker et al. (2009, 368, 380). See also Litman and Bridges (1986), Lacy (1987), Lacy and Blanchard (2003), and Gentzkow and Shapiro (2008), as well as Klinenberg's (2007) qualitative analysis of concentration's negative effects on local media.
17. As to the dynamics that facilitate the production of diverse content in monopoly or oligopoly conditions, see Doyle (2002, 13), Gamson and Latteier (2004), and Braun (2015).
18. Boczkowski (2010, 3, 95).
19. Cagé et al. (2017, 12).
20. Cagé (2019, 2).
21. Although not citing all these particular outlets, Zaller (1999, 16–18), makes this general point, citing Semetko et al. (1991) and Blumler and Gurevitch (2001), the latter as a pre-publisher manuscript.
22. Friedland and Alford (1991) and Thornton et al. (2012).
23. Bourdieu (1984; 1993; 2005).
24. Tunstall and Palmer (1991). Some studies (Thomas 1981; Agnès and Eveno 2010) mix the categories of owners, CEOs, and editors. See Sedel (2021a) for a sociologically circumscribed study of French news media "directors."
25. Knee et al. (2011, 3).
26. Ibid., 45.
27. Kennedy (2018); see also Sullivan (2020, 80–82).
28. Stern (2012).
29. Breed (1955), Bowers (1967), Bogart (1973), and Chomsky (1999; 2006).

30. Lukes (2004, 34, 69). Lukes is critical of the concept, but we value it as a supplement rather than as a replacement for power understood as domination.
31. Williams (1981, 33–56).
32. Bagdikian (2004).
33. Herman and Chomsky (1988, 3–14).
34. Ibid., 14.
35. Concerning composition and/or interlocking of news media company boards of directors, see Dreier (1982), An and Jin (2004), Simmons (2012), Ohlsson (2012), Benson (2018), and Saffer et al. (2021).
36. Gans (2005/1979) refers to a national journalistic "para-ideology," Tuchman (1980) to common "strategic rituals," and Gitlin (1980) and Ryan (1991) to the workings of "hegemony."
37. Bagdikian (1992, 204) specifically praises European audience funded newspapers, but he never carried out comparative research.
38. The remainder of this chapter draws and builds on Benson (2016; 2018; 2022).
39. As such, an inductive approach is crucial at the outset to ensure that the categories of analysis make room for the actually existing range of empirical phenomena. See, for example, Cagé and Huet (2021, 63–116) for France, or Ohlsson (2012; 2016) for Sweden. This "emic" knowledge must inform but not hinder the development of abstract "etic" categories justified on theoretical and heuristic principles that are necessary for generalizable comparative research (Bourdieu 1998; Wirth and Kolb 2004).
40. Curran (1991, 142–148).
41. Baker (1994a, 12, 18–19). Such non-ownership mechanisms of control could include organizational provisions that limit owner interference in editorial decision-making or provide journalists with some say over appointment of editors (see, e.g., Schwoebel 1969; 1970; Cagé and Huet 2021, 156–159).
42. Baker (2007, 198).
43. For comprehensive analyses of news media market failure and policy solutions, see Baker (2002) and Pickard (2020).
44. Djankov et al. (2003), Picard and van Weezel (2008), and Noam (2017). While useful, these approaches are either not comprehensive or mix distinct logics in ways that our approach is designed to avoid. For example, Picard and van Weezel's "private" category includes private equity, which we see as more closely aligned with (stock) market logic; they also designate employee ownership as a distinct form, when in our view it is better understood as a subform of private ownership (see Fedler and Pennington 2003), with the same degree of discretion in management styles and profit focus as at other privately owned outlets.
45. Friedland and Alford (1991) and Thornton et al. (2012). The use of institutional logics theory for media ownership research was introduced in Benson (2016; 2018) and empirically deployed in Benson et al. (2018). We draw on institutional logics in this section rather than Bourdieu's field theory, which we use elsewhere, because of its more pluralist conception of power and thus its greater facility in capturing the potential heterogeneity of ownership influences (Friedland and Alford 1991, 240–241; Friedland 2009). Bourdieu (2005) and others (Maares and Hanusch 2022) have usefully analyzed the conflict between an internal "autonomous" professional journalistic logic and an external "heteronomous" logic, with the latter (associated with political and economic power) understood as dominant. However, if distinct ownership forms are able to exert diverse effects on journalistic practice inside the professional journalistic field, we should find significant differences in news production along multiple axes, transcending the autonomy–heteronomy binary.
46. Friedland and Alford (1991, 240, 249) and Thornton et al. (2012, 73). For the most part, we do not analyze separately a "corporation" logic given its capture in recent decades by a profit-maximizing market logic (see Fligstein and Goldstein 2022). Empirical research may reveal the existence of other logics.
47. Thornton et al. (2012, 2).
48. Ibid.
49. Thornton et al. (2012, 73). This identification of societal civic values (civic solidarity) with the state, especially when there is a strong welfare state, is also developed by Lamont and Thévenot (2000), Benson and Saguy (2005), and Benson (2013), to differentiate France and the US (the latter with a more dominant "market" logic).
50. See Wright et al. (2024) for an analysis of international public media's vulnerability for purposes of political instrumentalism in the US and other leading democracies. Freedman (2019) argues

that even supposed paragons of domestic public service media, such as the *BBC*, may fall far short of civic ideals.

51. Thornton et al. (2012, 57–58, 60). When universities partner with news organizations, they create the potential for a mixing of two sub-types of professional logics: journalistic and *academic*. Concerning the co-existence of "multiple institutional logics" in the same organization, see Besharov and Smith (2014); for a similar approach applied to newsrooms drawing on Boltanski and Thévenot's (2006) "conventions of worth," see Raviola (2022).
52. Marshall Ingwerson, *Christian Science Monitor* managing editor, interview with Rodney Benson, May 2011, Boston.
53. Ryfe (2020).
54. Napoli (1997, 208).
55. Fligstein and Goldstein (2022, 7.4, 7.8); see also Ho (2009, 2–3).
56. Fligstein and Goldstein (2022, 7.14).
57. Applebaum and Batt (2014); Susca (2024, 22–25).
58. Susca (2024, 62–63).
59. To ensure consistency in our analysis, we generally define dominant shareholder in the same way as the closely related term "controlling shareholder": "any person who exercises or controls on their own or together with any person with whom they are acting in concert, 30 percent or more of the votes able to be cast on all or substantially all matters at general meetings of the company." See UK Financial Conduct Authority, "Controlling Shareholder," https://www.handbook.fca.org.uk/handbook/glossary/G3382.html. However, it is possible that a shareholder with a lower percentage control may still exert strong influence over the company.
60. Tifft and Jones (1999).
61. Fedler and Pennington (2003).
62. The limited partnership eventually adopted by almost all US venture capital firms was modeled on the French *société en commandite*, in which "passive" investors provide capital, but risk no liability, while general partners work closely with the "portfolio companies" (such as news media start-ups) in which they invest (Nicholas 2019, 146–150).
63. Charles Duhigg, "Letter from Silicon Valley: The Enablers," *The New Yorker*, November 30, 2020, 40–41.
64. See discussion in Benson (2013, 133–135; see also Benson 2016) and a general discussion of historical conceptions of civil society in Taylor (1990). For an analysis of civil society ownership, funding, and policy/advocacy support of journalism in the UK, see Fenton et al. (2010).
65. We thank Nikki Usher for suggesting this clarification.
66. Benson et al. (2017, 5, Table 1).
67. Some US *PBS* video content ("PBS Passport") is only available on-demand to "members" who donate $5 a month or more.
68. Syvertsen et al. (2014) and Benson et al. (2017, 10–11). Hallin and Mancini (2004, 55) refer to governmental intervention that transcends narrow partisan interests to "serve society as a whole" as "rational-legal authority": "a form of rule based on adherence to formal and universalistic rules of procedure."
69. Williams (2002) and Noam (2017).
70. Schudson (2007, 58).
71. Gans (2005). Among important recent works challenging the longstanding "Gans" consensus, see, for example, Anderson (2011), Usher (2014), Christin (2020), Nelson (2021), and Petre (2021). Nixon (2020) likewise emphasizes the importance of audience attention and consumption for news companies but uses a case study of (Alden Capital) Digital First to show the contemporary difficulty of effectively monetizing "digital audience labor" and thus the turn toward ownership consolidation economies of scale and drastic cost-cutting. See Chapter 3 for a discussion of Alden Capital.
72. Bourdieu (1984); see also Gaxie (1978).
73. Arthur Sulzberger, Jr., public comments at Columbia Graduate School of Journalism, New York, April 5, 2011, Rodney Benson field notes.
74. Baker (1994b).
75. Benson (2003).
76. Baker (1994b), Hamilton (2004), and Wu (2017).
77. Callahan (2018).
78. Murdock (1982).
79. Brüggemann et al. (2012).

80. "If you come to a V.C. and you say, I want to do a subscription business model, they'll say, well, I don't know—we don't have a whole lot of examples of that really blowing up, so why don't you just do advertising?" Tim Hwang, director of Harvard/MIT Ethics and Governance of AI Initiative and former public policy lead for AI at Google, interview with Ezra Klein, *Ezra Klein Show*, February 14, 2023, transcript available at https://www.nytimes.com/2023/02/14/podcasts/transcript-ezra-klein-interviews-tim-hwang.html.
81. See, for example, insider accounts such as Diamond (1993), Graham (1998), Tofel (2009), Abramson (2019), and Smith (2023), as well as the media management scholarship of Lardeau (2011), Küng (2015), Noam (2019), and Raviola (2022).
82. Wiik (2010, 144).
83. Nelson (2021, 48–50).
84. Navasky (2006) and Rusbridger (2018).
85. Andreas Gustavsson, *Dagens ETC* editor-in-chief, Zoom interview with Carl Ritter, February 2021. "Red" is shorthand for left and "Green" for environmentalist, in the newspaper's self-description as "red, green, and independent": see *Dagens ETC*, "About Us," https://www.etc.se/.
86. "There was an understanding inside the paper of his father [Punch Sulzberger] that the *Times* was edited by elites for elites . . . 'Our identity has not been primarily geographic, it has been demographic,' [editor] Max Frankel acknowledged" (Diamond 1993, 383).
87. Ibid., 391.
88. Leeds (2023).
89. Broadly speaking, our approach is sympathetic to Humprecht's (2016) emphasis on "configurationally complex" causation (citing Ragin 2008) assumed by the fuzzy set Qualitative Comparative Analysis that she uses, as well as Bourdieu's (1984) use of Multiple Correspondence Analysis. However, we use the term *ownership complex* to refer specifically to ownership form and its mutual imbrication at any given news outlet with funding and target audiences, as well as the agency that owners and their managers exert in shaping these combinations.
90. Picard and van Weezel (2008, 29).
91. Ohlsson (2016, 76–77, 84).
92. For studies that fruitfully focus on local situations and strategies, see, for example, Boczkowski (2005), Küng (2017), and Usher (2019).
93. Picard and van Weezel (2008, 29–30).
94. Baker (2002), Habermas (2006), Christians et al. (2009), Williams and Delli Carpini (2011), Benson (2013), and Hesmondhalgh (2014).
95. See Loicq and Rebillard (2013).
96. Hanitzsch et al. (2019).
97. Alexander (2016, 22–23).
98. Demsetz and Lehn (1985, 1161–1162); see also the discussion in Napoli (1997, 211).
99. Bowers (1967).
100. See Scott et al. (2017) and Wright et al. (2019) for a case of such blurring by a philanthropy-funded nonprofit news outlet.
101. Schiffrin (2021); see also Besley and Prat (2006) and Corneo (2006).

Chapter 2

1. For this chapter's historical synthesis, we consulted: for the US, Emery and Emery (1988), Kaplan (2002), and Schudson and Tifft (2005); for Sweden, Gustafsson and Rydén (2010), Djerf-Pierre and Weibull (2011), and Ohlsson (2012, 17–38); and for France, Popkin (1990), Censer (1994), Pradié (1995), Chalaby (1996), Thogmartin (1998), Eveno (2003), and Kuhn (2011).
2. Hadenius et al. (2009, 62).
3. Johan [Johan Jenny, since 2023] Ehrenberg, "Nu startar vi Stiftelsen ETC" [Now we are starting the ETC Foundation], *Dagens ETC*, June 19, 2020 (updated October 12, 2022), https://www.etc.se/ledare/nu-startar-vi-stiftelsen-etc.
4. Chalaby (1996).
5. Nasaw (2001) and Morris (2010).
6. Emery and Emery (1988, 627).
7. Gustafsson and Rydén (2010, 199–200).
8. Ohlsson (2015, 39–40).

9. According to Nordicom researcher Tobias Lindberg (email to Rodney Benson, March 28, 2024), Bonnier and Schibsted no longer measure "their printed and digital circulations, making it difficult to use that metric today." However, Lindberg said, available data on total market turnover shows that Bonnier Group newspapers increased their percentage of total newspaper market turnover from twenty-nine percent in 2015 to around forty-six percent in 2022. See also https://www.nordicom.gu.se/en/publications/nordic-news-media-global-competition, and https://mediemyndigheten.se/rapporter-och-analyser/medieutveckling/ (annual market reports, in Swedish). Regarding Bonnier's purchases since 2019, see Hanna Frick and Linnéa Kihlström, "Uppdaterad: Bonnier and Amedia köper Hall Media [Updated: Bonnier and Amedia buys Hall Media]," *Dagens Media*, February, 25, 2020, https://www.dagensmedia.se/medier/dagspress/uppdaterad-bonnier-och-amedia-koper-hall-media/.
10. Allern (2021).
11. Chalaby (1997, 629).
12. Chalaby (1997, 629–630).
13. Pradié (1995), Martin (1997), and Eveno (2003).
14. Pradié (1995, 137–146).
15. Charon (1991).
16. Sedel (2021a, 44–45).
17. France24, "Le Monde News Daily Sold to Billionaire Trio," *France24*, June 28, 2010, https://www.france24.com/en/20100628-france-le-monde-newspaper-sells-billionaire-trio-niel-pigasse-berge.
18. Küng (2015), Usher (2017), and Smith (2023).
19. Michael Calderone, "The Huffington Post Is Now HuffPost," *HuffPost*, April 25, 2017, https://www.huffpost.com/entry/huffington-post-huffpost-lydia-polgreen_n_58fce1cae4b00fa7de1522ee.
20. Synnöve Almer, "Nyheter 24.se ska gå runt om ett år" [Nyheter 24 should make profit in a year], *Dagens Media*, September 11, 2008, https://www.dagensmedia.se/alla-nyheter/nyheter/nyheter24se-ska-ga-runt-om-ett-ar/; Philip Wallin, "Nyheter 24 is Sold: 'Our Baby Couldn't Have Found a Better Home'", May 16, 2019, https://www.dagensmedia.se/medier/medier/nyheter-24-saljs-var-baby-kunde-inte-fatt-ett-battre-hem/.
21. Joseph Lichterman, "The Swedish Startup Kit is Rethinking Analytics for a Broader View of What Makes a Story Successful," *NiemanLab*, June 8, 2017, https://www.niemanlab.org/2017/06/the-swedish-startup-kit-is-rethinking-analytics-for-a-broader-view-of-what-makes-a-story-successful/; Lydia Farran-Lee, "Sajten Kit slutar med journalistik" [The KIT site stops producing journalism], *SVT Nyheter*, September 17, 2019, https://www.svt.se/kultur/sajten-kit-slutar-med-journalistik.
22. See, for example, Peter Kafka, "NBCUniversal Buys Big Chunks of Vox Media and Buzzfeed," *Vox*, August 12, 2015, https://www.vox.com/2015/8/12/11615536/nbcuniversal-buys-big-chunks-of-vox-media-and-buzzfeed, and Mark Sweney, "'Like Icarus—Now Everyone is Burnt': How Vice and Buzzfeed Fell to Earth," *The Guardian*, May 5, 2023, https://www.theguardian.com/media/2023/may/05/like-icarus-now-everyone-is-burnt-how-vice-and-buzzfeed-fell-to-earth.
23. Smith (2023, 32–34, 67–77).
24. See Clare Malone, "Jonah Peretti Has Regrets about BuzzFeed News," *New Yorker*, May 4, 2023, https://www.newyorker.com/news/annals-of-communications/jonah-peretti-has-regrets-about-buzzfeed-news. For information about how a SPAC differs from a traditional IPO (Initial Public Offering), see Max. H. Bazerman and Paresh Patel, "SPACS: What You Need to Know," *Harvard Business Review*, July–August 2021, https://hbr.org/2021/07/spacs-what-you-need-to-know. For our 2015–2016 content analysis, the *BuzzFeed* sample was gathered from the outlet's News section; *BuzzFeed News* did not have its own website until July 2018.
25. See Kennedy (2018) and Gretchen Frazee, "Why Billionaire Investors are Gambling on News Publications," *PBS NewsHour*, September 18, 2018, https://www.pbs.org/newshour/economy/making-sense/why-billionaire-investors-are-gambling-on-news-publications/.
26. Fedler and Pennington (2003); see also Picard and van Weezel (2008).
27. Fedler and Pennington (2003, 270).
28. Coulson (1994, 407–408); Demers and Wackman (1988, 65).
29. Analysis based on authors' research of the named newspaper websites, July 2021.
30. Thogmartin (1998, 196).
31. Rimbert (2005).

32. Regarding *Libération*'s development of a unique multi-genre journalistic style and format, see Benson (2013, 50–51); concerning *Le Monde*'s investigative reporting, see Berger (1992) and Marchetti (2009).
33. For detailed accounts of *Le Monde*'s internal operations during its final years of employee ownership, see Sedel (2004), Benson (2004), the investigative journalism of Péan and Cohen (2003), and the insider account of director Eric Fottorino (2014).
34. Fedler and Pennington (2003, 270).
35. For information about *Rue89*'s early company and individual angel investors, see *L'Obs*, "New Shareholders Help Street89's Development," July 17, 2008, https://www.nouvelobs.com/rue89/rue89-rue89/20080627.RUE4752/new-shareholders-help-street89-s-development.html.
36. Bruno and Nielsen (2012) and Raviola (2022).
37. Alfon (2017).
38. As of 2017, Benjamin and Ariane de Rothschild became the majority shareholders in *Slate.fr*. Alexandre Piquard, "'Slate.fr', ou les difficultés d'équilibrer un site d'information gratuit," *Le Monde*, August 18, 2017 (updated August 21, 2017), https://www.lemonde.fr/economie/article/2017/08/18/slate-ou-les-difficultes-d-equilibrer-un-site-d-information-gratuit_5173956_3234.html.
39. Pierre Haski, *Rue89* co-founder and former *Libération* foreign news editor and correspondent, interview with Julie Sedel, March 2011, Paris; Johan Hufnagel, *Slate.fr* co-founder and former online editor-in-chief at *Libération* and *20 Minutes*, interview with Rodney Benson, March 2023, Paris. Note: *Slate.fr* is the generally accepted name as well as the website address for the "French" Slate.
40. For the early history of US commercial television, see Barnouw (1990), McChesney (1995), and Pickard (2014).
41. Fligstein and Goldstein (2022).
42. Comcast Corporation, SEC (2021), Schedule 14A, https://www.sec.gov/Archives/edgar/data/1166691/000120677422001186/cmcsa4011221-def14a.htm.
43. Geraldine Fabrikant, "Walt Disney to Acquire ABC in $19 Billion Deal to Build a Giant for Entertainment," *New York Times*, August 1, 1995, A1, https://www.nytimes.com/1995/08/01/business/media-business-merger-walt-disney-acquire-abc-19-billion-deal-build-giant-for.html.
44. Bergreen (1980, 51–53); see also Halberstam (2000).
45. Date of CBS's first stock market listing provided by Paramount Company, https://www.paramount.com/company-history, accessed August 10, 2023.
46. Ibid.
47. See Jonathan Kandell, "Sumner Redstone Dies at 97," *New York Times*, August 12, 2020, https://www.nytimes.com/2020/08/12/obituaries/sumner-redstone-dead.html, and US Securities and Exchange Commission, Form 10-Q, Paramount Global, 13–4, https://ir.paramount.com/static-files/0111d53e-9def-4458-b106-c9e0f4cf655f, accessed August 10, 2023.
48. Ponce de Leon (2015, 230) and John Koblin, "Discovery's Shareholders Approve a Merger with WarnerMedia," *New York Times*, March 11, 2022, https://www.nytimes.com/2022/03/11/technology/discoverys-warnermedia-merger.html.
49. Madeline Berg, "What the Disney–Fox Deal Means for Rupert Murdoch's Fortune," *Forbes*, March 20, 2019, https://www.forbes.com/sites/maddieberg/2019/03/20/what-the-disney-fox-deal-means-for-rupert-murdochs-fortune/?sh=310523be312e. On the history of News Corporation and *Fox News*, see Peck (2019, ch. 1); for journalistic and insider accounts, see Sherman (2017) and Stelzer (2018).
50. Amy Tikkanen, "MSNBC: American Corporation," *Brittanica*, last updated August 8, 2023, https://www.britannica.com/topic/MSNBC.
51. Cranberg et al. (2001, 27).
52. Ibid., 27–32.
53. Cranberg et al. (2001, 2, 25–26).
54. Ibid., 33.
55. Abernathy (2016, 16).
56. Edmund Lee and Tiffany Hsu, "BuzzFeed to Acquire HuffPost from Verizon Media," *New York Times*, November 19, 2020 (updated June 23, 2021), https://www.nytimes.com/2020/11/19/business/media/buzzfeed-huffpost.html.
57. Michael Kinsley, "My History of Slate," *Slate*, June 18, 2006, https://slate.com/news-and-politics/2006/06/michael-kinsley-s-history-of-slate.html.
58. David Carr, "Microsoft Says It is Exploring the Sale of Slate Magazine," *New York Times*, July 23, 2004, https://www.nytimes.com/2004/07/23/business/media/microsoft-says-it-is-exploring-the-sale-of-slate-magazine.html; Kinsley, ibid.; Katie Robertson, "Slate, the Pioneering Web

Magazine, Struggles to Find Identity and Profit," *New York Times*, February 11, 2022, https://www.nytimes.com/2022/02/11/business/media/slate-departures.html.

59. The Bouygues family is the largest single shareholder in Bouygues, with 29.5 percent of shares. See Bouygues, "Ownership Structure," as of December 31, 2021, at https://www.bouygues.com/en/ownership-structure/, accessed April 27, 2022. This level of shareholding is clearly understood by the family itself as below the 30 percent "controlling" threshold. According to AFP (reported as source for "The Bouygues family exceeds the threshold of 25% of the capital of Bouygues," Batinfo.com, August 30, 2022, https://batinfo.com/en/actuality/the-bouygues-family-exceeds-the-threshold-of-25-in-the-capital-of-bouygues_21835), the "Bouygues families 'do not plan to take control of the Bouygues company.'"
60. *Reuters*, "TF1 veut cesser la parution de *Metronews* et supprimer 60 emplois" [TF1 wants to stop publishing Metronews and cut 60 jobs], May 21, 2015, https://www.reuters.com/article/tf1-metronews-idFRL5N0YC4JE20150521; *Libération*, "Médias: LCI, et son site, font peau neuve," August 29, 2016, https://archive.wikiwix.com/cache/index2.php?url=http%3A%2F%2Fwww.liberation.fr%2Fdirect%2Felement%2Fmedias-lci-et-son-site-font-peau-neuve_46230%2F#federation=archive.wikiwix.com&tab=url.
61. *Le Figaro* is directly owned by the Société du Figaro, which is in turn owned by Le Groupe Figaro (which also owns CCM Benchmark and Figaro Classifieds), part of Groupe Dassault (also sometimes called Groupe industriel Marcel Dassault), which is a private holding group taking the form of a Société par Actions Simplifiée (SAS) entirely owned by the Dassault family. The Groupe Dassault is also the dominant shareholder in stock market-traded company Dassault Aviation and other industrial companies. While *Le Figaro* is not directly owned by a stock market-traded company (as with Disney's ownership of *ABC*), it is integrated into the suite of companies, some stock market-traded, some not, owned by the private holding company Groupe Dassault. We thus consider it a borderline case between stock market dominant shareholder and private ownership, but categorize it as stock market dominant shareholder because of its integration in the complex infrastructure linking Groupe Dassault and the traded Dassault Aviation.
62. Laurent Joffrin, "A nos lecteurs; Rachat de 'Libé' par SFR: ce que ça change" [To our readers; Purchase of Libé by SFR: what it changes], *Libération*, April 25, 2016, https://www.liberation.fr/france/2016/04/25/rachat-de-libe-par-sfr-ce-que-ca-change_1448594/?redirected=1.
63. Matthew Fleischer, "The Huffington Post Heads to France," *Adweek*, October 10, 2011, https://www.adweek.com/performance-marketing/the-huffington-post-heads-to-france/. Fleischer reports that "HuffPo [Verizon] and its two [French] media partners will be equal shareholders." As such, *Le HuffPost* is a hybrid of stock market widely held and private ownership. However, given that the French partners control more than 30 percent of the shares in a company that is half-owned by a stock market-traded entity, it also has much in common with stock market dominant shareholder ownership, which is how we classify it for our analysis.
64. Tinius Trust, "Tinius Trust Foundation," accessed August 6, 2023, https://schibsted.com/sustainability/tinius-trust-foundation/ and Tinius Trust, "Corporate Governance Principles", accessed August 6, 2023, https://tinius.com/about-us/corporate-governance-principles/.
65. Ohlsson (2016, 44).
66. Jacob Johannesson, "Telias köp av Bonnier Broadcasting slutfört" [Telia's Purchase of Bonnier Broadcasting Completed], *Dagens Industri*, December, 2, 2019, https://www.di.se/live/telias-kop-av-bonnier-broadcasting-slutfort/.
67. Strömbäck and Nord (2008, 113) and Asp (2017, 38).
68. *Kinnevik*, "Kinnevik divests Metro Sweden," February 15, 2017, Kinnevik press release, no longer available online. According to Hadenius and Weibull (1999, 138), in the 1990s, *Metro* was "co-sponsored by the [Stockholm] metropolitan transit authority, which [had] two pages in each issue."
69. Amanda Ernst, "Metro Sells U.S. Papers to Ex-CEO," *Adweek*, May 11, 2009, https://www.adweek.com/performance-marketing/metro-sells-u-s-papers-to-ex-ceo/.
70. Susca (2024, 65–96).
71. See McKay Coppins, "A Secretive Hedge Fund is Gutting Newsrooms: Inside Alden Capital," *The Atlantic*, October 14, 2021, https://www.theatlantic.com/magazine/archive/2021/11/alden-global-capital-killing-americas-newspapers/620171/.
72. See Ken Doctor, "The Gannett–Gatehouse Merger is Really Happening," *NiemanLab*, October 9, 2019, https://www.niemanlab.org/2019/10/newsonomics-the-gannett-gatehouse-merger-is-really-happening-but-expect-to-see-more-than-10-of-jobs-cut-off-the-top/.
73. Cagé and Huet (2021, 94–102, 112–116, 133–151).

74. Ohlsson (2012; 2018) and Achtenhagen et al. (2018). The Axel and Margaret Ax:son Johnson Foundation for Public Benefit, the employer of co-author Mattias Hessérus and a partial funder of this book's research, is a nonprofit scholarly research "foundation for public benefit" that owns an AB company magazine and cable channel.
75. The newspaper *Fria Tidningar* had nonprofit cooperative ownership from 1999 to 2001, followed by worker cooperative ownership from 2001 to 2016, after which time it reverted to the standard commercial AB ownership (Madelene Axelsson, *Fria Tidningar* domestic editor, telephone interview with Marcus Nilsen, July 2020; Fria Tidningen, "Fria Tidningar," ND, last accessed October 5, 2023, https://www.fria.nu/omfria). See also this documentary, posted May 29, 2015, about "economic democracy" and worker ownership produced by Fria Tidningar: https://geo.coop/story/can-we-do-it-ourselves.
76. Sandlund (2001, 324–325).
77. Mentor Medier only lists the twenty biggest shareholders, which together have 42.37 percent of the voting rights. Fourteen of the top 20, with 27.69 percent of voting rights, have a clear church and/or Christian connection. No single shareholder is permitted to control more than five percent of voting shares. See Mentor Medier, "Årsrapport 2016" [Annual report 2016], accessed October 13, 2023, https://assets.website-files.com/5c99fee86af083e2f3a274ef/5ca5d53541698e07e4fc0373_Mentor-Medier_aarsmelding-2016-print.pdf.
78. The Center Party sold its local newspapers in 2005 to a consortium of Stampen, Mittmedia, and Lidköpings-Gruppen (Ohlsson 2016, 47). The Social Democratic party-owned company A-pressen went bankrupt in 1992, after which its newspapers were closed or taken over by local workers' organizations (Ohlsson 2016, 64).
79. Hadenius and Weibull (1999, 144).
80. Ohlsson (2012, 13).
81. Ohlsson (2016, 16).
82. Ohlsson (2012, 13).
83. Ohlsson (2018).
84. Sigurd Allern, professor of journalism, Department of Media and Communication, University of Oslo, personal communication with Rodney Benson, March 2015, Toulouse. This is also true for some of the leading US "nonprofits": at *ProPublica*, Paul Steiger, the former *Wall Street Journal* editor who was its founding editor-in-chief, was paid a "competitive" annual salary of $570,000. See Joe Pompeo, "ProPublica's Editor In Chief Makes More Than Half A Million Dollars," *BusinessInsider*, August 10, 2010, https://www.businessinsider.com/propublicas-editor-in-chief-makes-more-than-half-a-million-dollars-2010-8/.
85. Ohlsson (2018).
86. Jonas Ohlsson, director, Nordicom-University of Gothenburg, interview with Rodney Benson, October 2017, Gothenburg.
87. Ibid.
88. Malmsten (2022, 222–228). See also: Ida Yttergren and Andreas Lindberg, "Bonnier News och Amedia köper mediekoncernen Mittmedia" [Bonnier News and Amedia buy the media group Mittmedia], *Dagens Nyheter*, February 8, 2019, https://www.dn.se/ekonomi/uppgifter-bonnier-koper-mediekoncernen-mittmedia/.
89. Anders Westermark, Stiftelsen Skelleftepress chairman and former *Norran* CEO, interview with Mattias Hessérus, November 2023, Stockholm.
90. Sanna Gustavsson and Åsa Asplid, "Bonnier vinner: Köper 28 svenska lokaltidningar" [Bonnier wins: Buys 28 Swedish local newspapers], *Expressen*, February 8, 2019 (updated June 10, 2021), https://www.expressen.se/nyheter/uppgifter-bonnier-koper-28-svenska-lokaltidningar/; Anders Westermark interview with Hessérus, 2023.
91. As Westermark told Hessérus (ibid.): "In all contracts that I'm aware of where a foundation has handed over the media operation, and in our case *Norran*, one has made sure that there are a number of issues that one is in agreement about like the appointment of the political editor and that they are not allowed to change the newspaper's political orientation, etc."
92. Ibid.
93. *Libération*, "*L'Humanité*: 1 million de francs," December 11, 2000, https://www.liberation.fr/medias/2000/12/11/l-humanite-1-million-de-francs_347229/; *L'Obs*, "Qui possède quoi? *L'Humanité*" [Who owns what? L'Humanité], January 24, 2007 (updated September 2, 2008), https://www.nouvelobs.com/medias/medias-pouvoirs/20070124.OBS8585/qui-possede-quoi.html; Frantz Durupt, "Pour ses 112 ans, *L'Humanité* a besoin d'argent," *Libération*, April 18, 2016, https://www.liberation.fr/futurs/2016/04/18/pour-ses-112-ans-l-humanite-a-besoin-d-argent_1447016/.

94. Cagé and Huet (2021, 112–116). See also *La Lettre*, "Pourquoi L'Huma change de statut" [Why L'Huma changed its status], July 12, 2016 and *La Croix*, "Coup de pouce à l'entreprise solidaire de presse" [A helping hand for the solidarity press company], September 29, 2020.
95. Cagé and Huet, ibid.; Olivier Holmey, "News Unfolds Like a Saga," *NiemanLab*, June 19, 2019, https://www.niemanlab.org/2019/06/news-unfolds-like-a-saga-the-french-news-site-les-jours-wants-to-marry-narrative-depth-and-investigative-reporting.
96. Eveno (2008) and Kuhn (2011).
97. Frisque (2010) and Gapsys-Hutin (2011). In the 1990 change, *Ouest-France*'s ownership was officially transferred to a nonprofit association ("Association of the Law of 1901") titled "Association for the support of the Principles of Humanist Democracy," over which the founding Hutin family still exerts considerable control.
98. For the history of the Lenfest Institute's ownership of the *Philadelphia Inquirer*, see Lenfest Institute, "About," ND, accessed October 6, 2023, https://www.lenfestinstitute.org/about/; regarding the *Salt Lake Tribune*, see Emily Anderson, "Going Nonprofit Puts *Salt Lake Tribune* on Path to Sustainability," *Northwestern/Medill Local News Initiative*, January 19, 2022, https://localnewsinitiative.northwestern.edu/posts/2022/01/19/salt-lake-nonprofit/; and regarding the *Tampa Bay Times* (until 2012 the *St. Petersburg Times*), see Ellis (2014, 205–207).
99. Anderson, ibid.
100. According to Edwy Plenel ("Comment Mediapart a construit son indépendence," *Mediapart*, March 16, 2008, https://www.mediapart.fr/journal/france/090308/comment-mediapart-construit-son-independance), two of *Mediapart*'s original six founders had a business or academic background in information technologies. Regarding its economic model and success, see Alfon (2017) and Edwy Plenel, "Mediapart in 2020: Our Results and Figures in Detail," *Billet de Blog, Mediapart*, March 17, 2021, https://blogs.mediapart.fr/edwy-plenel/blog/170321/mediapart-2020-our-results-and-figures-detail.
101. Edwy Plenel, *Mediapart* co-founder, president, and publishing editor, remarks to NYU visiting group, June 2016, Paris. As to the formalization of nonprofit ownership of *Mediapart*, see François Bonnet, Laurent Mauduit, Edwy Plenel, and Marie-Hélène Smiejan-Wanneroy, "Mediapart Guarantees Its Future Independence," July 2, 2019, *Mediapart*, https://www.mediapart.fr/en/journal/france/020719/mediapart-guarantees-its-future-independence, and Sandrine Cassini, "'Mediapart' modifie sa gouvernance pour préserver son indépendance," *Le Monde*, July 2, 2019, https://www.lemonde.fr/actualite-medias/article/2019/07/02/mediapart-modifie-sa-gouvernance-pour-preserver-son-independance_5484502_3236.html. According to Cassini, after *Mediapart*'s conversion to a nonprofit, Plenel and the other journalist co-founders who were the largest individual investors collectively received a payout of 6.8 million euros, more than five times their original investments; Xavier Niel and the other Friends of *Mediapart*, as a group, received 2.7 million euros. At least one of the major early investors opted to contribute his earnings to the new nonprofit.
102. This section's discussion of US nonprofits draws on Benson (2018), Konieczna (2018; 2019), and Birnbauer (2019). According to Walker (2021), between 2008 and 2020, the total number of US newsroom employees fell from 114,000 to 85,000, a twenty-six percent decline. The biggest decline came in newspaper jobs, which fell fifty-seven percent, from 71,000 in 2008 to 31,000 in 2020.
103. For a legal analysis of 501(c)(3) ownership for journalism, see Usher and Layser (2010), and Westenskow and Carter (2021). Relating to the rise of partisan nonprofits, see Holcomb et al. (2011) and Buozis and Konieczna (2023).
104. Birnbauer (2019, 125–144) and Konieczna (2018).
105. Birnbauer ibid., 145–150.
106. Given the predominance of investigative reporting websites among the earliest members, INN originally meant "Investigative News Network" (Chuck Lewis, *Center for Public Integrity* (*CPI*) founding executive editor and *Investigative Reporting Workshop* (*IRW*) executive editor, Zoom interview with Rodney Benson, February 2021). Lewis was a co-founder of the original INN.
107. INN [Institute for NonProfit News] 2020 Index (based on 2019 survey data), https://inn.org/research/inn-index/inn-index-2020/.
108. Sweden Department of Culture, Swedish Government Official Reports, Medieutredningen [the Media Investigation], "*En gränsöverskridande mediepolitik: för upplysning, engagemang och ansvar: slutbetänkande* [A cross-border media policy: for enlightenment, engagement and responsibility] (Stockholm: Wolters Kluwer, 2016), 162, http://www.regeringen.se/rattsd

okument/statens-offentliga-utredningar/2016/11/sou-201680; Carlo (2017); and Powers and Vera Zambrano (2016).

109. Håkan A. Bengtsson, Arenagruppen CEO, in an email to Carl Ritter (January 14, 2021), estimates that in 2020 LO donations accounted for about sixty percent of *Dagens Arena* revenues.
110. Peter Santesson, *Kvartal* editor-in-chief, interview with Rodney Benson, October 2016, Stockholm. In a 2020 "manifesto" published on its website, a new editor-in-chief referred to *Kvartal*'s financial basis in "large contributions from a few" and the need to raise more contributions from small donors. See Jörgen Huitfeldt, "Det kvartalistiska manifestet" [The Quarterlist Manifesto], *Kvartal*, November 15, 2020, https://kvartal.se/artiklar/det-kvartalistiska-manifestet and Jörgen Huitfeldt, "Kvartal vänder blad [The Quarterly is turning a page], *Kvartal*, October 25, 2022, https://kvartal.se/artiklar/kvartal-vander-blad/.
111. Jean-Christophe Boulanger, SPIIL director, interview with Julie Sedel, 2016, Paris. The term "union" (syndicat) is used more broadly in France than in the US to refer to associations that may or may not directly represent workers. On the rise of the French concept of journalistic "independence" and its various incarnations, see Sedel (2021c) and Pacouret and Ouakrat (2021).
112. Didier Pourquery, *The Conversation France* director, interview with Julie Sedel, December 2020, Paris. *The Conversation France* is funded by major US foundations including Gates and Carnegie, as well as Google and French government subsidies. See Carlo (2017) and Google News Initiative, "Digital News Innovation Fund," ND, last accessed October 6, 2023, https://newsinitiative.withgoogle.com/dnifund/dni-projects/?country=FRA.
113. Hervé Kempf, *Reporterre* director, interview with Julie Sedel, June 2016, Paris; Ivan du Roy and Agnes Rousseaux, *Basta!* directors, interview with Rodney Benson and Julie Sedel, June 2016, Montreuil. The major long-term funder of Basta! is the French-Swiss Léopold Mayer Foundation. Basta! has also received grants from the Google Fund as well as significant French local and national government subsidies.
114. See, for example, Josephi (2013), Lei (2016), and Repnikova (2017).
115. See Benson et al. (2017, 5–6); CPB (2016); Nakamura (2019); Skatteverket [Swedish Tax Agency], "Public service-avgift" [Public Service Fee], ND, accessed July 5, 2024, https://www.skatteverket.se/privat/skatter/arbeteochinkomst/askattsedelochskattetabeller/publicserviceavgift.4.22501d9e166a8cb399f31dd.html; and Elsa Keslassy, "France Scraps TV License Fee That Finances Bulk of Broadcasters' Budgets," *Variety*, July 25, 2022, https://variety.com/2022/tv/news/france-tv-license-fee-1235324450/.
116. Hadenius (1998, 29–30, 316–317).
117. Ibid., 320.
118. For information on the foundations, see Förvatlningsstiftelsen, "Om stiftelsen" [About the foundation], accessed October 14, 2023, http://www.forvaltningsstiftelsen.se/, then go to the "Om.stiftelsen" page.
119. Benson and Powers (2011, 52) and Benson et al. (2017).
120. For further discussion of the "arms-length" principle, which is common across the Nordic countries, see Syvertsen et al. (2014).
121. Hadenius et al. (2009, 88).
122. Benson et al. (2017, 5). The countries in the study were Canada, Denmark, Finland, France, Germany, Japan, Netherlands, New Zealand, Norway, Sweden, the UK, and the US. Similar patterns were confirmed with updated data in a more diverse global sample of thirty-three countries (Neff and Pickard 2021).
123. Thomas (1976, 1–3).
124. Concerning radio under Vichy, see Cazenave and Ulmann-Mauriat (1995, 121–122).
125. Mercier (1996) and Chalaby (2002).
126. "The France Télévisions Group," accessed July 8, 2024, https://www.francetvpub.fr/en/the-france-televisions-group/; "France-médias-monde", accessed July 8, 2024, https://www.francemediasmonde.com/en/; Arte, "Arte, the European Culture Television," April 28, 2016, http://www.arte.tv/sites/en/corporate/qui-sommes-nous-cluster/publications/?lang=en (Internet Archive); Radio France, "Nous Connaître," accessed July 8, 2024, https://www.radiofrance.com/nous-connaitre. Regarding the history of the French "audio-visual" landscape, see Bourdon (1994), Chalaby (2002), and Kuhn (2011).
127. European Platform of Regulatory Authorities (EPRA), "Two New Members for the French CSA," January 29, 2015, https://www.epra.org/news_items/two-new-members-for-the-fre

nch-csa. According to EPRA (citing "Website of the CSA"), from 2015 until January 2017, CSA had eight members, as part of a transition from the previous regulation specifying a nine-member board. For additional information on the appointment process during this time period, see also: European Platform of Regulatory Authorities (EPRA), "New Composition for the French CSA," February 18, 2019, https://www.epra.org/news_items/new-composition-of-the-french-csa.

128. ARCOM, "Gouvernance," accessed July 9, 2024; https://www.arcom.fr/nous-connaitre/notre-institution/gouvernance.
129. For information about composition of the France Télévisions board of directors, see: https://www.francetelevisions.fr/groupe/notre-organisation/le-conseil-dadministration-139#, accessed July 23, 2024; for information about the Radio France board of directors, see: https://www.radiofrance.com/conseil-dadministration, accessed July 23, 2024.
130. See McChesney (1995; 2015) and Pickard (2014) for histories of US radio and television, with a focus on news.
131. CPB (1967). See also Usher et al. (2012).
132. Ibid. See also Starr (2000, 26).
133. *Current*, "By-laws of Public Broadcasting Service, 2000," February 6, 2000, https://current.org/2000/02/by-laws-of-public-broadcasting-service-2000/.
134. NPR, "About NPR: NPR Board of Directors," ND, accessed October 20, 2023, https://www.npr.org/about-npr/182676957/npr-board-of-directors.
135. Starr (2000). See also CPB (2016) and Dru Sefton, "Beyond Politics, Public Media Audiences and Trump Supporters Have Some Things in Common," *Current*, April 7, 2017, https://current.org/2017/04/beyond-politics-public-media-audiences-and-trump-supporters-have-some-things-in-common/.
136. Benson et al. (2017, 5).
137. Pew Research Center, "Digital: Top 50 Online News Entities (2015)" [based on industry standard ComScore Data], April 29, 2015, http://www.journalism.org/media-indicators/digital-top-50-online-news-entities-2015/, accessed on *Wayback Machine*, May 10, 2023.
138. Cook (1998) and Sparrow (1999).
139. In this classification of journalistic professional logics, we build on Hanitzsch et al.'s (2019, 174) global survey-based study of journalists, which finds that basic reporting and analysis are the most universally valued journalistic roles. Pluralism (letting people express their views) is also highly valued but less so than information.
140. Patrick Le Lay, former TF1 CEO, interview with Julie Sedel, April 2012, Paris.
141. These US findings accord with conclusions based on a much larger sample of nonprofits by the US Institute for Nonprofit News (INN), 2021 Index (based on 2020 survey data), https://inn.org/research/inn-index/inn-index-2021/. The INN study found the primary missions of its member nonprofits (which include all of the leading national and local nonprofits) to be analytical and explanatory journalism (thirty-nine percent), investigative (thirty-three percent), and news and events (twenty-nine percent).
142. Paul Goupil, former *Ouest-France* deputy editor (Zoom interview with Rodney Benson, November 2021), recounts that *Ouest-France*'s long-time publisher, the Hutin family, is careful not to stray too far from the "Bishops" in the paper's ideological positioning.
143. Notably, the *Washington Post*'s ethics policy on "conflict of interest" (https://www.washingtonpost.com/policies-and-standards/#ethics, last accessed on October 6, 2023), speaks only to journalists' own potential conflicts of interests and has nothing to say about how the *Washington Post* should write about owner Jeff Bezos's economic interests (see Chapter 7). However, in a public statement explaining the adoption of the new masthead "Democracy dies in darkness," the *Washington Post* staff explained, "The newspaper's duty is to its readers and to the public at large, and not to the private interests of its owners" (cited in Örnebring and Karlsson 2022, 197).
144. See Newman et al. (2016) and Methods Appendix section on content analysis.
145. See, for example, Perrin and Duggan (2015).
146. Pew Research Center (2018) showed that *SVT/SR* were named as "their main news source" by a far larger percentage of Swedish adults than any other outlet: thirty-nine percent, versus seventeen percent for *Aftonbladet*, ten percent for *TV4*, and six percent for *Dagens Nyheter*.
147. For data on audience size for US nonprofits, see also Hindman (2018). Online audience research companies have consistently shown that *Ouest-France*'s website is one of the most visited in France (see, e.g., Table 1.2); for this reason, we interpreted the Reuters's Institute

category of "regional/local paper website," the "title" with the third highest weekly usage, as a proxy for *Ouest-France*.

148. Steve Waldman, "Legacy Media Needs to be Transformed, not Discarded," *Nieman Reports*, February 23, 2023, https://niemanreports.org/articles/legacy-media-local-news/.
149. Lacy (1991, 38).
150. See, for example, Picard (1994), Cranberg et al. (2001), Ohlsson (2012; 2013), Cagé and Godechot (2017), Benson (2018), Saffer et al. (2021), and Sedel (2021a; 2021b).
151. Benson (2018) and Sedel (2021b).
152. Perrin and Duggan (2015).
153. Ksiazek et al. (2010) and Lindell and Mikkelsen Båge (2023).
154. Media Insight Project (2018) and Benson (2020, 95).
155. In the US, it is only at a handful of nonprofits, such as the *San Francisco Public Press*, the *Chicago City Bureau*, or the Detroit *Outlier*, where a proactive effort is being made to reach less elite audiences. Such a project is hampered by donating foundations' focus on "impact" as measured by policy change, which tends to incentivize a target audience of elites able to directly or indirectly shape public policies. See the discussion in Benson (2018; 2020).
156. Of the approximately forty countries across world regions included in the Reuters Institute's annual digital news report, Sweden, with twenty-two percent, had among the lowest percentage of news avoiders, versus thirty-three percent for France and forty-one percent for the US (Reuters Institute 2019 Digital News Report 2019, 25, reutersinstitute.politics.ox.ac.uk/sites/default/files/2019-06/DNR_2019_FINAL_0.pdf). Sweden was conversely among the highest in the Reuters sample in the percentage of its population paying for "any online news in the last week" (thirty percent, second after Norway), significantly higher than the US (twenty-one percent) and France (eleven percent) (Reuters Institute 2021 Digital News Report 2021, 13, https://reutersinstitute.politics.ox.ac.uk/digital-news-report/2021). The proportion of the public that "trusts news most of the time" was fifty percent in Sweden, thirty percent in France, and twenty-nine percent in the US (ibid., 18).
157. On the construction and use of categories of right and left in France, see Le Digol 2012; for an exemplary comparative study of audience political leaning, sensitive to each national context, which we draw on for many of our outlet classifications, see Fletcher et al. 2020.
158. Audience and owner partisan preference variables are correlated at .649 ($p < .001$) for the entire fifty-one outlet sample; within-national field correlations are 0.439 ($p < .05$) for the US, 0.559 for Sweden ($p < .05$), and 0.784 for France ($p = .001$).
159. According to a 2020 survey of twenty-eight countries conducted by the Edelman public relations firm, an average of fifty-six percent of persons agreed with the assertion that capitalism currently "did more harm than good." France had the third highest lack of trust in capitalism at sixty-nine percent. The US was among the six countries with majorities disagreeing with this assertion. Sweden was not included in the sample. See Mark John, "Capitalism Seen Doing 'More Harm Than Good' in Global Survey," *Reuters Business News*, January 20, 2020, https://www.reuters.com/article/us-davos-meeting-trust/capitalism-seen-doing-more-harm-than-good-in-global-survey-idUSKBN1ZJ0CW and Edelman Report, https://www.edelman.com/trust/2020-trust-barometer.
160. The US is the world leader in advertising spending per person, at $650.65 in 2018. Sweden was ranked fifth worldwide at $403.22, the highest in Europe after Norway. France was ranked twelfth worldwide, at $238.05. This data was accessed on April 6, 2022, from Insider Intelligence, eMarketer, http://www.emarketer.com/Article/Global-Ad-Spending-Growth-Double-This-Year/1010997/1.
161. Newman et al. (2021, 18).
162. Allern and Blach-Ørsten (2011) and Allern and Pollack (2019).

Chapter 3

1. Such contradictions, according to Des Freedman (2015, 285), are especially characteristic of capitalist control of media. We argue that similar dynamic processes operate in all ownership forms, due to tensions generated both within and across institutional logics.
2. Charlie Firestone, executive director of the Aspen Institute Communication and Society Program, interview with Rodney Benson, May 2011, Washington, DC.

3. Lacy and Blanchard (2003). Among the many in-depth scholarly and insider accounts, see Squires (1993), Cranberg et al. (2001), McCord (2001), Merritt (2005), Soloski (2005), and O'Shea (2011).
4. Isaac Josephson, *ABC News* vice president for product development, remarks and responses to questions in Rodney Benson's NYU graduate seminar on cultural production, March 2012, New York.
5. Paul S. Mason, *LinkTV* CEO and former *ABC News* executive producer, interview with Rodney Benson, April 2013, Denver.
6. Patrick Le Lay, former *TF1* CEO, interview with Julie Sedel, April 2012, Paris. Le Lay emphasized that making money did not translate into his direct involvement with the newsroom. He viewed this as a "world apart" that "doesn't interest me." But he did admit to playing a major role in hiring and firing senior managers, including journalists.
7. See the Tinius homepage on the Schibsted website at https://schibsted.com/sustainability/tinius-trust-foundation/ (original in English, accessed October 6, 2023).
8. Barland (2013).
9. In 2024, the news media operation was sold to the Tinius Trust, thus creating two companies: a news media company (Schibsted Media) owned by the Tinius Trust and a stock market-traded marketplaces company (Schibsted Marketplaces, including Blocket). See "Schibsted ASA completes sale of news media operations," Schibsted.com, June 7, 2024, https://schibsted.com/news/schibsted-asa-completes-sale-of-news-media-operations/.
10. Jan Helin, *SVT* programming director and former *Aftonbladet* editor-in-chief and CEO, Zoom interview with Rodney Benson, August 2020.
11. Ibid.
12. Emanuel Karlsten, former *Aftonbladet* digital consultant and former *Dagen* digital editor, interview with Rodney Benson, October 2017, Gothenburg.
13. Jonas Ohlsson, Nordicom director, interview with Rodney Benson, October 2017, Gothenburg.
14. Freeman, quoted in McKay Coppins, "A Secretive Hedge Fund is Gutting Newsrooms: Inside Alden Global Capital," *The Atlantic*, October 14, 2021, https://www.theatlantic.com/magazine/archive/2021/11/alden-global-capital-killing-americas-newspapers/620171/. As Coppins notes, however, the Tribune Company, which was Alden's single largest purchase, was solvent and profitable at the time of the purchase in the spring of 2021.
15. Geneva Overholser, former editor-in-chief of the *Des Moines Register*, remarks at NYU Institute for Public Knowledge book launch for *Trump and the Media* (Cambridge, MA: MIT, 2018), April 18, 2018, New York, Rodney Benson field notes. See also Gilbert Cranberg, "A Swan Song in Des Moines," *Columbia Journalism Review*, May–June 1995, 19.
16. Coppins, "A Secretive Hedge Fund," citing Abernathy (2016). See also LeBrun et al. (2022, 20) for evidence that local newspapers purchased by Alden and other "predatory corporate" buyers experienced "a significant decrease in locally focused content" and a "significant increase in the concentration of locally focused content (fewer areas served)."
17. Tom Weber, "Twin Cities Provide a Tale of Newspaper Woe and Redemption," *MPR News*, May 29, 2018, https://www.mprnews.org/story/2018/05/29/twin-cities-newspapers-star-tribune-pioneer-press-alden-global. For an argument that the *Minneapolis Star Tribune* has also benefited from highly competent management, see Rick Edmonds, "Why Does the Star Tribune Outperform the Pack of Metros? An Update," *Poynter*, May 2, 2018, https://www.poynter.org/business-work/2018/why-does-the-star-tribune-outperform-the-pack-of-metros-an-update/.
18. Strömbäck and Nord (2008, 112). In 2024, as discussed in Chapter 4, the Swedish press subsidies were changed to avoid the emergence of news deserts, keeping at least one newspaper alive in each locality; see Sveriges riksdag [Swedish Parliament], "Ett hållbart mediestöd för hela landet" [A Sustainable Media Subsidy for the Whole Country], 9, accessed July 5, 2024, https://www.riksdagen.se/sv/dokument-och-lagar/dokument/betankande/ett-hallbart-mediestod-for-hela-landet_hb01ku3/.
19. See Glen Taylor, "Glen Taylor: Why I'm Proud to Own the *Star Tribune*," *Minneapolis Star Tribune*, August 22, 2021, https://www.startribune.com/glen-taylor-why-im-proud-to-own-the-star-tribune/600090046/.
20. Weber, "Twin Cities."
21. Pickard (2020, 72); see also Meyer (2009).

22. Susca (2024), an excerpt from chapter 4 of *Hedged*, as published in *NiemanReports*, "'A Lot of People Got Really Rich Off of What Happened Here:' How Hedge Funds Helped Destroy Local News," October 10, 2023, https://niemanreports.org/articles/hedge-funds-local-news-book/.
23. Laura Frank, *Rocky Mountain PBS*, president and general manager of news, interview with Rodney Benson, April 2013, Denver. In 2016, Frank was elected chair of the board of directors of the Institute for Nonprofit News; she has founded and led a number of nonprofit consortiums, most recently COLab, the Colorado News Collaborative.
24. Alexander (2016).
25. Susca (2024, 19–21).
26. These remarks and subsequent Paton quotes are from John Paton, *The Independent* (UK) chairman of the board, *The Guardian* (UK) former chair of the Board of Directors, and former Digital First Media CEO, Zoom interview with Rodney Benson, November 2020. For other accounts of Digital First's commercial strategies during this period, see Nixon (2020) and Dan Kennedy, "How to Get Rich Plundering Newspapers," *GBH* (Boston public media), October 4, 2017, https://www.wgbh.org/news/commentary/2017-10-04/how-to-get-rich-plundering-newspapers.
27. Quoted in Dan Kennedy, "Aggressive Cost-cutting Already Diminished *Boston Herald*," *Media Nation*, February 14, 2018, https://dankennedy.net/2018/02/14/aggressive-cost-cutter-buys-an-already-diminished-boston-herald/.
28. Information about *HuffPost* in this section is provided by a *HuffPost* staffer, Zoom interview with Rodney Benson, 2021.
29. Ibid.
30. Braun (2015, 110–112).
31. John Paton interview with Benson, 2020.
32. Küng (2017, 126–127).
33. Diamond (1993, 375–376).
34. Leeds (2023).
35. "The *New York Times* Names Joe Kahn its Next Executive Editor," *NiemanLab*, April 19, 2022, https://www.niemanlab.org/2022/04/the-new-york-times-names-joe-kahn-its-next-executive-editor/. See also Leeds (2023).
36. Quoted in Paul Farhi, "*Washington Post* To Be Sold to Jeff Bezos, the Founder of Amazon," *Washington Post*, August 5, 2013, https://www.washingtonpost.com/national/washington-post-to-be-sold-to-jeff-bezos/2013/08/05/ca537c9e-fe0c-11e2-9711-3708310f6f4d_story.html.
37. Marc Tracy, "How Marty Baron and Jeff Bezos Remade The Washington Post," *New York Times*, February 27, 2021, https://www.nytimes.com/2021/02/27/business/marty-baron-jeff-bezos-washington-post.html.
38. Benjamin Mullen and Katie Robertson, "A Decade Ago, Jeff Bezos Bought a Newspaper. Now He's Paying Attention to It Again," *New York Times*, July 22, 2023, https://www.nytimes.com/2023/07/22/business/media/jeff-bezos-washington-post.html
39. Suki Dardarian, *Minneapolis Star Tribune* editor and senior vice president, remarks at Online Panel, "The Digital Transformation of The Metro Daily," hosted by the Harvard Kennedy School's Shorenstein Center on Media, Politics, and Public Policy, moderated by Jennifer Preston, senior fellow at the Shorenstein Center's Technology and Social Change Project, May 10, 2022, https://shorensteincenter.org/new-event/digital-transformation-metro-daily/. Although one of course expects employees to generally speak favorably of their bosses in public, it is at least worth noting that in the same online panel, the editors of the family-owned *Boston Globe* and *Seattle Times* also credited their owners with providing crucial resources and other support.
40. Isaac Josephson, former Hearst Newspapers head of product and former *ABC News* vice president for product development, email to Rodney Benson, December 3, 2023.
41. Ibid.
42. Benson (2017) and Benson (2019, 81).
43. Benjamin Mullin and Amrith Ramkumar, "BuzzFeed Suffers Wave of SPAC Investor Withdrawals Before Going Public," *Wall Street Journal*, December 2, 2021, https://www.wsj.com/articles/buzzfeed-suffers-wave-of-spac-investor-withdrawals-before-going-public-11638472756.

44. K. A. Dilday, "Crisis at *Libération*," *The Nation*, November 16, 2006, https://www.thenation.com/article/archive/crisis-liberation/. See also Eveno (2008, 85–87).
45. Laurent Joffrin, former *Libération* director, interview with Julie Sedel, April 2012, Paris; Dupuy (2010). Note: Joffrin returned to *Libération* as editor-in-chief from 2014 to 2020.
46. de Rochegonde and Sénéjoux (2017, 176–182). This strategy of joining "harvesting" (maximizing revenues) in the declining print sector with "investing" in the rising digital sector was also successfully pursued by the *Deseret News* in Salt Lake City, Utah (Küng 2017, 101–102).
47. Mediatique (2012, 7).
48. Pickard (2020, 94).
49. Karen Dunlap, Poynter Institute president, cited in Picard and van Weezel (2008, 27). The Poynter Institute nevertheless had the flexibility to temporarily stop pulling dividends from the *Times* when its revenues dropped after the 2008 financial crisis (Ellis 2014, 201).
50. Sture Bergman, CEO of VK Media (a foundation-owned northern Sweden media group, which includes the newspaper *Västerbottens-kuriren*), interview with Mattias Hessérus, May 2011, Stockholm.
51. Anders Westermark, *Norran* CEO, interview with Rodney Benson, October 2016, Stockholm.
52. Ibid. After the 2019 sale, Westermark told us that "keeping a lot of assets [in the foundation]" preserved the capacity of the foundation "to take [*Norran*] back" if the need should arise (Anders Westermark, Chairman of Stiftelsen Skelleftepress and former CEO of *Norran*, interview with Mattias Hessérus, November 2023, Stockholm).
53. Paul Goupil, former *Ouest-France* deputy editor, Zoom interview with Rodney Benson, November 2021.
54. The *New York Times*'s estimated newsroom budget of $234 million in 2016 is calculated based on the company's total revenues and industry data suggesting that commercial newsrooms spend fifteen percent of their total revenues on news operations. In 2016, the New York Times Co.'s total revenues were $1.56 billion (New York Times Co. Annual Report 2016, https://www.nytco.com/investors/annual-reports/). See Ken Doctor, "The newsonomics of Pulitzers, paywalls, and investing in the newsroom," *NiemanLab*, April 18, 2013, https://www.niemanlab.org/2013/04/the-newsonomics-of-pulitzers-paywalls-and-investing-in-the-newsroom/, for an estimate of 13 to 20 percent, based on unspecified sources and Inland Press Association 2011 survey data of a large sample of U.S. newspapers (see, however, Simone Flueckiger, "Publisher spend: A bigger focus on the newsroom," WAN-IFRA (World Association of News Publishers), April 22, 2021, https://wan-ifra.org/2021/04/publisher-spend-a-bigger-focus-on-the-newsroom/, for survey data suggesting that the proportion of revenues devoted to newsrooms may have increased somewhat in recent years). Our estimate of $30 million newsroom expenses for a strong regional newspaper such as the *Minneapolis Star Tribune* is likewise calculated as fifteen percent of its $230 million total revenues reported in a 2018 Forbes report: https://www.forbes.com/sites/tonysilber/2018/04/11/star-tribune-publisher-newspapers-can-survive-but-things-have-to-change-lots-of-things/?sh=41d69e5fb10f. According to the INN 2021 Index (https://inn.org/research/inn-index/inn-index-2021/), among its 268 responding member outlets (94 percent of all members), thirty-six percent of member outlets had total revenues of less than $250,000; thirty-three percent had revenues from $250 to $1 million; and thirty-two percent had $1 million or higher.
55. Andrew Donohue, "This is the Beginning of the End for the *Union-Tribune*," *Voice of San Diego*, October 31, 2023, https://voiceofsandiego.org/2023/10/31/this-is-the-beginning-of-the-end-for-the-union-tribune/; *Voice of San Diego*, "Our Team," accessed November 1, 2023, https://voiceofsandiego.org/about-us/our-team/.
56. With respect to nonprofit editorial investments, see Institute for Nonprofit News (2018); regarding legacy newspapers, see Edmonds, "A New Look."
57. See, for example, Abernathy (2016) and Sims (2017).
58. Figures are derived from "ProPublica 2021 Annual Report" (PDF), on "Reports & Financials" page, https://www.propublica.org/reports, accessed June 23, 2022.
59. Nygren and Nord (2019, 22).
60. Klas Wolf-Watz, *SR* national news editor-in-chief, Zoom interview with Carl Ritter, January 2021.
61. Charlotta Friborg, *SVT* national news editor-in-chief, Zoom interview with Carl Ritter, January 2021. Nevertheless, *SVT* director Jan Helin (interview with Benson, 2020), expressed concerns about the vulnerability to *SVT* funding introduced by the recent shift from a license fee to a designated governmental tax (see Chapter 4 of this book).

Chapter 4

1. Scott Kraft, "It's a Whole New World for *Le Monde*," *Los Angeles Times*, January 13, 1995.
2. Squires (1993, 72–73).
3. Laurent Joffrin, former *Libération* director, interview with Julie Sedel, April 2012, Paris.
4. Benson (2000), Coddington (2015).
5. Underwood (1995) and McCord (2001). Isaac Josephson (email to Benson, December 3, 2023), former *ABC News* vice president for product development and Hearst Newspapers head of product, insists from his own experience that MBAs were "less of a detriment (forcing bloodless, profit-minded perspectives) and more of a benefit (for the most part, good humans dedicated to the mission of news-as-cornerstone-of-democracy), and putting their experience to work in service of that mission . . . [because] journalists need to be paid." Similarly, newspaper chain CEOs in Sweden, Denmark, and Norway told Sjøvaag and Owren (2023, 777, 780) "that the best way to secure the journalistic institution is to stay financially sound," which in turn they saw as closely linked to "securing editorial autonomy."
6. For analysis of the rise of this "entrepreneurial" mindset in the US journalistic field, see Vos and Singer (2016); concerning similar developments in the French journalistic field, see Sedel (2021a).
7. Jonas Nordling, *Dagens Arena* editor-in-chief, telephone interview with Erik Thyselius, August 2020.
8. Anders Westermark, *Norran* CEO, interview with Rodney Benson, October 2016, Stockholm.
9. Mougeotte (2021, 336).
10. Johan Hansson, CEO of Stampen (owner of *Göteborgs-Posten* and other western Swedish newspapers), interview with Rodney Benson, October 2017, Gothenburg.
11. Ibid.
12. Christin (2018; 2020), Petre (2021), and Smith (2023).
13. Bourdieu (1984; 1993), Küng (2017), and Noam (2019).
14. Antoine Guelaud, *TF1* news director, interview with Julie Sedel, 2011, Paris. On the importance of "cultural style" in attracting and retaining a mass audience, see Peck (2019).
15. Ron Paul won more than two million votes, almost eleven percent, in the Republican presidential primaries of 2008.
16. Isaac Josephson remarks and responses to questions in Rodney Benson's NYU graduate seminar on cultural production, March 2012, New York.
17. With regard to free shoppers with no editorial content, see Baker (1994b); concerning commercial alternative news weeklies in the US, see Benson (2003) and Klinenberg (2007).
18. Johan Hansson interview with Benson, 2017. Hansson, who prior to joining Stampen was a Metro executive based in Hong Kong, said that other than the worldwide format of numerous, short articles, each *Metro* outlet had ample "editorial" autonomy over its news content. See Lamour (2017) on the worldwide rise of *Metro* and other free urban dailies.
19. Lardeau (2011, 301).
20. Former *20 Minutes* journalist quoted in Lardeau (2011, 300).
21. Frédéric Filloux, former *Libération* managing editor and former *20 Minutes* editor-in-chief, interview with Rodney Benson, April 2018, Austin, Texas.
22. Ibid.
23. Lardeau (2011, 312–313).
24. Ibid.
25. Isaac Josephson remarks, 2012.
26. Bo Hedin, consultant to *Nyheter24*, and former *Aftonbladet* news editor, interview with Rodney Benson, October 2017, Stockholm. Hedin described *Nyheter24*'s audience as: "for young people . . . 15–35." Peter Scheffer, owner of the company Life of Svea, which acquired *Nyheter24* in 2019, identified the outlet's target group as women aged 18–45, in Patrick Micu, "Nyheter 24 köps upp av kvinnoprofilerat mediehus" [Nyheter 24 is bought by a media house with a female profile], *Expressen*, May 16, 2019 (updated June 9, 2021), https://www.expressen.se/dinapengar/tech/nyheter-24-kops-upp-av-kvinnoinriktat-mediehus/. Likewise, *BuzzFeed* has a primarily young, female audience (Küng 2015).
27. Pickard (2020, 77).
28. Küng (2015), Tandoc Jr. (2018), Abramson (2019).
29. There is a close analogy here to what Caitlin Petre (2021, 122) found at the now defunct *Gawker*, in which "viral" news beats explicitly aiming to maximize traffic were widely understood within the organization to be subsidizing the core journalistic mission.

30. Frédéric Filloux interview with Benson, 2018.
31. Rosalind Adams, "What the Fuck Just Happened?", *BuzzFeed News*, December 7, 2016, https://www.buzzfeednews.com/article/rosalindadams/intake.
32. Frédéric Filloux interview with Benson, 2018. According to Ben Smith's (2023, 280) memoir of his time as editor-in-chief of *BuzzFeed News*, Peretti "always wished we could find a less conventional way to do journalism—more memes, fewer things that looked like *New York Times* articles—but he appreciated the attention and prestige it brought."
33. Luke Winkie, "More Digital Media Companies Want to Go Public. Can Their Newsrooms Survive?" *NiemanLab*, April 21, 2022, https://www.niemanlab.org/2022/04/more-digital-media-companies-want-to-go-public-can-their-newsrooms-survive/.
34. In the early 2000s (2002 and 2004 averaged), US newspapers earned eighty-seven percent of their revenues from advertising, the highest proportion in the world, compared to thirty-nine percent for France (2002 and 2003 averaged), near the bottom of the range (World Association of Newspapers 2007).
35. In 2016, US newspapers as a whole earned $18.3 billion (sixty-three percent) from advertising and $10.9 billion (thirty-seven percent) from circulation; it was only in 2020, the first time in the contemporary era, that US newspaper circulation revenues exceeded those from advertising. See Pew Research Center, Newspapers Fact Sheet, June 29, 2021, https://www.pewresearch.org/journalism/fact-sheet/newspapers/. Worldwide, the shift had occurred five years earlier: see Rick Edmonds, "Worldwide Newspaper Circulation Revenues Pass Advertising for the First Time," *Poynter*, June 1, 2015, https://www.poynter.org/reporting-editing/2015/worldwide-newspaper-circulation-revenues-pass-advertising-for-the-first-time/. For Tribune Publishing revenue data, see Business Wire, "Tribune Publishing Company," May 4, 2016, https://www.businesswire.com/news/home/20160504006408/en/Tribune-Publishing-Company-Reports-2016-First-Quarter-Results; for Gannett revenue data, see the company's *2016 Annual Report*: https://www.annualreports.com/HostedData/AnnualReportArchive/g/NYSE_GCI_2016.pdf, accessed April 30, 2023.
36. With respect to this willed ignorance about audiences at the *Chicago Tribune* even in recent years, see Nelson (2021, 48).
37. O'Shea (2011, 275). In contrast, Angelucci and Cagé (2019) found that when advertising declined, newspapers were often forced to reduce the amount or quality of the journalistic content that they produced.
38. Ken Doctor, "Newsonomics: Inside the New *L.A. Times*," *NiemanLab*, March 27, 2019, https://www.niemanlab.org/2019/03/newsonomics-inside-the-new-l-a-times-a-100-year-vision-that-bets-on-tech-and-top-notch-journalism/.
39. Martin Schori, former *KIT* news editor, Zoom interview with Carl Ritter, March 2021. As our content analysis in Chapter 5 shows, *KIT* did indeed provide more in-depth news than most other outlets.
40. Lydia Farran-Lee, "Sajten Kit slutar med journalistik" [The KIT site stops producing journalism], *SVT Nyheter*, September 17, 2019, https://www.svt.se/kultur/sajten-kit-slutar-med-journalistik.
41. Ibid.; see also Smith (2023, 230, 269–275, 279).
42. Smith (2023, 31).
43. *HuffPost* staffer, Zoom interview with Rodney Benson, 2021. Unlike the US *HuffPost*, the French version has been profitable, according to Louis Dreyfus, CEO of the Le Monde Group, *HuffPost-France*'s primary French co-owner. See WAN-IFRA Staff, "The New *Le Monde*: From an Institution to an Entrepreneurial Adventure," *World Association of News Publishers*, June 15, 2016, https://wan-ifra.org/2016/06/the-new-le-monde-from-an-institution-to-an-entrepreneurial-adventure/.
44. This and all subsequent quotes from Marshall Ingwerson, *Christian Science Monitor* managing editor, are from an interview with Rodney Benson, May 2011, Boston. For additional research on the *Monitor* during this time period, see Usher (2012) and Groves and Brown (2018).
45. Groves and Brown (2018, 101).
46. This analysis, that the endowment followed by other donations (including continuing church subsidies), made up about seventy percent of the *Monitor*'s 2016 revenues, is based on figures provided in Brown and Groves (2020) and in Rick Edmonds, "*Christian Science Monitor* Sees Traffic, Revenues Rising," *Poynter*, May 2, 2012, https://www.poynter.org/reporting-editing/2012/christian-science-monitor-sees-traffic-revenues-rising-after-3-years-of-web-first-strategy/. Groves confirmed that this estimate is roughly correct for that time period in an email to Benson, September 12, 2021.

47. See Lucia Moses, "How the *Washington Post* Grew Digital Subscriptions 145 Percent," *Digiday*, July 12, 2016, https://digiday.com/media/washington-post-grew-digital-subscriptions-145-percent/; and Rick Edmonds, "Why Does the *Star Tribune* Outperform the Pack of Metros? An Update," *Poynter*, May 2, 2018, https://www.poynter.org/business-work/2018/why-does-the-star-tribune-outperform-the-pack-of-metros-an-update/.
48. World Economic Forum, "These are the most popular paid subscription news websites," April 29, 2021, https://www.weforum.org/agenda/2021/04/ranked-paid-subscription-news-websites-nyt-washing-post-wsj/.
49. Júlio Lubianco, "Baron on Bezos Ownership," *Knight Center/ISOJ*, May 3, 2021, https://isoj.org/baron-on-bezos-ownership-of-the-washington-post-i-dont-think-that-we-would-have-been-a-success-without-his-involvement/.
50. Local Media Association, "This Is What Has Been Key," January 26, 2019, https://localmedia.org/2019/01/this-is-what-has-been-key-to-the-washington-posts-digital-subscription-success/.
51. See Benjamin Mullen and Katie Robertson, "A Decade Ago, Jeff Bezos Bought a Newspaper. Now He's Paying Attention to It Again," *New York Times*, July 22, 2023, https://www.nytimes.com/2023/07/22/business/media/jeff-bezos-washington-post.html.
52. Edmonds, "Why Does the *Star Tribune* Outperform the Pack"; Brian Veseling, "How the *Star Tribune* Aims to Retain Its 100,000 Digital Subscribers," *WAN-IFRA World Association of News Publishers*, January 12, 2023, https://wan-ifra.org/2023/01/how-the-star-tribune-aims-to-retain-its-100000-digital-subscribers/.
53. Dominique Quinio, *La Croix* editor, interview with Julie Sedel, July 2011, Paris.
54. Media Insight Project (2018) and Benson (2020, 95).
55. *Le Canard enchaîné* CEO, interview with Julie Sedel, March 2011, Paris.
56. Jade Lindgaard, *Mediapart* reporter, interview with Rodney Benson and Julie Sedel, June 2016, Paris.
57. Edwy Plenel, *Mediapart* president and co-founder, remarks to NYU visiting group, June 2016, Paris.
58. Hubert Beuve-Méry, *Paroles écrites: Memoires* (Paris: Bernard Grasset, 1991), 128, cited in Boltanski and Esquerre (2022, 131).
59. Jade Lindgaard interview with Benson and Sedel, 2016.
60. Edwy Plenel quoted in Lucinda Southern, "How French Publisher Mediapart Has Used Political Tumult to Drive Subscriptions," *Digiday*, March 28, 2017, https://digiday.com/media/mediapart-grown-140000-paying-subscribers/.
61. Edwy Plenel interview with Julie Sedel, October 2017, Paris.
62. Edwy Plenel remarks, 2016. Wagemans et al. (2016) and Alfon (2017).
63. Arthur Sulzberger, Jr., public comments at Columbia Graduate School of Journalism, New York, April 5, 2011, Rodney Benson field notes.
64. At a Columbia University book party held in April 2016, a prominent *New York Times* columnist told a group of listeners that the expensive luxury advertising in the "T" Sunday fashion magazine was "keeping the newspaper afloat" (Rodney Benson field notes). See also Ava Sirrah, "Tow Report: Guide to Native Advertising," *Columbia Journalism Review*, September 6, 2019, https://www.cjr.org/tow_center_reports/native-ads.php, and Sirrah (2021).
65. Patience Haggin, "*New York Times* Profit Soars with Ad Business Rebound," *Wall Street Journal*, November 3, 2021, https://www.wsj.com/articles/new-york-times-profit-soars-amid-ad-business-rebound-11635950670. See also Ken Doctor, "Newsonomics: The *New York Times*' new CEO, Meredith Levien," *NiemanLab*, July 30, 2020, https://www.niemanlab.org/2020/07/newsonomics-the-new-york-times-new-ceo-meredith-levien-on-building-a-world-class-digital-media-business-and-a-tech-company/.
66. Lars Truedson, Institute for Media Studies director, interview with Rodney Benson, October 2016, Stockholm.
67. Bonnier News CEO Anders Eriksson, quoted in Simon Nilsson, "Så gick DN 2017" [This is how DN performed in 2017], *Dagens Media*, February 13, 2018, https://www.dagensmedia.se/medier/dagspress/sa-gick-dn-2017-6898637. For subscriber numbers, see Caspar Opitz, "*Dagens Nyheter* slår rekord i antal prenumeranter" [*Dagens Nyheter* Reaches New Record Number of Subscribers]," *Dagens Nyheter*, April 27, 2020 (updated January 8, 2021), https://www.dn.se/kultur-noje/dagens-nyheter-slar-rekord-i-antal-prenumeranter/.
68. Antheaume (2021).
69. Louis Dreyfus, Le Monde Group CEO, interview with Julie Sedel, 2011, Paris.

70. WAN-IFRA Staff, "The New *Le Monde*."
71. *La Correspondance de la Presse*, "Jérôme Fenoglio réélu pour un second mandat comme directeur du 'Monde'; le quotidien poursuit sa recherche d'abonnés chez les 18–34 ans et à l'international,' July 5, 2021.
72. Pew Research Center (2016b), Lindell and Hovden (2018), Usher (2021), and Media Insight Project, "Digital subscribers: What motivates them to pay and how they are different from print readers," American Press Institute, February 27, 2018, https://americanpressinstitute.org/digital-subscribers-versus-print/.
73. The 2016 estimate of 45,000 SvD digital subscribers is calculated based on information provided in: Erik Jerdén, "Stor ökning av digitala prenumeranter för SvD" [Big Increase in Digital Subscriptions for SvD], *Svenska Dagbladet*, March 16, 2018, https://www.svd.se/a/rLGaXK/stor-okning-av-digitala-prenumeranter-for-svd. The 2020 figure is from Janne Næss, "Från kris till vinstlyft för storstadspressen 2020—och festen fortsätter i år" [From Crisis to Profit Increase for the City Press 2020—and the Party Continues This Year], *Dagens Media*, November 16, 2021, https://www.dagensmedia.se/medier/dagspress/fran-kris-till-vinstlyft-for-storstadspressen-2020-och-festen-fortsatter-i-ar/.
74. Næss, ibid.
75. Fredric Karén, former *Svenska Dagbladet* editor-in-chief, telephone interview with Erik Thyselius, August 2020.
76. See "Bilan 31-12-2016 de la Société du Figaro" [December 31, 2016 Balance Sheet of the Figaro company], *Société*, accessed July 12, 2022, https://www.societe.com/bilan/societe-du-figaro-54207775520161231l.html, and "Société du Figaro," *InfoGreffe*, accessed July 12, 2022, https://www.infogreffe.fr/entreprise-societe/542077755-societe-du-figaro-750154B077750000.html.
77. Joux (2017).
78. Antheaume (2021).
79. To make digital subscriptions a sustainable revenue source, media industry analysts have estimated that at least two percent of the total digital audience must be converted to subscribers. In the US, other than the *New York Times*, the *Wall Street Journal*, and the *Washington Post*, the two percent target had by 2019 only been approached (but still not fully attained) by two other newspapers: the *Boston Globe*, and the *Minneapolis Star Tribune*. See Keach Hagey, Lukas I. Alpert, and Yaryna Serkez, "In News Industry, a Stark Divide Between Haves and Have-Nots," *Wall Street Journal*, May 4, 2019, https://www.wsj.com/graphics/local-newspapers-stark-divide/.
80. Cecilia Oscarsson, "Stampen Medias digitala prenumernater ökar kraftigt" [Strong Increase of Digital Subscriptions for Stampen Media], *Göteborgs-Posten*, November 4, 2021, https://www.gp.se/ekonomi/stampen-medias-digitala-prenumeranter-okar-kraftigt.965b25af-63a3-4870-9d43-5c898b3d5f55.
81. Johan Hansson interview with Benson, 2017. For an in-depth profile of Stampen and *Göteborgs-Posten* from 2011 to 2016, see Raviola (2022, 53–78).
82. Jean-François Polo, "Bayard: les assomptionnistes au coeur des médias" [Bayard: The Assumptionists at the heart of the media], June 8, 2010 (updated August 6, 2019), *Les Echos*, https://www.lesechos.fr/2010/06/bayard-les-assomptionnistes-au-coeur-des-medias-1086359.
83. See Société Nouvelle Du Journal *L'Humanité*, "Fiche entreprise: chiffres d'affaires, bilan et résultat" [Company sheet: turnover, balance sheet and results], accessed July 12, 2022, https://www.verif.com/bilans-gratuits/SOCIETE-NOUVELLE-DU-JOURNAL-L-HUMANITE-562085308/.
84. Patrick Le Hyaric, "Comptes 2016 de *L'Humanité*: Une amélioration à conforter," *L'Humanité*, July 12, 2017, https://www.humanite.fr/culture-et-savoirs/presse-ecrite/comptes-2016-de-lhumanite-une-amelioration-conforter-638745.
85. For a history of the public discourse around *Libération*'s "crises," see Chevret-Castellani (2016).
86. Stern (2012, 99).
87. Sedel (2021c, 46).
88. This and all subsequent remarks attributed to Johan Hufnagel, former online editor-in-chief of *Libération* and *20 Minutes*, and co-founder of *Slate.fr*, are from an interview with Rodney Benson, March 2023, Paris.
89. Lucinda Southern, "After Two Decades of Losses, French Left-wing Daily *Liberation's* [sic] Pivots (Officially) to Non-profit Status," *Digiday*, May 18, 2020, https://digiday.com/media/after-22-years-of-losses-french-left-wing-daily-liberations-pivots-officially-to-non-profit-status/;

90. Pierre de Gasquet, "Dov Alfon, l'espion qui aimait *Libé*" [Dov Alfon, the spy who loved *Libé*], *Les Echos*, October 15, 2020,
91. Pacouret and Ouakrat (2021) and Sedel (2021c).
92. *La Correspondence de la Presse*, "'*Libération* souhaite fédérer 110,000 abonnés en 2023" [Libération aims to bring together 110,000 subscribers in 2023], September 18, 2020; see also de Gasquet, "Dov Alfon, l'espion qui aimait *Libé*." *Libération* gained its first digital subscribers as part of the SFR Presse group plan established by then owner SFR that provided all SFR clients access to a suite of news media titles for a flat fee.
93. Bødker (2017).
94. In 2015, the private *Vice* company self-reported that it had generated about $915 million in revenues and that the majority of these revenues derived from "content sales to broadcasters." See Sydney Ember and Andrew Ross Sorkin, "As Vice Moves More to TV . . . ," *New York Times*, May 3, 2015, https://www.nytimes.com/2015/05/04/business/media/as-vice-moves-more-to-tv-it-tries-to-keep-brash-voice.html.
95. *Le Monde*'s Louis Dreyfus reported to a World Association of News Publishers conference on June 13, 2016 (WAN-IFRA Staff, "The New *Le Monde*") that eighty percent of *Le Monde*'s revenues were still coming from print. See also World Association of Newspapers (2007) for historic data on French newspapers' reliance on reader funding.
96. Online panel, "The Digital Transformation of The Metro Daily," hosted by the Harvard Kennedy School's Shorenstein Center on Media, Politics, and Public Policy, moderated by Jennifer Preston, senior fellow at the Shorenstein Center's Technology and Social Change Project, May 10, 2022, https://shorensteincenter.org/new-event/digital-transformation-metro-daily/. The question on accessibility was posed by Rodney Benson.
97. Cécile Prieur, *Le Monde* deputy editor for digital innovation, email to Rodney Benson, January 28, 2019 (since November 2020, Prieur has been executive editor of *L'Obs*). See also Cécile Prieur, "Let's Open the Gates to Paid Content Models: It Is Becoming Urgent to Work on How We Can Expand the Reach of Paid Quality Journalism to Everyone," *Medium*, December 1, 2018, https://medium.com/jsk-class-of-2019/lets-open-the-gates-to-paid-content-news-models-e4062c70b7ed.
98. A $3 per month fee is paid indirectly to *Fox News* by some 87 million US cable subscribers even though the *Fox News* channel's average audience rarely exceeds 3 million; *CNN* has a similar disproportion between total cable subscribers and its own cable audiences. Fee revenue figures are from Pew Research Center, Cable News Fact Sheet, July 13, 2021, https://www.pewresearch.org/journalism/fact-sheet/cable-news/.
99. Pew Research Center, Cable News Fact Sheet, July 13, 2021, https://www.pewresearch.org/journalism/fact-sheet/cable-news/.
100. Hadenius et al. (2009, 142–143); in France, however, Wallez (2017) stresses the positive civic and economic benefits for *Ouest-France* from its ongoing competition with the neighboring regional newspaper, *Le Télégramme*.
101. Paul Goupil, former *Ouest-France* deputy editor, Zoom interview with Rodney Benson, November 2021.
102. Felicia Ferreira, *Dagen* CEO and editor-in-chief, telephone interview with Eric Thyselius, August 2020.
103. Andreas Gustavsson, *Dagens ETC* editor-in-chief, Zoom interview with Carl Ritter, February 2021.
104. Wallez (2017, 228–234).
105. Thomas Manfredh, "Så blev *Dagen* en allkristen tidning" [How *Dagen* Became a Newspaper for All Christians], *Dagen*, March 28, 2019, https://www.dagen.se/nyheter/2019/03/28/sa-blev-dagen-en-allkristen-tidning/.
106. For research on levels and types of direct and indirect public support for news media, see Benson and Powers (2011), Nielsen and Linnebank (2011), Benson et al. (2017), and Neff and Pickard (2021).
107. Santhanam and Rosenstiel (2011).
108. For information about the nonprofit 501(c)(3) New Jersey Civic Information Consortium, which has disbursed 81 grants totaling $5.5 million in funding $5 million through 2023, see the organization's website (https://njcivicinfo.org/about/) and Stonbely et al. (2020). Regarding California's initiative, see NiemanLab, "The State of California Will Fund $25 Million in Local Reporting Fellowships," *NiemanLab*, September 8, 2022, https://www.niemanlab.org/2022/09/the-state-of-california-will-fund-25-million-in-local-reporting-fellowships/.

109. Ohlsson (2013, 40–41). See also Myndigheten för press, radio och tv [The Authority for Press, Radio, and Television], "Beviljat driftstöd" [Granted operating support] and "Beviljat distributionsstöd" [Granted distribution support], accessed January 13, 2022, https://www.mprt.se/stod-till-medier/beviljade-stod/. Small, hyperlocal subscription-based newspapers in Sweden reported receiving thirty-five percent of their funding from press subsidies (Leckner et al. 2019, 79).
110. Myndigheten för press, radio och tv [The Authority for Press, Radio and Television], "Beviljade stöd och protokoll" [Granted Supports and Protocols], accessed January 13, 2022, https://www.mprt.se/stod-till-medier/beviljade-stod/.
111. Felicia Ferreira interview with Thyselius, 2020.
112. Sandra Laville, "Swedish Newspaper Stops Taking Adverts from Fossil Fuel Firms," *The Guardian*, September 26, 2019, https://www.theguardian.com/environment/2019/sep/26/swedish-newspaper-stops-taking-adverts-from-fossil-fuel-firms/.
113. Ibid.; The estimate that two percent of revenues come from advertising was provided by *Dagens ETC* owner and founder Johan Ehrenberg in an email to Carl Ritter, January 13, 2021.
114. Andreas Gustavsson interview with Ritter, 2021. Thirty-seven percent of revenues derived from press subsidies is a rough estimate provided by Ehrenberg, email to Ritter, 2021. In 2018, the ETC newspaper group was ordered to pay back 8 million SEK in press subsidies because they had inflated their subscription numbers by handing out free subscriptions to receive higher subsidies; see Johanna Palm, "ETC betalar tillbaka delar av tidigare presstöd" [ETC repays parts of previous press support], *SVT Nyheter*, September 3, 2018, https://www.svt.se/kultur/medier/etc-betalar-tillbaka-presstod.
115. Email from Johan Ehrenberg to Ritter, 2021.
116. Sveriges riksdag [Swedish Parliament], "Ett hållbart mediestöd för hela landet" [A Sustainable Media Subsidy for the Whole Country], https://www.riksdagen.se/sv/dokument-och-lagar/dokument/betankande/ett-hallbart-mediestod-for-hela-landet_hb01ku3/, accessed July 5, 2024; Mediemyndigheten, "Sök mediestöd" [Apply for Media Subsidy], https://mediemyndigheten.se/stod-till-medier/sok-mediestod-2024/, accessed July 5, 2024.
117. Sveriges Radio [Swedish Radio], "Tufft för andratidningarna när nytt mediestöd kommer" [Tough for Second Newspapers with the Arrival of New Media Subsidy], https://sverigesradio.se/artikel/tufft-for-andratidningarna-nar-nytt-mediestod-kommer, accessed July 5, 2024; Sveriges Tidskrifter [Sweden's Periodicals], "Vinnare och förlorare på det nya mediestödet" [The New Media Subsidy's Winners and Losers], https://sverigestidskrifter.se/tjanster/guider-verktyg/stor-guide-ar-det-vart-att-soka-mediestod/vinnare-och-forlorare-pa-det-nya-mediestodet/, accessed July 5, 2024.
118. Lardeau and Le Floch (2013).
119. Pierre Haski, *Rue89* co-founder and former *Libération* foreign news editor and correspondent, interview with Julie Sedel, 2011, Paris; *Les Jours* co-founders (Augustin Naepels, Isabelle Roberts, Charlotte Rotman), interview with Julie Sedel and Rodney Benson, June 2016, Paris.
120. Lardeau and Le Floch (2013).
121. Laurent Joffrin interview with Sedel, 2012.
122. The French Ministry of Culture, "Press Aid," https://www.culture.gouv.fr/Thematiques/Presse/Aides-a-la-Presse/Tableaux-des-titres-et-groupes-de-presse-aides-en-2016. *Ouest-France*'s subsidy was particularly high in 2016 because it received a special grant to support the modernization of its website and distribution networks.
123. Laurent Joffrin interview with Sedel, 2012. According to Joffrin, "They never spoke about [content], but one never knows if it comes into play or not. Maybe yes, maybe no. But in any case, she [the government official] never says 'Say, you're going [too] strong right now' . . . She never says a word about the content of the newspaper."
124. Lardeau and Le Floch (2013, 203).
125. Chuck Lewis, *Center for Public Integrity* (*CPI*) founding executive editor and *Investigative Reporting Workshop* (*IRW*) executive editor, Zoom interview with Rodney Benson, February 2021.
126. Ragan Rhyne, *ProPublica* senior vice president for development, interview with Rodney Benson, November 2016, New York.
127. Ibid.

128. Joel Kramer, *MinnPost* co-founder, CEO, and editor, telephone interview with Rodney Benson, June 2012.
129. Håkan A. Bengtsson, Arenagruppen CEO, email to Carl Ritter, January 14, 2021; Jonas Nordling interview with Thyselius, 2020.
130. Jonas Nordling interview with Thyselius, 2020.
131. Based on data provided in CPB (2016, Table 2), we calculate that sixty-three percent of US public television and eighty-six percent of public radio revenues derived from non-governmental mostly philanthropic sources.
132. Bill Moyers, prominent *PBS* producer and commentator (and former *CBS* and *NBC* correspondent and commentator), letter to Rodney Benson, December 5, 2013.
133. David Fanning, *PBS Frontline* executive producer, public remarks, panel on public media, Free Press conference, Boston, April 2011, Rodney Benson field notes. *PBS* CEO and President Paula Kerger added later during the same panel: We can't "let the federal government off the hook . . . Anyone that gets a whiff of 'perhaps we could manage without federal appropriations'—that's license to say let's cut it off at the knees." *Frontline* continues to do award-winning, substantial investigative documentaries, which do not show up in our content analysis of *PBS* online news articles.
134. Paula Kerger, *PBS* CEO, interview with Alexander Heffner, *PBS*, "The Public Imperative," video aired July 16, 2016, https://www.njpbs.org/programs/the-open-mind/open-mind-public-imperative/.
135. For evidence of the active internal coordination of funding model and target audiences at *NPR*, see Chávez (2021).
136. Benson et al. (2017, 5–6); Elsa Keslassy, "France Scraps TV License Fee That Finances Bulk of Broadcasters' Budgets," *Variety*, July 25, 2022, https://variety.com/2022/tv/news/france-tv-license-fee-1235324450/.
137. France Télévisions official, interview with Julie Sedel, 2012, Paris.
138. See Online Appendix Table 2.1b and Bergström et al. (2019) for data showing that Swedish public media still reach a broad, omnibus audience (versus *Dagens Nyheter* and *Svenska Dagbladet*, which reach much more elite audiences).
139. Skatteverket [Swedish Tax Agency], "Public service-avgift" [Public Service Fee], ND, accessed July 5, 2024, https://www.skatteverket.se/privat/skatter/arbeteochinkomst/askattsedelochskattetabeller/publicserviceavgift.4.22501d9e166a8cb399f31dd.html. See also Nakamura (2019).
140. Under certain circumstances *SVT* has the right to accept sponsorships, up to twenty times per year, for major public happenings such as sport events. The rationale behind this deviation from the main principle is the increasing market prices of broadcasting rights for some high-profile events. However, *SVT* is not allowed to collaborate with sponsors, but is only allowed to show the name on the screen. See: *SVT*, "Frågor och svar om reklam, logotyper och sponsring i SVT" [Questions and Answers about advertising, logos and sponsorship], accessed July, 11, 2024, https://www.svt.se/kontakt/fragor-och-svar-om-reklam-logotyper-och-sponsring-i-svt.
141. Johan Lindén, former *SVT* senior advisor and commissioning editor, interview with Rodney Benson, October 2016, Stockholm.
142. Lars Truedson interview with Benson, 2016.
143. Klas Wolf-Watz, *SR* national news editor-in-chief, Zoom interview with Carl Ritter, January 2021.
144. Charlotta Friborg, *SVT* national news editor-in-chief, Zoom interview with Carl Ritter, January 2021. *SVT* Programming Director Jan Helin (Zoom interview with Rodney Benson, August 2020) likewise emphasized that *SVT* has "a very broad audience if you compare it to [US] National Public Radio, which is brilliant journalism but it's clearly an elite project, and that is not the case in Swedish public service" media.
145. For data on the greater proportion of university graduates among public TV viewers than *TF1* viewers in France, see Online Appendix Table 2.1c. We do not present data on commercial TV for Sweden, but see Lindell and Hovden (2018, 647–648): "Those lacking in cultural capital more often dislike the Swedish public television broadcaster (*SVT*)—but they like the commercial TV channels (*TV3*, *Kanal 5*, and *TV6*)."
146. See Emily Bell and Taylor Owen, "The Platform Press," *Columbia Journalism Review*, March 29, 2017, https://www.cjr.org/tow_center_reports/platform-press-how-silicon-valley-reengineered-journalism.php.

Chapter 5

1. Hanitzsch et al. (2019).
2. Baker (2002) and Christians et al. (2009).
3. Charlie Firestone, executive director of the Aspen Institute Communication and Society Program (interview with Rodney Benson, May 2011, Washington, DC), used the *New York Times* as an example of the potential synergy between market-driven and public service goals: "What makes [the *New York Times*] their money is their brand, and their brand is made up of different elements, and one is that they are the paper of record and they do international reporting, and they do some investigative reporting." See the discussion in Benson (2016, 38–39).
4. The remainder of this chapter presents new indicators that differ from and extend the raw percentage findings and analysis provided in Benson et al. (2018).
5. See, for example, Fink and Schudson (2014) and Benson (2013, ch. 7).
6. The finding that civil society ownership fosters the highest proportion of public service news is strengthened by the fact that many civil society-owned outlets are locally or regionally oriented and thus arguably disadvantaged by the inclusion of international news in the PSI mean.
7. *Norran*, funded primarily by advertising and serving an omnibus audience, has a PSI score of 1.50. It is the only civil society outlet in our sample that had an advertising-omnibus audience strategy as of 2016.
8. Hamilton (2004, 71).
9. We distinguish between public affairs and light/sensational news rather than the common opposition between hard (breaking) and soft (feature) news because in our view it captures more precisely the fundamental opposition between information that is "democratically useful," "politically relevant" (Williams and Delli Carpini 2011) and substantively "important" versus news that is primarily entertaining and simply "interesting" (Cook 1998).
10. Isaac Josephson, former *ABC News* vice president for product development, remarks and responses to questions in Rodney Benson's NYU graduate seminar on cultural production, March 2012, New York. In a December 3, 2023 email to Benson, Josephson emphasized that "media and advertising strategies evolve at a rapid rate, and what was true in 2012 may be less true today—or at least reflective of a slightly outdated approach." Indeed, Josephson described a situation in 2012 in which there was an "expectation that we were going to replace 1-to-1 the revenue that the broadcast side was generating" (Josephson remarks, 2012). In subsequent years, as the large platforms began taking an ever larger share of digital advertising revenues, the notion that news websites could ever generate significant profits from advertising alone has lost its appeal; in addition, compared to newspapers, legacy television's offline revenues have remained relatively stable. As such, as Cornia et al. (2019, 697) find, in more recent years broadcasters have tended to "look at digital news" as having "more value for branding than for business."
11. Hallin and Mancini (2004, 29).
12. To be clear, our news content categories do not capture the social properties of actors mentioned in the news, such as the representation of poor or otherwise marginalized individuals or the organizations that seek to represent them. Previous research (e.g., Clarke 2014; Martin 2008; Martin 2019; Capuzza 2016; Robinson 2018; Dixon et al. 2019; Callison and Young 2020) has shown that the visibility and non-stereotyped representations of marginalized voices, whether by class, race/ethnicity, indigenous status, gender, or sexuality, tends to be low across most news media. Further research is needed to see if pluralism at this level is higher or not at philanthropy funded and civil society outlets.
13. Philanthropic funding, $p = .112$; online-only medium, $p = .119$.
14. *HuffPost* staffer, interview with Rodney Benson, 2021. For the announcement of the end of blogging at *HuffPost*, see https://variety.com/2018/digital/news/huffington-post-ends-unpaid-contributor-blogger-program-1202668053/.
15. Hanitzsch et al. (2019, 173) documented the higher value professional journalists around the world place on their "monitorial role" (which includes provision of political information and scrutinization of politics and business) over all other professional roles. Journalists from the US, Sweden, and France had similar scores for this informational "monitorial" role performance (ibid., 179, 181–182). In the US, distinct from Sweden and France, the component role of "provid[ing] political information" was ranked more highly than the role of "let people express their views" (Hanitzsch et al. 2019, Appendix 1, Tables A.3 and A.4).

16. Saitta (2004, 231).
17. For research on the longstanding invisibility of labor voices in most US "corporate" commercial news media, see Martin (2008; 2019).
18. Bourdieu (1993, 55–61).

Chapter 6

1. Mancini (2012, 263).
2. Hanitzsch et al. (2019, 174).
3. Nechushtai (2018) makes a compelling case that the US has changed enough in recent years that it is no longer a "liberal" but rather a "liberal-polarized pluralist" system (to use the categories of Hallin and Mancini 2004), but this enduring refusal by most US journalists of partisan labels suggests that such a transformation is still ongoing.
4. Mancini (2012, 263).
5. Hervé Kempf, *Reporterre* founder and editor-in-chief, interview with Julie Sedel, July 2016, Paris.
6. Jan Helin, *SVT* programming director and former *Aftonbladet* editor-in-chief and CEO, Zoom interview with Rodney Benson, August 2020.
7. Djankov et al. (2003).
8. Hallin and Mancini (2004, 56) and Syvertsen et al. (2014).
9. Dragomir (2018), Freedman (2019), and Wright et al. (2024).
10. Syvertsen et al. (2014) and Benson et al. (2017).
11. Johan Lindén, former *SVT* senior advisor and commissioning editor, interview with Rodney Benson, October 2016, Stockholm. On the threat to public media posed by right-wing populist parties, see Holtz-Bacha (2021).
12. In France, commercial television is subject to many of the same regulations as public television; further, because *TF1* is owned by the Bouygues company, which has many contracts with the state, the potential for government pressure on *TF1* is nearly if not as great as for public TV. See Kuhn (2013, 129).
13. Jean-Luc Hees, Groupe Radio-France CEO, interview with Julie Sedel, March 2011, Paris.
14. Ibid.
15. *France Télévisions* former editor-in-chief, interview with Julie Sedel, 2011, Paris.
16. Jean-Luc Hees interview with Sedel, 2011. See also Daniel Psenny, "Jean-Luc Hees: 'Je ne m'appele pas Domenech" [My name is not Domenech], *Le Monde*, June 23, 2010 (updated February 26, 2014), https://www.lemonde.fr/actualite-medias/article/2010/06/23/jean-luc-hees-je-ne-m-appelle-pas-domenech_1377459_3236.html and Jean-Baptiste Chastand, "Radio France condamnée pour le licenciement de Stéphane Guillon" [Radio France condemned for the dismissal of Stéphane Guillon], *Le Monde*, January 28, 2011, https://www.lemonde.fr/actualite-medias/article/2011/01/28/radio-france-condamnee-pour-le-licenciement-de-stephane-guillon_1471734_3236.html.
17. Delphine Ernotte, *France Télévisions* CEO, interview with Julie Sedel, 2017, Paris. See also discussion in Sedel (2021a, 130), and in Duhamel and Duhamel (2008), who reported frequent government pressure on their programs on French public television.
18. CPB (1967); see also Starr (2000) and Hoynes (2007).
19. Stephen Labaton and Lorne Manley, "Republican Chairman Exerts Pressure on PBS, Alleging Biases," *New York Times*, May 2, 2005, https://www.nytimes.com/2005/05/02/arts/television/republican-chairman-exerts-pressure-on-pbs-alleging-biases.html.
20. Joshua Benton, "Trump Wants to Kill Federal Funding for PBS and NPR (again); It Won't Happen, But It's Still Damaging," *NiemanLab*, March 11, 2019, https://www.niemanlab.org/2019/03/trump-wants-to-kill-federal-funding-for-pbs-and-npr-again-it-wont-happen-but-its-still-damaging/.
21. Bennett (2016).
22. Regarding right-wing attacks on public media, see Holtz-Bacha (2021) and Jan Schaffer, "Much Vitriol Aimed at 'PBS NewsHour' Newscasts," *CPB [Corporation for Public Broadcasting] Ombudsman*, January 11, 2021, https://www.cpb.org/ombudsman/Much-Vitriol-Aimed-PBS-NewsHour-Newscasts.
23. Cushion (2012).

24. Concerning generally high levels of trust in and belief in the importance of public media, see Benson et al. (2017), Neff and Pickard (2021), and Nielsen and Fletcher (2023).
25. See Baker (1994b), McManus (2009), and Pickard (2020) for syntheses of this literature.
26. Socolow (2010), Jacobs and Townsley (2011), and Berry and Sobieraj (2013).
27. John Cassidy, "Murdoch's Game," *The New Yorker*, October 16, 2006; Pasadeos and Renfro (1988). As Pasadeos (1984) documents, Murdoch first implemented his sensationalist style in the US in 1973 at the *San Antonio* [Texas] *News*.
28. See, e.g., *PBS NewsHour*, "Inside the unprecedented partnership between Fox News and the Trump White House," March 5, 2019, https://www.pbs.org/newshour/show/inside-the-unprecedented-partnership-between-fox-news-and-the-trump-white-house.
29. McKnight (2010, 304).
30. Shawcross (1997, 98).
31. Nicholas Confessore, "How Tucker Carlson Reshaped Fox News – and Became Trump's Heir," *New York Times*, April 30, 2022, https://www.nytimes.com/2022/04/30/us/tucker-carlson-fox-news.html. See also Benson (2012), Stelzer (2018), Peck (2019), and Bauer et al. (2021).
32. *Le Monde* (with AFP), "Serge Dassault prend le contrôle de la Socpresse" [Serge Dassault takes control of Socpresse], *Le Monde*, March 11, 2004, https://www.lemonde.fr/archives/article/2004/03/11/serge-dassault-prend-le-controle-de-la-socpresse_356415_1819218.html.
33. *Le Monde*, "Dassault veut une presse aux 'idées saines'" [Dassault wants a press with 'healthy ideas'], *Le Monde*, December 12, 2004, https://www.lemonde.fr/archives/article/2004/12/12/p-m-dassault-veut-une-presse-aux-idees-saines-p_4304972_1819218.html.
34. Nicolas Beytout, former *Le Figaro* editor-in-chief, interview with Julie Sedel, 2012, Paris.
35. Ibid.
36. Page (1996, 19).
37. Hanretty (2014).
38. Daniel Chomsky (1999; 2006). Chomsky found evidence in the archives of both political and economic instrumentalism.
39. Downie (2020, 222–223, 304–305, 319). One wonders, however, if such an arrangement could have persisted if the disagreements had been more frequent.
40. See, e.g., Edmund Lee, "*Washington Post* Finds Itself in the Middle of the Jeff Bezos Story," *New York Times*, February 11, 2019, https://www.nytimes.com/2019/02/11/business/media/washington-post-jeff-bezos.html.
41. Anders Frostell, Eskilstuna-Kuriren Foundation chairman, interview with Mattias Hessérus, 2011, Stockholm.
42. Olle Lidbom, Norstedts Förlagsgrupp Publishing head of marketing and publicity, interview with Rodney Benson, October 2016, Stockholm.
43. Anna Gullberg, *Gefle Dagblad* editor-in-chief, telephone interview with Erik Thyselius, August 2020.
44. Anders Westermark, *Norran* CEO, interview with Mattias Hessérus, May 2011, Stockholm.
45. Anders Westermark, *Norran* CEO, interview with Rodney Benson, October 2016, Stockholm.
46. Anders Westermark interview with Hessérus, 2011.
47. Pierre Zarka, former *L'Humanité* director, interview with Julie Sedel, 2011, Paris.
48. Ibid.
49. Ibid. Concerning changes at *L'Humanité* in the early 2000s and since, see Arboit (2002), Eveno (2004), and Nicolas Madelaine, "Nouveau départ pour 'L'Huma,'" *Les Echos*, December 30, 2019.
50. Clay Jones, *Christian Science Monitor* chief editorial writer, interview with Rodney Benson, May 2011, Boston. Benson witnessed Jones talking on the phone with a board member who gave him approval to use a particular cartoon in the print magazine.
51. *La Croix* desk editor quoted in Lardeau (2011, 279).
52. Dominique Quinio, *La Croix* director, interview with Julie Sedel, July 2011, Paris.
53. Emmanuel Karlsten, former *Dagen* digital editor and *Aftonbladet* digital consultant, interview with Rodney Benson, October 2017, Gothenburg.
54. Felicia Ferreira, *Dagen* CEO and editor-in-chief, telephone interview with Eric Thyselius, August 2020.
55. Emmanuel Karlsten interview with Benson, 2017.
56. Joel Kramer, *MinnPost* co-founder, CEO, and editor, telephone interview with Rodney Benson, June 2012. Josh Wilson, founder of Newsfunders.org, which long provided the umbrella educational and arts association ownership for the nonprofit *San Francisco Public Press*, likewise stressed that "legally you can't be for a politician or legislation if you're a 501(c)(3)" (personal communication with Rodney Benson, Boston, May 2011).

57. Andrew Donohue, *Voice of San Diego* editor, interview with Rodney Benson, July 2011, San Diego. Since 2013, Donohue has been a senior editor at *CIR/Reveal.*
58. Patterson and Donsbach (1996), McMane (2012), Strömback et al. (2012), and Hassell et al. (2022).
59. Patrick Le Lay, former *TF1* CEO, interview with Julie Sedel, April 2012, Paris. For evidence that *TF1* is broadly perceived to lean more to the right than its actual audience does, see Nami Sumida, Mason Walker, and Amy Mitchell, "News Media Attitudes in France: 5. Where users place outlets' ideologies," *Pew Research Center*, April 23, 2019, https://www.pewresearch.org/journalism/2019/04/23/where-users-place-outlets-ideologies/.
60. Lord et al. (1979), Rabin and Schrag (1999), and Anand et al. (2007). Long before the current era of partisan polarization, surveyed journalists in the early 1970s ranked the "political opinions" of readers as a greater influence on their work than their own political views or those of their editors (Flegel and Chaffee 1971, discussed in Örnebring and Karlsson 2022, 177).
61. Levendusky (2013).
62. Gentzkow and Shapiro (2010). To measure political slant in news, they examined "the set of all phrases used by members of Congress in the 2005 Congressional Record, and identif[ied] those that are used much more frequently by one party than another" and then "index[ed] newspapers by the extent to which the use of politically charged phrases in their news coverage resembles the use of the same phrases in the speech of a congressional Democrat or Republican" (36). They based audience measurements on the primary metropolitan statistical area where each paper's headquarters is located. This includes newspapers with significant *national* print and/or digital audiences, such as *USA Today*, the *New York Times*, the *Wall Street Journal*, and the *Washington Post.* Their study did not include the *Christian Science Monitor* or digital-only media with little or no single geographic based audience.
63. Benkler et al. (2018, 15, 75–82).
64. Étienne Mougeotte, former *TF1* programming director, interview with Julie Sedel, 2012, Paris.
65. Isaac Josephson, former *ABC News* vice president for product development, remarks and responses to questions in Rodney Benson's NYU graduate seminar on cultural production, March 2012, New York.
66. In 2020, *USA Today* decided to break with this long tradition to endorse Democratic presidential candidate Joe Biden against Republican incumbent Donald Trump.
67. Dahlgren (2019, 301) documents that "ideological leaning seems to play a limited role in the use of [Swedish] public service news over time, and individuals on the political left and right both use public service news slightly more than those in the center"; similarly, Skovsgaard et al. (2016, 542) showed that while ideological preferences played a role in selective exposure to party leader interviews on public television (right-leaning audiences more likely to watch interviews with right-wing candidates and vice versa), "the effect of political interest was significantly greater than partisan leaning."
68. Djerf-Pierre and Weibull (2011).
69. Prior (2007).
70. Jones (2012) and Peck (2019).
71. Fredric Karén, former *Svenska Dagbladet* editor-in-chief, telephone interview with Erik Thyselius, August 2020.
72. Martin Schori, former *KIT* news editor, Zoom interview with Carl Ritter, March 2021.
73. Abramson (2019, 115).
74. Tandoc Jr. (2018, 208), and Abramson (2019, 140).
75. Pickard (2020), and Smith (2023, 211–212, 275).
76. Gabszewicz et al. (2002) show that the more a media outlet relies on advertising, the more it tends to conform to the opinion of the median reader. For additional evidence that advertising exerts an ideological homogenizing and centering effect, see Baker (1994b).
77. Jonas Nordling, *Dagens Arena* editor-in-chief, telephone interview with Erik Thyselius, August 2020.
78. Ferrucci (2020, 253, 257). See also Usher (2013) and discussion in Örnebring and Karlsson (2022, 222–223).
79. US foundation official, interview with Rodney Benson, 2013.
80. Rosenstiel et al. (2016). Similar patterns were evident in Media Impact Funders (2023).
81. Nisbet et al. (2018, fig. 4, available at: https://shorensteincenter.org/funding-the-news-foundations-and-nonprofit-media/, accessed May 24, 2022).
82. Rosenstiel et al. (2016).

83. Chuck Lewis, *Center for Public Integrity* (*CPI*) founding executive editor and *Investigative Reporting Workshop* (*IRW*) executive editor, Zoom interview with Rodney Benson, February 2021.
84. Ibid.
85. Holcomb et al. (2011).
86. Soloski (1989, 226).
87. Page (1996, 19).
88. Groseclose and Milyo (2005, 1199).
89. *Washington Post* high-level editor, personal communication with Rodney Benson, 2022.
90. *New York Times* editorial page subeditor, personal communication with Rodney Benson, 2016.
91. Anders Westermark interview with Hessérus, 2011.
92. On Swedish cultural journalism's "dual focus on politics and artistic expression," see Riegert and Roosvall (2017, 89).
93. Anders Frostell, chairman of the Eskilstuna-Kuriren foundation (owner of newspapers in central Sweden) and Stiftelsen Pressorganisation foundation (thirty percent owner of the Mittmedia group, including *Gefle Dagblad*), interview with Rodney Benson, October 2016, Stockholm.
94. Ibid. Frostell attributed this hands-off approach to "agreements" with the former owners, as well as a "strong history of the newspapers being Social Democratic or Center party papers": "It's probably commercially right that they are still what they are, and also I think it would be very provocative if we did [change them]."
95. Anders Enström, *Barometern* editor-in-chief, telephone interview with Erik Thyselius, August 2020.
96. Anders Westermark interview with Benson, 2016.
97. Page (1996, 109–112).
98. Page (1996, 70–71). Groseclose and Milyo (2005) found similar results for the *Journal*. As the *Journal*'s opinion section has become even more conservative under Rupert Murdoch's ownership (Wagner and Collins 2014), tensions between the news and opinion sections have increased. See Adam Piore, "Breaking Right," *Columbia Journalism Review*, Fall 2021, https://www.cjr.org/special_report/breaking_right_wall_street_journal_stubborn_murdoch.php.
99. Jacobs and Townsley (2011), Benson et al. (2012), and Berry and Sobieraj (2013).
100. Clay Jones interview with Benson, 2011.
101. In their interview-based study of US conservative media news workers, Nadler et al. (2020) find support for "conventional notions of fairness and balance" but also for "radical subjectivity" and the idea that "all reporters . . . ought to be transparent about their political and other biases—trusting in the audience to assess the veracity of news on the basis of 'authenticity.'"
102. Lemieux and Schmalzbauer (2000) and Gans (2005). Wiik (2010, 85) finds that Swedish journalists strongly embrace the ideal of "letting different opinions be heard," followed at some distance by "objectivity" and "neutrality."
103. Smith (2023, 244).
104. Alexis Benveniste, "Shep Smith breaks his silence about why he left Fox News," *CNN Business*, January 20, 2021, https://www.cnn.com/2021/01/20/media/shep-smith-fox-amanpour/index.html.
105. Emmanuel Berretta, "*Figaro*: quand la rédaction a ses vapeurs" [*Figaro*: when the editorial staff is fuming], *Le Point.fr*, September 2, 2012, https://www.lepoint.fr/economie/figaro-quand-la-redaction-a-ses-vapeurs-09-02-2012-1429383_28.php.
106. Schwoebel (1969; 1970) and Dupuy (2010).
107. Eisendrath (1979).
108. Cagé and Huet (2021, 153–164).
109. Aude Dassonville, "'JDD': des députés déposent une proposition de loi transpartisane pour l'indépendance des rédactions" [*Journal du Dimanche*: deputies table a transpartisan bill for the independence of editorial staff], *Le Monde*, July 19, 2023, https://www.lemonde.fr/economie/article/2023/07/19/jdd-des-deputes-deposent-une-proposition-de-loi-transpartisane-pour-l-independance-des-redactions_6182595_3234.html.
110. Swedish Intellectual Property Office (PRV), "Responsible editor," last edited October 17, 2022, https://www.prv.se/en/periodicals/applying-for-a-certificate-of-publication/responsible-editor/.
111. CSA [now ARCOM] requires that during election periods all radio and television news must accord a certain amount of time to all political parties, regarding their "representativeness and their implication in the campaign." See CSA [Arcom], "Pendant une élection" [During an

election], n.d., accessed September 16, 2023, https://www.csa.fr/Proteger/Garantie-des-droits-et-libertes/Proteger-le-pluralisme-politique/Pendant-une-election.

112. The Swedish Press and Broadcasting Authority, accessed July 7, 2024, https://mediemyndigheten.se/anmala-program/.
113. Fredric Karén interview with Thyselius, 2020.
114. For the text of the *Journal's* editorial agreement (*Wall Street Journal*, June 29, 2007), see https://www.wsj.com/articles/SB118315620615153545. See also Julie Moss, "Whatever Happened to the WSJ Editorial Integrity Committee?", *Poynter*, July 13, 2011, https://www.poynter.org/newsletters/2011/whatever-happened-to-the-wsj-editorial-integrity-committee/.
115. Piore, "Breaking Right."
116. Johan Hansson, CEO of Stampen (owner of *Göteborgs-Posten* and other western Swedish newspapers), interview with Rodney Benson, October 2017, Gothenburg. Hansson magnifies the convergence between the *Times* and *Göteborgs-Posten* by playing down differences in the meaning of the word "liberal" in Sweden and the US. However, the larger point about the power of tradition to shape an outlet's "agenda" remains valid.
117. Jan Helin interview with Benson, 2020. According to *Aftonbladet's* official homepage, as of 2023 LO had nine percent of ownership shares and Schibsted owned the remaining ninety-one percent. See https://www.aftonbladet.se/omaftonbladet/a/rAjLze/historien-om-aftonbladet, accessed September 15, 2023.
118. Laurent Joffrin, former *Libération* director, interview with Julie Sedel, April 2012, Paris.
119. Johan Hufnagel, former online editor-in-chief of *Libération* and *20 Minutes*, and co-founder of *Slate.fr*, interview with Rodney Benson, March 2023, Paris.
120. Page (1996, 112–116).
121. It is possible that the level of within-field differences in partisan favorability or intensity between media outlets with different structural characteristics could vary between election and non-election periods or between campaigns with different types of political candidates (such as populist politicians): to the extent that this is the case, our relational scales would not entirely control for divergent conditions in the US, Sweden, and France during 2015 and 2016. Nevertheless, hopefully our framework and findings provide a useful baseline for future research across a range of societies and circumstances.
122. In regard to primary definers, see Hall et al. (1978); concerning news media "indexing," see Bennett (2016).
123. Fredric Karén interview with Thyselius, 2020.
124. For other studies of the outsized attention to Trump during 2015 and 2016, see Wells et al. (2016) and Patterson (2016).
125. The one news outlet where Trump is highlighted, but in which mentions of Hillary Clinton and President Obama are close behind, is the conservative Fox News. Overt and sharp contrasts between the parties is an essential part of Fox's news and commentary formula. See Peck (2019).
126. Lee Fang, "While War on Media Escalates, CBS Chief Praises Trump's Deregulatory Agenda," *The Intercept*, February 24, 2017, https://theintercept.com/2017/02/24/cbs-fcc-trump/.
127. Carlson, Robinson, and Lewis (2021, 59–61) and Cook (1998). With respect to Trump and US news media, see also Boczkowski and Papacharissi (2018).
128. Paul Bond, "Leslie Moonves on Donald Trump," *The Hollywood Reporter*, February 29, 2016, http://www.hollywoodreporter.com/news/leslie-moonves-donald-trump-may-871464. Interestingly, though, CBS had the fewest Trump mentions of the nine US stock market-traded media outlets in our sample.
129. Brandenburg (2005, 312). A score of 0 could thus be produced either by all mentions being neutral, by positive and negative mentions in perfect balance, or some combination of neutral and balanced positive and negative mentions. For a slightly different approach, see Hopmann et al. (2016, 97–100).
130. Holcomb et al. (2011) use a different methodology to create a 0–100 "ideological" index for US nonprofits that indexes their degree of deviation from neutrality without directly indicating left or right slant.
131. Across the fifty-one news outlet sample, news and opinion Partisan Favorability ratio scores were correlated at .248, $p < .10$; outlets' opinion articles had an average Partisan Intensity ratio score of 1.56 versus 1.21 for their news articles. The opinion-news gap in Partisan Intensity ratio scores was larger in the US (1.78 opinion, 1.15 news) and Sweden (1.67 opinion, 1.32 news) than in France, where there was essentially no difference (1.14 opinion, 1.17 news).

132. For audience subscription-funded media, the partisan favorability (1–4 *scale*) score is 1.89 for outlets with left-leaning audiences, 2.83 for neutral/balanced audiences, and 3.50 for right-leaning audiences ($p = .058$), a wider gap than for all outlets. For outlets with other types of primary funding, differences in partisan favorability by audience partisan preferences are not statistically significant.
133. Business Favorability and Partisan (Right) Favorability scores are positively correlated at 0.283 ($p < .05$).
134. Benkler et al. (2018, 75–82). To be fair, Benkler et al.'s important book is avowedly US-specific and analyzes far right outlets and aspects of news content that are not part of our study.

Chapter 7

1. Napoli (1997, 211).
2. Bourdieu (2005), Christians et al. (2009, 104).
3. Wasko (2001).
4. Turow (1997, 265).
5. Williams (2002, 456).
6. Davis and Craft (2000). For a useful discussion of the challenges involved in fully documenting all of the owners/investors of any news outlet, especially when it is privately held, see Cagé and Godechot (2017).
7. Frank Washkuch, "Murdoch: Too Much Editing at WSJ," *PR Week*, May 29, 2008, https://www.prweek.com/article/1252542/murdoch-editing-wsj.
8. Hardy (2013, 89).
9. Hardy (2013, 89–90). See also Hardy (2010).
10. See ETC, "ETC-företagen" [The ETC Companies], ND, accessed September 15, 2023, https://www.etc.se/meny#foretagen.
11. Scott et al. (2017), Wright et al. (2019). See also Browne (2010) and Benson (2018).
12. Wright et al. (2019, 683, 688). In a companion article, Scott et al. (2017, 181–182) find that IRIN did, however, shift toward a greater focus on reporting with measurable "impact" (on social problems amenable to changes in policies or practices); they argue that this focus was "informed as much by the anticipated desires of potential donors, as it was by its existing donor."
13. Wright et al. (2019, 686). See also Koehn and Ueng (2010).
14. Wright et al. (2019, 686, 688–690).
15. Michael Moss and Geraldinen Fabrikant, "Once Trusted Mortgage Pioneers, Now Scrutinized," *New York Times*, December 24, 2008, https://www.nytimes.com/2008/12/25/business/25sandler.html.
16. Jeff Horwitz, "The Education of Herb and Marion Sandler," *Columbia Journalism Review*, March/April 2010, https://archives.cjr.org/feature/the_education_of_herb_and_marion.php.
17. Ragan Rhyne, *ProPublica* senior vice president for development, interview with Rodney Benson, November 2016, New York.
18. Ibid.
19. Frank Ahrens, "And Now a Word About Our Sponsor," *Washington Post*, May 21, 1999; *NPR*, "Sponsors: Fiscal Year 2008," https://media.npr.org/documents/about/annualreports/NPRSponsorsDonors08.pdf
20. *Le Figaro*, with AFP, "Enquête sur l'eau: pas d'intervention de Delphine Ernotte (Elise Lucet)" [Water investigation: no intervention by Delphine Ernotte], *Le Figaro*, March 13, 2018, https://www.lefigaro.fr/flash-actu/2018/03/13/97001-20180313FILWWW00355-enquete-sur-l-eau-pas-d-intervention-de-delphine-ernotte-elise-lucet.php.
21. Portions of the US research previously appeared in Neff and Benson (2021).
22. See Online Appendix Tables 7.1a–7.1c for complete listing of ownership interests for each outlet.
23. Given the public prominence and news value of some owners, we tested whether media companies owned by (or associated with) newsworthy companies (*ABC News*–Disney, *CNN*–Time Warner, *HuffPost*–Verizon, and *Washington Post*–Amazon) mention these companies more often than other media. We found significant promotional "surpluses" at *ABC News* (Disney appearing in 2.8 percent of items, versus 1.0 percent in all other outlets) and *CNN* (Time Warner mentioned in 0.5 percent of items versus 0.1 percent at other outlets), but not at *HuffPost* and the *Washington Post*. See Neff and Benson (2021, 2112–2113).
24. Outlets with omnibus audiences had an average OMI score of 34.7 versus 19.1 for outlets with elite audiences ($n = 28$, $p = .186$).

25. Bruce Kushnick, "Verizon's $300 Million Shell Game in Boston and Cross-subsidizing Wireless," *Huffington Post*, May 24, 2016, https://www.huffpost.com/entry/verizons-300-million-shel_b_10113124.
26. Our content sample period coincided with a strike by Verizon workers. For additional analysis of the differences between staff and non-staff coverage of owners' interests, which in general did not exhibit a clear pattern across ownership forms, see Neff and Benson (2021, 2115).
27. Bruce Kushnick, the blogger critical of Verizon, suspected that the main motivation for shuttering the blogging program was to avert the threat of a lawsuit that would have forced *HuffPost* to financially compensate its heretofore unpaid bloggers. See Bruce Kushnick, "How Verizon Ruined HuffPost," *Medium*, September 30, 2020, https://kushnickbruce.medium.com/how-verizon-ruined-huffpost-d5d698cda886.
28. Average favorability scores were 0.029 for outlets with omnibus audiences and 0.014 for outlets with elite audiences (ns).
29. Baker (1994b), Pickard (2020).
30. Ryan (1991), Martin (2008; 2019), Starkman (2014).
31. Saffer et al. (2021, 456–458, 463).
32. Joshua Benton, "*The L.A. Times* Uses Its Physician Owner to Help Explain the Science Behind the Coronavirus," *NiemanLab*, March 18, 2020, https://www.niemanlab.org/2020/03/the-l-a-times-uses-its-physician-owner-to-help-explain-the-science-behind-the-coronavirus/.
33. Véronique Guillermard, "L'État commande le nouveau Rafale" [The State Orders the New Rafale], *Le Figaro*, January 10, 2014, https://www.lefigaro.fr/societes/2014/01/10/20005-20140110ARTFIG00525-l-etat-commande-le-nouveau-rafale.php. The article was criticized in Frédéric Lemaire, "*Le Figaro* se pame devant le Rafale" [Le Figaro Swoons in Front of the Rafale], *Acrimed*, January 17, 2014, https://www.acrimed.org/Le-Figaro-se-pame-devant-le-Rafale. According to the *New York Times*, shortly after Dassault purchased *Le Figaro* in 2004, concerns about the owner using the newspaper to push "his business interests" were raised in a nearly unanimous vote by the newspaper's society of journalists (a "nonunion body representing staff"); the *Times* referred to "media reports [that] said there had already been two cases of interference." See: "Figaro journalists vow independence," *New York Times*, September 22, 2004, https://www.nytimes.com/2004/09/22/business/worldbusiness/figaro-journalists-vow-independence.html.
34. Jérémie Fabre, "Les Dassault fêtent la vente du Rafale" [The Dassaults Celebrate the Sale of the Rafale], *Acrimed*, March 3, 2015, https://www.acrimed.org/Les-Dassault-fetent-la-vente-du-Rafale.
35. La rédaction de *Mediapart* [The editors of *Mediapart*], "Les journalistes du '*Parisien*' dénoncent l'emprise de Bernard Arnault" [*Le Parisien* Journalists Denounce the Influence of Bernard Arnault], *Mediapart*, February 25, 2018 (citing reporting originally in *Arrêt sur images*), https://www.mediapart.fr/journal/france/250218/les-journalistes-du-parisien-denoncent-l-emprise-de-bernard-arnault.
36. Mathias Reymond, "La 'marque' *Radio Classique* au service de son maître LVMH" [The Radio Classique 'Brand' at the Service of Its Master LVMH], *Acrimed*, December 11, 2020, https://www.acrimed.org/La-marque-Radio-Classique-au-service-de-son.
37. Martin Coutellier, "Fusions dans le monde des télécoms: banale convergence de vues à *Libération*" [Mergers in the World of Telecoms: Banal Convergence of Views at *Libération*], *Acrimed*, August 21, 2015, https://www.acrimed.org/Fusions-dans-le-monde-des-telecoms-banale-convergence-de-vues-a-Liberation.
38. Sophia Aït Kaci, "D'après *Le Monde*, Xavier Niel, proprietaire du *Monde*, est un 'aventurier exceptionnel'" [According to *Le Monde*, Xavier Niel, Owner of *Le Monde*, is an 'Exceptional Adventurer'], *Acrimed*, November 30, 2016, https://www.acrimed.org/D-apres-Le-Monde-Xavier-Niel-proprietaire-du.
39. Concerning Bolloré and Vivendi, see Amaury de Rochegonde, "Antoine Genton (I-Télé): La grève nous fait mal, nous n'informons pas" [The Strike Hurts Us, We Aren't Reporting the News], *Stratégies*, October 26, 2016, https://www.strategies.fr/actualites/medias/1049949W/antoine-genton-i-tele-la-greve-nous-fait-mal-.html, and "De quoi C-News est-elle le nom?" [What is C-News?], *Stratégies*, November 9, 2016, https://www.strategies.fr/actualites/medias/1050997W/de-quoi-c-news-est-elle-le-nom-.html. Concerning Credit Mutuel and its newspapers, see Alexandra Turpin, "Crédit Mutuel/EBRA: Le Syndicat national des journalistes (SNJ) dénonce une opération d'auto-promotion déguisée en journalisme" [Crédit Mutuel/EBRA: The National Journalists' Union (SNJ) Denounces Self-promotion Disguised as Journalism], *Correspondance de la Presse*, July 6, 2012.
40. Gustafsson (2008, 333).
41. Jim Romanesko, "'NBC Nightly News' Ignores GE Tax Controversy," *Poynter*, March 30, 2011, https://www.poynter.org/reporting-editing/2011/nbc-nightly-news-ignores-ge-tax-controversy/.

42. Brian Stelter, "A Donation Clouds Fox News Report," *New York Times*, October 31, 2010, https://www.nytimes.com/2010/11/01/business/media/01fox.html.
43. Steve Myers, "When It Comes to Disclosing Potential Conflicts of Interest, *New York Times* Shouldn't Throw Stones at Arrington," *Poynter*, September 14, 2011, https://www.poynter.org/reporting-editing/2011/when-it-comes-to-disclosing-potential-conflicts-of-interest-new-york-times-shouldnt-throw-stones-at-arrington/.
44. Dan Kennedy, "Conflicts of Interest and the New Media Moguls," *Media Nation*, January 13, 2014, https://dankennedy.net/2014/01/13/conflicts-of-interest-and-the-new-media-moguls/.
45. Edward Wong, "Bloomberg News is Said to Curb Articles that Might Anger China," *New York Times*, November 8, 2013, https://www.nytimes.com/2013/11/09/world/asia/bloomberg-news-is-said-to-curb-articles-that-might-anger-china.html; Margaret Sullivan [NYT "public editor"], "The Thorny Challenge of Covering China," *New York Times*, December 8, 2013, https://www.nytimes.com/2013/12/08/public-editor/the-thorny-challenge-of-covering-china.html.
46. Ken Doctor, "Newsonomics: The Financialization of News is Dimming the Lights of the Local Press; An Unfortunate Series of Recent Events," *NeimanLab*, February 19, 2016, https://www.niemanlab.org/2016/02/newsonomics-the-financialization-of-news-is-dimming-the-lights-of-the-local-press/; Sydney Ember, "In Sheldon Adelson's Newsroom, Looser Purse Strings and a Tighter Leash," *New York Times*, May 22, 2016, https://www.nytimes.com/2016/05/23/business/media/in-adelsons-newsroom-looser-purse-strings-and-a-tighter-leash.html.
47. According to Tony Todd, "French billionaire Senator Dassault 'paid for votes', *France24*, September 16, 2013, https://www.france24.com/en/20130916-french-billionaire-senator-dassault-paid-votes, the charges against Dassault originally appeared in the satirical investigative weekly *Le Canard Enchainé* and were also the subject of additional reporting by *Mediapart*. Julie Morel, "Exercise: Que trouve-t-on dans le panier d'achat de Serge Dassault" [Exercise: What's In Serge Dassault's Shopping Cart?], *Acrimed*, September 26, 2013, https://www.acrimed.org/Exercice-Que-trouve-t-on-dans-le-panier-d-achat-de-Serge-Dassault; Frédéric Lemaire, "Mise en examen de Serge Dassault: *Le Figaro* soigne son propriétaire" [Indictment of Serge Dassault: *Le Figaro* Looks After Its Owner], *Acrimed*, April 11, 2014, https://www.acrimed.org/Mise-en-examen-de-Serge-Dassault-Le-Figaro-soigne-son-proprietaire; Henri Maler and Jérémie Fabre, "Les 53 millions d'argent de poche de Serge Dassault? *Le Figaro* n'en sait rien" [Serge Dassault's 53 Million in Pocket Money? *Le Figaro* Knows Nothing About It], *Acrimed*, November 19, 2014, https://www.acrimed.org/Les-53-millions-d-argent-de-poche-de-Serge-Dassault-Le-Figaro-n-en-sait-rien.
48. de Rochegonde and Sénéjoux (2017, 87).
49. Xavier Ternisien, "Francis Morel évincé du '*Figaro*' pour 'incompatibilité d'humeur' avec Serge Dassault" [Francis Morel Ousted from *Le Figaro* for 'Incompatibility of Temperament' with Serge Dassault], *Le Monde*, January 25, 2011, https://www.lemonde.fr/actualite-medias/article/2011/01/25/francis-morel-evince-du-figaro-pour-incompatibilite-d-humeur-avec-serge-dassault_1470537_3236.html. See also de Rochegonde and Sénéjoux (2017, 91).
50. Francis Morel, former *Le Figaro* director, interview with Julie Sedel, February 2011, Paris. See also Sedel (2021a, 88), concerning how confidentiality clauses often limit the information former top editors can legally share with researchers.
51. de Rochegonde and Sénéjoux (2017, 99–100).
52. de Rochegonde and Sénéjoux (2017, 235–237).
53. Denis Perais, "Nicolas Barré, un bon 'Samaritaine' . . . , en service commandé pour son propriétaire" [Nicolas Barré, a good 'Samaritaine' . . . , on duty for his owner], *Acrimed*, February 23, 2015, https://www.acrimed.org/Nicolas-Barre-un-bon-Samaritaine-en-service-commande-pour-son-proprietaire. Perais argued that editor Barré's remarks were in direct violation of *Les Echos*' ethical charter, notably: "Journalists undertake to present the facts with rigor and honesty, this principle also applying without reservation when these facts are directly or indirectly linked to their shareholders and/or managers."
54. de Rochegonde and Sénéjoux (2017, 207–208).
55. Ibid., 208; Marc Baudriller, "Altice: pourquoi Drahi fait volte-face dans les médias" [Altice: Why Drahi is Making an About-face in the Media], *Challenges*, May 22, 2020, https://www.challenges.fr/media/altice-pourquoi-drahi-fait-volte-face-dans-les-medias_711406. If the story of the conversation with Hollande is true, Drahi was following a well-worn pattern of wealthy French businesspersons saving a media outlet as a favor to a president. According to press historian Patrick Eveno, in 1997, François Pinault purchased the conservative news magazine *Le Point*

as a token of friendship to President Jacques Chirac, who saw that the center-left *Le Monde* was prepared to buy it, and Chirac wanted to make sure the magazine continued to be associated with the center-right (quoted in Gilles Fontaine, "Le pouvoir médiatico-politique les fascine" [Media-political Power Fascinates Them], *Challenges*, July 8, 2021).

56. de Rochegonde and Sénéjoux (2017, 215). de Rochegonde and Sénéjoux (2017, 205) suggest that owning media allows Drahi to "politicize his dossier" and in so doing buy a certain protection. Given that his business model relies on extensive debt, if he were ever to be threatened with bankruptcy, they argue, journalists and government officials would know that it's not just him, but also *Libération*, as well as the weekly *L'Express* and the cable news channel *BFMTV*, that could collapse "like dominoes."
57. Sébastian Fontenelle, "Chez *Libération*, Pierre Marcelle de nouveau censuré" [At *Libération*, Pierre Marcelle Censored Again], *Acrimed*, September 27, 2014, https://www.acrimed.org/Chez-Liberation-Pierre-Marcelle-de-nouveau-censure.
58. Martin Coutellier, "Pierre Bergé regrètte l'independance éditoriale du *Monde*" [Pierre Bergé Regrets the Editorial Independence of *Le Monde*], *Acrimed*, February 13, 2015, https://www.acrimed.org/Pierre-Berge-regrette-l-independance-editoriale-du-Monde.
59. "Quand le Crédit Mutuel verrouille . . . l'information (SNJ)" [When Crédit Mutuel Locks . . . the Information], SNJ statement posted by *Acrimed*, January 6, 2012, https://www.acrimed.org/Quand-le-Credit-Mutuel-verrouille-l-information-SNJ.
60. Malin Ekman, "Hur påverkas journalistiken när medier agerar riskkapitalister" [How is Journalism Affected When Media Act as Venture Capitalists?], *Svenska Dagbladet*, November 13, 2014, https://www.svd.se/hur-paverkas-journalistiken-nar-medier-agerar-riskkapitalister; Christopher Jungstedt, "Mediecheferna: Ingen risk för trovärdighetsproblem" [Media Executives: No Risk for Credibility Problems], *Svenska Dagbladet*, November 13, 2014, https://www.svd.se/mediecheferna-ingen-risk-for-trovardighetsproblem.
61. FI [FI, financial markets government authority], "HQ banks tillstånd återkallas" [HQ Banking License is Being Revoked], August 28, 2010, https://www.fi.se/sv/publicerat/sanktioner/finansiella-foretag/2010/hq-banks-tillstand-aterkallas/; Alexander Zeilon Lund, "Ingen överklagan i HQ-målet" [No Appeal in the HQ Case], *Svenska Dagbladet*, July 11, 2016, https://www.svd.se/a/b8y2g/ingen-overklagan-i-hq-malet.
62. Johanna Cederblad, "Hårdgranskad Qviberg vill 'kvalitetssäkra' news website" [Scrutinized Qviberg Wants to 'Safeguard Quality' for News Website], *Svenska Dagbladet*, December 16, 2016, https://www.svd.se/a/y2jlJ/hardgranskad-qviberg-vill-kvalitetssakra-nyhetssajt.
63. Malin Ekman, "Olämpligt att Metrotoppen rekryteras bland HQ-vänner" [Inappropriate that Metro Top Executive Recruited among HQ friends], *Svenska Dagbladet*, April 20, 2017, https://www.svd.se/a/JmbdR/olampligt-att-metrotoppen-rekryteras-bland-hq-vanner.
64. Chang Frick, "Qviberg om journalisten som skrev Metros tiggarartikel: 'En typisk stalinist som vi borde bli av med'" [Qviberg on the Journalist Who Wrote Metro's Beggar Article: "A Typical Stalinist that We Ought to Get Rid Of"], *Nyheter Idag*, May, 12, 2017, https://nyheteridag.se/qviberg-om-journalisten-som-skrev-metros-tiggarartikel-en-typisk-stalinist-som-vi-borde-bli-av-med/; *Nyheter Idag* describes itself as a news platform with "no direct connection to any political organization" that rests "on both a libertarian and a liberal conservative foundation." *Nyheter Idag*, "Om oss/Kontakt" [About us/Contact], ND, accessed September 15, 2023, nyheteridag.se/om-oss-kontakt.
65. Johan Hellekant, "Politiker: Avtal med Metro har överlevt sig självt" [Politician: Agreement with Metro has Survived Itself], *Svenska Dagbladet*, May 13, 2017, https://www.svd.se/a/3Awwv/politiker-avtal-med-metro-har-overlevt-sig-sjalvt; Alexander Zeilon Lund, "TV4 avbryter samarbete efter Qvibergs uttalanden" [TV4 Ends Collaboration After Qviberg's Comments], *Svenska Dagbladet*, May 15, 2017, https://www.svd.se/a/vR1zm/tv4-avbryter-samarbete-efter-qvibergs-uttalanden.
66. Jonas Fröberg, "Qvibergs tid med Metro—detta har hänt" [Qviberg's Time with Metro—This Has Happened], *Svenska Dagbladet*, May 21, 2017, https://www.svd.se/a/dK1Wz/qvibergs-tid-med-metro-detta-har-hant.
67. We interpret infrequent ownership interest mentions as a lack of promotional economic instrumentalism; however, it might also be evidence of "suppression" or what Colistra (2012, 2018) terms "agenda-cutting" in relation to news about ownership interests. Mentions or lack of mentions of ownership interests thus need to be analyzed in context.
68. Hilgartner and Bosk (1988).
69. Quoted in Hardy (2013, 96, fn. 2).

70. Sandrine Cassini, "Bolloré, Arnault, Niel . . . Le Sénat auditionne les milliardaires des médias" [Bolloré, Arnault, Niel . . . Media Billionaires Testify Before Senate], *Le Monde*, January 19, 2022, https://www.lemonde.fr/actualite-medias/article/2022/01/19/bollore-arnault-niel-le-senat-auditionne-les-milliardaires-des-medias_6110050_3236.html.
71. DellaVigna and Hermle (2017) conducted a large study comparing movie reviews published in multiple outlets owned by News Corp. and Time Warner, both conglomerates with film divisions. They found that movies produced by the companies' own studios received more positive reviews than movies produced by other studios; however, after controlling for "correlation from taste," the authors concluded that there was no organizational bias and speculated that this may be partly due to the high value placed on media professional reputation.
72. de Rochegonde and Sénéjoux (2017, 245).
73. Marie Johansson Flyckt, Hallpressen (later Hall Media), responsible publisher and editor-in-chief, telephone interview with Erik Thyselius, August 2020.
74. Ibid.
75. Didier Si Ammour, "Avec les journalistes, il a tout compris" [With Journalists, He Understood Everything], *Stratégies*, December 19, 2013; Rochegonde and Sénéjoux (2017, 175–177), referring to Odile Benyahia-Kouider's *Un si petit monde*, (Paris: Fayard, 2011). See also Robin Andraca, CheckNews, "Xavier Niel a-t-il bien dit: 'Quand les journalistes m'emmerdent, je prends une participation dans leur canard et ensuite ils me foutent la paix"?, *Libération*, March 6, 2018, https://www.liberation.fr/checknews/2018/03/06/xavier-niel-a-t-il-bien-dit-quand-les-journalistes-m-emmerdent-je-prends-une-participation-dans-leur_1653285/.
76. Pew Research Center (2000, 3).
77. Matthieu Pelloli, president of *Le Parisien*'s société de journalistes (journalists' association), quoted in de Rochegonde and Sénéjoux (2017, 235).
78. Paul Goupil, former *Ouest-France* deputy editor, Zoom interview with Rodney Benson, November 2021.
79. Guy Rolnik, *Haaretz* deputy publisher and clinical professor of strategic management at the University of Chicago Booth School of Business, personal communication with Rodney Benson, 2016.
80. de Rochegonde and Sénéjoux (2017, 241–242).
81. Cohen et al. (2008), Stelzer (2018, 44–45).
82. Didier Si Ammour, "Avec les journalistes, il a tout compris."
83. de Rochegonde and Sénéjoux (2017, 164–167).
84. See the insider account of Stelzer (2018, 76) and Jonathan Mahler and Jim Rutenberg, "How Rupert Murdoch's Empire of Influence Remade the World, Part I: Imperial Reach," *The New York Times Magazine*, April 3, 2019, https://www.nytimes.com/interactive/2019/04/03/magazine/rupert-murdoch-fox-news-trump.html.

Conclusion

1. Lukes (2004, 34, 69).
2. Alexander (2016, 23).
3. Benkler et al. (2018, 75–82).
4. Napoli (1997), Tichenor et al. (1980, 49), and Usher (2019).
5. Esping-Andersen (1990), Jepperson and Meyer (1991), Pinto and Mary (2021), and Syvertsen et al. (2014).
6. Rebillard (2020).
7. See, for example, Berthaut (2013).
8. Benson et al. (2018, 293).
9. See, for example, Stone (1987), Lacy and Fico (1990), and Demers (1996). But see critical reviews of these conclusions in Baker (1994a) and Roppen (1998).
10. See, for example, Blumler et al. (1986), Blumler and Gurevitch (2001), Esser (2008), and Cushion (2012).
11. Curran et al. (2009). See also Albæk et al. (2014) and Tambini (2015).
12. Dimitrova and Strömbäck (2012). See also Asp (2017).
13. de Vreese et al. (2016, 176).
14. Cushion (2022).

15. Humprecht (2016, 105–107).
16. Coulson and Hansen (1995), Lacy and Blanchard (2003), Edmonds (2004), Dunaway (2008), Ferrucci (2015), Rohlinger and Proffitt (2016); but also see Abdenour (2018) and Beam (2008) for partly contradictory conclusions.
17. Hamilton (2004, 189).
18. Coulson and Hansen (1995).
19. Dunaway (2008; 2011).
20. Humprecht (2016, 17).
21. Sims (2017, 20).
22. Ewens et al. (2022, abstract, 1–6).
23. Hamilton (2016, 44–47, 183–189); Steven Waldman, "Legacy Media Needs to be Transformed, not Discarded," *Nieman Reports*, February 23, 2023, https://niemanreports.org/articles/legacy-media-local-news/. Waldman includes some stock market dominant shareholder-owned outlets in his category of "family-owned." Knobel (2018, 24) found that the amount of "accountability reporting" had increased between 1991 and 2011 at leading US private and stock market dominant shareholder-owned legacy newspapers, but she did not compare them to widely held stock market-traded outlets.
24. Ellis (2014, 135).
25. See Cranberg et al. (2001, 155–196), which documents that several large stock market-traded groups beyond the fabled *New York Times*, *Washington Post*, and Dow-Jones companies (in the latter two cases, no longer) have had dual stock structures with a majority of voting shares controlled by a family, individual, or trust (A. H. Belo, Central Newspapers, E. W. Scripps, McClatchy, Media General, Inc., and Pulitzer).
26. Patel and Manes (2013) and Institute for Nonprofit News (2018).
27. Neff et al. (2022).
28. Ferrucci (2014; 2015), Carpenter et al. (2016), Benson et al. (2018), and Neff et al. (2022).
29. Usher and Kim-Leffingwell (2023, 18).
30. Konieczna (2013; 2014).
31. Djerf-Pierre and Weibull (2011, 304).
32. Ohlsson (2016, 85).
33. Humprecht (2016, 143–144, 152).
34. Study by Erling Sivertsen, cited in Skogerbø (1997, 111). See also Benson (2013, 160–162).
35. Ostertag and Tuchman (2012), Konieczna (2018), Benson (2018), Ferrucci and Nelson (2019), and Ryfe (2020).
36. Herman and Chomsky (1988), Baker (1994b, 44–70), and McChesney (2015).
37. Sjøvaag (2016).
38. For exceptions, see Hamilton (2004), Benson (2013), Usher (2021), and Neff et al. (2022).
39. de Vreese et al. (2016), Mellado et al. (2020), and Mellado (2021).
40. Humprecht (2016, 111).
41. Stringer and Paterson (2019).
42. See Steinmetz (2004) for a compelling argument for how contextualized but generalizable knowledge can be generated from a theoretically focused analysis of multiple individual or small-N comparative case studies. See, for example, Aday et al. (2005), Groeling (2008), Puglisi (2011), Benson (2013), Wagner and Collins (2014), and Lainé (2019).
43. Groseclose and Milyo (2005, 1192). For critiques of their methodology, however, see reviews of Groseclose and Milyo (ibid.) and Groseclose (2011) by Nyhan (2012), as well as Nolan McCarty, Justin H. Gross, Cosma Rohilla Shalizi, Andrew Gelman, Nancy J. Rosenblum, and Kathleen Hall Jamieson in the same special issue of *Perspectives on Politics*.
44. See data presented in Groseclose and Milyo (2005, 1220, table IV). Groeling's (2008) smaller sample comparison of US national television coverage of presidential approval polls of a Democratic and a Republican president when they held office showed CBS (dominant shareholder) and NBC (widely held) more on the left, Fox News (dominant shareholder) on the right, with ABC (widely held) closest to the middle.
45. Asp (2017, 103–114).
46. Gentzkow and Shapiro (2010) did not analyze differences based on ownership form (which in their sample would include stock market widely held and dominant shareholder, and private), but it could be fruitful to re-analyze their data to see if any patterns emerge (e.g., see their Figure 4.1, on page 47).

47. Garz and Rickardsson (2022, 18–21).
48. Stanford business scholars Gregory Martin and Joshua McCrain (2019) found that "right-leaning phrases" increased dramatically at local stations after their purchase by Sinclair, changes without any self-evident "business logic" given that they correlated with losses of audience to their competitors (synthesis provided by Edmund L. Andrews, "Media Consolidation Means Less Local News, More Right Wing Slant," Stanford Graduate School of Business website, https://www.gsb.stanford.edu/insights/media-consolidation-means-less-local-news-more-right-wing-slant). Anand et al. (2007, 661) posit that "owner ideology can play a greater role in small markets." See also Jacey Fortin and Jonah Engel Bromwich, "Sinclair Made Dozens of Local News Anchors Recite the Same Script," *The New York Times*, April 2, 2018, https://www.nytimes.com/2018/04/02/business/media/sinclair-news-anchors-script.html/. However, Blankenship and Vargo (2021) compared six television channels before and after purchase by Sinclair and did not find a "clear conservative shift" in coverage but did find a decline in local and party politics coverage.
49. Groseclose and Milyo (2005, 1220).
50. Holcomb et al. (2011).
51. Williams (2002, 465). For other studies on cross-promotion in US television news, see Cleary and Adams-Bloom (2009a, 2009b), Hendrickson and Wilkins (2009), and the discussion in Neff and Benson (2021).
52. Saffer et al. (2021, 17–18, 23).
53. Williams (2002, 466), and Saffer et al. (2021, 17–18, 23).
54. Hardy (2013, 89–90). See also Panis et al. (2015) and Lee et al. (2020).
55. Gilens and Hertzman (2000). See also Herzog and Scerbinina (2021).
56. Chadwick (2013).
57. Berry and Sobieraj (2013), Hemmer (2016), Nadler et al. (2020), and Bauer et al. (2021).
58. Davey Alba and Jack Nicas, "As Local News Dies, a Pay-for-Play Network Rises in Its Place," *New York Times*, October 18, 2020, https://www.nytimes.com/2020/10/18/technology/timpone-local-news-metric-media.html.
59. Graves and Konieczna (2015).
60. For notable recent in-depth case studies with findings relevant to ownership form differences, see Brown and Groves (2010), Lardeau (2011), Usher et al. (2012), Raviola (2022), and Petre (2022).
61. See, for example, Ferrucci et al. (2017).
62. Hansen and Goligoski (2018, 69–76), Newman and Gallo (2019), and Brevini (2023).
63. Cagé (2016; 2021).
64. Reich and Hanitzsch (2013) and Mellado et al. (2020).
65. Štětka (2012) and Mazumdar (2021).
66. Usher (2013). See also Figenschou (2013).
67. Singh (2004) and Lei (2016).
68. Cheruiyot et al. (2021).
69. Mellor (2007) and Kraidy (2012).
70. Chris Carroll, "'They'll Only Kill You If the Denial of Revenue Does Not Bring You Down': Despite Government and Commercial Pressure—and, Sometimes, Physical Threats—Incisive Investigative Work is Getting Done across AFRICA," *NiemanReports* (Winter 2018), August 14, 2017, https://niemanreports.org/articles/theyll-only-kill-you-if-the-denial-of-revenue-does-not-bring-you-down/.

Appendix II

1. For insights on in-depth interviewing of elites, see Laurens (2007), Ortner (2010), and Mikecz (2012); see also Bourdieu (2000) for a general theoretical and methodological discussion of in-depth interviewing.
2. See, for example, the methodological discussion in Bélair-Gagnon et al. (2019, 564), drawing on Fereday and Muir-Cochrane (2006).
3. See Ortner's (2010, 218–221) discussion of the value of attending such public forums—what she terms "interface ethnography"—for gaining inside information and contacts from difficult to access media elites.

4. Jean-G. Padioleau, "Résumé de la communication de J.-G. Padioleau: La Face cachée du *Monde* de P. Péan et Ph. Cohen: opportunités pour la science sociale," Seminar, "Temps, Médias et Société," at Fondation Nationale des Sciences Politiques, Paris, March 14, 2003, previously referenced in Benson (2004). See also Ortner (2010).
5. The term is used by Paul Lopes (2019) to describes the source materials he used for his study of prominent musical artists and filmmakers.
6. Nechushtai and Zalmanson (2021, 2035).
7. In 2019, the newly established Swedish Ethical Review Authority interpreted privacy protections in research to prohibit searches of publicly available sources on the political views of individuals, including public figures, without prior consent. In 2023, 2,489 scholars protested, in an open letter to the government, against an ethical review process deemed draconian and counter to the spirit of free and independent research. (2489 Swedish scholars, "Systemet för etikprövningar är ett akut hot mot forskningen" [The System for Ethics Reviews is an acute threat to research], *Dagens Nyheter*, May 15, 2023 (updated May 17, 2023), https://www.dn.se/debatt/systemet-for-etikprovningar-ett-akut-hot-mot-forskningen/). On May 17, 2023, the minister of education, Mats Persson, announced that he was sympathetic to the criticism and that the government would conduct an investigation of the current system to protect the academic freedom of Swedish scholars. (Mats Persson, "Reglerna för forskarna ska ses över" [The Rules for the Researchers will be reviewed], *Svenska Dagbladet*, May 17, 2023, https://www.svd.se/a/abpA9M/mats-persson-reglerna-for-etikprovning-ska-ses-over).
8. Williams (1981, 19).
9. On purposive sampling, see Patton (1990).
10. Starkman (2014).
11. See Nielsen (1997) and Lee and Treadwell (2013).

Bibliography

Aalberg, Toril, and James Curran, eds. 2011. *How Media Inform Democracy.* London: Routledge.

Aalberg, Toril, Stylianos Papathanassopoulos, Stuart Soroka, James Curran, Kaori Hayashi, Shanto Iyengar, et al. 2013. "International TV News, Foreign Affairs Interest and Public Knowledge." *Journalism Studies* 14, no. 3: 387–406.

Abdenour, Jesse. 2018. "Inspecting the Investigators: An Analysis of Television Investigative Journalism and Factors Leading to Its Production." *Journalism & Mass Communication Quarterly* 95, no. 4: 1058–1078.

Abernathy, Penelope Muse. 2016. "The Rise of a New Media Baron and the Emerging Threat of News Deserts." Center for Innovation and Sustainability in Local Media, UNC School of Media and Journalism, Chapel Hill, North Carolina. http://newspaperownership.com/newspaper-ownership-report/.

Abramson, Jill. 2019. *Merchants of Truth.* New York: Simon & Schuster.

Achtenhagen, Leona, Stefan Melesko, and Mart Ots. 2018. "Upholding the 4th Estate—Exploring the Corporate Governance of the Media Ownership Form of Business Foundations." *International Journal of Media Management* 20, no. 2: 129–150.

Aday, Sean, Steven Livingston, and Maeve Hebert. 2005. "Embedding the Truth: A Cross-Cultural Analysis of Objectivity and Television Coverage of the Iraq War." *International Journal of Press/Politics* 10, no. 1: 3–21.

Agnès, Yves, and Patrick Eveno. 2010. *Ils ont fait la presse: L'histoire des journaux en France en 40 portraits.* Paris: Vuibert.

Albæk, Erik, Arjen Van Dalen, Nael Jebril, and Claes H. de Vreese. 2014. *Political Journalism in Comparative Perspective.* Cambridge, UK: Cambridge University Press.

Alexander, Jeffrey. 2016. "Introduction: Journalism, Democratic Culture, and Creative Reconstruction." In *The Crisis of Journalism Reconsidered*, edited by J. Alexander, E. B. Breese, and M. Luengo, 1–30. Cambridge, UK: Cambridge University Press.

Alfon, Dov. 2017. "Mediapart: A Viable Model?" Stigler Case No. 1, March 13, University of Chicago Stigler Center for the Study of the Economy and the State. https://research.chicagobooth.edu/~/media/9F86BCAEF28941B2A55663969C34929B.pdf.

Allern, Sigurd. 2021. "Mediekapitalet: Ägarskap, kontroll och ideologisk hegemoni i svenska nyhetsmedier." In *Klass i Sverige: Ojämlikheten, makten och politiken i det 21:a århundradet*, edited by D. Suhonen, G. Therborn, and J. Weithz, 411–428. Stockholm: Arkiv forlag & Katalys.

Allern, Sigurd, and Mark Blach-Ørsten. 2011. "The News Media as a Political Institution: A Scandinavian Perspective." *Journalism Studies* 12, no. 1: 92–105.

Allern, Sigurd, and Ester Pollack. 2019. "Journalism as a Public Good: A Scandinavian Perspective." *Journalism* 20, no. 11: 1423–1439.

An, Soontae, and Hyung Seung Jin. 2004. "Interlocking of Newspaper Companies with Financial Institutions and Leading Advertisers." *Journalism & Mass Communication Quarterly* 81, 3: 578–600.

Anand, Bharat, Rafael Di Tella, and Alexander Galetovic. 2007. "Information or Opinion? Media Bias as Product Differentiation." *Journal of Economics & Management* Strategy 16, no. 3: 635–682.

Anderson, C. W. 2011. "Between Creative and Quantified Audiences: Web Metrics and Changing Patterns of Newswork in Local US Newsrooms." *Journalism* 12, no. 5: 550–566.

Anderson, C. W. 2013. *Rebuilding the News*. Philadelphia, PA: Temple University Press.

Angelucci, Charles, and Julia Cagé. 2019. "Newspapers in Times of Low Advertising Revenues." *American Economic Journal: Microeconomics* 11, no. 3: 319–364.

Antheaume, Alice. 2021. *"France." Digital News Report 2021*. Oxford: Reuters Institute for the Study of Journalism.

Applebaum, Eileen, and Rosemary Batt. 2014. *Private Equity at Work*. New York: Russell Sage Foundation.

Arboit, Gérald. 2002. "La nouvelle économie politique de L'Humanité." *Annuaire Français de relations internationals* 3: 822–840.

Asp, Kent. 2017. *Public service-TV: vårt offentliga rum: en utvärdering*. Institutionen för journalistik, medier och kommunikation, Göteborg: Göteborgs universitet.

Bagdikian, Ben. 1983. *The Media Monopoly*. 1st ed. Boston: Beacon Press.

Bagdikian, Ben . 1992. *The Media Monopoly*. 4th ed. Boston: Beacon Press

Bagdikian, Ben. 2004. *The New Media Monopoly*. Boston: Beacon.

Baker, C. Edwin. 1994a. "Ownership of Newspapers: The View from Positivist Social Science." Research Paper R-12, The Joan Shorenstein Center for Press, Politics, and Public Policy, Harvard University.

Baker, C. Edwin. 1994b. *Advertising and a Democratic Press*. Princeton, NJ: Princeton University Press.

Baker, C. Edwin. 2002. *Media, Markets, and Democracy*. Cambridge, UK: Cambridge University Press.

Baker, C. Edwin. 2007. *Media Concentration and Democracy: Why Ownership Matters*. Cambridge, UK: Cambridge University Press.

Barland, Jens. 2013. "Innovation of New Revenue Streams in Digital Media: Journalism as Customer Relationship." *Nordicom Review* 34: 99–112.

Barnouw, Erik. 1990. *Tube of Plenty*. 2nd ed. Oxford: Oxford University Press.

Bauer, A. J., Anthony Nadler, and Jacob L. Nelson. 2021. "What is Fox News? Partisan Journalism, Misinformation, and the Problem of Classification." *Electronic News* 16, no. 1: 18–29.

Beam, Randal A. 2008. "Content in Publicly, Privately Owned Newspapers More Alike Than Different." *Newspaper Research Journal* 29, no. 4: 74–80.

Becker, Lee, Tudor Vlad, and Nancy Nusser. 2007. "An Evaluation of Press Freedom Indicators." *International Communication Gazette* 69, no. 1: 5–28.

Becker, Lee B., C. Ann Hollifield, Adam Jacobsson, Eva-Maria Jacobsson, and Tudor Vlad. 2009. "Is More Always Better? Examining the Adverse Effects of Competition on Media Performance." *Journalism Studies* 10, no. 3: 368–385.

Bélair-Gagnon, Valérie, Jacob L. Nelson, and Seth C. Lewis. 2019. "Audience Engagement, Reciprocity, and the Pursuit of Community Connectedness in Public Media Journalism." *Journalism Practice* 13, no. 5: 558–575.

Benkler, Yochai, Robert Faris, and Hal Roberts. 2018. *Network Propaganda*. New York: Oxford University Press.

Bennett, W. Lance. 2016. "Indexing Theory." In *The International Encyclopedia of Political Communication*. New York: Wiley. https://doi.org/10.1002/9781118541555.wbiepc180.

Benson, Rodney. 2000. "La logique du profit dans les médias américains." *Actes de la recherche en sciences sociales* 131–132: 107–115. [Republished in English as "Tearing Down the Wall in American Journalism," *Core: International Journal of the Humanities* 1, no. 1 (2001): 102–113.]

Benson, Rodney. 2003. "Commercialism and Critique: California's Alternative Weeklies." In *Contesting Media Power: Alternative Media in a Networked World*, edited by J. Curran and N. Couldry, 111–127. Lanham, MD: Rowman and Littlefield.

Benson, Rodney. 2004. "La fin du Monde?: Tradition and Change in the French Press." *French Politics, Culture & Society* 22, no. 1: 108–126.

Benson, Rodney. 2012. "Murdoch in the United States? Kingmaker or Ringmaster?" *Global Media and Communication* 8, no. 1: 4–7.

Benson, Rodney. 2013. *Shaping Immigration News: A French-American Comparison.* Cambridge, UK: Cambridge University Press.

Benson, Rodney. 2016. "Institutional Forms of Media Ownership and their Modes of Power." In *The Journalistic Institution Reexamined*, edited by M. Eide, L. O. Larsen, and H. Sjøvaag, 27–48. Chicago: Intellect/University of Chicago.

Benson, Rodney. 2017. "Métamorphoses du paysage médiatique américain." *Le Monde Diplomatique* September: 18–19.

Benson, Rodney. 2018. "Can Foundations Solve the Journalism Crisis?" *Journalism* 19, no. 8: 1059–1077.

Benson, Rodney (interview with Eric Darras). 2019. "How Media Ownership Matters in the U.S.: Beyond the Concentration Debate." *Sociétés Contemporaines* 113: 71–83.

Benson, Rodney. 2020. "Journalism and Inclusion." In *Rethinking Media Research for Changing Societies*, edited by M. Powers and A. Russell, 91–104. Cambridge, UK: Cambridge University Press.

Benson, Rodney. 2022. "A Conceptual and Methodological Framework for International Comparative Media Ownership Research." Paper prepared for Zoom presentation at the annual conference of the Association Française de Science Politique, July 6, Lille.

Benson, Rodney, Mark Blach-Ørsten, Matthew Powers, Ida Willig, and Sandra Vera Zambrano. 2012. "Media Systems Online and Off: Comparing the Form of News in the U.S., Denmark, and France." *Journal of Communication* 62: 21–38.

Benson, Rodney, Timothy Neff, and Mattias Hessérus. 2018. "Media Ownership and Public Service News: How Strong are Institutional Logics?" *International Journal of Press/Politics* 23, no. 3: 275–298.

Benson, Rodney, and Erik Neveu, eds. 2005. *Bourdieu and the Journalistic Field.* Cambridge, UK: Polity.

Benson, Rodney, and Matthew Powers. 2011. *Public Media and Political Independence* Washington, DC: Free Press. http://rodneybenson.org/publications/books/policy-reports/.

Benson Rodney, Matthew Powers, and Timothy Neff. 2017. "Public Media Autonomy and Accountability: Best and Worst Policy Practices in 12 Leading Democracies." *International Journal of Communication* 11: 1–22.

Benson, Rodney, and Abigail C. Saguy. 2005. "Constructing Social Problems in an Age of Globalization: A French-American Comparison." *American Sociological Review* 70, no. 2: 233–259.

Berger, Françoise. 1992. *Journaux intimes: Les aventures tragi comiques sous François Mitterrand.* Paris: R. Laffont.

Bergreen, Laurence. 1980. *Look Now, Pay Later: The Rise of Network Broadcasting.* New York: Doubleday & Co.

Bergström, Annika, Jesper Strömbäck, and Sofia Arkhede. 2019. "Towards Rising Inequalities in Newspaper and Television News Consumption? A Longitudinal Analysis, 2000–2016." *European Journal of Communication* 34, no. 2: 175–189.

Berry, Jeffrey M., and Sarah Sobieraj. 2013. *The Outrage Industry.* Oxford: Oxford University Press.

Berthaut, Jérôme. 2013. *La banlieue du '20 heures'.* Marseille: Agone.

Besharov, Marya L., and Wendy K. Smith. 2014. "Multiple Institutional Logics in Organizations: Explaining Their Varied Nature and Implications." *Academy of Management Review* 39, no. 3: 364–381.

Besley, Timothy, and Andrea Prat. 2006. "Handcuffs for the Grabbing Hand? Media Capture and Government Accountability." *American Economic Review* 96, no. 3: 720–736.

Birnbauer, Bill. 2019. *The Rise of Nonprofit Investigative Journalism in the United States.* New York: Routledge

Blankenship, Justin C., and Chris J. Vargo. 2021. "The Effect of Corporate Media Ownership on the Depth of Local Coverage and Issue Agendas: A Computational Case Study of Six Sinclair TV Station Websites." *Electronic News* 15, no. 3–4: 139–158.

Blumler, Jay G., Malcolm Brynin, and T. J. Nossiter. 1986. "Broadcasting Finance and Programme Quality: An International Review." *European Journal of Communication* 1, no. 3: 343–364.

Blumler, Jay G., and Michael Gurevitch. 2001. "Americanization Reconsidered: U.K.–U.S. Campaign Communication Comparisons Across Time." In *Mediated Politics*, edited by W. L. Bennett and R. M. Entman, 380–406. Cambridge, UK: Cambridge University Press.

Boczkowski, Pablo J. 2005. *Digitizing the News*. Cambridge, MA: The MIT Press.

Boczkowski, Pablo J. 2010. *News at Work: Imitation in an Age of Information Abundance*. Chicago: University of Chicago Press.

Boczkowski, Pablo J., and Zizi Papacharissi, eds. 2018. *Trump and the Media*. Cambridge, MA: The MIT Press.

Bødker, Henrik. 2017. "Vice Media Inc.: Youth, Lifestyle—and News." *Journalism* 18, no. 1: 27–43.

Bogart, Leo. 1973. "The Management of Mass Media: An Agenda for Research." *Public Opinion Quarterly* 34, no. 4: 580–589.

Bogart, Leo. 2004. "Reflections on Content Quality in Newspapers." *Newspaper Research Journal* 25, no. 1: 40–53.

Boltanski, Luc, and Arnaud Esquerre. 2022. *Qu'est-ce que l'actualité politique?* Paris: Gallimard.

Boltanski, Luc, and Laurent Thévenot. 2006. *On Justification*. Princeton, NJ: Princeton University Press.

Bourdieu, Pierre. 1984. *Distinction*. Cambridge, MA: Harvard University Press.

Bourdieu, Pierre. 1993. *The Field of Cultural Production*. New York: Columbia.

Bourdieu, Pierre. 1998. "Social Space and Symbolic Space." In *Practical Reason*, 1–13. Stanford, CA: Stanford University Press.

Bourdieu, Pierre. 2000. "Understanding." In *The Weight of the World*, 607–626. Stanford, CA: Stanford University Press.

Bourdieu, Pierre. 2005. "The Political Field, the Social Science Field, and the Journalistic Field." In *Bourdieu and the Journalistic Field*, edited by R. Benson and E. Neveu, 29–48. Cambridge, UK: Polity.

Bourdieu, Pierre, Jean-Claude Chamboredon, and Jean-Claude Passeron. 1991. *The Craft of Sociology: Epistemological Preliminaries*. Berlin: Walter de Gruyter.

Bourdon, Jérôme. 1994. *Haute Fidelité: Pouvoir et Télévision, 1935–1994*. Paris: Seuil.

Bowers, David R. 1967. "A Report on Activity by Publishers in Directing Newsroom Decisions." *Journalism & Mass Communication Quarterly* 44: 43–52.

Brandenburg, Heinz. 2005. "Political Bias in the Irish Media: A Qualitative Study of Campaign Coverage during the 2002 General Election." *Irish Political Studies* 20, no. 3: 297–322.

Braun, Joshua A. 2015. *This Program is Brought to You By . . . : Distributing Television News Online*. New Haven, CT: Yale University Press.

Breed, Warren. 1955. "Social Control in the Newsroom: A Functional Analysis." *Social Forces* 33, no. 4: 326–335.

Brevini, Benedetta. 2023. "Global Digital Lords and Privatisation of Media Policy: The Australian Media Bargaining Code." *Javnost—The Public* 30, no. 2: 268–283.

Brown, Carrie, and Jonathan Groves. 2010. "New Media, Enduring Values: How Three News Organizations Managed Change in an Age of Uncertainty." *Electronic News* 4, no. 3: 131–145.

Brown, Carrie, and Jonathan Groves. 2020. *Transforming Newsrooms*. London: Routledge.

Browne, Harry. 2010. "Foundation-funded Journalism: Reasons to be Wary of Charitable Support." *Journalism Studies* 11, no. 6: 889–903.

Brüggemann, Michael, Frank Esser, and Edda Humprecht. 2012. "The Strategic Repertoire of Publishers in the Media Crisis." *Journalism Studies* 13, no. 5: 742–752.

Brüggemann, Michael, Sven Engesser, Florin Büchel, Edda Humprecht, and Laia Castro. 2014. "Hallin and Mancini Revisited: Four Empirical Types of Western Media Systems." *Journal of Communication* 64, no. 6: 1037–165.

Bruno, Nicola, and Rasmus Kleis Nielsen. 2012. *Survival is Success: Journalistic Online Start-ups in Western Europe.* Oxford: Reuters Institute for the Study of Journalism.

Buozis, Michael, and Magda Konieczna. 2023. "Conservative News Nonprofits: Claiming Legitimacy Without Transparency." *Journalism* 24, no. 6: 1211–1231.

Cagé, Julia. 2016. *Saving the Media.* Cambridge, MA: Harvard University Press.

Cagé, Julia. 2019. "Media Competition, Information Provision and Political Participation: Evidence from French Local Newspapers and Elections, 1944–2014." *Journal of Public Economics* 185: 104077. https://doi.org/10.1016/j.jpubeco.2019.104077.

Cagé, Julia. 2021. "From Philanthropy to Democracy: Rethinking Governance and Funding of High-Quality News in the Digital Age." In *Digital Technology and Democratic Theory*, edited by L. Bernholz et al., 241–273. Chicago: University of Chicago Press.

Cagé, Julia, and Olivier Godechot. 2017. "Who Owns the Media? The Media Independence Project." Sciences Po Report.

Cagé, Julia, Nicolas Hervé, and Marie-Luce Viaud. 2017. *L'information à tout prix.* Paris: Institut National de l'Audiovisuel.

Cagé, Julia, and Benoît Huet. 2021. *L'information est un bien public.* Paris: Seuil.

Callahan, David. 2018. *The Givers: Wealth, Power and Philanthropy in a New Gilded Age.* New York: Vintage.

Callison, Candis, and Mary Lynn Young. 2020. *Reckoning: Journalism's Limits and Possibilities.* Oxford: Oxford University Press.

Capuzza, Jamie Colette. 2016. "Improvements Still Needed for Transgender Coverage." *Newspaper Research Journal* 37, no. 1: 82–94.

Carlo, Anne-Lise. 2017. *Philanthropic Journalism Funding in France.* Report commissioned by the European Journalism Centre. Paris: Centre de formation des journalistes.

Carlson, Matt, Sue Robinson, and Seth C. Lewis. 2021. *News After Trump.* New York: Oxford University Press.

Carpenter, Serena, Jan Boehmer, and Frederick Fico. 2016. "The Measurement of Journalistic Role Enactments: A Study of Organizational Constraints and Support in For-Profit and Nonprofit Journalism." *Journalism & Mass Communication Quarterly* 93, no. 3: 587–608.

Cazenave, Elisabeth, and Caroline Ulmann-Mauriat. 1995. *Presse, radio et télévision en France de 1631 à nos jours.* Paris: Hachette.

Censer, Jack. 1994. *The French Press in the Age of Enlightenment.* New York: Routledge.

Chadwick, Andrew. 2013. *The Hybrid Media System.* Oxford: Oxford University Press.

Chalaby, Jean K. 1996. "Journalism as an Anglo-American Invention: A Comparison of the Development of French and Anglo-American Journalism, 1830s–1920s." *European Journal of Communication* 11, no. 3: 303–326.

Chalaby, Jean K. 1997. "No Ordinary Press Owners: Press Barons as a Weberian Ideal Type." *Media, Culture & Society* 19, no. 4: 621–641.

Chalaby, Jean K. 2002. *The de Gaulle Presidency and the Media.* London: Palgrave Macmillan.

Charon, Jean-Marie. 1991. *La presse en France, de 1945 à nos jours.* Paris: Seuil.

Chávez, Christopher. 2021. *The Sound of Exclusion: NPR and the Latinx Public.* Tucson: University of Arizona Press.

Cheruiyot, David, J. Siguru Wahutu, Admire Mare, George Ogola, and Hayes Mawindi Mabweazara. 2021. "Making News Outside Legacy Media: Peripheral Actors Within an African Communication Ecology." *African Journalism Studies* 42, no. 4: 1–14.

Chevret-Castellani, Christine. 2016. "Libération: discours sur les crises d'un quotidien." *Communication langages* 3: 3–23.

Chomsky, Daniel. 1999. "The Mechanisms of Management Control at the *New York Times.*" *Media, Culture & Society* 21: 579–599.

Chomsky, Daniel. 2006. "'An Interested Reader': Measuring Ownership Control at the New York Times." *Critical Studies in Media Communication* 23, no. 1: 1–18.

Christians, Clifford G., Theodore L. Glasser, Denis McQuail, Kaarle Nordenstreng, and Robert A. White. 2009. *Normative Theories of the Media*. Urbana: University of Illinois Press.

Christin, Angèle. 2018. "Counting Clicks: Quantification and Variation in Web Journalism in the United States and France." *American Journal of Sociology* 123, no. 5: 1382–1415.

Christin, Angèle. 2020. *Metrics at Work*. Princeton, NJ: Princeton University Press.

Clarke, Debra M. 2014. *Journalism and Political Exclusion*. Montreal: McGill-Queen's University Press.

Cleary, Johanna, and Terry Adams-Bloom. 2009a. "Selling News: Behind the Content of Cable and Broadcast Morning Shows." *Electronic News* 3, no. 1: 13–31.

Cleary, Johanna, and Terry Adams-Bloom. 2009b. "The Family Business: Entertainment Products and the Network Morning News Shows." *Mass Communication & Society* 12, no. 1: 78–96.

Coddington, Mark. 2015. "The Wall Becomes a Curtain." In *Boundaries of Journalism*, edited by M. Carlson and S. C. Lewis, 67–82. London: Routledge.

Cohen, Jonathan, Yariv Tsfati, and Tamir Sheafer. 2008. "The Influence of Presumed Media Influence in Politics: Do Politicians' Perceptions of Media Power Matter?" *Public Opinion Quarterly* 72, no. 2: 331–344.

Colistra, Rita. 2012. "Shaping and Cutting the Media Agenda: Television Reporters' Perceptions of Agenda- and Frame-building and Agenda-cutting Influences." *Journalism & Communication Monographs* 14, no. 2: 85–146.

Colistra, Rita. 2018. "Power Pressures and Pocketbook Concerns: Perceptions of Organizational Influences on News Content in the Television Industry." *International Journal of Communication* 12: 1790–1810.

Compaine, Benjamin M. 1995. "The Impact of Ownership on Content: Does it Matter?" *Cardozo Arts & Entertainment* 13: 755–780.

Cook, Timothy E. 1998. *Governing with the News*. Chicago: University of Chicago Press.

Corneo, Giacomo. 2006. "Media Capture in a Democracy: The Role of Wealth Concentration." *Journal of Public Economics* 90, no. 1–2: 37–58.

Cornia, Alessio, Annika Sehl, and Rasmus Kleis Nielsen. 2019. "Comparing Legacy Media Responses to the Changing Business of News: Cross-national Similarities and Differences across Media Types." *International Communication Gazette* 81, no. 6–7–8: 686–706.

Coulson, David C. 1994. "Impact of Ownership on Newspaper Quality." *Journalism Quarterly* 71, no. 2: 403–410.

Coulson, David C., and Anne Hansen. 1995. "The *Louisville Courier-Journal*'s News Content After Purchase by Gannett." *Journalism & Mass Communication Quarterly* 72, no. 1: 205–215.

Coulson, David C., and Stephen Lacy. 1996. "Journalists' Perceptions of How Newspaper and Broadcast News Competition Affects Newspaper Content." *Journalism & Mass Communication Quarterly* 73, no. 2: 354–363.

CPB [Corporation for Public Broadcasting]. 1967. Public Broadcasting Act of 1967. https://www.cpb.org/aboutpb/act/.

CPB [Corporation for Public Broadcasting]. 2016. *Public Broadcasting Revenue Fiscal Year 2016*. Washington, DC: CPB.

Cranberg, Gilbert, Randall Bezanson, and John Soloski. 2001. *Taking Stock: Journalism and the Publicly Traded Newspaper Company*. Ames: Iowa State University Press.

Curran, James. 1991. "Mass Media and Democracy: A Reappraisal." In *Mass Media and Society*, edited by J. Curran and M. Gurevitch, 82–117. London: Arnold.

Curran, James, Shanto Iyengar, Anker Brink Lund, and Inka Salovaara-Moring. 2009. "Media System, Public Knowledge and Democracy: A Comparative Study." *European Journal of Communication* 24, no. 1: 5–26.

Curran, James, and Jean Seaton. 2009. *Power Without Responsibility*. 7th ed. London: Routledge.

Cushion, Stephen. 2012. *The Democratic Value of News: Why Public Service Media Matter.* London: Palgrave MacMillan.

Cushion, Stephen. 2022. "Are Public Service Media Distinctive from the Market? Interpreting the Political Information Environments of BBC and Commercial News in the United Kingdom." *European Journal of Communication* 37, no. 1: 3–20.

Dahlgren, Peter M. 2019. "Selective Exposure to Public Service News over Thirty Years: The Role of Ideological Leaning, Party Support, and Political Interest." *International Journal of Press/Politics* 24, no. 3: 293–314.

Davis, Charles, and Stephanie Craft. 2000. "New Media Synergy: Emergence of Institutional Conflicts of Interest." *Journal of Mass Media Ethics* 15, no. 4: 219–231.

de Rochegonde, Amaury, and Richard Sénéjoux. 2017. *Médias: Les Nouveaux Empires.* Paris: First Editions.

de Vreese, Claes H., Frank Esser, and David Nicolas Hopmann, eds. 2016. *Comparing Political Journalism.* New York: Routledge.

DellaVigna, Stefano, and Johannes Hermle. 2017. "Does Conflict of Interest Lead to Biased Coverage? Evidence from Movie Reviews." *Review of Economic Studies* 84, no. 4: 1510–1550.

Demers, David Pearce. 1996. *The Menace of the Corporate Newspaper: Fact or Fiction?* Ames: Iowa State University Press.

Demers, David Pearce, and Daniel B. Wackman. 1988. "Effect of Chain Ownership on Newspaper Management Goals." *Newspaper Research Journal* 9, no. 2: 59–68.

Demsetz, Harold, and Kenneth Lehn. 1985. "The Structure of Corporate Ownership: Causes and Consequences." *Journal of Political Economy* 93, no. 6: 1155–1177.

Diamond, Edwin. 1993. *Behind the Times: Inside the New* New York Times. New York: Villard/Random House.

Dimitrova, Daniela V., and Jesper Strömbäck. 2012. "Election News in Sweden and the United States: A Comparative Study of Sources and Media Frames." *Journalism* 13, no. 5: 604–619.

Dixon, Travis L., Kristopher R. Weeks, and Marisa A. Smith. 2019. "Media Constructions of Culture, Race, and Ethnicity." In Oxford Research Encyclopedia of Communication, edited by M. Powers. New York: Oxford University Press. https://doi.org/10.1093/acrefore/9780190228613.013.502.

Djankov, Simeon, Caralee McLiesh, Tatiana Nenova, and Andrei Shleifer. 2003. "Who Owns the Media?" *Journal of Law and Economics* 46, no. 2: 341–382.

Djerf-Pierre, Monika, and Lennart Weibull. 2011. "From Idealist-Entrepreneur to Corporate Executive: Provincial Newspaper Editors' and Publishers' Ways-of-Thinking from the mid-1800s to the Present." *Journalism Studies* 12, no. 3: 294–310.

Downie, Len. 2020. *All About the Story: News, Power, Politics, and the Washington Post.* New York: PublicAffairs.

Doyle, Gillian. 2002. *Media Ownership.* London: Sage.

Dragomir, Marius. 2018. "Control the Money, Control the Media: How Government Uses Funding to Keep Media in Line." *Journalism* 19, no. 8: 1131–1148.

Dreier, Peter. 1982. "The Position of the Press in the U.S. Power Structure." *Social Problems* 29, no. 3: 298–310.

Dudouet, François-Xavier. 2019. "L'argent dirige-t-il les entreprises?" *Regards croisés sur l'économie* 24, no. 1: 163–171.

Duhamel, Alain, and Patrice Duhamel. 2008. *Cartes sur table.* Paris: Plon.

Dunaway, Johanna. 2008. "Markets, Ownership, and the Quality of Campaign News Coverage." *Journal of Politics* 70, no. 4: 1193–1202.

Dunaway, Johanna. 2011. "Institutional Effects on the Information Quality of Campaign News." *Journalism Studies* 12, no. 1: 27–44.

Dupuy, Camille. 2010. "L'entreprise de presse en conflit. *Libération* et *Le Monde* en restructuration." *Travail et Emploi* 124: 29–42.

Dupuy, Camille. 2014. "Repenser les acteurs et la négociation collective au travail. Le cas des sociétés de journalistes dans les entreprises de presse." *Négociations* 1: 51–64.

Duval, Julien. 2004. *Critique de la raison journalistique : Les transformations de la presse économique en France.* Paris : Seuil.

Edmonds, Rick. 2004. "News Staffing, News Budgets and News Capacity." *Newspaper Research Journal* 25, no. 1: 98–109.

Edwards, Lee. 2020. "Transparency, Publicity, Democracy, and Markets: Inhabiting Tensions Through Hybridity." *American Behavioral Scientist* 64, no. 11: 1545–1564.

Eisendrath, Charles R. 1979. "Politics and Journalism: The French Connection." *Columbia Journalism Review* 18, no. 1 (May): 58.

Ellis, Gavin. 2014. *Trust Ownership and the Future of News.* New York: Palgrave Macmillan.

Emery, Michael, and Edwin Emery. 1988. *The Press and America.* Englewood Cliffs, NJ: Prentice-Hall.

Esping-Andersen, Gøsta. 1990. *The Three Worlds of Welfare Capitalism.* Cambridge, UK: Polity.

Esser, Frank. 2008. "Dimensions of Political News Cultures: Sound Bite and Image Bite News in France, Germany, Great Britain, and the United States." *International Journal of Press/Politics* 13, no. 4: 401–428.

Esser, Frank, Claes de Vreese, and David Nicolas Hoppmann. 2016. "The Explanatory Logic: Factors that Shape Political News." In *Comparing Political Journalism*, edited by C. de Vreese, F. Esser, and D. N. Hopmann, 10–21. London: Routledge.

Eveno, Patrick. 2003. *L'argent de la presse française des années 1820 à nos jours.* Paris: CTHS.

Eveno, Patrick. 2004. "Du l'organe du Parti au journal d'opinion: *L'Humanité*, une entreprise politique." In *L'Humanité de Jaurès à nos jours*, edited by C. Delporte, C. Pennetier, J-F. Sirinelli, and S. Wolikow, 199–228. Paris: Nouveau Monde.

Eveno, Patrick. 2008. *La Presse Quotidienne Nationale.* Paris: Vuibert.

Ewens, Michael, Arpit Gupta, and Sabrina T. Howell. 2022. "Local Journalism under Private Equity Ownership." National Bureau of Economic Research: NBER Working Paper #29743.

Fedler, Fred, and Robert Pennington. 2003. "Employee-owned Dailies: The Triumph of Economic Self Interest over Journalistic Ideals." *International Journal on Media Management* 5, no. 4: 262–274.

Fenton, Natalie, Des Freedman, and Tamara Witschge. 2010. "Protecting the News: Civil Society and the Media." *Geopolitics, History, and International Relations* 2, no. 2: 31–72.

Fereday, Jennifer, and Elmear Muir-Cochrane. 2006. "Demonstrating Rigor Using Thematic Analysis." *International Journal of Qualitative Methods* 5, no. 1: 80–92.

Ferrucci, Patrick. 2014. "Public Journalism No More: The Digitally Native News Nonprofit and Public Service Journalism." *Journalism* 6, no. 7: 904–919.

Ferrucci, Patrick. 2015. "Murder Incorporated: Market Orientation and Coverage of the Annie Le Investigation." *Electronic News* 9, no. 2: 108–121.

Ferrucci, Patrick. 2020. "It Is In the Numbers: How Market Orientation Impacts Journalists' Use of News Metrics." *Journalism* 21, no. 2: 244–261.

Ferrucci, Patrick, and Jacob L. Nelson. 2019. "The New Advertisers: How Foundation Funding Impacts Journalism." *Media and Communication* 7, no. 4: 45–55.

Ferrucci, Patrick, Frank Michael Russell, Heesook Choi, Margaret Duffy and Esther Thorson. 2017. "Times Are a Changin': How a Merger Affects the Construction of News Processes." *Journalism Studies* 18, no. 3: 247–264.

Figenschou, Tine. 2013. *Al-Jazeera and the Global Media Landscape.* London: Routledge.

Fink, Katherine, and Michael Schudson. 2014. "The Rise of Contextual Journalism, 1950s–2000s." *Journalism* 15, no. 1: 3–20.

Flegel, Ruth C., and Steven H. Chaffee. 1971. "Influences of Editors, Readers, and Personal Opinions on Reporters." *Journalism Quarterly* 48, no. 4: 645–651.

Fletcher, Richard, Alessio Cornia, and Rasmus Kleis Nielsen. 2020. "How Polarized Are Online and Offline News Audiences? A Comparative Analysis of Twelve Countries." *International Journal of Press/Politics* 25, no. 2: 169–195.

Fligstein, Neil, and Adam Goldstein. 2022. "The Legacy of Shareholder Value Capitalism." *Annual Review of Sociology* 48. Review in advance posted online on February 15. https://doi.org/10.1146/annurev-soc-030420-120827.

Fottorino, Eric. 2014. *Mon tour du 'Monde'*. Paris: Gallimard Folio.

Freedman, Des. 2008. *The Politics of Media Policy*. Cambridge, UK: Polity.

Freedman, Des. 2015. "Paradigms of Media Power." *Communication, Culture & Critique* 8: 273–289.

Freedman, Des. 2019. "'Public Service' and the Journalism Crisis: Is the BBC the Answer?" *Television & New Media* 20, no. 3: 203–218.

Friedland, Roger. 2009. "The Endless Fields of Pierre Bourdieu." *Organization* 16, no. 6: 887–917.

Friedland, Roger, and Robert Alford. 1991. "Bringing Society Back In." In *The New Institutionalism in Organizational Analysis*, edited by W. W. Powell and P. J. DiMaggio, 232–263. Chicago: University of Chicago Press.

Frisque, Cégolène. 2010. "Des espaces médiatiques et politiques locaux?" *Revue française de science politique* 60, no. 5: 951-973.

Gabszewicz, Jean J., Didier Laussel, and Nathalie Sonnac. 2002. "Press Advertising and the Political Differentiation of Newspapers." *Journal of Public Economic Theory* 4, no. 3: 317–334.

Gamson, Joshua, and Pearl Latteier. 2004. "Do Media Monsters Devour Diversity?" *Contexts*, 3, no. Summer: 26–32.

Gans, Herbert. 2005 [1979]. *Deciding What's News*. Evanston, IL: Northwestern University Press.

Gapsys-Hutin, Jeanne-Emmanuelle. 2011. "Ensuring Independence at *Ouest-France*." In *Is There a Better Structure for News Providers?*, edited by D. A. L. Levy and R. G. Picard, 85–95. Oxford, UK: Reuters Institute for the Study of Journalism.

Garz, Marcel, and Jonna Rickardsson. 2022. "Ownership and Media Slant: Evidence from Swedish Newspapers." *Kyklos* 76: 18–40.

Gatien, Emmanuelle. 2012. *Prétendre à l'excellence: Prix Albert Londres, prix journalistiques et transformations du journalisme*. Clermont-Ferrand: Fondation Varenne.

Gaxie, Daniel. 1978. *Le Cens Caché: Inégalités culturelles et ségrégation politique*. Paris: Seuil.

Gentzkow, Matthew, and Jesse M. Shapiro. 2008. "Competition and Truth in the Market for News." *Journal of Economic Perspectives* 22, no. 2: 133–154.

Gentzkow, Matthew, and Jesse M. Shapiro. 2010. "What Drives Media Slant? Evidence from U.S. Daily Newspapers." *Econometrica* 78, no. 1: 35–71.

Gilens, Martin, and Craig Hertzman. 2000. "Corporate Ownership and News Bias: Newspaper Coverage of the 1996 Telecommunications Act." *Journal of Politics* 62, no. 2: 369–386.

Gill, Matthew J. 2017. "Chi-square." In *The SAGE Encyclopedia of Communication Research Methods*, edited by M. Allen, 128–132. London: Sage.

Gitlin, Todd. 1980. *The Whole World Is Watching*. Berkeley, CA: University of California Press.

Gitlin, Todd. 2000 [1983]. *Inside Prime Time*. 1st ed. (with a new introduction). Berkeley, CA: University of California Press.

Graham, Katharine. 1998. *Personal History*. New York: Vintage.

Graves, Lucas, and Magda Konieczna. 2015. "Sharing the News: Journalistic Collaboration as Field Repair." *International Journal of Communication* 9: 1966–1984.

Grieco, Elizabeth. 2020. "Americans' Main Sources of Political News Vary by Party and Age." Pew Research Center. April 1. https://www.pewresearch.org/fact-tank/2020/04/01/americans-main-sources-for-political-news-vary-by-party-and-age/.

Groeling, Tim. 2008. "Who's the Fairest of Them All? An Empirical Test for Partisan Bias on ABC, CBS, NBC, and Fox News." *Presidential Studies Quarterly* 38, no. 4: 631–657.

Groseclose, Tim. 2011. *Left Turn: How Liberal Media Bias Distorts the American Mind*. New York: St. Martin's Press.

Groseclose, Tim, and Jeffrey Milyo. 2005. "A Measure of Media Bias." *Quarterly Journal of Economics* CCX, no. 4: 1191–1237.

Grossman, Guy, Yotam Margalit, and Tamar Mitts. 2022. "How the Ultrarich use Media Ownership as a Political Investment." *Journal of Politics* 84, no. 4: 1913–1931.

Groves, Jonathan, and Carrie Brown. 2018. "Changing 'Habits of Thought': An Examination of Eight Years of Digital Evolution at the *Christian Science Monitor*." *#ISOJ* [International Symposium on Online Journalism] 8, no. 1: 89–108.

Gustafsson, Karl Erik. 2008. "End-game Strategies in the Swedish National Tabloid Industry." *Nordicom Review* 29, no. 2: 325–334.

Gustafsson, Karl Erik, and Per Rydén. 2010. *A History of the Press in Sweden*. Göteborg: Nordicom.

Guyot, Jacques. 2009. "Political-economic Factors Shaping News Culture." In *Making the News: Journalism and News Cultures in Europe*, edited by P. Preston, 92–109. London: Routledge.

Gwet, K. L. 2008. "Computing Inter-Rater Reliability and Its Variance in the Presence of High Agreement." *British Journal of Mathematical and Statistical Psychology* 61: 29–48.

Habermas, Jürgen. 2006. "Political Communication in Media Society: Does Democracy Still Enjoy an Epistemic Dimension?" *Communication Theory* 16: 411–426.

Hadenius, Stig. 1998. *Kampen om monopolet—Sveriges Radio och TV under 1900-talet*. Stockholm: Prisma.

Hadenius, Stig, and Lennart Weibull. 1999. "The Swedish Newspaper System in the Late 1990s: Tradition and Transition." *Nordicom Review* 20, no. 1: 129–152.

Hadenius, Stig, Lennart Weibull, and Ingela Wadbring. 2009. *Massmedier: Press, radio och tv i den digitala tidsåldern*. Stockholm: Ekerlids Förlag.

Halberstam, David. 2000. *The Powers That Be*. Urbana: University of Illinois Press.

Hall, Stuart. 1982. "The Rediscovery of 'Ideology': Return of the Repressed in Media Studies." In *Culture, Society and the Media*, edited by M. Gurevitch, T. Bennett, J. Curran, and J. Woollcott, 52–86. London: Routledge.

Hall, Stuart, Chas Critcher, Tony Jefferson, John Clark, and Brian Roberts. 1978. *Policing the Crisis*. London: Macmillan.

Hallin, Daniel C., and Paolo Mancini. 2004. *Comparing Media Systems*. Cambridge, UK: Cambridge University Press.

Hamilton, James. 2004. *All the News that's Fit to Sell*. Princeton, NJ: Princeton University Press.

Hamilton, James. 2016. *Democracy's Detectives*. Cambridge, MA: Harvard University Press.

Hanitzsch, Thomas, Folker Hanusch, Jyotika Ramaprasad, and Arnold S. de Beer, eds. 2019. *Worlds of Journalism*. New York: Columbia University Press.

Hanretty, Chris. 2014. "Media Outlets and Their Moguls: Why Concentrated Individual or Family Ownership is Bad for Editorial Independence." *European Journal of Communication* 29, no. 3: 335–350.

Hansen, Elizabeth, and Emily Goligoski. 2018. "Guide to Audience Revenue and Engagement." Tow Center for Digital Journalism, Columbia University. https://academiccommons.columbia.edu/doi/10.7916/D86T1ZNN/download.

Hardy, Jonathan. 2010. *Cross-Media Promotion*. Bern, Switzerland: Peter Lang.

Hardy, Jonathan. 2013. "Cross-Media Promotion and Media Synergy: Practices, Problems, and Policy Responses." In *The Routledge Companion to Advertising and Promotional Culture*, edited by M. P. McAllister and E. West, 83–98. London: Routledge.

Hardy, Jonathan. 2014. *Critical Political Economy of the Media*. London: Routledge.

Hassell, Hans J. G., Matthew R. Miles, and Kevin Reuning. 2022. "Does the Ideology of the Newsroom Affect the Provision of Media Slant?" *Political Communication* 39, no. 2: 184–201.

Hemmer, Nicole. 2016. *Messengers of the Right: Conservative Media and the Transformation of American Politics*. Philadelphia: University of Pennsylvania Press.

Hendrickson, Elizabeth, and Lee Wilkins. 2009. "The Wages of Synergy." *Journalism Practice* 3, no. 4: 377–391.

Herman, Edward S., and Noam Chomsky. 1988. *Manufacturing Consent*. New York: Pantheon Books.

Herzog, Christian, and Alise Scerbinina. 2021. "'Self-centered, Self-promoting, and Self-legitimizing': CNN's Portrayal of Media Ownership Concentration in the U.S." *Atlantic Journal of Communication* 29, no. 5: 328–344.

Hesmondhalgh, David. 2014. "The Menace of Instrumentalism in Media Industries Research and Education." *Media Industries Journal* 1, no. 1: 21–26.

Hilgartner, Stephen, and Charles L. Bosk. 1988. "The Rise and Fall of Social Problems: A Public Arenas Model." *American Journal of Sociology* 94, no. 1: 53–78.

Hindman, Matthew. 2018. *The Internet Trap*. Princeton, NJ: Princeton University Press.

Ho, Karen. 2009. *Liquidated: An Ethnography of Wall Street*. Durham, NC: Duke University Press.

Holcomb, Jesse, Tom Rosenstiel, Amy Mitchell, Kevin Caldwell, Tricia Sartor, and Nancy Vogt. 2011. "Non-Profit News: Assessing a New Landscape in Journalism." Pew Research Center. July 18. https://www.pewresearch.org/journalism/2011/07/18/special-features/.

Holtz-Bacha, Christina. 2021. "The Kiss of Death: Public Service Media under Right-wing Populist Attack." *European Journal of Communication* 36, no. 3: 221–237.

Hopmann, David Nicolas, Peter van Aelst, Susana Salgado, and Guido Legnante. 2016. "Political Balance." In *Comparing Political Journalism*, edited by C. de Vreese, F. Esser, and D. N. Hopmann, 92–111. London: Routledge.

Horwitz, Robert. 2005. "On Media Concentration and the Diversity Question." *Information Society* 21, no. 3: 181–204.

Hoynes, William. 2007. "Public Broadcasting for the 21st Century: Notes on an Agenda for Reform." *Critical Studies in Media Communication* 24, no. 4: 370–376.

Humprecht, Edda. 2016. *Shaping Online News Performance: Political News in Six Western Democracies*. New York: Palgrave Macmillan.

IFOP [Institut français d'opinion publique]. 2012. "Analyse du vote selon les habitudes médias." (In partnership with *Marianne*.) April. https://www.ifop.com/publication/analyse-du-vote-selon-les-habitudes-medias/.

IFOP [Institut français d'opinion publique]. 2014. "Analyse du vote au premier tour des élections municipales en fonction des habitudes médias. (In partnership with *Marianne*.) March 23. https://www.ifop.com/publication/analyse-du-vote-au-premier-tour-des-elections-municipales-en-fonction-des-habitudes-medias/.

Institut Montaigne. 2019. "Media Polarization 'À La Française'? Comparing the French and American Ecosystems." Paris. https://www.institutmontaigne.org/en/publications/media-polarization-la-francaise.

Institute for Nonprofit News. 2018. "INN Index 2018." https://inn.org/research/inn-index/inn-index-2018/.

Jacobs, Ronald N., and Eleanor Townsley. 2011. *The Space of Opinion*. Oxford: Oxford University Press.

Jeambar, Denis. 2012. *Portraits crachés*. Paris: J'ai lu.

Jepperson, Ronald J., and John W. Meyer. 1991. "The Public Order and the Construction of Formal Organizations." In *The New Institutionalism in Organizational Analysis*, edited by W. W. Powell and P. DiMaggio, 204–231. Chicago: University of Chicago Press.

Jones, Jeffrey P. 2012. "The 'New' News as No 'News': US Cable News Channels as Branded Political Entertainment Television." *Media International Australia* 144, no. 1: 146–155.

Jonsson, Sverker. 2002. "TV förändrar världen" [TV Changes the World]." In *Den svenska pressens historia 4 Bland andra massmedier (efter 1945)*, edited by L.-A. Engblom, K. E. Gustafsson, and P. Rydén, 134–247. Stockholm: Ekerlid.

Josephi, Beate. 2013. "How Much Democracy Does Journalism Need?" *Journalism* 14, no. 4: 474–489.

Joux, Alexandre. 2017. "Stratégies de marques et stratégies éditoriales du Groupe Figaro." *Réseaux* 5, no. 205: 117–143.

Jung, Jaemin, and Hoyeon Kim. 2011. "A Clash of Journalism and Ownership: CNN's Movie Coverage." *Journal of Media and Communication Studies* 3, no. 2: 71–79.

Kaplan, Richard L. 2002. *Politics and the American Press.* Cambridge, UK: Cambridge University Press.

Kennedy, Dan. 2018. *The Return of the Moguls.* Lebanon, NH: ForeEdge.

Klinenberg, Eric. 2007. *Fighting for Air.* New York: Metropolitan Books.

Knee, Jonathan, Bruce Greenwald, and Ana Seave. 2011. *The Curse of the Mogul.* New York: Portfolio.

Knobel, Beth. 2018. *The Watchdog Still Barks: How Accountability Reporting Evolved for the Digital Age.* New York: Fordham University Press.

Koehn, Daryl, and Joe Ueng. 2010. "Is Philanthropy Being Used by Corporate Wrongdoers to Buy Good Will?" *Journal of Management and Governance* 14, no. 1: 1–16.

Konieczna, Magda. 2013. "The Effect of the Nonprofit Business Model on News Content: A Case Study." Paper presented at the International Communication Association annual meeting, London.

Konieczna, Magda. 2014. "Do Old Norms Have a Place in New Media? A Case Study of the Nonprofit MinnPost." *Journalism Practice* 8, no. 1: 49–64.

Konieczna, Magda. 2018. *Journalism without Profit.* Oxford: Oxford University Press.

Konieczna, Magda. 2019. "Nonprofit News: An Exploration of a Changing Field." In *The International Encyclopedia of Journalism Studies*, edited by T. P. Vos and F. Hanusch, 1–7. Hoboken: John Wiley & Sons.

Kraidy, Marwan M., 2012. "The Rise of Transnational Media Systems." In *Comparing Media Systems Beyond the Western World*, edited by D. Hallin and P. Mancini, 177–200. Cambridge, UK: Cambridge University Press.

Kreiss, Daniel. 2019. "The Social Identity of Journalists." *Journalism* 20, no. 1: 27–31.

Kruskal, William H., and W. Allen Wallis. 1952. "Use of Ranks in One-Criterion Variance Analysis." *Journal of the American Statistical Association* 47: 583–621.

Ksiazek, Thomas B., Edward C. Malthouse, and James G. Webster. 2010. "News-seekers and Avoiders: Exploring Patterns of Total News Consumption Across Media and the Relationship to Civic Participation." *Journal of Broadcasting and Electronic Media* 54, no. 4: 551–568.

Kuhn, Raymond. 2011. *The Media in Contemporary France.* New York: Open University Press.

Kuhn, Raymond. 2013. "The Media and the Executive in France: An Unequal Power Relationship." *European Journal of Communication* 28, no. 2: 122–135.

Küng, Lucy. 2015. *Innovators in Digital News.* London: Bloomsbury Publishing.

Küng, Lucy. 2017. *Strategic Management in the Media.* 2nd ed. London: Sage.

Lacy, Stephen. 1987. "The Effects of Intracity Competition on Daily Newspaper Content." *Journalism Quarterly* 64: 281–290.

Lacy, Stephen. 1991. "Effects of Group Ownership on Daily Newspaper Content." *Journal of Media Economics* 4, no. 1: 35–47.

Lacy, Stephen, and Alan Blanchard. 2003. "The Impact of Public Ownership, Profits, and Competition on Number of Newsroom Employees and Starting Salaries in Mid-Sized Daily Newspapers." *Journalism & Mass Communication Quarterly* 80, no. 4: 949–968.

Lacy, Stephen, and Frederick Fico. 1990. "Newspaper Quality & Ownership: Rating the Groups." *Newspaper Research Journal* 11, no. 2: 42–56.

Lacy, Stephen, and Tom Rosenstiel. 2015. "Defining and Measuring Quality Journalism." Report prepared for Rutgers School of Communication and Information.

Lahire, Bernard, ed. 2001. *Le travail sociologique de Pierre Bourdieu: dettes et critiques.* Paris: La découverte.

Lainé, Michael. 2019. "Are the Media Biased? Evidence from France." *Journal of Economic Issues* 53, no. 3: 774–798.

Lamont, Michèle, and Laurent Thévenot, eds. 2000. *Rethinking Comparative Cultural Sociology.* Cambridge, UK: Cambridge University Press.

Lamour, Christian. 2017. "News for Free in the Late-modern Metropolis: An Exploration of Differentiated Social Worlds." *Global Media and Communication* 13, no. 3: 213–227.

Lardeau, Matthieu. 2011. "Changement institutionnel et managérialisation: Transformation de la presse quotidienne nationale française et des pratiques professionelles journalistiques (1944–2010)." PhD diss., Université Paul Cézanne Aix-Marseille III.

Lardeau, Matthieu, and Patrick Le Floch. 2013. "France: Press Subsidies—Inefficient but Enduring." In *State Aid for Newspapers*, edited by P. Murschetz, 195–214. Berlin: Springer-Verlag.

Laurens, Sylvain. 2007. "Pourquoi et comment poser les questions qui fâchent? Réflexions sur les dilemmes récurrents que posent les entretiens avec des 'imposants.'" *Genèses* 69: 112–127.

Le Digol, Christophe. 2012. "Comment penser le clivage gauche-droite?" In *Gauche-droite: Genèse d'un clivage politique*, edited by J. Le Bohec and C. Le Digol, 1–17. Paris: Presses Universitaires de France.

LeBrun, Benjamin, Kaitlyn Todd, and Andrew Piper. 2022. "Buying the News: A Quantitative Study of the Effects of Corporate Acquisition on Local News." *New Media & Society* 26, no. 4: 2189–2212. https://doi.org/10.1177/14614448221079030.

Leckner, Sara, Carina Tenor, and Gunnar Nygren. 2019. "What About the Hyperlocals? The Drivers, Organization and Economy of Independent News Media in Sweden." *Journalism Practice* 13, no. 1: 68–89.

Lee, Allan, and Gregory Treadwell. 2013. "Online News Style—Poking a Hornet's Nest." *Pacific Journalism Review* 19, no. 1: 264–281.

Lee, Na Yeon, Kanghui Baek, Jung Kun Pae, Sun Ho Jeong, and Nakwon Jung. 2020. "Self-coverage for Public Interest or Self-promotion: How Media Cross-ownership Structures Affect News Content in South Korea." *Journalism* 21, no. 12: 2025–2043.

Leeds, Tyler. 2023. "The Journalistic Field in the Platform Economy: The *New York Times* and the Inverted Pyramid." *Social Problems* 70, no. 3: 849–867.

Lei, Ya-Wen. 2016. "Freeing the Press: How Field Environment Explains Critical News Reporting in China." *American Journal of Sociology* 122, no. 1: 1–48.

Lemieux, Cyril, and John Schmalzbauer. 2000. "Involvement and Detachment among French and American Journalists: To Be or Not To Be a 'Real' Professional." In *Rethinking Comparative Cultural Sociology*, edited by M. Lamont and L. Thévenot, 148–169. Cambridge, UK: Cambridge University Press.

Levendusky, Matthew. 2013. *How Partisan Media Polarize America*. Chicago: University of Chicago Press.

Lindell, Johan, and Else Mikkelsen Båge. 2023. "Disconnecting from Digital News: News Avoidance and the Ignored Role of Social Class." *Journalism* 24, no. 9: 1980–1997.

Lindell, Johan, and Jan Fredrik Hovden. 2018. "Distinctions in the Media Welfare State: Audience-fragmentation in Post-egalitarian Sweden." *Media, Culture & Society* 40, no. 5: 639–655.

Litman, Barry R., and Janet Bridges. 1986. "An Economic Analysis of Daily Newspaper Performance." *Newspaper Research Journal* 7, no. 3: 9–26.

Loicq, Marlène, and Frank Rebillard, eds. 2013. *Pluralisme de l'information et media diversity*. Brussels: De Boeck Supérieur.

Lopes, Paul. 2019. *Art Rebels*. Princeton, NJ: Princeton University Press.

Lord, Charles G., Lee Ross, and Mark R. Lepper. 1979. "Biased Assimilation and Attitude Polarization: The Effects of Prior Theories on Subsequently Considered Evidence." *Journal of Personality and Social Psychology* 37, no. 11: 2098–2109.

Lukes, Steven. 2004. *Power: A Radical View*. New York: Palgrave Macmillan.

Maares, Phoebe, and Folker Hanusch. 2022. "Interpretations of the Journalistic Field: A Systematic Analysis of How Journalism Scholarship Appropriates Bourdieusian Thought." *Journalism* 23, no. 4: 736–754.

Malmsten, Anders. 2022. *Press stopp*. Stockholm: Ekerlids Förlag.

Mancini, Paolo. 2012. "Instrumentalism of the Media vs. Political Parallelism." *Chinese Journal of Communication* 5, no. 3: 262–280.

Marchetti, Dominique. 2009. "The Revelations of Investigative Journalism in France." *Global Media and Communication* 5, no. 3: 368–388.

Martin, Christopher R. 2008. "'Upscale' News Audiences and the Transformation of Labour News." *Journalism Studies* 9, no. 2: 178–194.

Martin, Christopher R. 2019. *No Longer Newsworthy: How the Mainstream Media Abandoned the Working Class.* Ithaca, NY: Cornell University Press.

Martin, Gregory J., and Joshua McCrain. 2019. "Local News and National Politics." *American Political Science Review* 113, no. 2: 372–384.

Martin, Marc. 1997. *Médias et journalistes de la République.* Paris: Odile Jacob.

Mazumdar, Suruchi. 2021. "Profit versus Partisan Causes in Diverse Ownership Models: A Case Study of Mainstream Newspapers in East Indian City of Kolkata." *Asia Pacific Media Educator* 31, no. 2: 229–247.

McChesney, Robert W. 1995. *Telecommunications, Mass Media, and Democracy: The Battle for the Control of U.S. Broadcasting, 1928–1935.* Oxford: Oxford University Press.

McChesney, Robert W. 2015. *Rich Media, Poor Democracy.* New York: The New Press.

McCord, Richard. 2001. *The Chain Gang: One Newspaper Versus the Gannett Empire.* Columbia: University of Missouri Press.

McKnight, David. 2010. "Rupert Murdoch's News Corporation: A Media Institution with a Mission." *Historical Journal of Film, Radio and Television* 30, no. 3: 303–316.

McMane, Aralynn Abare. 2012. "The French Journalist." In *The Global Journalist in the 21st Century,* edited by D. H. Weaver and L. Willnat, 187–203. Milton Park, UK: Taylor & Francis.

McManus, John. 1995. "A Market-Based Model of News Production." *Communication Theory* 5, no. 4: 301–338.

McManus, John. 2009. "The Commercialization of News." In *The Handbook of Journalism Studies,* edited by K. Wahl-Jorgensen and T. Hanitzsch, 218–233. New York: Routledge.

Media Impact Funders. 2023. "Journalism and Philanthropy: Growth, Diversity, and Potential Conflicts of Interest." August 23. https://mediaimpactfunders.org/reports/journalism-and-philanthropy-growth-diversity-and-potential-conflicts-of-interest/.

Media Insight Project. 2018. "Respondents' Demographics and News Behaviors." February 27. https://americanpressinstitute.org/publications/reports/survey-research/subscribers-appendix-1/.

Mediatique. 2012. "A Report for Ofcom (Annex 6 to Ofcom's Advice to the Secretary of State for Culture, Olympics, Media and Sport): The Provision of News in the UK." June. https://www.ofcom.org.uk/__data/assets/pdf_file/0030/54597/annex6.pdf.pdf.

Mellado, Claudia, ed. 2021. *Beyond Journalistic Norms: Role Performance and News in Comparative Perspective.* London: Routledge.

Mellado, Claudia, Cornelia Mothes, Daniel C. Hallin, María Luisa Humanes, Maria Lauber, Jacques Mick et al. 2020. "Investigating the Gap between Newspaper Journalists' Role Conceptions and Role Performance in Nine European, Asian, and Latin American Countries." *International Journal of Press/Politics* 25, no. 4: 552–575.

Mellor, Noha. 2007. *Modern Arab Journalism.* Edinburgh: Edinburgh University Press.

Mercier, Arnaud. 1996. *Le journal télévisé.* Paris: Presses de la FNSP.

Merritt, Davis. 2005. *Knightfall: Knight Ridder and How the Erosion of Newspaper Journalism is Putting Democracy at Risk.* New York: AMACOM/American Management Association.

Meyer, Philip. 2009. *The Vanishing Newspaper.*2nd ed. Columbia: University of Missouri Press.

Mikecz, Robert. 2012. "Interviewing Elites: Addressing Methodological Issues." *Qualitative Inquiry* 18, no. 6: 482–493.

Ministère de la culture [Culture Ministry, France]. 2022. Aides à la presse. https://www.culture.gouv.fr/Thematiques/Presse/Aides-a-la-Presse.

Mitchell, Amy, Jeffrey Gottfried, Jocelyn Kiley, and Katerina Eva Matsa. 2014. "Political Polarization & Media Habits." Pew Research Center. October 21. https://www.pewresearch.org/journalism/2014/10/21/political-polarization-media-habits/.

Morris, James McGrath. 2010. *Pulitzer: A Life in Politics, Print, and Power.* New York: Harper Perennial.

Mougeotte, Étienne. 2021. *Pouvoirs.* Paris: Calmann-Levy

Murdock, Graham. 1982. "Large Corporations and the Control of the Communications Industries." In *Culture, Society and the Media,* 1st ed., edited by M. Gurevitch et al., 118–150. London: Routledge.

Nadler, Anthony, A. J. Bauer, and Magda Konieczna. 2020. "Conservative Newswork: A Report on the Values and Practices of Online Journalists on the Right." Tow Report, Tow Center for Digital Journalism. *Columbia Journalism Review.* March 31. https://www.cjr.org/tow_center_reports/conservative-newswork-report-on-the-values-and-practices-of-online-journalists-on-the-right.php.

Nakamura, Yoshiko. 2019. "Public Service Broadcasting in Europe: Accelerated Funding Reforms and Opaque Future." 27th JAMCO [Japan Media Communication Center] Online International Symposium. March. https://www.jamco.or.jp/en/symposium/27/7/.

Napoli, Philip M. 1997. "A Principal-Agent Approach to the Study of Media Organizations: Toward a Theory of the Media Firm." *Political Communication* 14: 207–219.

Nasaw, David. 2001. *The Chief: The Life of William Randolph Hearst.* Boston: Mariner.

Navasky, Victor S. 2006. *A Matter of Opinion.* New York: Picador.

Nechushtai, Efrat. 2018. "From Liberal to Polarized Liberal? Contemporary U.S. News in Hallin and Mancini's Typology of News Systems." *International Journal of Press/Politics* 23, no. 2: 183–201.

Nechushtai, Efrat, and Lior Zalmanson. 2021. "'Stay Informed', 'Become an Insider' or 'Drive Change': Repackaging Newspaper Subscriptions in the Digital Age." *Journalism* 22, no. 8: 2035–2052.

Neff, Timothy, and Rodney Benson. 2021. "News You Can Use to Promote Your Interests: Media Ownership Forms and Economic Instrumentalism." *Journalism Studies* 22, no. 15: 2103–2121.

Neff, Timothy, and Victor Pickard. 2021. "Funding Democracy: Public Media and Democratic Health in 33 Countries." *International Journal of Press/Politics.* doi:10.1177/19401612211060255.

Neff, Timothy, Pawel Popiel, and Victor Pickard. 2022. "Philadelphia's News Media System: Which Audiences are Underserved?" *Journal of Communication* 72, no. 4: 476–487.

Nelson, Jacob L. 2021. *Imagined Audiences: How Journalists Perceive and Pursue the Public.* Oxford: Oxford University Press.

Nelson, Jacob L., and James G. Webster. 2017. "The Myth of Partisan Selective Exposure: A Portrait of the Online Political News Audience." *Social Media + Society* (July): 1–13.

Neuharth, Allen Harold. 1989. *Confessions of an S.O.B.* New York: Doubleday Business.

Neveu, Erik. 2019. *Sociologie du journalisme.* Paris: La Découverte.

Newman, Nic, with Richard Fletcher, David A. L. Levy, and Rasmus Kleis Nielsen. 2016. *Reuters Institute Digital News Report 2016.* Oxford: Reuters Institute for the Study of Journalism.

Newman, Nic, with Richard Fletcher, Anne Schulz, Simge Andi, Craig T. Robertson, and Rasmus Kleis Nielsen. 2021. *Reuters Institute Digital News Report 2021.* Oxford: Reuters Institute for the Study of Journalism.

Newman, Nic, and Nathan Gallo. 2019. "Report: News Podcasts and the Opportunities for Publishers." December. Oxford: Reuters Institute for the Study of Journalism. https://ora.ox.ac.uk/objects/uuid:e3d070ec-cd72-4f44-b234-ec1dda4aa1f0.

Nicholas, Tom. 2019. *VC: An American History.* Cambridge, MA: Harvard University Press.

Nicholls, Tom, Nabeelah Shabbir, and Rasmus Kleis Nielsen. 2016. *Digital-Born News Media in Europe.* Oxford: Reuters Institute for the Study of Journalism.

Nielsen, Jakob. 1997. "How Users Read on the Web." Nielsen Norman Group. October 1. https://www.nngroup.com/articles/how-users-read-on-the-web/.

Nielsen, Rasmus Kleis, and Richard Fletcher. 2023. "The Importance of Public Service Media for Individuals and for Society." *Reuters Institute Digital News Report 2023*. https://reutersinstitute.politics.ox.ac.uk/digital-news-report/2023/importance-public-service-media-individuals-society.

Nielsen, Rasmus Kleis, and Geert Linnebank. 2011. *Public Support for the Media: A Six-Country Overview of Direct and Indirect Subsidies*. Oxford: Reuters Institute for the Study of Journalism.

Nisbet, Matthew, John Wihbey, Silje Kristiansen, and Aleszu Bajak. 2018. "Funding the News: Foundations and Nonprofit Media." Harvard Shorenstein Center. June 18, figure 4. https://shorensteincenter.org/funding-the-news-foundations-and-nonprofit-media/.

Nixon, Brice. 2020. "The Business of News in the Attention Economy: Audience Labor and MediaNews Group's Efforts to Capitalize on News Consumption." *Journalism* 21, no. 1: 73–94.

Noam, Eli M. 2016a. "Introduction." In *Who Owns the World's Media?*, edited by E. M. Noam and The International Media Concentration Collaboration, 3–15. Oxford: Oxford Scholarship Online.

Noam, Eli M. 2016b. "National Media Concentrations Compared." In *Who Owns the World's Media?*, edited by E. M. Noam and The International Media Concentration Collaboration, 1017–1041. Oxford: Oxford Scholarship Online.

Noam, Eli M. 2016c. "Findings: The Questions Addressed, From A to Z." In *Who Owns the World's Media?*, edited by E. M. Noam and The International Media Concentration Collaboration, 1303–1344. Oxford: Oxford Scholarship Online.

Noam, Eli M. 2017. "Beyond the Mogul: From Media Conglomerates to Portfolio Media." *Journalism*. https://doi.org/10.1177/1464884917725941.

Noam, Eli M. 2019. *Media and Digital Management*. 1st ed. New York: Palgrave Macmillan.

Noam, Eli, and Paul Mutter. 2016. "Media Concentration in the United States." In *Who Owns the World's Media?*, edited by E. M. Noam and The International Media Concentration Collaboration, 500–572. Oxford: Oxford Scholarship Online.

Noam, Eli, and The International Media Concentration Collaboration. 2016. *Who Owns the World's Media?: Media Concentration and Ownership Around the World*. Oxford: Oxford Scholarship Online.

Nord, Lars W., and Jesper Strömbäck. 2014. "It Didn't Happen Here: Commercialization and Political News Coverage in Swedish Television 1998–2010." *Comparing Political Communication Across Time and Space*, edited by M. J. Canel and K. Voltmer, 192–209. New York: Palgrave Macmillan.

Nygren, Gunnar, and Karolina Olga Nord. 2019. "Svenska nyhetsredaktioner 2019: Krympande redaktioner—nätverksproduktion och läsardata i centrum" [Swedish Newsrooms 2019: Shrinking Newsrooms—Networked Production and a Focus on Reader Data]. In *Mediestudiers årsbok—tillståndet för journalistiken 2018/2019* [*The Annual Review of Media Studies: The State of Journalism 2018/2019*], edited by L. Truedson, 22–57. Stockholm: Institutet för mediestudier.

Nyhan, Brendan. 2012. "Does the US Media Have a Liberal Bias? A Discussion of Tim Groseclose's 'Left Turn': How Liberal Bias Distorts the American Mind." *Perspectives on Politics* 10, no. 3: 767–771.

Ohlsson, Jonas. 2012. "The Practice of Newspaper Ownership." PhD diss., University of Bergen, Norway.

Ohlsson, Jonas. 2013. "Boardroom Empires? A Study of Ownership in the Swedish Press." *Nordicom Review* 34, no. s1: 11–24.

Ohlsson, Jonas. 2014. "Fading Support for the Swedish Press Support." *Journal of Media Business Studies* 11, no. 1: 39–60.

Ohlsson, Jonas. 2015. *The Nordic Media Market 2015*. Gothenburg: Nordicom.

Ohlsson, Jonas. 2016. *Den Svenska mediemarknaden 2016: ägare, företag, medier* [*The Swedish Media Market 2016: Owners, Companies, Media*]. Gothenburg: Nordicom.

Ohlsson, Jonas. 2018. "Foundation Ownership in the Swedish Press." Nordicom/University of Gothenburg Research Paper.

Ohlsson, Jonas, Johan Lindell, and Sofia Arkhede. 2017. "A Matter of Cultural Distinction: News Consumption in the Online Media Landscape." *European Journal of Communication* 32, no. 2: 116–130.

Örnebring, Henrik, and Michael Karlsson. 2022. *Journalistic Autonomy*. Columbia: University of Missouri Press.

Ortner, Sherry B. 2010. "Access: Reflections on studying up in Hollywood." *Ethnography* 11, no. 2: 211–233.

O'Shea, James. 2011. *The Deal from Hell: How Moguls and Wall Street Plundered Great American Newspapers*. New York: Public Affairs.

Ostertag, Stephen, and Gaye Tuchman. 2012. "When Innovation Meets Legacy." *Information, Community & Society* 15, no. 6: 909–931.

Pacouret, Jérôme, and Alan Ouakrat. 2021. "Les conditions économiques légitimes de production d'une information numérique 'de qualité." *Politiques de communication* 16: 53–84.

Page, Benjamin. 1996. *Who Deliberates?* Chicago: University of Chicago Press.

Panis, Koen, Hilde Van den Bulck, Birte Veerschraegen, Miriam van der Burg, and Steve Paulussen. 2015. "Does Media Cross-Ownership Translate into Cross-Promotion?" *Journalism Studies* 16, no. 6: 868–886.

Pasadeos, Yorgo. 1984. "Applications of Measures of Sensationalism to a Murdoch-owned Daily in the San Antonio Market." *Newspaper Research Journal* 5, no. 4: 9–17.

Pasadeos, Yorgo, and Paula Renfro. 1988. "Rupert Murdoch's Style: The *New York Post*." *Newspaper Research Journal* 9, no. 4: 25–33.

Patel, Mayur, and Michael Manes. 2013. "Finding a Foothold: How Nonprofit News Ventures Seek Sustainability." Miami: Knight Foundation. https://knightfoundation.org/reports/finding-foothold.

Patterson, Thomas E. 2016. "Pre-Primary News Coverage of the 2016 Presidential Race: Trump's Rise, Sanders' Emergence, Clinton's Struggle." Shorenstein Center on Media, Politics, and Public Policy. June 13. https://shorensteincenter.org/pre-primary-news-coverage-2016-trump-clinton-sanders/.

Patterson, Thomas E., and Wolfgang Donsbach. 1996. "News Decisions: Journalists as Partisan Actors." *Political Communication* 13, no. 4: 455–468.

Patton, Michael Quinn. 1990. *Qualitative Evaluation and Research Methods*. 2nd ed. Newbury Park, CA: Sage.

Péan, Pierre, and Philippe Cohen. 2003. *La face cachée du Monde*. Paris: Fayard.

Peck, Reece. 2019. *Fox Populism*. Cambridge, UK: Cambridge University Press.

Perrin, Andrew, and Maeve Duggan. 2015. "Americans' Internet Access: 2000–2015." Pew Research Center. http://www.pewinternet.org/2015/06/26/americans-internet-access-2000-2015/.

Petre, Caitlin. 2021. *All the News That's Fit to Click: How Metrics are Transforming the Work of Journalists*. Princeton, NJ: Princeton University Press.

Petre, Caitlin. 2022. "When Workers Own the Newsroom: Media Ownership, Journalistic Working Conditions, and the Case of Defector Media." Paper presented to the August 2022 Media Sociology Symposium, American Sociological Association annual conference, CITAMS Plenary. https://citams.org/media-sociology-symposium/.

Pew Research Center. 2000. "Self Censorship: How Often and Why." http://www.pewresearch.org/wp-content/uploads/sites/4/legacy-pdf/39.pdf.

Pew Research Center. 2010. "Section 4: Who is Listening, Watching, Reading—and Why." *Americans Spending More Time Following the News*. September 24. https://www.pewresearch.org/politics/2010/09/12/section-4-who-is-listening-watching-reading-and-why/.

Pew Research Center. 2012. "Demographics and Political Views of News Audiences." September 27. https://www.pewresearch.org/politics/2012/09/27/section-4-demographics-and-political-views-of-news-audiences/.

Pew Research Center. 2013. *Non-Profit Journalism: A Growing but Fragile Part of the U.S. News System*. Washington, DC: Pew Research Center. http://www.journalism.org/2013/06/10/nonprofit-journalism/.

Pew Research Center. 2016a. "Ideological Placement of Each Source's Audience." January 26. https://www.pewresearch.org/pj_14-10-21_mediapolarization-08-2/.

Pew Research Center. 2016b. "A Wider Ideological Gap Between More and Less Educated Adults." https://www.pewresearch.org/politics/2016/04/26/a-wider-ideological-gap-between-more-and-less-educated-adults/.

Pew Research Center. 2018. "News Media and Political Attitudes in Sweden." https://www.pewresearch.org/global/fact-sheet/news-media-and-political-attitudes-in-sweden/.

Pew Research Center. 2019. "Where Users Place Outlets' Ideologies." *News Media Attitudes in France*. April 23. https://www.pewresearch.org/journalism/2019/04/23/where-users-place-outlets-ideologies/.

Pew Research Center. 2020. "Americans are Divided by Party in the Sources They Turn to for Political News." *U.S. Media Polarization and the 2020 Election: A Nation Divided*. January 24. https://www.pewresearch.org/journalism/2020/01/24/americans-are-divided-by-party-in-the-sources-they-turn-to-for-political-news/.

Pew Research Center. 2021. "Newspapers Fact Sheet." June 29. https://www.pewresearch.org/journalism/fact-sheet/newspapers/.

Picard, Robert G. 1994. "Institutional Ownership of Publicly Traded U.S. Newspaper Companies." *Journal of Media Economics* 7: 49–64.

Picard, Robert G. 2004. "Commercialism and Newspaper Quality." *Newspaper Research Journal* 25, no. 1: 54–65.

Picard, Robert G., Mart Ots, and Madison Forsander. 2016. "Media Ownership and Concentration in Sweden." In *Who Owns the World's Media?*, edited by E. M. Noam and The International Media Concentration Collaboration, 338–357. Oxford: Oxford Scholarship Online.

Picard, Robert, and Aldo van Weezel. 2008. "Capital and Control: Consequences of Different Forms of Newspaper Ownership." *The International Journal on Media Management* 10: 22–31.

Pickard, Victor. 2014. *America's Battle for Media Democracy*. Cambridge, UK: Cambridge University Press.

Pickard, Victor. 2020. *Democracy without Journalism?* Oxford: Oxford University Press.

Pinto, Aurélie, and Philippe Mary. 2021. *Sociologie du cinéma*. Paris: La Découverte.

Ponce de Leon, Charles L. 2015. *That's the Way It Is: A History of Television News in America*. Chicago: University of Chicago Press.

Popkin, Jeremy. 1990. *Revolutionary News: The Press in France, 1789–1799*. Durham, NC: Duke University Press.

Powers, Matthew, and Sandra Vera Zambrano. 2016. "Explaining the Formation of Online News Startups in France and the United States: A Field Analysis." *Journal of Communication* 66, no. 5: 857–877.

Powers, Matthew, and Sandra Vera Zambrano. 2023. *The Journalist's Predicament*. New York: Columbia University Press.

Pradié, Christian. 1995. "La presse, le capitalisme et le lecteur." PhD diss., L'université Grenoble 3 Stendhal.

Price, Cindy J. 2003. "Interfering Owners or Meddling Advertisers: How Network Television News Correspondents Feel about Ownership and Advertiser Influence on News Stories." *Journal of Media Economics* 16, no. 3: 175–188.

Prior, Markus. 2007. *Post-Broadcast Democracy*. Cambridge, UK: Cambridge University Press.

Puglisi, Riccardo. 2011. "Being *The New York Times*: The Political Behaviour of a Newspaper." *B.E. Journal of Economic Analysis & Policy* 11, no. 1: 1–34.

Rabin, Matthew, and Joel L. Schrag. 1999. "First Impressions Matter: A Model of Confirmatory Bias." *Quarterly Journal of Economics* 114, no. 1: 37–82.

Ragin, Charles. 2008. *Redesigning Social Inquiry*. Chicago: University Of Chicago Press.

Raviola, Elena. 2022. *Organizing Independence: Negotiations Between Journalism and Management in News Organizations*. Cheltenham, UK: Edward Elgar

Rebillard, Franck. 2020. "Funding Print and Online News Media in France: Developments and Challenges." In *The Independence of the News Media*, edited by L. Ballarini, 7–17. London: Palgrave.

Reese, Stephen D. 2021. *The Crisis of the Institutional Press*. Cambridge, UK: Polity.

Reese, Stephen D., and Pamela J. Shoemaker. 2016. "A Media Sociology for the Networked Public Sphere: The Hierarchy of Influences Model." *Mass Communication and Society* 19: 389–410.

Reich, Zvi, and Thomas Hanitzsch. 2013. "Determinants of Journalists' Professional Autonomy: Individual and National Level Factors Matter More than Organizational Ones." *Mass Communication and Society* 16, no. 1: 133–156.

Repnikova, Maria. 2017. *Media Politics in China: Improvising Power under Authoritarianism*. Cambridge, UK: Cambridge University Press.

Reuters Institute for the Study of Journalism. 2016. "*Reuters Institute Digital News Report 2016*." reutersinstitute.politics.ox.ac.uk/sites/default/files/research/files/Digital%2520News%2520Report%25202016.pdf.

Reuters Institute for the Study of Journalism. 2019. "*Reuters Institute Digital News Report 2019*." https://www.reutersagency.com/wp-content/uploads/2020/08/reuters-institute-digital-news-report-2019.pdf.

Reuters Institute for the Study of Journalism. 2021. "*Reuters Institute Digital News Report 2021*." https://reutersinstitute.politics.ox.ac.uk/digital-news-report/2021.

Riegert, Kristina, and Anna Roosvall. 2017. "Cultural Journalism as a Contribution to Democratic Discourse in Sweden." In *Cultural Journalism in the Nordic Countries*, edited by N. N. Kristensen and K. Riegert, 89–108. Göteborg: Nordicom.

Rimbert, Pierre. 2005. *Libération, de Sartre à Rothschild*. Paris: Seuil, coll. Raisons d'agir.

Robinson, Sue. 2018. *Networked News, Racial Divides*. Cambridge, UK: Cambridge University Press.

Rohlinger, Deana, and Jennifer M. Proffitt. 2016. "How Much Does Ownership Matter? Deliberative Discourse in Local Media Coverage of the Terri Schiavo Case." *Journalism* 18, no. 10: 1271 1291.

Roppen, Johann. 1998. "The Problem of No-Effects of Media Concentration." *Nordicom Review* 19, no. 1: 115–124.

Rosenstiel, Tom, William Buzenberg, Marjorie Connelly, and Kevin Loker. 2016. "Charting New Ground: The Ethical Terrain of Nonprofit Journalism." American Press Institute. https://www.americanpressinstitute.org/publications/reports/nonprofit-news/.

Ruotsalainen, Juho, Jaana Hujanen, and Mikko Villi. 2021. "A Future of Journalism beyond the Objectivity–Dialogue Divide? Hybridity in the News of Entrepreneurial Journalists." *Journalism* 22, no. 9: 2240–2258.

Rusbridger, Alan. 2018. *Breaking News*. New York: FSG.

Ryan, Charlotte. 1991. *Prime Time Activism*. Boston: South End Press

Ryfe, David M. 2012. *Can Journalism Survive? An Inside Look at American Newsrooms*. Cambridge, UK: Polity.

Ryfe, David M. 2016. *Journalism and the Public*. Cambridge, UK: Polity.

Ryfe, David M. 2020. "The Economics of News and the Practice of News Production." *Journalism Studies* 22, no. 1: 60–76.

Saffer, Adam J., Deborah L. Dwyer, Jennifer L. Harker, Christopher E. Etheridge, Mariam Turner, and Daniel Riffe. 2021. "Interlocking among American Newspaper Organizations Revisited: 'Pressure from the Top' and Its Influence on Newsroom and Content." *Mass Communication and Society* 24, no. 3: 441–469.

Saitta, Eugénie. 2004. "*L'Humanité*, de l'organe de parti au journal communiste: 1999–2000." In *L'Humanité de Jaurès à nos jours*, edited by C. Delporte, C. Pennetier, and J. Sirinelli, 229–243. Paris: Nouveau Monde Editions.

Sandlund, Elisabeth. 2001. "Beredskap och repression (1936–1945)." In *Den svenska pressens historia III*, edited by Karl Erik Gustafsson and Per Rydén, 266–381. Stockholm: Ekerlids förlag.

Santhanam, Laura Houston, and Tom Rosenstiel. 2011. "Why U.S. Newspapers Suffer More than Others." *The State of the News Media 2010.* Pew Research Center. https://www.pewresearch.org/journalism/2011/03/19/why-u-s-newspapers-suffer-more-than-others/.

Schiffrin, Anya, ed. 2021. *Media Capture.* New York: Columbia University Press.

Schudson, Michael. 2007. "Owning Up." *Columbia Journalism Review*, January 1, https://www.cjr.org/review/owning_up_a_new_book_stops_sho.php/.

Schudson, Michael. 2011. *Sociology of News.* 2nd ed. New York: W.W. Norton.

Schudson, Michael, and Susan E. Tifft. 2005. "American Journalism in Historical Perspective." In *The Press*, edited by G. Overholser and K. H. Jamieson, 17–47. New York: Oxford University Press.

Schwoebel, Jean. 1969. *La Presse, le pouvoir et l'argent.* Paris: Seuil.

Schwoebel, Jean. 1970. "Balance of Power." *Columbia Journalism Review* (Summer), https://www.cjr.org/60th/balance-of-power-jean-schwoebel-le-monde-miracle.php/.

Scott, Martin, Mel Bunce, and Kate Wright. 2017. "Donor Power and the News: The Influence of Foundation Funding on International Public Service Journalism." *International Journal of Press/Politics* 22, no. 2: 163–184.

Sedel, Julie. 2004. "La nouvelle formule du *Monde*." *Questions de communication* 6: 299–315.

Sedel, Julie. 2021a. *Dirigeants de médias: Sociologie d'un groupe patronal.* Rennes: PUR.

Sedel, Julie. 2021b. "Tel proprietaire, tel dirigeant de presse?" *Politiques de communication* 2, no. 15: 169–195.

Sedel, Julie. 2021c. "Construire l'indépendance en label de qualité." *Politiques de communication* 1, no. 16: 13–51.

Sedel, Julie. 2022. *Sociologie des dirigeants de presse.* Paris: La Découverte.

Semetko, Holli, Jay G. Blumler, Michael Gurevitch, and David Weaver, with Steve Barkin and G. Cleveland Wilhoit. 1991. *The Formation of Campaign Agendas: A Comparative Analysis of Party and Media Roles in Recent American and British Elections.* Mahwah, NJ: Lawrence Erlbaum.

Shawcross, William. 1997. *Murdoch: The Making of a Media Empire.* New York: Touchstone.

Shehata, Adam. 2010. "Marking Journalistic Independence: Official Dominance and the Rule of Product Substitution in Swedish Press Coverage." *European Journal of Communication* 25, no. 2: 123–137.

Sherman, Gabriel. 2017. *The Loudest Voice in the Room.* New York: Random House.

Simmons, Charlene. 2012. "Will You Be on Our Board of Directors? We Need Help: Media Corporations, Environmental Change, and Resource Dependency Theory." *Journalism & Mass Communication Quarterly* 89, no. 1: 55–72.

Sims, Patrick. 2017. "Does Ownership Affect Reporting?" In *Report: Thwarting the Emergence of News Deserts*, 18–27. Center for Innovation and Sustainability in Local Media/University of North Carolina School of Media and Journalism. March. https://www.cislm.org/resources/report/thwarting-the-emergence-of-news-deserts/.

Singh, Shailendra. 2004. "Media Ownership in Oceania: Three Case Studies in Fiji, Papua New Guinea and Tonga." *Pacific Journalism Review* 10, no. 2: 47–68.

Sirrah, Ava. 2021. "Invisible Ads." PhD diss., Columbia University School of Journalism.

Sjøvaag, Helle. 2016. "Introducing the Paywall: A Case Study of Content Changes in Three Online Newspapers." *Journalism Practice* 10, no. 3: 304–322.

Sjøvaag, Helle, and Thomas Owren. 2023. "Risk Perception in Newspaper Chains: Threat, Uncertainties and Corporate Boundary Work." *Journalism* 24, no. 4: 767–784.

Skogerbø, Eli. 1997. "The Press Subsidy System in Norway: Controversial Past, Unpredictable Future?" *European Journal of Communication* 12, no. 1: 99–118.

Skovsgaard, Morten, Adam Shehata, and Jesper Strömbäck. 2016. "Opportunity Structures for Selective Exposure: Investigating Selective Exposure and Learning in Swedish Election Campaigns Using Panel Survey Data." *International Journal of Press/Politics* 21, no. 4: 527–546.

Smith, Ben. 2023. *Traffic*. New York: Penguin Press.

Socolow, Michael J. 2010. "A Profitable Public Sphere: The Creation of the *New York Times* Op-Ed Page." *Journalism & Mass Communication Quarterly* 87, no. 2: 281–296.

Soloski, John. 1989. "News Reporting and Professionalism: Some Constraints on the Reporting of News." *Media, Culture & Society* 11: 207–228.

Soloski, John. 2005. "Taking Stock Redux: Corporate Ownership and Journalism of Publicly Traded Newspaper Companies." In *Corporate Governance of Media Companies*, edited by R. Picard, 59–76. Jönköping, Sweden: Jönköping International Business School Ltd.

Sparrow, Bartholomew. 1999. *Uncertain Guardians: The News Media as a Political Institution*. Baltimore, MD: Johns Hopkins University Press.

Squires, James D. 1993. *Read All About It: The Corporate Takeover of America's Newspapers*. New York: Times Books.

Starkman, Dean. 2014. *The Watchdog that Didn't Bite*. New York: Columbia University Press.

Starr, Jerold M. 2000. *Air Wars: The Fight to Reclaim Public Broadcasting*. Boston: Beacon.

Steinmetz, George. 2004. "Odious Comparisons: Incommensurability, the Case Study, and 'Small N's' in Sociology." *Sociological Theory* 22, no. 3: 371–400.

Stelzer, Irwin. 2018. *The Murdoch Method: Notes on Running a Media Empire*. New York: Pegasus Books.

Stern, Jean. 2012. *Les patrons de la presse nationale: Tous mauvais*. Paris: La Fabrique Editions.

Štětka, Václav. 2012. "From Multinationals to Business Tycoons: Media Ownership and Journalistic Autonomy in Eastern and Central Europe." *International Journal of Press/Politics* 17, no. 4: 433–456.

Stonbely, Sarah, Matthew S. Weber, and Christopher Satullo. 2020. "Innovation in Public Funding for Local Journalism: A Case Study of New Jersey's 2018 Civic Information Bill." *Digital Journalism* 8, no. 6: 740–757.

Stone, Gerald F. 1987. *Examining Newspapers: What Research Reveals About America's Newspapers*. Newbury Park, CA: Sage.

Stringer, Paul, and Chris Paterson. 2019. "Redressing the Balance? An Examination of Sourcing Practices at Two Digital Natives: BuzzFeed and Vice." Paper presented at Annual Conference of International Communication Association, Washington, DC, May.

Strömbäck, Jesper, and Lars W. Nord. 2008. "Media and Politics in Sweden." In *Communicating Politics: Political Communication in the Nordic Countries*, edited by J. Strömbäck, M. Ørsten, and T. Aalberg, 103–121. Gothenburg: Nordicom.

Strömbäck, Jesper and Lars W. Nord. 2017. *Mest spelgestaltningar och strukturell partiskhet: En analys av svensk valrörelsejournalistik 2002–2014* [Mostly Game Framing and Structural Partisanship: An Analysis of Swedish Election Campaign Journalism 2002–2014]. Sundsvall: Demicom, Mid Sweden University.

Strömbäck, Jesper, Lars Nord, and Adam Shehata. 2012. "Swedish Journalists: Between Professionalization and Commercialization." In *The Global Journalist in the 21st Century*, edited by D. H. Wilhoit and L. Willnat, 316–319. New York: Routledge.

Sullivan, Margaret. 2020. *Ghosting the News: Local Journalism and the Crisis of American Democracy*. New York: Columbia Global Reports.

Susca, Margot. 2024. *Hedged: How Private Investment Funds Helped Destroy American Newspapers and Undermine Democracy*. Champaign: University of Illinois Press.

Syvertsen, Trine, Gunn Enli, Ole J. Mjøs, and Hallvard Moe. 2014. *The Media Welfare State: Nordic Media in the Digital Era*. Ann Arbor: University of Michigan Press.

Tambini, Damian. 2015. "Five Theses on Public Media and Digitization: From a 56-country Study." *International Journal of Communication* 9: 1400–1424.

Tandoc Jr., Edson C. 2018. "Five Ways BuzzFeed is Preserving (or Transforming) the Journalistic Field." *Journalism* 19, no. 2: 200–216.

Taylor, Charles. 1990. "Modes of Civil Society." *Public Culture* 3, no. 1: 95–118.

Thogmartin, Clyde. 1998. *The National Daily Press of France.* Birmingham, AL: Summa Publications.

Thomas, Dana L. 1981. *The Media Moguls: From Joseph Pulitzer to William S. Paley.* New York: G.P. Putnam's Sons.

Thomas, Ruth. 1976. *Broadcasting and Democracy in France.* Philadelphia, PA: Temple University Press.

Thornton, Patricia H., William Ocasio, and Michael Lounsbury. 2012. *The Institutional Logics Perspective.* New York: Oxford University Press.

Tichenor, Phillip J., George A. Donohue, and Clarice N. Olien. 1980. *Community Conflict and the Press.* Beverly Hills, CA: Sage.

Tifft, Susan E., and Alex S. Jones. 1999. *The Trust: The Private and Powerful Family Behind the New York Times.* New York: Little, Brown & Co.

Tofel, Richard J. 2009. *Restless Genius: Barney Kilgore, The Wall Street Journal, and the Invention of Modern Journalism.* New York: St. Martin's Press.

Tuchman, Gaye. 1980. *Making News.* New York: Free Press.

Tunstall, Jeremy, and Michael Palmer. 1991. *Media Moguls.* London: Routledge.

Turow, Joseph. 1997. *Media Systems in Society.* 2nd ed. White Plains, NY: Longman.

Underwood, Doug. 1995. *When MBAs Rule the Newsroom.* New York: Columbia University Press.

Usher, Nikki. 2012. "Going Web-First at the *Christian Science Monitor*: A Three-Part Study of Change." *International Journal of Communication* 6: 1898–1917.

Usher, Nikki. 2013. "Al Jazeera English Online: Understanding Web Metrics and News Production When a Quantified Audience is Not a Commodified Audience." *Digital Journalism* 1, no. 3: 335–351.

Usher, Nikki. 2014. *Making News at the New York Times.* Ann Arbor: University of Michigan Press.

Usher, Nikki. 2017. "Venture-backed News Startups and the Field of Journalism." *Digital Journalism* 5, no. 9: 1116–1133.

Usher, Nikki. 2019. "Putting Place in the Center of Journalism Research: A Way Forward to Understand Challenges to Trust and Knowledge in News." *Journalism and Mass Communication Monographs* 21, no. 2: 84–196.

Usher, Nikki. 2021. *News for the Rich, White, and Blue.* New York: Columbia University Press.

Usher, Nikki, and Sanghoon Kim-Leffingwell. 2023. "How Loud Does the Watchdog Bark? A Reconsideration of Losing Local Journalism, News Nonprofits, and Political Corruption." *International Journal of Press/Politics.* First published online July 22. https://doi.org/10.1177/19401612231186939.

Usher, Nikki, and Michelle Layser. 2010. "The Quest to Save Journalism: A Legal Analysis of New Models for Newspapers from Nonprofit Tax-Exempt Organizations to L3Cs." *Utah Law Review* 4: 1315–1371.

Usher, Nikki, Patricia Riley, and Vikki Porter. 2012. "NPR Online: Public Service Communication at the Center of National Public Radio." In *Histories of Public Service Broadcasters on the Web*, edited by M. Burns and N. Brügger, 31–48. New York: Peter Lang.

Vos, Tim P., and Jane B. Singer. 2016. "Media Discourse About Entrepreneurial Journalism: Implications for Journalistic Capital." *Journalism Practice* 10, no. 2: 143–159.

Wagemans, Andrea, Tamara Witschge, and Mark Deuze. 2016. "Ideology as Resource in Entrepreneurial Journalism: The French Online News Startup *Mediapart*." *Journalism Practice* 10, no. 2: 160–177.

Wagner, Michael W., and Timothy P. Collins. 2014. "Does Ownership Matter? The Case of Rupert Murdoch's Purchase of the *Wall Street Journal*." *Journalism Practice* 8, no. 6: 758–771. http://dx.doi.org/10.1080/17512786.2014.882063.

Walker, Mason. 2021. "U.S. Newsroom Employment has Fallen." Pew Research Center. July 13. https://www.pewresearch.org/fact-tank/2021/07/13/u-s-newsroom-employment-has-fallen-26-since-2008/.

Wallez, Philippe. 2017. "Local and Regional Information in the Age of Electronic Media: A Comparative Study." PhD diss., Aix-Marseille Université.

Wasko, Janet. 2001. "Challenging Disney Myths." *Journal of Communication Inquiry* 25, no. 3: 237–257.

Wells, Chris, Dhavan V. Shah, Jon C. Pevehouse, JungHwan Yang, Ayellet Pelled, Frederick Boehm et al. 2016. "How Trump Drove Coverage to the Nomination: Hybrid Media Campaigning." *Political Communication* 33, no. 4: 669–676.

Westenskow, Rosalie C., and Edward L. Carter. 2021. "Journalism as a Public Good: How the Nonprofit News Model Can Save Us from Ourselves." *Communication Law and Policy* 26, no. 3: 336–375.

Wiik, Jenny. 2010. "Journalism in Transition: The Professional Identity of Swedish Journalists." PhD diss., University of Gothenburg.

Williams, Bruce A., and Michael X. Delli Carpini. 2011. *After Broadcast News*. Cambridge, UK: Cambridge University Press.

Williams, Dmitri. 2002. "Synergy Bias: Conglomerates and Promotion in the News." *Journal of Broadcasting & Electronic Media* 46, no. 3: 453–472.

Williams, Raymond. 1974. *Television: Technology and Cultural Form*. London: Routledge.

Williams, Raymond. 1981. *The Sociology of Culture*. Chicago: University of Chicago Press.

Winseck, Dwayne. 2008. "The State of Media Ownership and Media Markets: Competition or Concentration and Why Should We Care?" *Sociology Compass* 2, no. 1: 34–47.

Wirth, Werner, and Steffen Kolb. 2004. "Designs and Methods of Comparative Political Communication Research." In *Comparing Political Communication*, edited by F. Esser and B. Pfetsch, 87–111. Cambridge, UK: Cambridge University Press.

Wood, Tim, and Melissa Aronczyk. 2020. "Publicity and Transparency." *American Behavioral Scientist* 64, no. 11: 1531–1544.

World Association of Newspapers [WAN]. 2007. *World Press Trends*. Paris: World Association of Newspapers and ZenithOptimedia.

Wright, Kate, Martin Scott, and Mel Bunce. 2019. "Foundation-funded Journalism, Philanthrocapitalism and Tainted Donors." *Journalism Studies* 20, no. 5: 675–695.

Wright, Kate, Martin Scott, and Mel Bunce. 2024. *Capturing News, Capturing Democracy: Trump and the Voice of America*. Oxford: Oxford University Press.

Wu, Tim. 2017. *The Attention Merchants*. New York: Vintage.

Zaller, John. 1999. "Market competition and news quality." Paper Prepared for Presentation at the 1999 Annual Meetings of the American Political Science Association, Atlanta, GA.

Zeldes, Geri Alumit, Frederick Fico, and Arvind Diddi. 2012. "Differences in the Way Broadcast, Cable and Public TV Reporters Used Women and Non-White Sources to Cover the 2008 Presidential Race." *Mass Communication and Society* 15, no. 6: 831–851.

Zelizer, Barbie. 2004. *Taking Journalism Seriously*. Thousand Oaks, CA: Sage.

Index

For the benefit of digital users, indexed terms that span two pages (e.g., 52–53) may, on occasion, appear on only one of those pages.

Tables and figures are indicated by an italic *t* and *f* following the page number.